M000079646

ZAGAT
2013

London
Restaurants

LOCAL EDITORS
Sholto Douglas-Home and Susan Kessler
with Claire Coleman
STAFF EDITOR
Bill Corsello

Published and distributed by
Zagat Survey, LLC
76 Ninth Avenue
New York, NY 10011
T: 212.977.6000
E: london@zagat.com
plus.google.com/local

ACKNOWLEDGMENTS

We're grateful to our local editors, Sholto Douglas-Home, a London restaurant critic for over two decades, Susan Kessler, cookbook author and consultant for numerous lifestyle publications in the U.K. and the U.S., and Claire Coleman, lifestyle journalist and all-around epicurean enthusiast.

We also thank Rob Anker, Deborah Bennett, Karen Bonham, Max, Fiz and Rebecca Coleman, Ricki Conway, Alex, Louis and Tallula Douglas-Home, Sarah Drinkwater, Rosanne Johnston, Larry Kessler, Michele Laudig, Pamela Lester, Margaret Levin, Mike Lima, Jamie Selzer and Ben Whine, as well as the following members of our staff: Danielle Borovoy (editor), Brian Albert, Sean Beachell, Maryanne Bertollo, Reni Chin, Larry Cohn, Nicole Diaz, Kelly Dobkin, Jeff Freier, Alison Gainor, Matthew Hamm, Justin Hartung, Marc Henson, Ryutaro Ishikane, Natalie Lebert, Mike Liao, Vivian Ma, James Mulcahy, Polina Paley, Amanda Spurlock, Chris Walsh, Jacqueline Wasilczyk, Sharon Yates, Anna Zappia and Kyle Zolner.

The reviews in this guide are based on public opinion surveys. The ratings reflect the average scores given by the survey participants who voted on each establishment. The text is based on quotes from, or paraphrasings of, the surveyors' comments. Phone numbers, addresses and other factual data were correct to the best of our knowledge when published in this guide.

© 2012 Zagat Survey, LLC
ISBN-13: 978-1-60478-512-8
ISBN-10: 1-60478-512-8
Printed in the
United States of America

Contents

Ratings & Symbols

Zagat Top Spot	Name	Symbols		Cuisine	Zagat Ratings			
					FOOD	DECOR	SERVICE	COST

Area, Address & Contact

Z Tim & Nina's ◑ *British*

Covent Garden | West St., WC2H 9NQ | 020-7123-4567 | www.zagat.com

| | | | | | ▽ 23 | 5 | 9 | £15 |

Review, surveyor comments in quotes

After "cracking success" in NYC (with "a pop-up that lasted 33 years"), "culinary innovators" T&N have joined forces with some "astonishingly creative" chefs from the Google cafeteria to create this "mind-blowing" Modern Brit gastropub in Covent Garden; ok, the setting's "dreary" and "staff have no personality", but at least it's "cheap."

Ratings

Food, Decor & **Service** are rated on a 30-point scale.

26	– 30	extraordinary to perfection
21	– 25	very good to excellent
16	– 20	good to very good
11	– 15	fair to good
0	– 10	poor to fair
▽		low response | less reliable

Cost

The price of dinner with a drink and service; lunch is usually 25% to 30% less. For unrated **newcomers,** the price range is as follows:

I	£20 and below	E	£41 to £60
M	£21 to £40	VE	£61 or above

Symbols

Z	highest ratings, popularity and importance
◑	serves after 11 PM
S M	closed on Sunday or Monday
⊄	no credit cards accepted

Maps

Index maps show restaurants with the highest Food ratings in those areas.

Phone

From outside the U.K., dial international code (e.g. 011 from the U.S.) +44, then omit the first zero of the listed number.

About This Survey

- 1,351 restaurants covered
- 9,583 surveyors
- 62 notable openings
- Winners: **Waterside Inn** (Food), **Sketch – The Lecture Room & Library** (Decor), **Roganic** (Service), **The Wolseley** (Favourite Restaurant), **Wagamama** (Favourite Chain)
- No. 1 Newcomer: **Pitt Cue Co.**

SURVEY STATS: London surveyors report eating out an average of 2.2 times per week, less frequently than their counterparts in Paris and New York (both at 3.0) . . . Service remains the No. 1 dining-out irritant (cited by 73%), followed by noise (10%) . . . If service isn't included, surveyors tip an average of 11.8% . . . 30% say they're spending more per meal than a year ago, 56% say the same and 14% say less . . . Favourite cuisines: Italian (25%), French (17%), Japanese (14%) – only one in 10 names British their favourite . . . A famous chef at the helm would make 44% more likely to patronise a restaurant, 6% less likely . . . 73% say locally sourced, organic and/or sustainable ingredients are somewhat to extremely important to them, 56% are willing to pay more for it . . . On a 30-point scale, London rates 25 for culinary diversity, 22 for creativity, 14 for hospitality and 13 for table availability.

TECH TALK: 53% book via phone, 40% use the Internet . . . 36% have downloaded restaurant-related smart-phone apps . . . 23% follow restaurants via social media, 16% "check-in" to a restaurant on social media when they arrive . . . 45% feel texting, e-mailing or talking on the phone whilst dining is rude and inappropriate, 49% deem it acceptable in moderation, 4% say it's perfectly acceptable . . . Regarding diners who photograph their food, 12% find it inappropriate, 66% call it acceptable in moderation, 18% feel it's perfectly acceptable.

PEDIGREED PREMIERES: Hix Belgravia and **Tramshed** (Mark Hix), **Cinnamon Soho** (Vivek Singh), **Bread Street Kitchen** (Gordon Ramsay), **Cut at 45 Park Lane** (Wolfgang Puck), **Union Jacks** (Jamie Oliver), **Sette** (Frankie Dettori), **Brasserie Zédel** and **The Delaunay** (**The Wolseley**'s Chris Corbin and Jeremy King), **Mishkin's** (**Polpo**'s Russell Norman), **Aurelia** (**Zuma**'s Arjun Waney), **Novikov** (prolific Moscow-based restaurateur Arkady Novikov), **34** (the Caprice group), **Downtown Mayfair** (the **C London** folks).

CHEFS FROM ABROAD BET ON LONDON: Cotidie (Italy's Bruno Barbieri), **Granger** (Australia's Bill Granger), **Hedone** (Sweden's Mikael Jonsson), **Kitchen 264 @ The Collection** (Israel's Oded Oren), **Lima** (Peru's Virgilio Martinez).

HOT NEIGHBOURHOODS FOR NEWCOMERS: Covent Garden (**Leon de Bruxelles, Meat Market, Suda, 10 Cases** et al.), Mayfair (**Alyn Williams at the Westbury, Arts Club, Burger & Lobster** et al.), Soho (**Ceviche, Copita, Ducksoup, La Bodega Negra, Mele e Pere, Pitt Cue Co., Tapasia, 10 Greek Street** et al.).

London   Sholto Douglas-Home
11 September, 2012

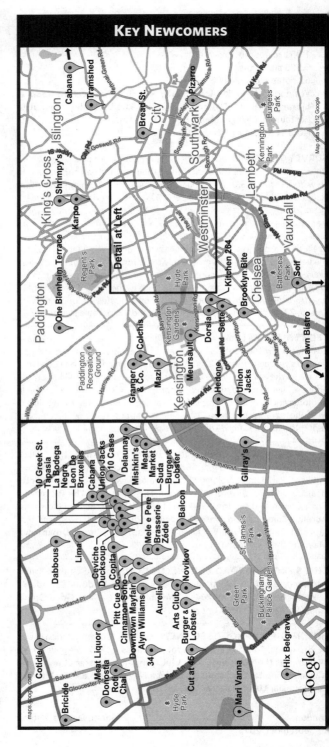

KEY NEWCOMERS

Upper map:

- Cabana
- Tramshed
- Bread St.
- Pizarro
- City
- Southwark
- Lambeth
- Shrimpy's
- King's Cross
- Islington
- Karpo
- Westminster
- Kitchen 264
- Brooklyn Bite
- Chelsea
- Soif
- One Blenheim Terrace
- Paddington
- Regent's Park
- Detail at Left
- Hyde Park
- Colchis
- Granger & Co.
- Mazi
- Meursault
- Kensington
- Dorsia
- Sette
- Hedone
- Union Jacks
- Lawn Bistro
- Map data ©2012 Google

Lower map (Detail):

- 10 Greek St.
- Tapasia
- La Bodega Negra
- Leon De Bruxelles
- Cabana
- Union Jacks
- 10 Cases
- Delaunay
- Mishkin's
- Meat Market
- Suda
- Burger & Lobster
- Gillray's
- Dabbous
- Lima
- Ceviche
- Ducksoup
- Copita
- Mele e Pere
- Brasserie Zédel
- Balcon
- Whitehall
- Pitt Cue Co.
- Cinnamon Soho
- Downtown Mayfair
- Alyn Williams
- Aurelia
- Arts Club
- Novikov
- St. James's Park
- Cotidie
- Meat Liquor
- Donostia
- Roti Chai
- 34
- Burger & Lobster
- Cut at 45
- Green Park
- Buckingham Palace Gardens
- Briciole
- Hyde Park
- Mari Vanna
- Hix Belgravia
- Google

maps.sbdg.com

Key Newcomers

Our editors' picks amongst this year's arrivals. See full list at p. 30.

NOTABLE NAMES

Aurelia
Brasserie Zédel
Bread Street Kitchen
Cinnamon Soho
Cut at 45 Park Lane
The Delaunay
Downtown Mayfair
Hix Belgravia
Novikov
Pizarro
Sette
34
Tramshed
Union Jacks

CHEFS TO WATCH

Alyn Williams at The Westbury
Briciole
Dabbous
Lawn Bistro
One Blenheim Terrace

AMERICAN-STYLE CASUAL

Brooklyn Bite
Burger & Lobster
Meat Liquor
Meat Market
Mishkin's
Pitt Cue Co.
Shrimpy's

WINE HAVENS

Meursault
Soif
10 Cases

INTERNATIONAL INTRIGUE

Colchis
Cotidie
Granger & Co.
Hedone
Kitchen 264 @ The Collection
Leon de Bruxelles
Mari Vanna
Mazi

LATIN LEANINGS

Cabana
Ceviche
Copita
Donostia
La Bodega Negra
Lima
Pizarro

HOTEL ADDITIONS

Balcon
Gillray's
Karpo

MORE WESTENDERS

Arts Club
Dorsia
Ducksoup
Mele e Pere
Roti Chai
Suda
Tapasia
10 Greek Street

ABOVE AND BEYOND:

Scheduled to debut soon after deadline were **Banca** (from the **Aurelia** owners), **Tramontana Brindisa** (**Brindisa** group), **SushiSamba** and **Duck and Waffle** (in the City's Heron Tower) and **Bubbledogs,** marrying champagne and hot dogs. Also, **Polpo** sibling **Polpetto,** closed at press time, hoped to relocate sometime in the summer.

On the horizon were **Cafe Colbert** (**The Wolseley** owners), **Chicken Shop** (**Soho House** and **Pizza East** owners), **Granary Square Kitchen** (chef **Bruno Loubet**), **Green Man & French Horn** (**Terroirs** owners), **Outlaw's Seafood & Grill** at the Capital Hotel (from Cornish chef **Nathan Outlaw**), plus **HKK** and **Chrysan** (**Hakkasan** owners). Big names coming from NYC include **Balthazar, La Esquina, STK** and **Standard Grill.** Premieres from renowned international names include **Moreno Cedroni at the Baglioni** (from the eponymous Italian chef), **Bo London** (Hong Kong's **Alvin Leung**) and **Okku** (a Japanese restaurant from Dubai).

Favourites

This list is plotted on the map at the back of this book.

1. Wolseley | *European*
2. Hakkasan | *Chinese*
3. Le Gavroche | *French*
4. Ivy | *British/European*
5. River Café | *Italian*
6. Ledbury | *French*
7. Gordon Ramsay/68 | *French*
8. J. Sheekey | *Seafood*
9. Dinner by Heston | *British*
10. Gordon Ramsay/Clar. | *Euro.*
11. Hawksmoor | *Chophouse*
12. Chez Bruce | *British*
13. Zuma | *Japanese*
14. L'Atelier/Robuchon | *French*
15. 101 Thai Kitchen | *Thai*
16. Alain Ducasse/ Dorchester | *Fr.*
17. Yauatcha | *Chinese*
18. Scott's | *Seafood*
19. Ottolenghi | *Bakery/Med.*
20. Rules | *Chophouse*
21. 1 Lombard Street | *French*
22. Amaya | *Indian*
23. Pollen St. Social | *British*
24. Bodeans | *BBQ*
25. Blue Elephant | *Thai*
26. Nobu London | *Japanese*
27. Square | *French*
28. Bar Boulud | *French*
29. Cinnamon Club | *Indian*
30. St. John | *British*
31. Goodman | *Chophouse*
32. Roka | *Japanese*
33. Chez Gérard | *French*
34. Arbutus | *European*
35. Clos Maggiore | *French*
36. Fat Duck (Bray) | *British*
37. Annie's | *British*
38. La Trompette | *Euro./Fr.*
39. Le Caprice | *British/European*
40. Maze | *French*
41. Zafferano | *Italian*
42. Barrafina | *Spanish*
43. Pied à Terre | *French*
44. Locanda Locatelli | *Italian*
45. Asia de Cuba | *Asian/Cuban*
46. Marcus Wareing | *French*
47. Boca di Lupo/Gelupo | *Italian*
48. Galvin at Windows | *French*
49. Moro | *African/Spanish*
50. Oxo Tower | *European*

FAVOURITE CHAINS

1. Wagamama | *Japanese*
2. Pizza Express | *Pizza*
3. Nando's | *Portuguese*
4. Gaucho | *Argent./Chophouse*
5. Café Rouge | *French*
6. Zizzi | *Pizza*
7. Jamie's Italian | *Italian*
8. Busaba Eathai | *Thai*
9. Wahaca | *Mexican*
10. Gourmet Burger | *Burgers*

Many of the above restaurants are among the London area's most expensive, but if popularity were calibrated to price, a number of other restaurants would surely join their ranks. To illustrate this, we have added lists of Best Buys on pages 15 and 16.

Top Food

29 Waterside Inn (Bray) | *French*

28 Dinings | *Japanese*
Le Gavroche | *French*
Barrafina | *Spanish*
Roganic | *British*
Petrus | *French*
Ledbury | *French*
Gordon Ramsay/68 | *Fr.*
Yashin Sushi | *Japanese*
Square | *French*
Chez Bruce | *British*
Pitt Cue Co. | *BBQ*
Gauthier Soho | *French*
Harwood Arms | *British*
Le Manoir/Quat
   (Great Milton) | *Fr.*
L'Atelier/Robuchon | *French*
Pearl | *French*
José | *Spanish*
French Table | *Fr./Med.*
Hunan* | *Chinese*
La Trompette* | *Euro./Fr.*

27 Fat Duck (Bray) | *European*
Pied à Terre | *French*
Babur | *Indian*
Marcus Wareing* | *French*

River Café | *Italian*
Morito | *African/Spanish*
Alain Ducasse/Dorchester | *Fr.*
Jin Kichi | *Japanese*
Umu | *Japanese*
La Petite Maison | *Med.*
Rasoi Vineet Bhatia* | *Indian*
Zucca* | *Italian*
Nobu London | *Japanese*
Roussillon | *French*
Zuma | *Japanese*
L'Escargot | *French*
Yauatcha | *Chinese*
Pepper Tree | *Thai*
Glasshouse* | *European*
Koffmann's | *French*
L'Oranger | *French*
Moro | *African/Spanish*
North Road | *European*

26 Dinner by Heston | *British*
Hibiscus | *French*
Wilton's | *British/Seafood*
Hawksmoor | *Chophouse*
Brawn | *British/French*
Amaya | *Indian*

BY CUISINE

AMERICAN

25 Burger & Lobster
Cut at 45 Park Lane
Spuntino
22 Palm
Hoxton Grill

BBQ (INT'L)

28 Pitt Cue Co.
23 Asadal
Barbecoa
22 Bodeans
21 Rodizio Rico

BRITISH (MODERN)

28 Roganic
Chez Bruce
Harwood Arms
27 Fat Duck (Bray)
26 Dinner by Heston

BRITISH (TRAD.)

26 Wilton's
25 Rhodes 24
Bentley's
Goring Dining Rm.
French Horn (Sonning)
Hix at the Albemarle*

CHINESE

28 Hunan
27 Yauatcha
26 Hakkasan
Min Jiang
25 Mandarin Kitchen

CHOPHOUSES

26 Hawksmoor
Goodman
Santa Maria/Garufa
25 Gaucho
24 Rib Room

* Indicates a tie with restaurant above; excludes places with low votes

ECLECTIC

26 Viajante
Mosimann's
25 Modern Pantry
Light House
Providores

EUROPEAN (MODERN)

28 La Trompette
27 Glasshouse
North Road
26 Trinity
Dabbous

FISH 'N' CHIPS

25 North Sea
24 Golden Hind
Rock & Sole Plaice
23 Two Brothers Fish
20 Geales

FRENCH (BISTRO)

26 Brula
Bistrot Bruno Loubet
25 Comptoir Gascon
Galvin Bistrot
Le Café/Marché
Le Vacherin*

FRENCH (BRASSERIE)

25 Angelus
24 Le Colombier
Racine
22 Le Café Anglais
Brasserie Blanc
Côte

FRENCH (CLASSIC)

29 Waterside Inn (Bray)
28 Le Gavroche
27 L'Escargot
Koffmann's
L'Oranger

FRENCH (NEW)

28 Petrus
Ledbury
Gordon Ramsay/68
Square
Gauthier Soho

INDIAN

27 Babur
Rasoi Vineet Bhatia
26 Amaya
Trishna
Star of India

ITALIAN

27 River Café
Zucca
26 Apsleys
Mennula
Theo Randall

JAPANESE

28 Dinings
Yashin Sushi
27 Jin Kichi
Umu
Nobu London

LEBANESE

25 Ishbilia
24 Yalla Yalla
23 Fairuz
Maroush
Al Hamra

MEDITERRANEAN

28 French Table
27 La Petite Maison
26 Ottolenghi
23 Eagle
Oxo Tower Brass.

MEXICAN

24 Tortilla
23 Lupita
Cantina Laredo
Taqueria
Wahaca

PIZZA

26 Portobello Rist.
25 Rossopomodoro
Franco Manca
Osteria Basilico
24 Princi London

SEAFOOD

26 Wilton's
Scott's
Randall & Aubin
J. Sheekey
J. Sheekey Oyster

SPANISH

28 Barrafina
José
27 Morito
Moro
25 Dehesa

THAI

27 Pepper Tree
26 Nahm
24 Patara
101 Thai Kitchen
Thai Thai

VEGETARIAN

26 Chutneys
25 Food for Thought
Gate
24 222 Veggie Vegan
Rasa

BY SPECIAL FEATURE

BREAKFAST

25 Nopi
Roast*
23 Wolseley
22 Cecconi's
21 1 Lombard Brass.

LATE NIGHT

27 Yauatcha
26 Amaya
Roka
Nobu Berkeley
J. Sheekey

BRUNCH

25 Pizarro
Modern Pantry
Angelus
Providores
24 Le Caprice

MEET FOR A DRINK

27 Zuma
26 Hawksmoor
Hakkasan
25 Cinnamon Club
24 Bar Boulud

BUSINESS LUNCH

28 Le Gavroche
25 Galvin La Chapelle
L'Anima
Arbutus
Savoy Grill

NEWCOMERS (RATED)

28 Pitt Cue Co.
26 Dabbous
25 Pizarro
Burger & Lobster
Cut at 45 Park Ln.

CHILD-FRIENDLY

27 River Café
Zuma
Yauatcha
23 Tom's Kitchen
22 Bodeans

OLDE ENGLAND

26 Wilton's
25 French Horn (Sonning)
Rules
24 Hinds Head (Bray)
23 Sweetings

EXPERIMENTAL

28 Roganic
27 Fat Duck (Bray)
North Rd.
26 Hibiscus
Viajante

PEOPLE-WATCHING

27 La Petite Maison
Nobu London
Zuma
25 Pollen St. Social
21 Delaunay

GASTROPUBS

28 Harwood Arms
25 Anchor/Hope
24 Great Queen St.
23 Empress
Gun*

PRIVATE CLUBS

26 Mosimann's
25 Harry's Bar
23 George
Arts Club
22 Adam St.

HOTEL DINING

29 Waterside Inn
28 Le Manoir/Quat
Pearl (Renaissance/Ct.)
27 Marcus Wareing (Berkeley)
Alain Ducasse (Dorchester)

SMALL PLATES

28 Dinings
L'Atelier/Robuchon
Hunan
26 Brawn
Amaya

SUNDAY LUNCH (COUNTRY)

- 29] Waterside Inn (Bray)
- 28] Le Manoir/Quat (Great Milton)
- 25] French Horn (Sonning)
- 24] Hinds Head (Bray)
- 22] Aubergine

SUNDAY LUNCH (TOWN)

- 27] La Petite Maison
- 26] Hawksmoor
  Bistrot Bruno Loubet
- 25] Launceston Place
  Roast

TASTING MENUS

- 29] Waterside Inn (Bray)
- 28] Le Gavroche

Roganic
Petrus
Ledbury

TEA SERVICE (OTHER THAN HOTELS)

- 25] Modern Pantry
- 24] Ladurée
  Chor Bizarre
  La Fromagerie
- 23] Wolseley

WINNING WINE LISTS

- 29] Waterside Inn (Bray)
- 28] Le Gavroche
  Roganic
  Gordon Ramsay/68
  Square

BY LOCATION

BAYSWATER

- 25] Mandarin Kitchen
  Angelus
- 24] Bombay Palace
  Halepi
  Alounak

BELGRAVIA

- 28] Petrus
- 27] Marcus Wareing
  Koffmann's
- 26] Amaya
  Apsleys

BLOOMSBURY/ FITZROVIA

- 27] Pied à Terre
- 26] Roka
  Hakkasan
  Mennula
  Dabbous

BOROUGH

- 25] Roast
- 24] Wright Brothers
  Brindisa
- 23] Fish
- 22] Tas

CANARY WHARF

- 26] Roka
  Goodman
- 25] Gaucho
- 24] Plateau
  Tortilla

CHELSEA

- 28] Gordon Ramsay/68
- 27] Rasoi Vineet Bhatia
- 25] Rossopomodoro
  Medlar
  Gaucho

CHISWICK

- 28] La Trompette
- 26] Charlotte's Bistro
- 25] Franco Manca
  Le Vacherin
- 24] Sam's Brasserie

CITY

- 26] Hawksmoor
  Goodman
  Café Spice Namasté
- 25] Rhodes 24
  Galvin La Chapelle

CLERKENWELL/ FARRINGDON

- 27] Morito
  Moro
  North Road
- 26] Club Gascon
  Bistrot Bruno Loubet

COVENT GARDEN

- 28] L'Atelier/Robuchon
- 26] Hawksmoor
  J. Sheekey
  J. Sheekey Oyster
- 25] Rossopomodoro

HAMPSTEAD

27 Jin Kichi
25 Gaucho
23 Woodlands
   Artigiano
22 The Wells

ISLINGTON

26 Santa Maria/Garufa
   Ottolenghi
25 Antepliler Restaurant
   Gate
24 Rasa

KENSINGTON

28 Yashin Sushi
26 Kitchen W8
   Min Jiang
   Clarke's
25 Launceston Place

KNIGHTSBRIDGE

27 Zuma
26 Dinner by Heston
24 Rib Room
   Good Earth
   Patara

MARYLEBONE

28 Dinings
   Roganic
26 Trishna
   Locanda Locatelli
   Roux/Landau

MAYFAIR

28 Le Gavroche
   Square
27 Alain Ducasse/Dorchester
   Umu
   La Petite Maison

NOTTING HILL

28 Ledbury
26 Ottolenghi
   Assaggi
   Portobello Rist.
25 Rossopomodoro

PICCADILLY

25 Bentley's
   Gaucho
   Ritz
   Yoshino
24 Ladurée

PIMLICO

28 Hunan
26 Tinello
25 Kazan
24 About Thyme
23 La Poule au Pot

SHOREDITCH/HOXTON

26 Hawksmoor
   Brawn
   Song Que Café
25 St. John Bread/Wine
24 Eyre Brothers

SOHO

28 Barrafina
   Pitt Cue Co.
   Gauthier Soho
27 L'Escargot
   Yauatcha

SOUTH KENSINGTON

26 Star of India
25 L'Etranger
24 Patara
   Brindisa
   Cambio de Tercio

ST. JAMES'S

27 L'Oranger
26 Wilton's
25 Sake No Hana
24 Le Caprice
   Rowley's

VICTORIA

25 Goring Dining Rm.
22 Olivo
21 Mango Tree
20 Zizzi
   Prezzo

IN THE COUNTRY

29 Waterside Inn (Bray)
28 Le Manoir/Quat (Great Milton)
27 Fat Duck (Bray)
25 French Horn (Sonning)
24 Hinds Head (Bray)

Top Decor

28 Sketch/Lecture Room	Babylon
Sketch/Parlour	Alain Ducasse/Dorchester
Waterside Inn (Bray)	La Porte des Indes
Ritz	Gordon Ramsay/Claridge's
Bob Bob Ricard	Portrait
	Wapping Food
27 Les Trois Garçons	Greenhouse
Le Manoir/Quat (Great Milton)	Aqua Nueva
Clos Maggiore	Blue Elephant
Sketch/Gallery	Delaunay
Espelette	Apsleys
Mosimann's*	Roux/Landau*
Criterion	Hakkasan
	French Horn (Sonning)
26 Hélène Darroze	Savoy River*
Rhodes 24	
Petrus	**25** Pearl
Aqua Kyoto	Folly*
Galvin La Chapelle	Gordon Ramsay/68
Goring Dining Rm.	Le Gavroche
Wolseley	Galvin at Windows
Rules	

OUTDOORS

Boundary	Ledbury
Coq d'Argent	Le Pont de la Tour
Hush	Oxo Tower Brass.
La Famiglia	River Café
La Poule au Pot	Scott's

PRIVATE ROOMS

Amaya	Min Jiang
China Tang	Spice Market
Dinner by Heston	Square
L'Anima	Zafferano
Marcus Wareing	Zuma

ROMANCE

Clos Maggiore	Le Gavroche
Club Gascon	Les Trois Garçons
Crazy Bear	Marcus Wareing
Dinner by Heston	Rasoi Vineet Bhatia
Galvin at Windows	Sketch/Lecture Room
La Poule au Pot	34

VIEWS

Boundary	Oxo Tower Brass.
Dinner by Heston	Paramount
Galvin at Windows	Rhodes 24
Le Pont de la Tour	Smiths/Top Floor
Min Jiang	Waterside Inn (Bray)

Top Service

Best Buys

OTHER GOOD VALUES

ALL YOU CAN EAT

26 Chutneys
Ma Goa
222 Veggie Vegan
Blue Elephant
23 Bombay Brasserie
22 Khan's
La Porte des Indes
21 Rodizio Rico

BAKERIES

26 Ottolenghi
24 Princi London
Ladurée
22 Gail's
21 Baker & Spice

CHAINS

23 Wahaca
22 Tas
Byron
Côte
21 Wagamama

CHILD-FRIENDLY

24 Oliveto
23 Tom's Kitchen
22 Bodeans
19 Chuen Cheng Ku
Masala Zone

PIZZA

26 Portobello Rist.
25 Franco Manca
24 Oliveto
21 Pizza Express
20 Zizzi

TAKEAWAY

28 José
27 Jin Kichi
26 Ottolenghi
Kiku
Star of India
Café Spice Namasté
25 Lahore Kebab
Pizarro
Royal China Club
Tamarind

OTHER USEFUL LISTS*

LOCATION MAPS

* These lists include low vote places that do not qualify for top lists.

Special Features

Listings cover the best in each category and include names, locations and Food ratings. Multi-location restaurants' features may vary by branch.

BREAKFAST

(See also Hotel Dining)

🔲 Ottolenghi | **multi.**	26
Cinnamon Club | **SW1P**	25
Nopi | **W1B**	25
Providores | **W1U**	25
Roast | **SE1**	25
St. John Bread | **E1**	25
Ladurée | **SW1X**	24
La Fromagerie | **W1U**	24
Rivington Grill | **EC2A**	24
Tom's Deli | **W11**	24
Butlers Wharf | **SE1**	23
Coq d'Argent | **EC2R**	23
Fifteen | **N1**	23
Lutyens | **EC4**	23
Empress | **E9**	23
Tom's Kitchen | **SW3**	23
🔲 Wolseley | **W1J**	23
Cecconi's | **W1S**	22
Franco's | **SW1Y**	22
Portrait | **WC2H**	22
Troubadour | **SW5**	22
Baker & Spice | **multi.**	21
NEW Delaunay | **WC2B**	21
1 Lombard Brass. | **EC3V**	21
Riding Hse. Café | **W1W**	21
Simpson's/Strand | **WC2R**	21
🔲 Carluccio's | **multi.**	20
Fortnum's Fountain | **W1A**	20
York/Albany | **NW1**	20
Automat | **W1S**	19
Balans | **multi.**	19
Fifth Floor Cafe | **SW1X**	19
Julie's | **W11**	19
La Brasserie | **SW3**	19
Lucky 7 | **W2**	19
Patisserie Valerie | **multi.**	19
202 | **W11**	19
Aubaine | **multi.**	18
Café Boheme | **W1D**	18
🔲 Café Rouge | **multi.**	18
Giraffe | **multi.**	18
Inn the Park | **SW1A**	18
Raoul's | **W9**	17
Richoux | **multi.**	16

BRUNCH

Angelus | **W2**	25
Hélène Darroze | **W1K**	25
L'Etranger | **SW7**	25
Modern Pantry | **EC1V**	25
NEW Pizarro | **SE1**	25
Providores | **W1U**	25
Caravan | **EC1R**	24
Le Caprice | **SW1A**	24
Sam's Brass. | **W4**	24
Tom's Deli | **W11**	24
Annie's | **multi.**	23
Tom's Kitchen | **SW3**	23
Cecconi's | **W1S**	22
Portrait | **WC2H**	22
Sophie's | **SW10**	22
NEW Delaunay | **WC2B**	21
Motcombs | **SW1X**	21
Quadrato | **E14**	21
Riding Hse. Café | **W1W**	21
Christopher's | **WC2E**	20
PJ's B&G | **SW3**	20
Wapping Food | **E1W**	20
Automat | **W1S**	19
Fifth Floor Cafe | **SW1X**	19
Joe Allen | **WC2E**	19
Lucky 7 | **W2**	19
202 | **W11**	19
Villandry | **W1W**	19
Aubaine | **multi.**	18
Giraffe | **multi.**	18

BUSINESS DINING

🔲 Waterside Inn | **SL6**	29
🔲 French Table | **KT6**	28
🔲 Gauthier | **W1D**	28
🔲 Gordon Ramsay/68 | **SW3**	28
🔲 L'Atelier/Robuchon | **WC2H**	28
🔲 La Trompette | **W4**	28
🔲 Ledbury | **W11**	28
🔲 Le Gavroche | **W1K**	28
🔲 Le Manoir/Quat | **OX44**	28
Morgan M | **EC1A**	28
🔲 Petrus | **SW1X**	28
🔲 Roganic | **W1U**	28
🔲 Square | **W1J**	28
🔲 Alain Ducasse | **W1A**	27
Glasshouse | **TW9**	27
Koffmann's | **SW1X**	27
🔲 La Petite Maison | **W1K**	27
🔲 L'Escargot | **W1D**	27
L'Oranger | **SW1A**	27

🅩 Marcus Wareing | **SW1X**	27	
🅩 Nobu London | **W1K**	27	
North Rd. | **EC1M**	27	
🅩 Pied à Terre | **W1T**	27	
🅩 Rasoi Vineet | **SW3**	27	
🅩 River Café | **W6**	27	
NEW Roti Chai | **W1H**	27	
🅩 Umu | **W1J**	27	
🅩 Zuma | **SW7**	27	
🅩 Amaya | **SW1X**	26	
Apsleys | **SW1X**	26	
Bistrot Bruno Loubet | **EC1M**	26	
Clarke's | **W8**	26	
Club Gascon | **EC1A**	26	
NEW Dabbous | **W1T**	26	
🅩 Dinner/Heston | **SW1X**	26	
Goodman | **multi.**	26	
🅩 Gordon Ramsay/Clar. | **W1K**	26	
Greenhouse | **W1J**	26	
🅩 Hakkasan | **W1J**	26	
Hibiscus | **W1S**	26	
🅩 J. Sheekey | **WC2N**	26	
J. Sheekey Oyster | **WC2N**	26	
Kitchen W8 | **W8**	26	
Locanda Locatelli | **W1H**	26	
Magdalen | **SE1**	26	
Mennula | **W1T**	26	
Min Jiang | **W8**	26	
Murano | **W1J**	26	
Nahm | **SW1X**	26	
Nobu Berkeley | **W1J**	26	
Portobello | **W11**	26	
Roka | **W1T**	26	
Roux/Landau | **W1**	26	
🅩 Scott's | **W1K**	26	
Theo Randall | **W1J**	26	
Tinello | **SW1W**	26	
Trinity | **SW4**	26	
Viajante | **E2**	26	
Wilton's | **SW1Y**	26	
Amaranto | **W1J**	25	
Angelus | **W2**	25	
Arbutus | **W1D**	25	
Benares | **W1J**	25	
Bentley's | **W1B**	25	
Cinnamon Club | **SW1P**	25	
Cinnamon Kitchen | **EC2M**	25	
Corrigan's Mayfair | **W1K**	25	
NEW Cut/45 Park Ln. | **W1K**	25	
Dock Kitchen | **W10**	25	
Dorchester | **W1K**	25	
🅩 Espelette | **W1K**	25	
Fino | **W1T**	25	

Galvin at Windows | **W1K**	25
Galvin Bistrot | **W1U**	25
🅩 Galvin Chapelle/Cafe | **E1**	25
Goring | **SW1**	25
Hélène Darroze | **W1K**	25
Hereford Rd. | **W2**	25
Hix at the Albemarle | **W1S**	25
Kai Mayfair | **W1K**	25
Kazan | **SW1V**	25
L'Anima | **EC2A**	25
Launceston Pl. | **W8**	25
L'Autre Pied | **W1U**	25
Le Café/Marché | **EC1M**	25
L'Etranger | **SW7**	25
Maze | **W1K**	25
Medlar | **SW10**	25
Nopi | **W1B**	25
Poissonnerie/l'Avenue | **SW3**	25
🅩 Pollen St. Social | **W1S**	25
Providores | **W1U**	25
Quirinale | **SW1P**	25
Red Fort | **W1D**	25
Rhodes 24 | **EC2N**	25
🅩 Ritz | **W1J**	25
Roast | **SE1**	25
🅩 Rules | **WC2E**	25
Savoy Grill | **WC2**	25
St. John Hotel Rest. | **WC2H**	25
Tamarind | **W1J**	25
Texture | **W1H**	25
Tom Aikens | **SW3**	25
Zafferano | **SW1X**	25
Zaika | **W8**	25
Bar Boulud | **SW1X**	24
Bellamy's | **W1J**	24
Constancia | **SE1**	24
Hix Oyster | **EC1M**	24
🅩 Ivy | **WC2H**	24
JW Steak | **W1K**	24
Kenza | **EC2M**	24
La Genova | **W1K**	24
Le Caprice | **SW1A**	24
Le Cercle | **SW1X**	24
Maze Grill | **W1K**	24
Olivomare | **SW1W**	24
Orrery | **W1U**	24
Plateau | **E14**	24
Princess Garden | **W1K**	24
Rasa | **multi.**	24
Rib Room | **SW1X**	24
Roux/Parliament | **SW1P**	24
Tempo | **W1J**	24
Alba | **EC1Y**	23

Almeida	**N1**	23	Bank Westminster	**SW1E**	21
Bar Battu	**EC2V**	23	Cassis Bistro	**SW3**	21
Bonds	**EC2R**	23	Criterion	**W1J**	21
Boundary	**E2**	23	**NEW** Delaunay	**WC2B**	21
C London	**W1K**	23	**NEW** Downtown Mayfair	**W1S**	21
Empress of Sichuan	**WC2H**	23	Imperial City	**EC3V**	21
Il Convivio	**SW1W**	23	Langan's Bistro	**W1G**	21
Indigo	**WC2B**	23	Langan's Brass.	**W1JJ**	21
Le Pont/Tour	**SE1**	23	Marco Pierre White	**E1**	21
Lutyens	**EC4**	23	Odin's	**W1G**	21
Matsuri	**SW1Y**	23	1 Lombard Brass.	**EC3V**	21
Memories/China	**multi.**	23	Quadrato	**E14**	21
Miyama	**W1**	23	Quaglino's	**SW1Y**	21
1901	**EC2M**	23	Quo Vadis	**W1D**	21
Paramount	**WC1A**	23	Smiths/Dining Rm.	**EC1M**	21
Semplice Rist.	**W1S**	23	Caldesi	**W1U**	20
Shanghai Blues	**WC1V**	23	Christopher's	**WC2E**	20
Shepherd's	**SW1P**	23	Elena's L'Etoile	**W1T**	20
2 Sketch/Lecture	**W1S**	23	Gilgamesh	**NW1**	20
Smiths/Top Fl.	**EC1M**	23	Massimo	**SW1N**	20
Sumosan	**W1S**	23	Mews/Mayfair	**W1S**	20
Sweetings	**EC4N**	23	**NEW** Novikov	**W1J**	20
NEW 34	**W1K**	23	Santini	**SW1W**	20
Tom's Kitchen	**SW3**	23	Skylon	**SE1**	20
Wheeler's	**SW1A**	23	Waterloo	**SE1**	20
Wild Honey	**W1S**	23	York/Albany	**NW1**	20
Al Duca	**SW1Y**	22	Fakhreldine	**W1J**	19
Alloro	**W1S**	22	Les Deux	**WC2N**	19
NEW Alyn Williams	**W1S**	22	Prism	**EC3V**	19
NEW Aurelia	**W1S**	22	Whitechapel	**E1**	19
Belvedere	**W8**	22	Folly	**EC3V**	18
Brasserie Blanc	**EC2R**	22	Gilbert Scott	**NW1**	18
Cecconi's	**W1S**	22	Manicomio	**multi.**	18
Cigalon	**WC2A**	22	Only Running	**W1J**	18
Dean St.	**W1D**	22	St. Pancras	**NW1**	18
Fifth Floor	**SW1X**	22	Wallace	**W1U**	18
Green's	**multi.**	22	Luxe	**E1**	17
High Road Brass.	**W4**	22	Northbank	**EC4V**	15
Hix	**W1F**	22	**NEW** Brasserie Zédel	**W1F**	-
Incognico	**WC2H**	22	**NEW** Briciole	**W1H**	-
Le Café Anglais	**W2**	22	**NEW** Cinnamon Soho	**W1B**	-
Mercer	**EC2R**	22	**NEW** Colchis	**W2**	-
One-O-One	**SW1X**	22	**NEW** Cotidie	**W1U**	-
Oxo Tower	**SE1**	22	**NEW** Door	**EC3V**	-
Palm	**SW1X**	22	**NEW** Drift	**EC2**	-
Pantechnicon Rooms	**SW1X**	22	**NEW** Gillray's	**SE1**	-
Paternoster Chop	**EC4M**	22	**NEW** Hix Belgravia	**SW1X**	-
Polpo	**WC2E**	22	**NEW** Karpo	**NW1**	-
NEW Suda	**WC2E**	22	**NEW** La Bodega Negra	**W1D**	-
28-50 Wine	**EC4A**	22	**NEW** Lima	**W1T**	-
Amico Bio	**EC1A**	21	**NEW** Mari Vanna	**SW1X**	-
Avenue	**SW1A**	21	**NEW** Mele e Pere	**W1F**	-
Babbo	**W1S**	21	**NEW** Meursault	**SW7**	-

SPECIAL FEATURES

Foxtrot Oscar | **SW3**	19
Narrow | **E14**	18
Theo Randall	
Theo Randall | **W1J**	26
Gary Rhodes	
Rhodes 24 | **EC2N**	25
Rhodes W1 | **W1H**	23
Joël Robuchon	
☒ L'Atelier/Robuchon | **WC2H**	28
Simon Rogan	
☒ Roganic | **W1U**	28
Ruth Rogers	
☒ River Café | **W6**	27
Albert Roux	
Roux/Landau | **W1**	26
☒ Waterside Inn | **SL6**	29
Michel Roux Jr	
☒ Le Gavroche | **W1K**	28
Roux/Landau | **W1**	26
Roux/Parliament | **SW1P**	24
Vivek Singh	
Cinnamon Club | **SW1P**	25
Cinnamon Kitchen | **EC2M**	25
NEW Cinnamon Soho | **W1B**	–
Jun Tanaka	
☒ Pearl | **WC1V**	28
David Thompson	
Nahm | **SW1X**	26
Cyrus Todiwala	
Café Spice | **E1**	26
John Torode	
Smiths/Top Fl. | **EC1M**	23
Smiths/Dining Rm. | **EC1M**	21
Luxe | **E1**	17
Jean-Georges Vongerichten	
Spice Mkt. | **W1**	23
Marcus Wareing	
☒ Marcus Wareing | **SW1X**	27
Gilbert Scott | **NW1**	18
Marco Pierre White	
Wheeler's | **SW1A**	23
Marco Pierre White | **E1**	21
Frankie's | **multi.**	18

CHILD-FRIENDLY

(Besides the normal fast-food places; * children's menu available)

☒ Barrafina | **W1D**	28
☒ Chez Bruce | **SW17**	28
☒ Le Manoir/Quat* | **OX44**	28
☒**NEW** Pitt Cue Co. | **W1F**	28
Glasshouse | **TW9**	27

☒ Nobu London | **W1K**	27
☒ River Café | **W6**	27
☒ Yauatcha | **W1F**	27
☒ Zuma | **SW7**	27
Assaggi | **W2**	26
Books/Cooks | **W11**	26
Café Spice | **E1**	26
☒ Hakkasan | **multi.**	26
☒ Hawksmoor | **multi.**	26
Locanda Locatelli | **W1H**	26
Min Jiang | **W8**	26
☒ Ottolenghi | **multi.**	26
Randall/Aubin | **W1F**	26
NEW Burger & Lobster | **W1J**	25
Cinnamon Club | **SW1P**	25
Fino | **W1T**	25
☒ Gaucho | **multi.**	25
L'Etranger | **SW7**	25
Locanda Ottoemezzo | **W8**	25
☒ Ritz* | **W1J**	25
Royal China Club | **W1U**	25
☒ Rules | **WC2E**	25
Sabor* | **N1**	25
Yoshino | **W1J**	25
Zafferano | **SW1X**	25
Archipelago | **W1T**	24
☒ Blue Elephant | **SW6**	24
Ladurée | **multi.**	24
La Fromagerie | **W1U**	24
Le Caprice | **SW1A**	24
Mediterraneo* | **W11**	24
Oliveto | **SW1W**	24
Patara | **multi.**	24
Plateau* | **E14**	24
Popeseye | **multi.**	24
Princi London | **W1F**	24
Rasa | **multi.**	24
Tom's Deli | **W11**	24
Abbeville | **SW4**	23
Almeida | **N1**	23
Babylon* | **W8**	23
Bibendum | **SW3**	23
Bibendum Oyster | **SW3**	23
Caraffini | **SW1**	23
Churchill Arms | **W8**	23
Eagle | **EC1R**	23
E&O | **W11**	23
Fifteen | **N1**	23
Fish* | **SE1**	23
Frederick's* | **N1**	23
Indigo* | **WC2B**	23
La Porchetta | **multi.**	23

Maroush	**multi.**	23	Benihana	**multi.**	20
Mela	**WC2H**	23	Black & Blue	**SW7**	20
Oxo Tower Brass.*	**SE1**	23	Bluebird*	**SW3**	20
Petersham*	**TW10**	23	☑ Browns*	**multi.**	20
Royal China	**multi.**	23	Cafe Pacifico*	**WC2H**	20
Sale e Pepe	**SW1X**	23	☑ Carluccio's*	**multi.**	20
Shepherd's	**SW1P**	23	Chez Gérard*	**EC2N**	20
Tom's Kitchen*	**SW3**	23	Christopher's*	**WC2E**	20
Two Brothers Fish*	**N3**	23	Ed's Easy Diner*	**W1D**	20
☑ Wahaca*	**multi.**	23	Fortnum's Fountain	**W1A**	20
☑ Wolseley	**W1J**	23	Kensington Pl.*	**W8**	20
Al Duca	**SW1Y**	22	NEW Mishkin's	**WC2B**	20
☑ Bodeans*	**multi.**	22	PJ's B&G*	**multi.**	20
☑ Byron*	**multi.**	22	Santini	**SW1W**	20
Cecconi's	**W1S**	22	Semplice Bar Trattoria	**W1C**	20
Daphne's	**SW3**	22	Strada*	**multi.**	20
Daylesford*	**multi.**	22	☑ Zizzi*	**multi.**	20
Fora	**NW8**	22	Ask Italian*	**multi.**	19
Il Baretto	**W1U**	22	Buona Sera	**multi.**	19
Le Café Anglais	**W2**	22	Caravaggio	**EC3A**	19
Noura	**multi.**	22	Chuen Cheng Ku	**W1D**	19
Oxo Tower*	**SE1**	22	Fifth Floor Cafe*	**SW1X**	19
Pellicano	**SW3**	22	Great Eastern*	**EC2A**	19
Sophie's*	**SW10**	22	Itsu	**SW3**	19
Tas	**multi.**	22	Jenny Lo's Tea	**SW1W**	19
Abingdon	**W8**	21	Joe Allen	**WC2E**	19
Baker & Spice	**multi.**	21	Julie's*	**W11**	19
Belgo*	**multi.**	21	La Brasserie*	**SW3**	19
Big Easy*	**SW3**	21	Lucky 7*	**W2**	19
Cantina/Ponte	**SE1**	21	Masala Zone*	**multi.**	19
Cassis Bistro	**SW3**	21	Patisserie Valerie	**multi.**	19
Cheyne Walk	**SW3**	21	Real Greek*	**multi.**	19
Cigala	**WC1N**	21	Rocket	**W1S**	19
Citrus*	**W1J**	21	Smollensky's*	**WC2R**	19
NEW Delaunay	**WC2B**	21	Sticky Fingers*	**W8**	19
Elistano	**SW3**	21	202	**W11**	19
Gay Hussar	**W1D**	21	Villandry*	**W1W**	19
☑ Gourmet Burger*	**multi.**	21	Aubaine	**multi.**	18
Kettner's*	**W1D**	21	☑ Café Rouge*	**multi.**	18
La Famiglia	**SW10**	21	Cha Cha Moon	**W1F**	18
Lucio	**SW3**	21	Frankie's*	**SW3**	18
Mango Tree	**SW1X**	21	Giraffe*	**multi.**	18
Orso	**WC2E**	21	Inn the Park*	**SW1A**	18
☑ Pizza Express*	**multi.**	21	Manicomio	**SW3**	18
Quadrato*	**E14**	21	Porters English*	**WC2E**	18
Quaglino's*	**SW1Y**	21	Truc Vert	**W1K**	18
Ransome's	**SW11**	21	Yo! Sushi*	**multi.**	18
Red Pepper	**W9**	21	Hard Rock*	**W1K**	17
Reubens*	**W1U**	21	Raoul's*	**multi.**	17
San Lorenzo	**SW3**	21	Riccardo's	**SW3**	17
Sofra	**multi.**	21	Richoux*	**multi.**	16
☑ Wagamama*	**multi.**	21	Quilon	**SW1E**	-

DELIVERY/TAKEAWAY

(D=delivery, T=takeaway)

🗹 José	T	**SE1**	28
Ikeda	T	**W1K**	27
🗹 Jin Kichi	T	**NW3**	27
Café Spice	D, T	**E1**	26
Kiku	T	**W1J**	26
🗹 Ottolenghi	T	**multi.**	26
Star of India	T	**SW5**	26
Beiteddine	D, T	**SW1X**	25
🗹 Gaucho	T	**multi.**	25
Ishbilia	D, T	**SW1X**	25
Lahore Kebab House	T	**E1**	25
Ma Goa	T	**SW15**	25
Mandalay	T	**W2**	25
Mao Tai	T	**SW6**	25
North Sea	T	**WC1H**	25
𝗡𝗘𝗪 Pizarro	T	**SE1**	25
Royal China Club	T	**W1U**	25
Tamarind	D, T	**W1J**	25
Yoshino	T	**W1J**	25
Alounak	D, T	**multi.**	24
🗹 Blue Elephant	D, T	**SW6**	24
Chor Bizarre	T	**W1S**	24
Defune	T	**W1U**	24
Golden Dragon	T	**W1D**	24
Halepi	T	**W2**	24
La Fromagerie	D, T	**W1U**	24
Patara	T	**multi.**	24
Princi London	T	**W1F**	24
Rasa	T	**multi.**	24
Rock & Sole	T	**WC2H**	24
Salloos	T	**SW1X**	24
Tom's Deli	T	**W11**	24
Cantina Laredo	T	**WC2H**	23
Churchill Arms	T	**W8**	23
Fairuz	D, T	**W1H**	23
Koi	D, T	**W8**	23
La Porchetta	T	**multi.**	23
Matsuri	T	**SW1Y**	23
Mela	T	**WC2H**	23
Memories/China	T	**multi.**	23
Noor Jahan	T	**multi.**	23
Original Lahore	T	**NW4**	23
Royal China	T	**multi.**	23
Singapore Gdn.	D, T	**NW6**	23
Two Brothers Fish	T	**N3**	23
Al Waha	D	**W2**	22
Daylesford	T	**multi.**	22
Esarn Kheaw	T	**W12**	22
Khan's	T	**W2**	22
Kulu Kulu	T	**multi.**	22
La Porte/Indes	T	**W1H**	22
Noura	D, T	**multi.**	22
Thai Sq./Soho Thai	T	**multi.**	22
Tas	D, T	**multi.**	22
Baker & Spice	T	**multi.**	21
Big Easy	T	**SW3**	21
𝗡𝗘𝗪 Delaunay	T	**WC2B**	21
Harbour City	T	**W1D**	21
Imperial City	T	**EC3V**	21
Mango Tree	T	**SW1X**	21
Özer	T	**W1B**	21
🗹 Pizza Express	T	**multi.**	21
Red Pepper	T	**W9**	21
Reubens	T	**W1U**	21
🗹 Carluccio's	T	**multi.**	20
Ed's Easy Diner	T	**W1D**	20
Leon	T	**multi.**	20
Solly's	T	**NW11**	20
Strada	T	**multi.**	20
Ask Italian	T	**multi.**	19
Chuen Cheng Ku	T	**W1D**	19
Fakhreldine	D, T	**W1J**	19
Feng Sushi	D, T	**multi.**	19
Gopal's	T	**W1D**	19
Itsu	D, T	**SW3**	19
Jenny Lo's Tea	D, T	**SW1W**	19
Lucky 7	T	**W2**	19
Masala Zone	T	**multi.**	19
Sticky Fingers	T	**W8**	19
Villandry	T	**W1W**	19
Crazy Homies	T	**W2**	18
Giraffe	T	**multi.**	18
Inn the Park	T	**SW1A**	18
Manicomio	T	**multi.**	18
Truc Vert	D, T	**W1K**	18
Yo! Sushi	D, T	**multi.**	18
Riccardo's	T	**SW3**	17
Richoux	T	**multi.**	16

DINING ALONE

(Other than hotels and places
with counter service)

🗹 Yauatcha	**W1F**	27
🗹 Amaya	**SW1X**	26
Books/Cooks	**W11**	26
🗹 Hakkasan	**multi.**	26
🗹 Ottolenghi	**multi.**	26
Randall/Aubin	**W1F**	26
Comptoir Gascon	**EC1M**	25
Fino	**W1T**	25
Providores	**W1U**	25
St. John Bread	**E1**	25
Ladurée	**multi.**	24
La Fromagerie	**W1U**	24

Le Colombier | **SW3**	24
Princi London | **W1F**	24
Tom's Deli | **W11**	24
🏧 Busaba Eathai | **multi.**	23
Matsuri | **SW1Y**	23
Taqueria | **W11**	23
Tom's Kitchen | **multi.**	23
🏧 Wolseley | **W1J**	23
Daylesford | **multi.**	22
Gail's | **multi.**	22
Noura | **multi.**	22
Polpo | **W1F**	22
Portrait | **WC2H**	22
Baker & Spice | **multi.**	21
Mon Plaisir | **WC2H**	21
Ping Pong | **multi.**	21
🏧 Wagamama | **multi.**	21
🏧 Carluccio's | **multi.**	20
Chowki | **W1D**	20
Comptoir Libanais | **multi.**	20
Ed's Easy Diner | **multi.**	20
Fortnum's Fountain | **W1A**	20
Leon | **multi.**	20
New Culture Rev. | **multi.**	20
Tate Modern | **SE1**	20
Chuen Cheng Ku | **W1D**	19
Fifth Floor Cafe | **SW1X**	19
Jenny Lo's Tea | **SW1W**	19
Le Pain Quot. | **multi.**	19
Patisserie Valerie | **multi.**	19
Villandry | **W1W**	19
Aubaine | **multi.**	18
🏧 Café Rouge | **multi.**	18
Inn the Park | **SW1A**	18
Manicomio | **SW3**	18
Porters English | **WC2E**	18
Truc Vert | **W1K**	18
Yo! Sushi | **multi.**	18
Armani Caffé | **SW3**	17
Restaurant/Arts | **W1J**	17
Richoux | **multi.**	16

ENTERTAINMENT

(Call for days and times of
performances)

🏧 Hakkasan | DJ | **W1T**	26
Bentley's | piano | **W1B**	25
Le Café/Marché | jazz/piano | **EC1M**	25
🏧 Ritz | bands/piano | **W1J**	25
Le Caprice | piano | **SW1A**	24
Little Italy | DJ | **W1D**	24
Coq d'Argent | jazz | **EC2R**	23
Le Pont/Tour | piano | **SE1**	23
Maroush | belly dancing | **multi.**	23
Meson Don Felipe | guitarist | **SE1**	23
Oxo Tower Brass. | jazz | **SE1**	23
Bengal Clipper | piano | **SE1**	22
Boisdale | jazz | **SW1W**	22
Efes | varies | **W1W**	22
Notting Hill Brass. | jazz/piano | **W11**	22
Thai Sq./Soho Thai | DJ | **SW1Y**	22
Big Easy | bands | **SW3**	21
Ishtar | belly dancing | **W1U**	21
Langan's Brass. | varies | **W1JJ**	21
Quaglino's | varies | **SW1Y**	21
Simpson's/Strand | piano | **WC2R**	21
Souk | belly dancing | **WC2H**	21
Gilgamesh | DJ | **NW1**	20
Joe Allen | piano | **WC2E**	19
Floridita | Cuban/DJ | **W1F**	18

FIREPLACES

🏧 Waterside Inn | **SL6**	29
🏧 Harwood Arms | **SW6**	28
🏧 Pearl | **WC1V**	28
🏧 L'Escargot | **W1D**	27
Amaranto | **W1J**	25
Brunello | **SW7**	25
🏧 Clos Maggiore | **WC2E**	25
🏧 Espelette | **W1K**	25
French Horn | **RG4**	25
Goring | **SW1**	25
Hix at the Albemarle | **W1S**	25
Princess Victoria | **W12**	25
🏧 Rules | **WC2E**	25
Cambio/Tercio | **SW5**	24
Hinds Head | **SL6**	24
Le Cercle | **SW1X**	24
Palmerston | **SE22**	24
Abbeville | **SW4**	23
Al Hamra | **W1J**	23
Babylon | **W8**	23
Churchill Arms | **W8**	23
Gravetye Manor | **RH19**	23
Gun | **E14**	23
Sands End | **SW6**	23
Vapiano | **W1W**	23
Aubergine | **SL7**	22
Bam-Bou | **W1T**	22
Cottons | **NW1**	22
Daphne's | **SW3**	22
Hoxton Grill | **EC2A**	22
Il Baretto | **W1U**	22

Pantechnicon Rooms | **SW1X**	22
Wells | **NW3**	22
Anglesea Arms | **W6**	21
Cheyne Walk | **SW3**	21
Criterion | **W1J**	21
Grazing Goat | **W1**	21
Greig's | **W1J**	21
Lemonia | **NW1**	21
Thomas Cubitt | **SW1W**	21
Waterway | **W9**	21
Gazette | **SW12**	20
Old Bull & Bush | **NW3**	20
Pig's Ear | **SW3**	20
Sardo | **NW1**	20
Admiral Codrington | **SW3**	19
Cafe Med | **NW8**	19
Gopal's | **W1D**	19
Julie's | **W11**	19
Builders Arms | **SW3**	18
Grenadier | **SW1X**	18
Narrow | **E14**	18
Only Running | **W1J**	18
NEW Sonny's Kitchen | **SW13**	-

HISTORIC PLACES

(Year opened; * building)

1550 | Aubergine* | **SL7**	22
1550 | Fat Duck* | **SL6**	27
1598 | Graveye Manor* | **RH19**	23
1677 | Green's* | **SW1Y**	22
1680 | French Horn* | **RG4**	25
1690 | Giovanni's* | **WC2N**	25
1690 | Hinds Head | **SL6**	24
1690 | Wells* | **NW3**	22
1700 | Bellamy's* | **W1J**	24
1700 | Ransome's* | **SW11**	21
1720 | Grenadier* | **SW1X**	18
1721 | Old Bull & Bush | **NW3**	20
1740 | Bingham* | **TW10**	24
1741 | L'Escargot* | **W1D**	27
1742 | Princess/Shoreditch* | **EC2A**	21
1746 | Bleeding Heart* | **EC1N**	23
1750 | Food/Thought* | **WC2H**	25
1750 | Gauthier* | **W1D**	28
1750 | Gun* | **E14**	23
1755 | Randall/Aubin* | **W1F**	26
1760 | Auberge du Lac* | **AL8**	26
1762 | Bull & Last* | **NW5**	23
1776 | Tom's Kitchen* | **WC2R**	23
1779 | Sketch/Gallery* | **W1S**	22
1779 | Sketch/Lecture* | **W1S**	23

1780 | Andrew Edmunds* | **W1F**	24
1790 | Carluccio's* | **EC1A**	20
1790 | Rowley's* | **SW1Y**	24
1798 | Don* | **EC4N**	22
1798 | Rules* | **WC2E**	25
1800 | Anglesea Arms* | **W6**	21
1800 | Belvedere* | **W8**	22
1800 | Churchill Arms* | **W8**	23
1800 | Rocket* | **multi.**	19
1800 | Tokyo Diner* | **WC2H**	22
1810 | Angelus* | **W2**	25
1810 | Pig's Ear* | **SW3**	20
1820 | Builders Arms* | **SW3**	18
1820 | York/Albany* | **NW1**	20
1828 | Simpson's/Strand* | **WC2R**	21
1834 | Albion* | **N1**	22
1837 | Hix at the Albemarle* | **W1S**	25
1846 | Les Trois Garçons* | **E1**	23
1850 | Brumus* | **SW1Y**	23
1851 | Flemings Grill* | **W1J**	22
1855 | Baltic* | **SE1**	24
1855 | Bonds* | **EC2R**	23
1857 | Warrington* | **W9**	20
1865 | Petersham* | **TW10**	23
1867 | Kettner's* | **W1D**	21
1867 | Pantechnicon Rooms* | **SW1X**	22
1868 | St. Pancras* | **NW1**	18
1871 | Rock & Sole | **WC2H**	24
1873 | Gilbert Scott* | **NW1**	18
1874 | Criterion | **W1J**	21
1879 | Opera Tavern* | **WC2B**	24
1880 | Bombay Brass.* | **SW7**	23
1881 | Duke/Cambridge* | **N1**	22
1886 | Tuttons* | **WC2B**	19
1887 | Luxe* | **E1**	17
1888 | Da Mario* | **SW7**	19
1889 | Savoy Grill* | **WC2**	25
1889 | Savoy River* | **WC2**	22
1889 | Sweetings | **EC4N**	23
1890 | Bradley's* | **NW3**	23
1890 | La Fromagerie* | **W1U**	24
1890 | Maggie Jones's* | **W8**	23
1890 | Notting Hill Brass.* | **W11**	22
1890 | R.S.J.* | **SE1**	23
1890 | Wapping Food* | **E1W**	20
1896 | Elena's L'Etoile* | **W1T**	20
1896 | J. Sheekey* | **WC2N**	26
1897 | Espelette* | **W1K**	25
1897 | Hélène Darroze* | **W1K**	25
1898 | Duke of Sussex* | **W4**	23

1900	Annie's*	**W4**	23
1900	Artigiano*	**NW3**	23
1900	Balans*	**SW5**	19
1900	Brinkley's*	**SW10**	16
1900	Frontline*	**W2**	24
1900	Goodman*	**W1S**	26
1900	Julie's*	**W11**	19
1900	La Famiglia*	**SW10**	21
1900	Langan's Brass.*	**W1JJ**	21
1900	St. John Bread*	**E1**	25
1905	Almeida*	**N1**	23
1906	Ritz*	**W1J**	25
1910	Bocca/Gelupo*	**W1D**	26
1910	Goring*	**SW1**	25
1910	Viajante*	**E2**	26
1911	Bibendum*	**SW3**	23
1911	Bibendum Oyster*	**SW3**	23
1914	Golden Hind	**W1U**	24
1920	Orso*	**WC2E**	21
1920	Tamarind*	**W1J**	25
1921	Delaunay*	**WC2B**	21
1921	Patisserie Valerie*	**W1U**	19
1921	Wolseley*	**W1J**	23
1923	Bluebird*	**SW3**	20
1924	Prism*	**EC3V**	19
1926	Patisserie Valerie	**W1D**	19
1926	Quo Vadis	**W1D**	21
1926	Veeraswamy	**W1B**	25
1930	Bistrotheque*	**E2**	22
1930	Haché*	**NW1**	22
1930	Sale e Pepe*	**SW1X**	23
1931	Dorchester	**W1K**	25
1933	Babylon*	**W8**	23
1939	Geales	**W8**	20
1939	Lutyens*	**EC4**	23
1942	Mon Plaisir	**WC2H**	21
1947	Gessler/Daquise	**SW7**	25
1947	Punjab	**WC2H**	23
1950	Fortnum's Fountain	**W1A**	20
1950	Greig's	**W1J**	21
1952	Star of India	**SW5**	26
1953	Gay Hussar	**W1D**	21
1953	Guinea Grill	**W1J**	24
1954	Troubadour	**SW5**	22
1955	Brompton B&G*	**SW3**	19
1956	Pescatori	**W1T**	24
1959	Ebury Wine	**SW1W**	18
1960	Angus Steakhouse	**WC2H**	19
1960	Archipelago*	**W1T**	24
1961	Rib Room	**SW1X**	24
1962	La Poule au Pot	**SW1W**	23
1962	L'Oranger	**SW1A**	27

HOTEL DINING

Andaz Liverpool St.	
1901	**EC2M**	23
Baglioni Hotel	
Brunello	**SW7**	25
Belgraves Hotel	
NEW Hix Belgravia	**SW1X**	–
Berkeley	
Koffmann's	**SW1X**	27
Z Marcus Wareing	**SW1X**	27
Bingham Hotel	
Bingham	**TW10**	24
Blakes Hotel	
Blakes	**SW7**	19
Brown's Hotel	
Hix at the Albemarle	**W1S**	25
Church Street Hotel	
Angels & Gypsies	**SE5**	25
Claridge's	
Z Gordon Ramsay/Clar.	**W1K**	26
Cliveden Country House Hotel	
Cliveden Hse.	**SL6**	20
Connaught	
Z Espelette	**W1K**	25
Hélène Darroze	**W1K**	25
Corinthia Hotel London	
Massimo	**SW1N**	20
Crowne Plaza London	
Refettorio	**EC4V**	26
Crowne Plaza St. James Hotel	
Quilon	**SW1E**	–
Cumberland Hotel	
Rhodes W1	**W1H**	23
Dean Street Townhse.	
Dean St.	**W1D**	22
Dorchester	
Z Alain Ducasse	**W1A**	27
Dorchester	**W1K**	25
China Tang	**W1K**	22
Flemings Hotel	
Flemings Grill	**W1J**	22
45 Park Ln.	
NEW Cut/45 Park Ln.	**W1K**	25
Four Seasons Canary Wharf	
Quadrato	**E14**	21
Four Seasons Park Ln.	
Amaranto	**W1J**	25
French Horn Hotel	
French Horn	**RG4**	25
Goring Hotel	
Goring	**SW1**	25

LATE DINING

(Weekday closing hour)

Ishbilia | 12 AM | **SW1X**	25
Lahore Kebab House | varies | **E1**	25
New Mayflower | 4 AM | **W1D**	25
Paradise | varies | **W10**	25
Sabor | varies | **N1**	25
St. John Hotel Rest. | 1.30 AM | **WC2H**	25
Texture | 12 AM | **W1H**	25
Alounak | varies | **multi.**	24
Asia de Cuba | varies | **WC2N**	24
805 | varies | **SE15**	24
Gaby's | 12 AM | **WC2H**	24
Halepi | 12 AM | **W2**	24
⊠ Ivy | 12 AM | **WC2H**	24
Le Caprice | 12 AM | **SW1A**	24
Little Italy | 4 AM | **W1D**	24
NEW Meat Liquor | varies | **W1G**	24
Opera Tavern | 12 AM | **WC2B**	24
Princi London | 12 AM | **W1F**	24
Tsunami | varies | **SW4**	24
Wright Brothers | 12 AM | **W1**	24
Al Hamra | 12 AM | **W1J**	23
Almeida | 1 AM | **N1**	23
Forge | 12 AM | **WC2E**	23
Four Seasons | varies | **W1D**	23
Frederick's | 12 AM | **N1**	23
Haz | 12 AM | **E1**	23
La Porchetta | 12 AM | **N10**	23
Maroush | varies | **multi.**	23
Mint Leaf | varies | **SW1Y**	23
Original Lahore | varies | **multi.**	23
Paramount | varies | **WC1A**	23
Spuntino | 12 AM | **W1D**	23
Sumosan | 12 AM | **W1S**	23
Vapiano | varies | **multi.**	23
⊠ Wolseley | 12 AM | **W1J**	23
Bam-Bou | 1 AM | **W1T**	22
Boisdale | 12 AM | **E14**	22
Brasserie Blanc | 12 AM | **SE1**	22
Cecconi's | 1 AM | **W1S**	22
Efes | 12 AM | **W1W**	22
Hoxton Grill | 12 AM | **EC2A**	22
Imperial China | 12 AM | **WC2H**	22
Las Iguanas | 12 AM | **KT1**	22
Le Deuxième | 12 AM | **WC2E**	22
Malabar | 12 AM | **W8**	22
Mr. Kong | 2.45 AM | **WC2H**	22
Sophie's | 12 AM | **WC2E**	22
Tokyo Diner | 12 AM | **WC2H**	22
Wasabi | varies | **SW1V**	22
Avenue | 1 AM | **SW1A**	21
Belgo | 11.30 PM | **SW4**	21
NEW Cabana | 12 AM | **WC2H**	21
Chiswell St. Dining | varies | **EC1**	21
Del'Aziz | 12 AM | **W12**	21
Greig's | 12 AM | **W1J**	21
Ishtar | 12 AM | **W1U**	21
Le Mercury | 1 AM | **N1**	21
Little Bay | 12 AM | **multi.**	21
Mr. Chow | 12 AM | **SW1X**	21
Orso | 12 AM | **WC2E**	21
Pasha | 12 AM | **SW7**	21
Ping Pong | varies | **multi.**	21
Rodizio Rico | 12 AM | **multi.**	21
⊠ Sketch/Parlour | 2 AM | **W1S**	21
Souk | 12 AM | **WC2H**	21
Union Cafe | 12 AM | **W1U**	21
Cafe Pacifico | 12 AM | **WC2H**	20
Gilgamesh | varies | **NW1**	20
Inamo | 12 AM | **SW1Y**	20
⊠ Jamie's Italian | varies | **E20**	20
New World | 12 AM | **W1D**	20
Pizza East | varies | **E1**	20
PJ's B&G | varies | **WC2E**	20
Angus Steakhouse | varies | **multi.**	19
Automat | 1 AM | **W1S**	19
Balans | varies | **multi.**	19
Blakes | 12 AM | **SW7**	19
Bumpkin | 12 AM | **multi.**	19
Buona Sera | 12 AM | **multi.**	19
Chuen Cheng Ku | 12 AM | **W1D**	19
Great Eastern | 12 AM | **EC2A**	19
Joe Allen | 12.45 AM | **WC2E**	19
Fulham/Kens. Wine Rooms | 12 AM | **SW6**	19
Maxwell's | 12 AM | **WC2E**	19
Rocket | 12 AM | **W1S**	19
Café Boheme | 2.30 AM | **W1D**	18
Ciro's Pizza | varies | **SW3**	18
Diner | 12 AM | **multi.**	18
Floridita | 1 AM | **W1F**	18
Montpeliano | 12 AM | **SW7**	18
All Star Lanes | varies | **E1**	17
NEW Bunga Bunga | varies | **SW11**	17
Giant Robot | varies | **EC1M**	17
Hard Rock | 12.30 AM | **W1K**	17
Hoxton Square | varies | **N1**	17
Luxe | 1 AM | **E1**	17
Planet Hollywood | 1 AM | **SW1Y**	16
Pix Pintxos | 12 AM | **WC2H**	13
NEW Brasserie Zédel | 12 AM | **W1F**	–
NEW Ceviche | 12 AM | **W1D**	–
NEW Colchis | 12 AM | **W2**	–
NEW Kitchen 264 | 12 AM | **SW3**	–

NEW La Bodega Negra | 1 AM | W1D

NEW Lowcountry | varies | SW6

NEW Mari Vanna | 12 AM | SW1X

NEW Mazi | 12 AM | W8

NEW Meursault | 1 AM | SW7

NEW Tapasia | 12 AM | W1D

NEWCOMERS

⧄ Pitt Cue Co.	W1F	28
Roti Chai	W1H	27
Dabbous	W1T	26
Burger & Lobster	W1J	25
Cut/45 Park Ln.	W1K	25
Pizarro	SE1	25
Meat Liquor	W1G	24
Balcon	SW1Y	23
Copita	W1F	23
10 Cases	WC2H	23
34	W1K	23
Alyn Williams	W1S	22
Aurelia	W1S	22
Hedone	W4	22
Suda	WC2E	22
Bread St. Kitchen	EC4M	21
Cabana	multi.	21
Chakra	W11	21
Delaunay	WC2B	21
Mishkin's	WC2B	20
Novikov	W1J	20
Union Jacks	multi.	20
Devonshire Arms	W4	19
Leon De Bruxelles	WC2H	19
Ducksoup	W1D	18
Granger & Co.	W11	18
Bunga Bunga	SW11	17
Brasserie Zédel	W1F	-
Briciole	W1H	-
Brooklyn Bite	SW3	-
Ceviche	W1D	-
Cinnamon Soho	W1B	-
Colchis	W2	-
Cotidie	W1U	-
Donostia	W1H	-
Door	EC3V	-
Drift	EC2	-
Georgina's	SW13	-
Gillray's	SE1	-
Hix Belgravia	SW1X	-
Karpo	NW1	-
Kitchen 264	SW3	-
La Bodega Negra	W1D	-
Lawn Bistro	SW19	-
Lima	W1T	-
Lowcountry	SW6	-
Mari Vanna	SW1X	-
Mazi	W8	-
Meat Market	WC2E	-
Mele e Pere	W1F	-
Meursault	SW7	-
1 Blenheim Terrace	NW8	-
Sette	SW3	-
Shrimpy's	N1C	-
Soif	SW11	-
Tapasia	W1D	-
10 Greek Street	W1D	-
Tramshed	EC2A	-
Wulumuchi	WC2H	-

OUTDOOR DINING

⧄ Barrafina	W1D	28
⧄ La Trompette	W4	28
⧄ Ledbury	W11	28
Moro	EC1R	27
⧄ River Café	W6	27
Bistrot Bruno Loubet	EC1M	26
Café Spice	E1	26
Roka	multi.	26
⧄ Scott's	W1K	26
Amaranto	W1J	25
Brunello	SW7	25
Cinnamon Kitchen	EC2M	25
Ishbilia	SW1X	25
L'Aventure	NW8	25
Modern Pantry	EC1V	25
Osteria Basilico	W11	25
Paradise	W10	25
⧄ Ritz	W1J	25
Archipelago	W1T	24
Le Colombier	SW3	24
Mediterraneo	W11	24
Olivomare	SW1W	24
Orrery	W1U	24
Plateau	E14	24
Tom's Deli	W11	24
Abbeville	SW4	23
Al Hamra	W1J	23
Almeida	N1	23
Artigiano	NW3	23
Babylon	W8	23
Boundary	E2	23
Butlers Wharf	SE1	23
Caraffini	SW1	23
Coq d'Argent	EC2R	23
Eagle	EC1R	23

E&O | **W11**	23
Fish | **SE1**	23
La Poule au Pot | **SW1W**	23
Le Pont/Tour | **SE1**	23
Oxo Tower Brass. | **SE1**	23
Rotunda | **N1**	23
Smiths/Top Fl. | **EC1M**	23
Albion | **N1**	22
Aqua Nueva | **W1B**	22
Bam-Bou | **W1T**	22
Belvedere | **W8**	22
Blueprint | **SE1**	22
Daylesford | **multi.**	22
Dean St. | **W1D**	22
El Gaucho | **SW3**	22
Oxo Tower | **SE1**	22
Pellicano | **SW3**	22
Abingdon | **W8**	21
Anglesea Arms | **W6**	21
Ark | **W8**	21
Bank Westminster | **SW1E**	21
Cantina/Ponte | **SE1**	21
Elistano | **SW3**	21
Hush | **W1S**	21
La Famiglia | **SW10**	21
Motcombs | **SW1X**	21
Osteria Antica | **SW11**	21
Özer | **W1B**	21
Quadrato | **E14**	21
Quo Vadis | **W1D**	21
Ransome's | **SW11**	21
Momo | **W1B**	20
Santini | **SW1W**	20
Semplice Bar Trattoria | **W1C**	20
Wapping Food | **E1W**	20
Admiral Codrington | **SW3**	19
Fifth Floor Cafe | **SW1X**	19
Julie's | **W11**	19
Rocket | **W1S**	19
202 | **W11**	19
Villandry | **W1W**	19
Aubaine | **SW3**	18
Builders Arms | **SW3**	18
Inn the Park | **SW1A**	18
Manicomio | **SW3**	18
Narrow | **E14**	18
Porters English | **WC2E**	18
Hard Rock | **W1K**	17
Riccardo's | **SW3**	17

PEOPLE-WATCHING

☒ Waterside Inn | **SL6**	29
☒ Gordon Ramsay/68 | **SW3**	28

☒ L'Atelier/Robuchon | **WC2H**	28
☒ La Trompette | **W4**	28
☒ Ledbury | **W11**	28
☒ La Petite Maison | **W1K**	27
☒ Marcus Wareing | **SW1X**	27
☒ Nobu London | **W1K**	27
☒ River Café | **W6**	27
☒ Yauatcha | **W1F**	27
☒ Zuma | **SW7**	27
☒ Amaya | **SW1X**	26
Club Gascon | **EC1A**	26
NEW Dabbous | **W1T**	26
☒ Hakkasan | **multi.**	26
☒ J. Sheekey | **WC2N**	26
J. Sheekey Oyster | **WC2N**	26
Locanda Locatelli | **W1H**	26
Nobu Berkeley | **W1J**	26
Roka | **W1T**	26
☒ Scott's | **W1K**	26
Wilton's | **SW1Y**	26
NEW Burger & Lobster | **W1J**	25
Cinnamon Club | **SW1P**	25
Cinnamon Kitchen | **EC2M**	25
Corrigan's Mayfair | **W1K**	25
Dehesa | **W1F**	25
Dock Kitchen | **W10**	25
Fino | **W1T**	25
Franco Manca | **multi.**	25
Galvin Bistrot | **W1U**	25
☒ Galvin Chapelle/Cafe | **E1**	25
Hereford Rd. | **W2**	25
Hix at the Albemarle | **W1S**	25
L'Anima | **EC2A**	25
Maze | **W1K**	25
Nopi | **W1B**	25
Osteria Basilico | **W11**	25
NEW Pizarro | **SE1**	25
☒ Pollen St. Social | **W1S**	25
Sake No Hana | **SW1A**	25
Savoy Grill | **WC2**	25
St. John Hotel Rest. | **WC2H**	25
Tom Aikens | **SW3**	25
Zafferano | **SW1X**	25
Asia de Cuba | **WC2N**	24
Bar Boulud | **SW1X**	24
Ba Shan | **W1S**	24
Bellamy's | **W1J**	24
Giaconda | **WC2H**	24
Great Queen St. | **WC2B**	24
Hix Oyster | **EC1M**	24
☒ Ivy | **WC2H**	24
Le Caprice | **SW1A**	24

Le Cercle | **SW1X**	24
Maze Grill | **W1K**	24
Olivomare | **SW1W**	24
Opera Tavern | **WC2B**	24
Princi London | **W1F**	24
Racine | **SW3**	24
Tom's Deli | **W11**	24
Abbeville | **SW4**	23
Aqua Kyoto | **W1B**	23
Bar Battu | **EC2V**	23
Barshu | **W1D**	23
Boundary | **E2**	23
Caraffini | **SW1**	23
C London | **W1K**	23
NEW Copita | **W1F**	23
Dishoom | **WC2H**	23
E&O | **W11**	23
Eight Over Eight | **SW3**	23
Fifteen | **N1**	23
Lutyens | **EC4**	23
Rotunda | **N1**	23
Semplice Rist. | **W1S**	23
2 Sketch/Lecture | **W1S**	23
Spice Mkt. | **W1**	23
Spuntino | **W1D**	23
Sumosan | **W1S**	23
NEW 34 | **W1K**	23
Tom's Kitchen | **SW3**	23
Tsuru | **multi.**	23
2 Wahaca | **multi.**	23
Wild Honey | **W1S**	23
2 Wolseley | **W1J**	23
NEW Aurelia | **W1S**	22
Bam-Bou | **W1T**	22
Cecconi's | **W1S**	22
Daphne's | **SW3**	22
Daylesford | **multi.**	22
Dean St. | **W1D**	22
Fifth Floor | **SW1X**	22
High Road Brass. | **W4**	22
Hix | **W1F**	22
Le Café Anglais | **W2**	22
Olivo | **SW1W**	22
Palm | **SW1X**	22
Pantechnicon Rooms | **SW1X**	22
Polpo | **multi.**	22
2 Sketch/Gallery | **W1S**	22
Sophie's | **SW10**	22
NEW Suda | **WC2E**	22
Avenue | **SW1A**	21
NEW Cabana | **E20**	21
Cassis Bistro | **SW3**	21

NEW Delaunay | **WC2B**	21
NEW Downtown Mayfair | **W1S**	21
Hush | **W1S**	21
La Famiglia | **SW10**	21
Lucio | **SW3**	21
Quaglino's | **SW1Y**	21
Quo Vadis | **W1D**	21
San Lorenzo | **SW3**	21
Tendido Cuatro | **SW6**	21
XO | **NW3**	21
Caldesi | **W1U**	20
Christopher's | **WC2E**	20
Gilgamesh | **NW1**	20
Inamo | **W1F**	20
Kensington Pl. | **W8**	20
Mews/Mayfair | **W1S**	20
NEW Mishkin's | **WC2B**	20
Momo | **W1B**	20
NEW Novikov | **W1J**	20
Pizza East | **E1**	20
PJ's B&G | **SW3**	20
Santini | **SW1W**	20
York/Albany | **NW1**	20
Admiral Codrington | **SW3**	19
NEW Devonshire Arms | **W4**	19
Joe Allen | **WC2E**	19
Les Deux | **WC2N**	19
Old Brewery | **SE10**	19
Rocca | **multi.**	19
202 | **W11**	19
Whitechapel | **E1**	19
Antidote | **W1**	18
Aubaine | **multi.**	18
Folly | **EC3V**	18
NEW Granger & Co. | **W11**	18
Manicomio | **SW3**	18
Narrow | **E14**	18
All Star Lanes | **WC1B**	17
Anthologist | **EC2V**	17
Luxe | **E1**	17
Riccardo's | **SW3**	17
NEW Brasserie Zédel | **W1F**	—
NEW Briciole | **W1H**	—
NEW Cinnamon Soho | **W1B**	—
NEW Drift | **EC2**	—
NEW Georgina's | **SW13**	—
NEW Kitchen 264 | **SW3**	—
NEW La Bodega Negra | **W1D**	—
NEW Lima | **W1T**	—
NEW Lowcountry | **SW6**	—
NEW Mele e Pere | **W1F**	—
NEW Sette | **SW3**	—

NEW Soif | **SW11**	-
NEW Tramshed | **EC2A**	-

POWER SCENES

🄩 Waterside Inn | **SL6**	29
🄩 Gordon Ramsay/68 | **SW3**	28
🄩 L'Atelier/Robuchon | **WC2H**	28
🄩 Ledbury | **W11**	28
🄩 Le Gavroche | **W1K**	28
🄩 Le Manoir/Quat | **OX44**	28
🄩 Petrus | **SW1X**	28
🄩 Square | **W1J**	28
🄩 Alain Ducasse | **W1A**	27
🄩 La Petite Maison | **W1K**	27
🄩 Marcus Wareing | **SW1X**	27
🄩 Nobu London | **W1K**	27
🄩 Umu | **W1J**	27
🄩 Zuma | **SW7**	27
Club Gascon | **EC1A**	26
Greenhouse | **W1J**	26
Hibiscus | **W1S**	26
🄩 J. Sheekey | **WC2N**	26
Murano | **W1J**	26
Nobu Berkeley | **W1J**	26
🄩 Scott's | **W1K**	26
Tinello | **SW1W**	26
Wilton's | **SW1Y**	26
Bentley's | **W1B**	25
Cinnamon Club | **SW1P**	25
Cinnamon Kitchen | **EC2M**	25
Corrigan's Mayfair | **W1K**	25
NEW Cut/45 Park Ln. | **W1K**	25
🄩 Galvin Chapelle/Cafe | **E1**	25
Goring | **SW1**	25
Hélène Darroze | **W1K**	25
Hix at the Albemarle | **W1S**	25
L'Anima | **EC2A**	25
Launceston Pl. | **W8**	25
Maze | **W1K**	25
Quirinale | **SW1P**	25
Rhodes 24 | **EC2N**	25
Sake No Hana | **SW1A**	25
Savoy Grill | **WC2**	25
Tom Aikens | **SW3**	25
Zafferano | **SW1X**	25
Bar Boulud | **SW1X**	24
🄩 Ivy | **WC2H**	24
Le Caprice | **SW1A**	24
Maze Grill | **W1K**	24
Tempo | **W1J**	24
Bonds | **EC2R**	23
Boundary | **E2**	23
C London | **W1K**	23

Lutyens | **EC4**	23
Semplice Rist. | **W1S**	23
Shepherd's | **SW1P**	23
🄩 Sketch/Lecture | **W1S**	23
NEW 34 | **W1K**	23
Wild Honey | **W1S**	23
🄩 Wolseley | **W1J**	23
NEW Aurelia | **W1S**	22
Cigalon | **WC2A**	22
Daphne's | **SW3**	22
Dean St. | **W1D**	22
Green's | **multi.**	22
🄩 1 Lombard | **EC3V**	22
Palm | **SW1X**	22
Avenue | **SW1A**	21
Babbo | **W1S**	21
NEW Delaunay | **WC2B**	21
Langan's Brass. | **W1JJ**	21
Quo Vadis | **W1D**	21
San Lorenzo | **SW3**	21
NEW Novikov | **W1J**	20
York/Albany | **NW1**	20
Caravaggio | **EC3A**	19
Prism | **EC3V**	19
Gilbert Scott | **NW1**	18
NEW Door | **EC3V**	-
NEW Gillray's | **SE1**	-
NEW Mari Vanna | **SW1X**	-

PRIVATE ROOMS

(Call for capacity)

🄩 Waterside Inn | **SL6**	29
🄩 Chez Bruce | **SW17**	28
🄩 Le Manoir/Quat | **OX44**	28
🄩 Pearl | **WC1V**	28
🄩 Square | **W1J**	28
🄩 Alain Ducasse | **W1A**	27
Koffmann's | **SW1X**	27
🄩 L'Escargot | **W1D**	27
L'Oranger | **SW1A**	27
🄩 Marcus Wareing | **SW1X**	27
🄩 Nobu London | **W1K**	27
🄩 Pied à Terre | **W1T**	27
🄩 Rasoi Vineet | **SW3**	27
🄩 Zuma | **SW7**	27
🄩 Amaya | **SW1X**	26
Auberge du Lac | **AL8**	26
🄩 Dinner/Heston | **SW1X**	26
🄩 Gordon Ramsay/Clar. | **W1K**	26
Greenhouse | **W1J**	26
🄩 Hakkasan | **W1T**	26
🄩 Hawksmoor | **E1**	26

Restaurant		Rating
Hibiscus	W1S	26
Min Jiang	W8	26
Murano	W1J	26
Nahm	SW1X	26
Patterson's	W1S	26
🔲 Scott's	W1K	26
St. John	EC1M	26
Vasco & Piero's	W1F	26
Wilton's	SW1Y	26
Benares	W1J	25
Bentley's	W1B	25
Brunello	SW7	25
Cinnamon Club	SW1P	25
Corrigan's Mayfair	W1K	25
Dehesa	W1F	25
French Horn	RG4	25
Ishbilia	SW1X	25
Kai Mayfair	W1K	25
L'Anima	EC2A	25
Launceston Pl.	W8	25
Mao Tai	SW6	25
Maze	W1K	25
Paradise	W10	25
Poissonnerie/l'Avenue	SW3	25
🔲 Rules	WC2E	25
Savoy Grill	WC2	25
Timo	W8	25
Tom Aikens	SW3	25
Veeraswamy	W1B	25
Zafferano	SW1X	25
Baltic	SE1	24
Cambio/Tercio	SW5	24
Chutney Mary	SW10	24
Guinea Grill	W1J	24
🔲 Ivy	WC2H	24
Le Cercle	SW1X	24
Le Colombier	SW3	24
Patara	SW3	24
Plateau	E14	24
Rasa	multi.	24
Rib Room	SW1X	24
Rivington Grill	EC2A	24
Tentazioni	SE1	24
Almeida	N1	23
Babylon	W8	23
Boundary	E2	23
C London	W1K	23
E&O	W11	23
Eight Over Eight	SW3	23
Fairuz	W1H	23
Il Convivio	SW1W	23
La Poule au Pot	SW1W	23
Le Pont/Tour	SE1	23
🔲 Les Trois Garçons	E1	23
Matsuri	SW1Y	23
Memories/China	SW1W	23
Mint Leaf	SW1Y	23
Royal China	multi.	23
Shepherd's	SW1P	23
🔲 Sketch/Lecture	W1S	23
Spice Mkt.	W1	23
Sumosan	W1S	23
Tom's Kitchen	SW3	23
Alloro	W1S	22
Bam-Bou	W1T	22
🔲 Bob Bob Ricard	W1F	22
China Tang	W1K	22
Cigalon	WC2A	22
Daphne's	SW3	22
Franco's	SW1Y	22
Green's	multi.	22
La Porte/Indes	W1H	22
Le Café Anglais	W2	22
Notting Hill Brass.	W11	22
Noura	W1J	22
🔲 1 Lombard	EC3V	22
One-O-One	SW1X	22
Palm	SW1X	22
Pellicano	SW3	22
Sartoria	W1S	22
Thai Sq./Soho Thai	multi.	22
Wells	NW3	22
Albannach	WC2N	21
Greig's	W1J	21
Hush	W1S	21
Mon Plaisir	WC2H	21
Motcombs	SW1X	21
Mr. Chow	SW1X	21
1 Lombard Brass.	EC3V	21
Pasha	SW7	21
Quaglino's	SW1Y	21
Quo Vadis	W1D	21
San Lorenzo	SW19	21
Smiths/Dining Rm.	EC1M	21
Thomas Cubitt	SW1W	21
Vivat Bacchus	EC4A	21
Benihana	multi.	20
Christopher's	WC2E	20
Gilgamesh	NW1	20
Kensington Pl.	W8	20
Massimo	SW1N	20
Santini	SW1W	20
Warrington	W9	20
York/Albany	NW1	20

Admiral Codrington | **SW3** — 19
Chuen Cheng Ku | **W1D** — 19
Julie's | **W11** — 19
Masala Zone | **multi.** — 19
Prism | **EC3V** — 19
Real Greek | **N1** — 19
Rocket | **W1S** — 19
Villandry | **W1W** — 19
Floridita | **W1F** — 18
Manicomio | **multi.** — 18
Narrow | **E14** — 18
All Star Lanes | **WC1B** — 17
NEW Sette | **SW3** — -
NEW Sonny's Kitchen | **SW13** — -

PUDDING SPECIALISTS

Z Waterside Inn | **SL6** — 29
Z Chez Bruce | **SW17** — 28
Z Gauthier | **W1D** — 28
Z Gordon Ramsay/68 | **SW3** — 28
Z L'Atelier/Robuchon | **WC2H** — 28
Z La Trompette | **W4** — 28
Z Ledbury | **W11** — 28
Z Le Gavroche | **W1K** — 28
Z Le Manoir/Quat | **OX44** — 28
Z Petrus | **SW1X** — 28
Z Square | **W1J** — 28
Z Alain Ducasse | **W1A** — 27
Z Fat Duck | **SL6** — 27
Glasshouse | **TW9** — 27
Koffmann's | **SW1X** — 27
L'Oranger | **SW1A** — 27
Z Marcus Wareing | **SW1X** — 27
Z Nobu London | **W1K** — 27
Z Pied à Terre | **W1T** — 27
Z Rasoi Vineet | **SW3** — 27
Z River Café | **W6** — 27
Z Yauatcha | **W1F** — 27
Z Zuma | **SW7** — 27
Z Amaya | **SW1X** — 26
Auberge du Lac | **AL8** — 26
Bistrot Bruno Loubet | **EC1M** — 26
Bocca/Gelupo | **W1D** — 26
Clarke's | **W8** — 26
Club Gascon | **EC1A** — 26
Z Dinner/Heston | **SW1X** — 26
Z Gordon Ramsay/Clar. | **W1K** — 26
Greenhouse | **W1J** — 26
Hibiscus | **W1S** — 26
Locanda Locatelli | **W1H** — 26
Murano | **W1J** — 26

Nobu Berkeley | **W1J** — 26
Oslo Court | **NW8** — 26
Z Ottolenghi | **multi.** — 26
Theo Randall | **W1J** — 26
Trinity | **SW4** — 26
NEW Cut/45 Park Ln. | **W1K** — 25
Galvin at Windows | **W1K** — 25
Galvin Bistrot | **W1U** — 25
Z Galvin Chapelle/Cafe | **E1** — 25
Hélène Darroze | **W1K** — 25
Launceston Pl. | **W8** — 25
Maze | **W1K** — 25
Z Pollen St. Social | **W1S** — 25
Providores | **W1U** — 25
Z Ritz | **W1J** — 25
Savoy Grill | **WC2** — 25
St. John Bread | **E1** — 25
St. John Hotel Rest. | **WC2H** — 25
Tom Aikens | **SW3** — 25
Zafferano | **SW1X** — 25
Asia de Cuba | **WC2N** — 24
Ladurée | **SW1X** — 24
Le Cercle | **SW1X** — 24
Orrery | **W1U** — 24
Plateau | **E14** — 24
Princi London | **W1F** — 24
Almeida | **N1** — 23
Bibendum | **SW3** — 23
C London | **W1K** — 23
Fifteen | **N1** — 23
Le Pont/Tour | **SE1** — 23
Rhodes W1 | **W1H** — 23
Semplice Rist. | **W1S** — 23
Z Sketch/Lecture | **W1S** — 23
Z Wolseley | **W1J** — 23
Aubergine | **SL7** — 22
Belvedere | **W8** — 22
Fifth Floor | **SW1X** — 22
Le Café Anglais | **W2** — 22
Palm | **SW1X** — 22
Z Sketch/Gallery | **W1S** — 22
Baker & Spice | **multi.** — 21
Cassis Bistro | **SW3** — 21
NEW Delaunay | **WC2B** — 21
Z Sketch/Parlour | **W1S** — 21
Fortnum's Fountain | **W1A** — 20
Blakes | **SW7** — 19
Patisserie Valerie | **multi.** — 19
Villandry | **W1W** — 19
Aubaine | **W1S** — 18
Gilbert Scott | **NW1** — 18
Richoux | **multi.** — 16

QUIET CONVERSATION

🄩 Waterside Inn	SL6	29
🄩 French Table	KT6	28
🄩 Le Gavroche	W1K	28
🄩 Le Manoir/Quat	OX44	28
Morgan M	EC1A	28
🄩 Petrus	SW1X	28
🄩 Alain Ducasse	W1A	27
Koffmann's	SW1X	27
L'Oranger	SW1A	27
🄩 Pied à Terre	W1T	27
🄩 Rasoi Vineet	SW3	27
Apsleys	SW1X	26
Clarke's	W8	26
Hibiscus	W1S	26
Kitchen W8	W8	26
Magdalen	SE1	26
Mennula	W1T	26
Min Jiang	W8	26
Murano	W1J	26
Nahm	SW1X	26
Theo Randall	W1J	26
Wilton's	SW1Y	26
Amaranto	W1J	25
Arbutus	W1D	25
Benares	W1J	25
🄩 Clos Maggiore	WC2E	25
🄩 Espelette	W1K	25
Goring	SW1	25
Hélène Darroze	W1K	25
Launceston Pl.	W8	25
L'Autre Pied	W1U	25
Medlar	SW10	25
Quirinale	SW1P	25
🄩 Ritz	W1J	25
Texture	W1H	25
Bingham	TW10	24
JW Steak	W1K	24
La Genova	W1K	24
Mediterraneo	W11	24
Orrery	W1U	24
Roux/Parliament	SW1P	24
Salloos	SW1X	24
Tempo	W1J	24
Il Convivio	SW1W	23
Indigo	WC2B	23
Koi	W8	23
Lutyens	EC4	23
Rhodes W1	W1H	23
🄩 Sketch/Lecture	W1S	23
Al Sultan	W1J	22

NEW Alyn Williams	W1S	22
Bengal Clipper	SE1	22
Cigalon	WC2A	22
Green's	multi.	22
One-O-One	SW1X	22
28-50 Wine	EC4A	22
Babbo	W1S	21
Bank Westminster	SW1E	21
Odin's	W1G	21
Quadrato	E14	21
Massimo	SW1N	20
Mews/Mayfair	W1S	20
Gilbert Scott	NW1	18
St. Pancras	NW1	18
Northbank	EC4V	15
NEW Briciole	W1H	-
NEW Colchis	W2	-
NEW Cotidie	W1U	-
NEW Door	EC3V	-
NEW Gillray's	SE1	-
NEW Hix Belgravia	SW1X	-
NEW Karpo	NW1	-
NEW Meursault	SW7	-
NEW Sette	SW3	-
NEW Sonny's Kitchen	SW13	-
NEW Wulumuchi	WC2H	-

ROMANTIC PLACES

🄩 Waterside Inn	SL6	29
🄩 Gordon Ramsay/68	SW3	28
🄩 L'Atelier/Robuchon	WC2H	28
🄩 La Trompette	W4	28
🄩 Ledbury	W11	28
🄩 Le Gavroche	W1K	28
🄩 Le Manoir/Quat	OX44	28
🄩 Petrus	SW1X	28
🄩 Square	W1J	28
🄩 Alain Ducasse	W1A	27
Koffmann's	SW1X	27
L'Oranger	SW1A	27
🄩 Marcus Wareing	SW1X	27
🄩 Nobu London	W1K	27
🄩 Rasoi Vineet	SW3	27
🄩 River Café	W6	27
🄩 Zuma	SW7	27
🄩 Dinner/Heston	SW1X	26
🄩 Amaya	SW1X	26
Apsleys	SW1X	26
Clarke's	W8	26
Club Gascon	EC1A	26
🄩 Gordon Ramsay/Clar.	W1K	26
Greenhouse	W1J	26

Oslo Court	**NW8**	26
Patterson's	**W1S**	26
Theo Randall	**W1J**	26
Trishna	**W1U**	26
Vasco & Piero's	**W1F**	26
Angelus	**W2**	25
Arbutus	**W1D**	25
Benares	**W1J**	25
Brunello	**SW7**	25
Café Japan	**NW11**	25
Cinnamon Club	**SW1P**	25
ⓩ Clos Maggiore	**WC2E**	25
Enoteca Turi	**SW15**	25
Galvin Bistrot	**W1U**	25
Goring	**SW1**	25
Hélène Darroze	**W1K**	25
Kai Mayfair	**W1K**	25
Launceston Pl.	**W8**	25
L'Autre Pied	**W1U**	25
L'Aventure	**NW8**	25
Le Café/Marché	**EC1M**	25
L'Etranger	**SW7**	25
Le Vacherin	**W4**	25
Maze	**W1K**	25
Poissonnerie/l'Avenue	**SW3**	25
Red Fort	**W1D**	25
ⓩ Ritz	**W1J**	25
Savoy Grill	**WC2**	25
Tamarind	**W1J**	25
Tom Aikens	**SW3**	25
Veeraswamy	**W1B**	25
Yoshino	**W1J**	25
Zaika	**W8**	25
Ziani	**SW3**	25
Baltic	**SE1**	24
Bar Boulud	**SW1X**	24
Bellamy's	**W1J**	24
Chor Bizarre	**W1S**	24
Chutney Mary	**SW10**	24
Defune	**W1U**	24
Latium	**W1T**	24
Le Cercle	**SW1X**	24
Le Colombier	**SW3**	24
Maze Grill	**W1K**	24
Orrery	**W1U**	24
Patara	**multi.**	24
Plateau	**E14**	24
Princess Garden	**W1K**	24
Racine	**SW3**	24
Rasa	**multi.**	24
Rib Room	**SW1X**	24
Roux/Parliament	**SW1P**	24

Tentazioni	**SE1**	24
Almeida	**N1**	23
Bibendum	**SW3**	23
Butlers Wharf	**SE1**	23
Coq d'Argent	**EC2R**	23
Fifteen	**N1**	23
Forge	**WC2E**	23
Il Convivio	**SW1W**	23
Indigo	**WC2B**	23
La Poule au Pot	**SW1W**	23
ⓩ Les Trois Garçons	**E1**	23
Mela	**WC2H**	23
Memories/China	**W8**	23
Royal China	**W2**	23
Semplice Rist.	**W1S**	23
ⓩ Sketch/Lecture	**W1S**	23
Al Duca	**SW1Y**	22
Alloro	**W1S**	22
ⓝⓔⓦ Alyn Williams	**W1S**	22
Belvedere	**W8**	22
Bengal Clipper	**SE1**	22
El Pirata	**W1J**	22
Fora	**NW8**	22
High Road Brass.	**W4**	22
Noura	**multi.**	22
Olivo	**SW1W**	22
One-O-One	**SW1X**	22
Oxo Tower	**SE1**	22
Pellicano	**SW3**	22
Sartoria	**W1S**	22
Sophie's	**multi.**	22
Abingdon	**W8**	21
Cigala	**WC1N**	21
Criterion	**W1J**	21
Langan's Bistro	**W1G**	21
Lucio	**SW3**	21
Özer	**W1B**	21
Sofra	**multi.**	21
Christopher's	**WC2E**	20
Kensington Pl.	**W8**	20
Sardo	**NW1**	20
Café des Amis	**WC2E**	19
Caravaggio	**EC3A**	19
Porters English	**WC2E**	18
Quilon	**SW1E**	–

SINGLES SCENES

ⓩ Morito	**EC1R**	27
Moro	**EC1R**	27
ⓩ Nobu London	**W1K**	27
ⓩ Zuma	**SW7**	27
ⓩ Hakkasan	**W1T**	26
Nobu Berkeley	**W1J**	26

Roka	**W1T**	26
Barrica	**W1T**	25
Fino	**W1T**	25
Maze	**W1K**	25
Sabor	**N1**	25
Asia de Cuba	**WC2N**	24
Kenza	**EC2M**	24
Le Cercle	**SW1X**	24
Aqua Kyoto	**W1B**	23
E&O	**W11**	23
Eight Over Eight	**SW3**	23
Fifteen	**N1**	23
Maroush	**multi.**	23
Oxo Tower Brass.	**SE1**	23
Spice Mkt.	**W1**	23
Sumosan	**W1S**	23
⊠ Wahaca	**W1F**	23
⊠ Bob Bob Ricard	**W1F**	22
Cecconi's	**W1S**	22
Oxo Tower	**SE1**	22
⊠ Sketch/Gallery	**W1S**	22
Sophie's	**multi.**	22
Albannach	**WC2N**	21
Avenue	**SW1A**	21
Bank Westminster	**SW1E**	21
Belgo	**multi.**	21
Big Easy	**SW3**	21
Bountiful Cow	**WC1R**	21
Enterprise	**SW3**	21
Hush	**W1S**	21
Kettner's	**W1D**	21
Medcalf	**EC1R**	21
Motcombs	**SW1X**	21
Ping Pong	**multi.**	21
Quaglino's	**SW1Y**	21
Smiths/Dining Rm.	**EC1M**	21
Waterway	**W9**	21
XO	**NW3**	21
Bluebird	**SW3**	20
⊠ Browns	**multi.**	20
Cafe Pacifico	**WC2H**	20
Christopher's	**WC2E**	20
Gilgamesh	**NW1**	20
Inamo	**W1F**	20
Mews/Mayfair	**W1S**	20
Momo	**W1B**	20
PJ's B&G	**SW3**	20
York/Albany	**NW1**	20
Admiral Codrington	**SW3**	19
Balans	**multi.**	19
Botanist	**SW1W**	19
Buona Sera	**multi.**	19

Circus	**WC2H**	19
Fifth Floor Cafe	**SW1X**	19
Real Greek	**multi.**	19
Sticky Fingers	**W8**	19
Ebury Wine	**SW1W**	18
Floridita	**W1F**	18
All Star Lanes	**E20**	17
Nozomi	**SW3**	16
𝗡𝗘𝗪 Kitchen 264	**SW3**	-
𝗡𝗘𝗪 La Bodega Negra	**W1D**	-

SLEEPERS

(Good food, but little known)

Sushi-Say	**NW2**	28
Zayna	**W1H**	28
Ikeda	**W1K**	27
Lamberts	**SW12**	27
Hot Stuff	**SW8**	26
Portal	**EC1M**	26
Refettorio	**EC4V**	26
Vasco & Piero's	**W1F**	26
Aurora	**W1F**	25
Beiteddine	**SW1X**	25
Chancery	**EC4A**	25
Gessler/Daquise	**SW7**	25
Giovanni's	**WC2N**	25
Goldmine	**W2**	25
Locanda Ottoemezzo	**W8**	25
Mandalay	**W2**	25
Mao Tai	**SW6**	25
Paradise	**W10**	25
Plum Valley	**W1D**	25
Princess Victoria	**W12**	25
Sabor	**N1**	25
Ten Ten Tei	**W1**	25
Timo	**W8**	25
Frontline	**W2**	24
Made/Camden	**NW1**	24
Palmerston	**SE22**	24
Tempo	**W1J**	24
Tentazioni	**SE1**	24
Tom Ilic	**SW8**	24
Verru	**W1U**	24
Bar Battu	**EC2V**	23
Bonds	**EC2R**	23
Brumus	**SW1Y**	23
Cellar Gascon	**EC1A**	23
Koi	**W8**	23
Meson Don Felipe	**SE1**	23
Original Lahore	**multi.**	23
Rotunda	**N1**	23
Sakura	**W1S**	23

Sands End | SW6 — 23
Tsuru | multi. — 23

SPECIAL OCCASIONS

☒ Waterside Inn | SL6 — 29
☒ Chez Bruce | SW17 — 28
☒ French Table | KT6 — 28
☒ Gauthier | W1D — 28
☒ Gordon Ramsay/68 | SW3 — 28
☒ L'Atelier/Robuchon | WC2H — 28
☒ La Trompette | W4 — 28
☒ Ledbury | W11 — 28
☒ Le Gavroche | W1K — 28
☒ Le Manoir/Quat | OX44 — 28
Morgan M | EC1A — 28
☒ Pearl | WC1V — 28
☒ Petrus | SW1X — 28
☒ Roganic | W1U — 28
☒ Square | W1J — 28
☒ Alain Ducasse | W1A — 27
☒ Fat Duck | SL6 — 27
Glasshouse | TW9 — 27
Koffmann's | SW1X — 27
☒ La Petite Maison | W1K — 27
L'Oranger | SW1A — 27
☒ Marcus Wareing | SW1X — 27
☒ Nobu London | W1K — 27
☒ Pied à Terre | W1T — 27
☒ Rasoi Vineet | SW3 — 27
☒ River Café | W6 — 27
☒ Umu | W1J — 27
☒ Zuma | SW7 — 27
☒ Amaya | SW1X — 26
Apsleys | SW1X — 26
Auberge du Lac | AL8 — 26
Clarke's | W8 — 26
Club Gascon | EC1A — 26
NEW Dabbous | W1T — 26
☒ Dinner/Heston | SW1X — 26
☒ Gordon Ramsay/Clar. | W1K — 26
Greenhouse | W1J — 26
☒ Hakkasan | multi. — 26
Hibiscus | W1S — 26
☒ J. Sheekey | WC2N — 26
Locanda Locatelli | W1H — 26
Min Jiang | W8 — 26
Murano | W1J — 26
Nahm | SW1X — 26
Nobu Berkeley | W1J — 26
☒ Scott's | W1K — 26
Theo Randall | W1J — 26
Tinello | SW1W — 26
Trinity | SW4 — 26

Wilton's | SW1Y — 26
Amaranto | W1J — 25
Angelus | W2 — 25
Bentley's | W1B — 25
Cinnamon Club | SW1P — 25
Cinnamon Kitchen | EC2M — 25
Corrigan's Mayfair | W1K — 25
NEW Cut/45 Park Ln. | W1K — 25
Dorchester | W1K — 25
Fino | W1T — 25
French Horn | RG4 — 25
Galvin at Windows | W1K — 25
Galvin Bistrot | W1U — 25
☒ Galvin Chapelle/Cafe | E1 — 25
Goring | SW1 — 25
Hélène Darroze | W1K — 25
Hix at the Albemarle | W1S — 25
Launceston Pl. | W8 — 25
Maze | W1K — 25
Medlar | SW10 — 25
☒ Pollen St. Social | W1S — 25
Providores | W1U — 25
☒ Ritz | W1J — 25
Roast | SE1 — 25
Savoy Grill | WC2 — 25
Texture | W1H — 25
Tom Aikens | SW3 — 25
Zafferano | SW1X — 25
Zaika | W8 — 25
Asia de Cuba | WC2N — 24
Bar Boulud | SW1X — 24
Chutney Mary | SW10 — 24
☒ Ivy | WC2H — 24
Le Caprice | SW1A — 24
Le Cercle | SW1X — 24
Maze Grill | W1K — 24
Orrery | W1U — 24
Plateau | E14 — 24
Racine | SW3 — 24
Roux/Parliament | SW1P — 24
Almeida | N1 — 23
C London | W1K — 23
Fifteen | N1 — 23
Le Pont/Tour | SE1 — 23
Lutyens | EC4 — 23
1901 | EC2M — 23
Paramount | WC1A — 23
Petersham | TW10 — 23
Rhodes W1 | W1H — 23
Semplice Rist. | W1S — 23
☒ Sketch/Lecture | W1S — 23
Smiths/Top Fl. | EC1M — 23

Spice Mkt. | **W1**	23
NEW 34 | **W1K**	23
Z Wolseley | **W1J**	23
NEW Alyn Williams | **W1S**	22
Aubergine | **SL7**	22
NEW Aurelia | **W1S**	22
Belvedere | **W8**	22
Cecconi's | **W1S**	22
Cigalon | **WC2A**	22
Daphne's | **SW3**	22
Dean St. | **W1D**	22
Green's | **multi.**	22
Le Café Anglais | **W2**	22
Palm | **SW1X**	22
Savoy River | **WC2**	22
Cassis Bistro | **SW3**	21
Criterion | **W1J**	21
NEW Delaunay | **WC2B**	21
Quaglino's | **SW1Y**	21
Quo Vadis | **W1D**	21
San Lorenzo | **SW3**	21
Smiths/Dining Rm. | **EC1M**	21
Massimo | **SW1N**	20
Momo | **W1B**	20
NEW Novikov | **W1J**	20
Santini | **SW1W**	20
Skylon | **SE1**	20
York/Albany | **NW1**	20
Floridita | **W1F**	18
Gilbert Scott | **NW1**	18
Luxe | **E1**	17
NEW Gillray's | **SE1**	-
NEW Meursault | **SW7**	-

TRENDY

Z Barrafina | **W1D**	28
Z Chez Bruce | **SW17**	28
Z Harwood Arms | **SW6**	28
Z L'Atelier/Robuchon | **WC2H**	28
Z La Trompette | **W4**	28
Z Ledbury | **W11**	28
ZNEW Pitt Cue Co. | **W1F**	28
Z Roganic | **W1U**	28
Z La Petite Maison | **W1K**	27
Z Morito | **EC1R**	27
Moro | **EC1R**	27
Z Nobu London | **W1K**	27
Z River Café | **W6**	27
Z Yauatcha | **W1F**	27
Z Zucca | **SE1**	27
Z Zuma | **SW7**	27
Z Amaya | **SW1X**	26
Assaggi | **W2**	26

Bistrot Bruno Loubet | **EC1M**	26
Bocca/Gelupo | **W1D**	26
Brawn | **E2**	26
Clarke's | **W8**	26
Club Gascon | **EC1A**	26
NEW Dabbous | **W1T**	26
Z Hakkasan | **multi.**	26
Z Hawksmoor | **multi.**	26
Z J. Sheekey | **WC2N**	26
J. Sheekey Oyster | **WC2N**	26
Locanda Locatelli | **W1H**	26
Nobu Berkeley | **W1J**	26
Z Ottolenghi | **multi.**	26
Refettorio | **EC4V**	26
Roka | **multi.**	26
Z Scott's | **W1K**	26
St. John | **EC1M**	26
Viajante | **E2**	26
Anchor/Hope | **SE1**	25
Angels & Gypsies | **SE5**	25
Barrica | **W1T**	25
NEW Burger & Lobster | **W1J**	25
Cinnamon Club | **SW1P**	25
Cinnamon Kitchen | **EC2M**	25
NEW Cut/45 Park Ln. | **W1K**	25
Dehesa | **W1F**	25
Dock Kitchen | **W10**	25
Fino | **W1T**	25
Franco Manca | **multi.**	25
Galvin Bistrot | **W1U**	25
Z Galvin Chapelle/Cafe | **E1**	25
Hereford Rd. | **W2**	25
L'Etranger | **SW7**	25
Maze | **W1K**	25
Nopi | **W1B**	25
NEW Pizarro | **SE1**	25
Z Pollen St. Social | **W1S**	25
Providores | **W1U**	25
Sake No Hana | **SW1A**	25
St. John Bread | **E1**	25
Tom Aikens | **SW3**	25
Zafferano | **SW1X**	25
Ziani | **SW3**	25
Asia de Cuba | **WC2N**	24
Bar Boulud | **SW1X**	24
Ba Shan | **W1S**	24
Brindisa | **multi.**	24
Constancia | **SE1**	24
Great Queen St. | **WC2B**	24
Hix Oyster | **EC1M**	24
Z Ivy | **WC2H**	24
Kenza | **EC2M**	24
La Fromagerie | **W1U**	24

Restaurant		Score
Le Caprice	SW1A	24
Le Cercle	SW1X	24
Le Colombier	SW3	24
Maze Grill	W1K	24
NEW Meat Liquor	W1G	24
Oliveto	SW1W	24
Olivomare	SW1W	24
Opera Tavern	WC2B	24
Princi London	W1F	24
Racine	SW3	24
Salt Yard	W1T	24
Tom's Deli	W11	24
Tsunami	multi.	24
Yalla Yalla	multi.	24
Aqua Kyoto	W1B	23
Bar Battu	EC2V	23
Barbecoa	EC4M	23
Barshu	W1D	23
Bibendum Oyster	SW3	23
Bincho	W1D	23
Z Busaba Eathai	multi.	23
Caraffini	SW1	23
C London	W1K	23
NEW Copita	W1F	23
Dishoom	WC2H	23
E&O	W11	23
Eight Over Eight	SW3	23
Fifteen	N1	23
Fish	SE1	23
Z Les Trois Garçons	E1	23
Mint Leaf	EC2R	23
Paramount	WC1A	23
Spice Mkt.	W1	23
Spuntino	W1D	23
Taqueria	W11	23
Tom's Kitchen	SW3	23
Z Wahaca	multi.	23
Z Wolseley	W1J	23
NEW Aurelia	W1S	22
Bam-Bou	W1T	22
Belvedere	W8	22
Z Bob Bob Ricard	W1F	22
Cecconi's	W1S	22
Chilango	multi.	22
Daphne's	SW3	22
Daylesford	multi.	22
Dean St.	W1D	22
El Pirata	W2	22
High Road Brass.	W4	22
Hix	W1F	22
Hoxton Grill	EC2A	22
Le Café Anglais	W2	22
Olivo	SW1W	22
Oxo Tower	SE1	22
Palm	SW1X	22
Polpo	multi.	22
Z Sketch/Gallery	W1S	22
Sophie's	SW10	22
NEW Suda	WC2E	22
Wells	NW3	22
Avenue	SW1A	21
Baker & Spice	multi.	21
Belgo	multi.	21
NEW Cabana	E20	21
Cassis Bistro	SW3	21
Cheyne Walk	SW3	21
Del'Aziz	multi.	21
NEW Downtown Mayfair	W1S	21
Elistano	SW3	21
Enterprise	SW3	21
Hush	W1S	21
Lucio	SW3	21
Orso	WC2E	21
Pasha	SW7	21
Ping Pong	multi.	21
Quo Vadis	W1D	21
San Lorenzo	SW3	21
Smiths/Dining Rm.	EC1M	21
Tendido Cuatro	SW6	21
Thomas Cubitt	SW1W	21
Z Wagamama	multi.	21
XO	NW3	21
Z Carluccio's	multi.	20
Christopher's	WC2E	20
Comptoir Libanais	multi.	20
Gilgamesh	NW1	20
Inamo	multi.	20
Z Jamie's Italian	multi.	20
Kensington Pl.	W8	20
Mews/Mayfair	W1S	20
NEW Mishkin's	WC2B	20
Momo	W1B	20
NEW Novikov	W1J	20
Pizza East	E1	20
PJ's B&G	SW3	20
Semplice Bar Trattoria	W1C	20
Wapping Food	E1W	20
Waterloo	SE1	20
York/Albany	NW1	20
Admiral Codrington	SW3	19
Blakes	SW7	19
Botanist	SW1W	19
Bumpkin	multi.	19
Circus	WC2H	19

Itsu	multi.	19
Les Deux	WC2N	19
Lucky 7	W2	19
Masala Zone	multi.	19
202	W11	19
Whitechapel	E1	19
Antidote	W1	18
Aubaine	multi.	18
Canteen	multi.	18
Crazy Homies	W2	18
Folly	EC3V	18
NEW Granger & Co.	W11	18
Manicomio	SW3	18
All Star Lanes	multi.	17
Anthologist	EC2V	17
Armani Caffé	SW3	17
Luxe	E1	17
Nozomi	SW3	16
Northbank	EC4V	15
Pix Pintxos	WC2H	13
NEW Brasserie Zédel	W1F	–
NEW Briciole	W1H	–
NEW Cinnamon Soho	W1B	–
NEW Cotidie	W1U	–
NEW Drift	EC2	–
NEW Georgina's	SW13	–
NEW Karpo	NW1	–
NEW Kitchen 264	SW3	–
NEW La Bodega Negra	W1D	–
NEW Lima	W1T	–
NEW Mele e Pere	W1F	–
NEW Sette	SW3	–
NEW Soif	SW11	–
NEW Tapasia	W1D	–
NEW Tramshed	EC2A	–

VIEWS

Z Waterside Inn	SL6	29
Z Le Manoir/Quat	OX44	28
Z Nobu London	W1K	27
Z River Café	W6	27
Auberge du Lac	AL8	26
Bistrot Bruno Loubet	EC1M	26
Z Dinner/Heston	SW1X	26
Greenhouse	W1J	26
Min Jiang	W8	26
Oslo Court	NW8	26
Roka	E14	26
French Horn	RG4	25
Galvin at Windows	W1K	25
Z Gaucho	multi.	25
Maze	W1K	25
Rhodes 24	EC2N	25
Roast	SE1	25
Bingham	TW10	24
Maze Grill	W1K	24
Orrery	W1U	24
Plateau	E14	24
Aqua Kyoto	W1B	23
Babylon	W8	23
Barbecoa	EC4M	23
Boundary	E2	23
Butlers Wharf	SE1	23
Coq d'Argent	EC2R	23
Fish	SE1	23
Gravetye Manor	RH19	23
Gun	E14	23
Haz	E14	23
Le Pont/Tour	SE1	23
Oxo Tower Brass.	SE1	23
Paramount	WC1A	23
Petersham	TW10	23
Rotunda	N1	23
Royal China	E14	23
Smiths/Top Fl.	EC1M	23
Tom's Kitchen	WC2R	23
Aqua Nueva	W1B	22
Aubergine	SL7	22
Belvedere	W8	22
Blueprint	SE1	22
Fernandez & Wells	WC2R	22
Oxo Tower	SE1	22
Portrait	WC2H	22
Savoy River	WC2	22
Thai Sq./Soho Thai	SW15	22
Cantina/Ponte	SE1	21
Cheyne Walk	SW3	21
Kettner's	W1D	21
Pho	E20	21
Quadrato	E14	21
Ransome's	SW11	21
Waterway	W9	21
Butcher & Grill	SW11	20
Skylon	SE1	20
Tate Modern	SE1	20
NEW Union Jacks	WC2H	20
Fakhreldine	W1J	19
Real Greek	SE1	19
Rocket	E14	19
Tuttons	WC2B	19
Dim T	SE1	18
Gilbert Scott	NW1	18
Inn the Park	SW1A	18
Narrow	E14	18
Northbank	EC4V	15

Restaurant	Area	Score
Ⓩ Waterside Inn	SL6	29
Ⓩ Chez Bruce	SW17	28
Ⓩ Gordon Ramsay/68	SW3	28
Ⓩ L'Atelier/Robuchon	WC2H	28
Ⓩ Ledbury	W11	28
Ⓩ Le Gavroche	W1K	28
Ⓩ Le Manoir/Quat	OX44	28
Morgan M	EC1A	28
Ⓩ Petrus	SW1X	28
Ⓩ Roganic	W1U	28
Ⓩ Square	W1J	28
Ⓩ Alain Ducasse	W1A	27
Ⓩ Fat Duck	SL6	27
Glasshouse	TW9	27
Koffmann's	SW1X	27
Ⓩ La Petite Maison	W1K	27
L'Oranger	SW1A	27
Ⓩ Marcus Wareing	SW1X	27
Ⓩ Nobu London	W1K	27
Ⓩ Pied à Terre	W1T	27
Ⓩ Rasoi Vineet	SW3	27
Ⓩ River Café	W6	27
Ⓩ Umu	W1J	27
Ⓩ Zuma	SW7	27
Ⓩ Amaya	SW1X	26
Apsleys	SW1X	26
Auberge du Lac	AL8	26
Bistrot Bruno Loubet	EC1M	26
Clarke's	W8	26
Club Gascon	EC1A	26
NEW Dabbous	W1T	26
Ⓩ Dinner/Heston	SW1X	26
Goodman	multi.	26
Ⓩ Gordon Ramsay/Clar.	W1K	26
Greenhouse	W1J	26
Ⓩ Hakkasan	multi.	26
Hibiscus	W1S	26
Ⓩ J. Sheekey	WC2N	26
J. Sheekey Oyster	WC2N	26
Kitchen W8	W8	26
Locanda Locatelli	W1H	26
Min Jiang	W8	26
Murano	W1J	26
Nahm	SW1X	26
Nobu Berkeley	W1J	26
Roka	W1T	26
Ⓩ Scott's	W1K	26
Theo Randall	W1J	26
Tinello	SW1W	26
Trinity	SW4	26
Viajante	E2	26
Wilton's	SW1Y	26
Amaranto	W1J	25
Arbutus	W1D	25
Benares	W1J	25
Bentley's	W1B	25
Cinnamon Club	SW1P	25
Cinnamon Kitchen	EC2M	25
Corrigan's Mayfair	W1K	25
NEW Cut/45 Park Ln.	W1K	25
Dock Kitchen	W10	25
Dorchester	W1K	25
Fino	W1T	25
Galvin at Windows	W1K	25
Galvin Bistrot	W1U	25
Ⓩ Galvin Chapelle/Cafe	E1	25
Hélène Darroze	W1K	25
Hix at the Albemarle	W1S	25
Kai Mayfair	W1K	25
Kazan	SW1V	25
L'Anima	EC2A	25
Launceston Pl.	W8	25
L'Autre Pied	W1U	25
Maze	W1K	25
Medlar	SW10	25
Nopi	W1B	25
Poissonnerie/l'Avenue	SW3	25
Ⓩ Pollen St. Social	W1S	25
Providores	W1U	25
Quirinale	SW1P	25
Red Fort	W1D	25
Rhodes 24	EC2N	25
Ⓩ Ritz	W1J	25
Roast	SE1	25
Sake No Hana	SW1A	25
Savoy Grill	WC2	25
Tamarind	W1J	25
Texture	W1H	25
Tom Aikens	SW3	25
Veeraswamy	W1B	25
Zafferano	SW1X	25
Zaika	W8	25
Asia de Cuba	WC2N	24
Bar Boulud	SW1X	24
Chutney Mary	SW10	24
Constancia	SE1	24
Ⓩ Ivy	WC2H	24
JW Steak	W1K	24
Le Caprice	SW1A	24
Maze Grill	W1K	24
NEW Meat Liquor	W1G	24

Orrery	**W1U**	24
Plateau	**E14**	24
Roux/Parliament	**SW1P**	24
Tempo	**W1J**	24
Almeida	**N1**	23
Bar Battu	**EC2V**	23
Bibendum	**SW3**	23
C London	**W1K**	23
Coq d'Argent	**EC2R**	23
Empress of Sichuan	**WC2H**	23
Fifteen	**N1**	23
Forge	**WC2E**	23
Le Pont/Tour	**SE1**	23
Lutyens	**EC4**	23
Matsuri	**SW1Y**	23
1901	**EC2M**	23
Paramount	**WC1A**	23
Rhodes W1	**W1H**	23
Semplice Rist.	**W1S**	23
Shanghai Blues	**WC1V**	23
☑ Sketch/Lecture	**W1S**	23
Smiths/Top Fl.	**EC1M**	23
Spice Mkt.	**W1**	23
Sumosan	**W1S**	23
NEW 34	**W1K**	23
Wheeler's	**SW1A**	23
Wild Honey	**W1S**	23
NEW Alyn Williams	**W1S**	22
Aubergine	**SL7**	22
NEW Aurelia	**W1S**	22
Belvedere	**W8**	22
Cecconi's	**W1S**	22
China Tang	**W1K**	22
Cigalon	**WC2A**	22
Daphne's	**SW3**	22
Fifth Floor	**SW1X**	22
Green's	**multi.**	22
Hix	**W1F**	22
Le Café Anglais	**W2**	22
One-O-One	**SW1X**	22
Oxo Tower	**SE1**	22
Palm	**SW1X**	22
Pantechnicon Rooms	**SW1X**	22
Sartoria	**W1S**	22
28-50 Wine	**EC4A**	22
Babbo	**W1S**	21
Bank Westminster	**SW1E**	21
Cassis Bistro	**SW3**	21
Criterion	**W1J**	21
NEW Delaunay	**WC2B**	21
NEW Downtown Mayfair	**W1S**	21
Langan's Brass.	**W1JJ**	21

Marco Pierre White	**E1**	21
Odin's	**W1G**	21
Quo Vadis	**W1D**	21
San Lorenzo	**SW3**	21
Caldesi	**W1U**	20
Christopher's	**WC2E**	20
Cliveden Hse.	**SL6**	20
Massimo	**SW1N**	20
NEW Novikov	**W1J**	20
Santini	**SW1W**	20
Skylon	**SE1**	20
York/Albany	**NW1**	20
Blakes	**SW7**	19
Caravaggio	**EC3A**	19
Les Deux	**WC2N**	19
Gilbert Scott	**NW1**	18
St. Pancras	**NW1**	18
Anthologist	**EC2V**	17
Luxe	**E1**	17
Northbank	**EC4V**	15
NEW Brasserie Zédel	**W1F**	-
NEW Cinnamon Soho	**W1B**	-
NEW Colchis	**W2**	-
NEW Cotidie	**W1U**	-
NEW Door	**EC3V**	-
NEW Drift	**EC2**	-
NEW Gillray's	**SE1**	-
NEW Hix Belgravia	**SW1X**	-
NEW Kitchen 264	**SW3**	-
NEW Lima	**W1T**	-
NEW Mele e Pere	**W1F**	-
NEW Meursault	**SW7**	-
NEW Sette	**SW3**	-
NEW Sonny's Kitchen	**SW13**	-
NEW Tramshed	**EC2A**	-

WINNING WINE LISTS

☑ Waterside Inn	**SL6**	29
☑ Chez Bruce	**SW17**	28
☑ French Table	**KT6**	28
☑ Gauthier	**W1D**	28
☑ Gordon Ramsay/68	**SW3**	28
☑ La Trompette	**W4**	28
☑ Ledbury	**W11**	28
☑ Le Gavroche	**W1K**	28
☑ Le Manoir/Quat	**OX44**	28
Morgan M	**EC1A**	28
☑ Petrus	**SW1X**	28
☑ Roganic	**W1U**	28
☑ Square	**W1J**	28
☑ Alain Ducasse	**W1A**	27
☑ Fat Duck	**SL6**	27

Glasshouse	TW9	27	
Koffmann's	SW1X	27	
▣ L'Escargot	W1D	27	
L'Oranger	SW1A	27	
▣ Marcus Wareing	SW1X	27	
▣ Pied à Terre	W1T	27	
▣ Umu	W1J	27	
▣ Zucca	SE1	27	
▣ Zuma	SW7	27	
Apsleys	SW1X	26	
Auberge du Lac	AL8	26	
Clarke's	W8	26	
Club Gascon	EC1A	26	
▣ Gordon Ramsay/Clar.	W1K	26	
Greenhouse	W1J	26	
▣ Hakkasan	multi.	26	
Hibiscus	W1S	26	
Locanda Locatelli	W1H	26	
Magdalen	SE1	26	
Murano	W1J	26	
Nahm	SW1X	26	
Roux/Landau	W1	26	
Theo Randall	W1J	26	
Wilton's	SW1Y	26	
Amaranto	W1J	25	
Angelus	W2	25	
Arbutus	W1D	25	
Cinnamon Club	SW1P	25	
NEW Cut/45 Park Ln.	W1K	25	
Dorchester	W1K	25	
Enoteca Turi	SW15	25	
Fino	W1T	25	
▣ Galvin Chapelle/Cafe	E1	25	
▣ Gaucho	multi.	25	
Hélène Darroze	W1K	25	
Hix at the Albemarle	W1S	25	
L'Etranger	SW7	25	
Ma Goa	SW15	25	
Maze	W1K	25	
Odette's	NW1	25	
Providores	W1U	25	
▣ Ritz	W1J	25	
Savoy Grill	WC2	25	
Texture	W1H	25	
Tom Aikens	SW3	25	
Zafferano	SW1X	25	
Andrew Edmunds	W1F	24	
Bar Boulud	SW1X	24	
Cambio/Tercio	SW5	24	
Chutney Mary	SW10	24	
Latium	W1T	24	
Le Cercle	SW1X	24	
Orrery	W1U	24	
Plateau	E14	24	
Rib Room	SW1X	24	
Tempo	W1J	24	
Bar Battu	EC2V	23	
C London	W1K	23	
Coq d'Argent	EC2R	23	
Fifteen	N1	23	
Forge	WC2E	23	
Gravetye Manor	RH19	23	
Il Convivio	SW1W	23	
Le Pont/Tour	SE1	23	
Lutyens	EC4	23	
R.S.J.	SE1	23	
▣ Sketch/Lecture	W1S	23	
NEW 10 Cases	WC2H	23	
NEW 34	W1K	23	
Vinoteca	EC1M	23	
Wild Honey	W1S	23	
Alloro	W1S	22	
NEW Alyn Williams	W1S	22	
Aubergine	SL7	22	
NEW Aurelia	W1S	22	
Belvedere	W8	22	
Cigalon	WC2A	22	
Don	EC4N	22	
Fifth Floor	SW1X	22	
Il Baretto	W1U	22	
▣ 1 Lombard	EC3V	22	
Sartoria	W1S	22	
28-50 Wine	EC4A	22	
Cassis Bistro	SW3	21	
Criterion	W1J	21	
Langan's Bistro	W1G	21	
Quo Vadis	W1D	21	
Ransome's	SW11	21	
Terroirs	WC2N	21	
Vivat Bacchus	multi.	21	
Christopher's	WC2E	20	
Cliveden Hse.	SL6	20	
NEW Novikov	W1J	20	
Waterloo	SE1	20	
Cantina Vino.	SE1	19	
Caravaggio	EC3A	19	
Fulham/Kens. Wine Rooms	W8	19	
Prism	EC3V	19	
Antidote	W1	18	
Ebury Wine	SW1W	18	
NEW Meursault	SW7	—	
NEW Soif	SW11	—	

Cuisines

Includes restaurant names, locations and Food ratings.

AFGHAN

Afghan Kitchen	**N1**	24

AMERICAN

NEW Burger & Lobster	**W1J**	25
NEW Cut/45 Park Ln.	**W1K**	25
JW Steak	**W1K**	24
Spuntino	**W1D**	23
Z Byron	**multi.**	22
Hoxton Grill	**EC2A**	22
Palm	**SW1X**	22
Sophie's	**multi.**	22
Big Easy	**SW3**	21
Christopher's	**WC2E**	20
Ed's Easy Diner	**multi.**	20
PJ's B&G	**multi.**	20
Automat	**W1S**	19
Joe Allen	**WC2E**	19
Lucky 7	**W2**	19
Maxwell's	**WC2E**	19
Smollensky's	**multi.**	19
Sticky Fingers	**W8**	19
Diner	**multi.**	18
All Star Lanes	**multi.**	17
Giant Robot	**EC1M**	17
Hard Rock	**W1K**	17
Planet Hollywood	**SW1Y**	16
NEW Lowcountry	**SW6**	–

ARGENTINEAN

Buen Ayre	**E8**	26
Santa Maria/Garufa	**multi.**	26
Z Gaucho	**multi.**	25
Constancia	**SE1**	24
El Gaucho	**multi.**	22

ASIAN

Nopi	**W1B**	25
Asia de Cuba	**WC2N**	24
E&O	**W11**	23
Eight Over Eight	**SW3**	23
Oxo Tower Brass.	**SE1**	23
Spice Mkt.	**W1**	23
Bam-Bou	**W1T**	22
Banana Tree	**multi.**	21
XO	**NW3**	21
Gilgamesh	**NW1**	20
namo	**multi.**	20
NEW Novikov	**W1J**	20
Circus	**WC2H**	19

Great Eastern	**EC2A**	19
NEW Tapasia	**W1D**	–

AUSTRALIAN

NEW Granger & Co.	**W11**	18

BAKERIES

Z Ottolenghi	**multi.**	26
Ladurée	**multi.**	24
Princi London	**W1F**	24
Gail's	**multi.**	22
Baker & Spice	**multi.**	21
Le Pain Quot.	**multi.**	19

BARBECUE

Z NEW Pitt Cue Co.	**W1F**	28
Barbecoa	**EC4M**	23
Z Bodeans	**multi.**	22

BELGIAN

Belgo	**multi.**	21
NEW Leon De Bruxelles	**WC2H**	19
Le Pain Quot.	**multi.**	19

BRAZILIAN

NEW Cabana	**multi.**	21
Rodizio Rico	**multi.**	21

BRITISH (MODERN)

Z Chez Bruce	**SW17**	28
Z Harwood Arms	**SW6**	28
Z Roganic	**W1U**	28
Z Fat Duck	**SL6**	27
Lamberts	**SW12**	27
Clarke's	**W8**	26
Z Dinner/Heston	**SW1X**	26
Patterson's	**W1S**	26
Randall/Aubin	**W1F**	26
St. John	**EC1M**	26
Anchor/Hope	**SE1**	25
Corrigan's Mayfair	**W1K**	25
Dorchester	**W1K**	25
Hereford Rd.	**W2**	25
Launceston Pl.	**W8**	25
Paradise	**W10**	25
Z Pollen St. Social	**W1S**	25
St. John Bread	**E1**	25
St. John Hotel Rest.	**WC2H**	25
Bevis Marks	**E1**	24
Bingham	**TW10**	24

Great Queen St. | **WC2B**	24
☑ Ivy | **WC2H**	24
Le Caprice | **SW1A**	24
Palmerston | **SE22**	24
Annie's | **multi.**	23
Babylon | **W8**	23
NEW Balcon | **SW1Y**	23
Bradley's | **NW3**	23
Frederick's | **N1**	23
Gravetye Manor | **RH19**	23
Gun | **E14**	23
1901 | **EC2M**	23
R.S.J. | **SE1**	23
Smiths/Top Fl. | **EC1M**	23
Empress | **E9**	23
Tom's Kitchen | **multi.**	23
Wild Honey | **W1S**	23
Adam St. | **WC2N**	22
Belvedere | **W8**	22
☑ Bob Bob Ricard | **W1F**	22
Cow | **W2**	22
Dean St. | **W1D**	22
Duke/Cambridge | **N1**	22
Hix | **W1F**	22
Portrait | **WC2H**	22
Anglesea Arms | **W6**	21
Avenue | **SW1A**	21
Chiswell St. Dining | **EC1**	21
Enterprise | **SW3**	21
Medcalf | **EC1R**	21
Princess/Shoreditch | **EC2A**	21
Ransome's | **SW11**	21
Smiths/Dining Rm. | **EC1M**	21
Soho Hse. | **W1D**	21
Union Cafe | **W1U**	21
Bluebird | **SW3**	20
English Pig | **SW1P**	20
Fox/Grapes | **SW19**	20
Kensington Pl. | **W8**	20
Mews/Mayfair | **W1S**	20
Waterloo | **SE1**	20
Admiral Codrington | **SW3**	19
Balans | **multi.**	19
Botanist | **SW1W**	19
Brompton B&G | **SW3**	19
Bumpkin | **multi.**	19
Fifth Floor Cafe | **SW1X**	19
Julie's | **W11**	19
National Dining Rooms | **WC2N**	19
Old Brewery | **SE10**	19
Prism | **EC3V**	19
Groucho Club | **W1D**	18

St. Pancras | **NW1**	18
Luxe | **E1**	17
Restaurant/Arts | **W1J**	17
Northbank | **EC4V**	15
NEW Tramshed | **EC2A**	-

BRITISH (TRADITIONAL)

Wilton's | **SW1Y**	26
Bentley's | **W1B**	25
French Horn | **RG4**	25
Goring | **SW1**	25
Hix at the Albemarle | **W1S**	25
Princess Victoria | **W12**	25
Rhodes 24 | **EC2N**	25
☑ Ritz | **W1J**	25
Roast | **SE1**	25
Savoy Grill | **WC2**	25
Frontline | **W2**	24
Hinds Head | **SL6**	24
Hix Oyster | **EC1M**	24
Rivington Grill | **multi.**	24
Rowley's | **SW1Y**	24
Abbeville | **SW4**	23
Bleeding Heart | **EC1N**	23
Boundary | **E2**	23
Bull & Last | **NW5**	23
Maggie Jones's | **W8**	23
Rotunda | **N1**	23
Shepherd's | **SW1P**	23
Albion | **N1**	22
Boisdale | **multi.**	22
Ffiona's | **W8**	22
Green's | **multi.**	22
Mercer | **EC2R**	22
Annabel's | **W1J**	21
Grazing Goat | **W1**	21
Langan's Bistro | **W1G**	21
Langan's Brass. | **W1JJ**	21
Mark's Club | **W1J**	21
Odin's | **W1G**	21
108 Marylebone | **W1U**	21
Quo Vadis | **W1D**	21
Simpson's/Strand | **WC2R**	21
☑ Sketch/Parlour | **W1S**	21
Thomas Cubitt | **SW1W**	21
☑ Browns | **multi.**	20
Butcher & Grill | **multi.**	20
Cliveden Hse. | **SL6**	20
Fortnum's Fountain | **W1A**	20
Pig's Ear | **SW3**	20
Warrington | **W9**	20
Foxtrot Oscar | **SW3**	19

Grumbles | **SW1V**	19
Tuttons | **WC2B**	19
Builders Arms | **SW3**	18
Canteen | **multi.**	18
Gilbert Scott | **NW1**	18
Grenadier | **SW1X**	18
Inn the Park | **SW1A**	18
Narrow | **E14**	18
Only Running | **W1J**	18
Porters English | **WC2E**	18
Richoux | **multi.**	16

BURGERS

Honest Burgers | **SW9**	27
NEW Burger & Lobster | **W1J**	25
NEW Meat Liquor | **W1G**	24
B Byron | **multi.**	22
Haché | **multi.**	22
B Gourmet Burger | **multi.**	21
Automat | **W1S**	19
Lucky 7 | **W2**	19
Maxwell's | **WC2E**	19
Sticky Fingers | **W8**	19
Diner | **multi.**	18
Hard Rock | **W1K**	17
NEW Meat Market | **WC2E**	-

BURMESE

Mandalay | **W2**	25

CALIFORNIAN

NEW Shrimpy's | **N1C**	-

CARIBBEAN

Cottons | **multi.**	22

CHINESE

(* dim sum specialist)

B Hunan | **SW1W**	28
B Yauatcha* | **W1F**	27
B Hakkasan* | **multi.**	26
Min Jiang* | **W8**	26
Goldmine | **W2**	25
Haozhan | **W1D**	25
Kai Mayfair | **W1K**	25
Mandarin Kitchen | **W2**	25
Mao Tai* | **SW6**	25
New Mayflower | **W1D**	25
Plum Valley | **W1D**	25
Royal China Club* | **W1U**	25
Ba Shan | **W1S**	24
Golden Dragon* | **W1D**	24
Good Earth | **multi.**	24
Pearl Liang* | **W2**	24

Princess Garden | **W1K**	24
Yming | **W1D**	24
Barshu | **W1D**	23
Empress of Sichuan | **WC2H**	23
Four Seasons | **multi.**	23
Lotus Floating | **E14**	23
Memories/China | **multi.**	23
Phoenix Palace* | **NW1**	23
Royal China | **multi.**	23
Shanghai Blues* | **WC1V**	23
China Tang* | **W1K**	22
Dragon Castle | **SE17**	22
Imperial China* | **WC2H**	22
Mr. Kong | **WC2H**	22
Harbour City* | **W1D**	21
Imperial City | **EC3V**	21
Joy King Lau* | **WC2H**	21
Mr. Chow | **SW1X**	21
Ping Pong* | **multi.**	21
New Culture Rev. | **multi.**	20
New World* | **W1D**	20
Chuen Cheng Ku* | **W1D**	19
Jenny Lo's Tea | **SW1W**	19
Wong Kei | **W1D**	19
Cha Cha Moon | **W1F**	18
Dim T* | **multi.**	18
NEW Wulumuchi | **WC2H**	-

CHOPHOUSES

Goodman | **multi.**	26
B Hawksmoor | **multi.**	26
Santa Maria/Garufa | **multi.**	26
NEW Cut/45 Park Ln. | **W1K**	25
B Gaucho | **multi.**	25
B Rules | **WC2E**	25
Constancia | **SE1**	24
Guinea Grill | **W1J**	24
Hix Oyster | **EC1M**	24
JW Steak | **W1K**	24
Le Relais | **multi.**	24
Maze Grill | **W1K**	24
Popeseye | **multi.**	24
Rib Room | **SW1X**	24
Butlers Wharf | **SE1**	23
NEW 34 | **W1K**	23
El Gaucho | **multi.**	22
Palm | **SW1X**	22
Paternoster Chop | **EC4M**	22
Sophie's | **multi.**	22
Bountiful Cow | **WC1R**	21
Greig's | **W1J**	21
Marco Pierre White | **E1**	21
Black & Blue | **multi.**	20

Christopher's	**WC2E**	20
Angus Steakhouse	**multi.**	19
Marco Pierre/King's	**SW3**	19
Smollensky's	**multi.**	19
NEW Door	**EC3V**	-
NEW Gillray's	**SE1**	-

CUBAN

Asia de Cuba	**WC2N**	24

DELIS

Reubens	**W1U**	21
NEW Mishkin's	**WC2B**	20

EASTERN EUROPEAN

Baltic	**SE1**	24
Verru	**W1U**	24

ECLECTIC

Books/Cooks	**W11**	26
☒ Mosimann's	**SW1X**	26
Viajante	**E2**	26
Light House	**SW19**	25
Modern Pantry	**EC1V**	25
Providores	**W1U**	25
Archipelago	**W1T**	24
Cape Town Fish	**W1F**	24
Tom's Deli	**W11**	24
Elk in the Woods	**N1**	23
Kopapa	**WC2H**	23
Daylesford	**multi.**	22
Troubadour	**SW5**	22
Motcombs	**SW1X**	21
Ransome's	**SW11**	21
Saf	**W8**	21
Draft House	**multi.**	20
Blakes	**SW7**	19
Cantina Vino.	**SE1**	19
Giraffe	**multi.**	18
NEW Granger & Co.	**W11**	18
Brinkley's	**SW10**	16
Brompton Quarter	**SW3**	16
Dans Le Noir	**EC1R**	13
NEW Hix Belgravia	**SW1X**	-
NEW Karpo	**NW1**	-

EUROPEAN (MODERN)

Corner Room	**E2**	29
☒ La Trompette	**W4**	28
Glasshouse	**TW9**	27
North Rd.	**EC1M**	27
Auberge du Lac	**AL8**	26
Charlotte's	**multi.**	26
NEW Dabbous	**W1T**	26
☒ Gordon Ramsay/Clar.	**W1K**	26
Kitchen W8	**W8**	26
Magdalen	**SE1**	26
Murano	**W1J**	26
Roux/Landau	**W1**	26
Trinity	**SW4**	26
Arbutus	**W1D**	25
Aurora	**W1F**	25
Chancery	**EC4A**	25
Chapters All Day	**SE3**	25
Dock Kitchen	**W10**	25
L'Autre Pied	**W1U**	25
Odette's	**NW1**	25
Texture	**W1H**	25
About Thyme	**SW1V**	24
Andrew Edmunds	**W1F**	24
Bingham	**TW10**	24
Caravan	**EC1R**	24
Giaconda	**WC2H**	24
☒ Ivy	**WC2H**	24
La Fromagerie	**multi.**	24
Le Caprice	**SW1A**	24
Made/Camden	**NW1**	24
Petersham Nurseries	**TW10**	24
Roux/Parliament	**SW1P**	24
Sam's Brass.	**W4**	24
Tom Ilic	**SW8**	24
NEW Arts Club	**W1S**	23
Bar Battu	**EC2V**	23
Brumus	**SW1Y**	23
Bumbles	**SW1W**	23
Camden Brass.	**NW1**	23
Forge	**WC2E**	23
Frederick's	**N1**	23
George	**W1K**	23
Indigo	**WC2B**	23
Paramount	**WC1A**	23
Petersham	**TW10**	23
Rhodes W1	**W1H**	23
☒ Sketch/Lecture	**W1S**	23
NEW 10 Cases	**WC2H**	23
Vinoteca	**multi.**	23
☒ Wolseley	**W1J**	23
NEW Alyn Williams	**W1S**	22
Blueprint	**SE1**	22
Don	**EC4N**	22
Fifth Floor	**SW1X**	22
Flemings Grill	**W1J**	22
NEW Hedone	**W4**	22
High Road Brass.	**W4**	22
Hix	**W1F**	22

CUISINES

✦ Les Trois Garçons | **E1**	23
Lutyens | **EC4**	23
Rhodes W1 | **W1H**	23
Aubergine | **SL7**	22
Belvedere | **W8**	22
Cigalon | **WC2A**	22
Incognico | **WC2H**	22
Le Suquet | **SW3**	22
✦ 1 Lombard | **EC3V**	22
One-O-One | **SW1X**	22
Savoy River | **WC2**	22
Annabel's | **W1J**	21
Cassis Bistro | **SW3**	21
Langan's Bistro | **W1G**	21
Le Mercury | **N1**	21
Mark's Club | **W1J**	21
Odin's | **W1G**	21
Cliveden Hse. | **SL6**	20
Elena's L'Etoile | **W1T**	20
Café des Amis | **WC2E**	19
Les Deux | **WC2N**	19
Villandry | **W1W**	19
Antidote | **W1**	18
Aubaine | **W1S**	18
Wallace | **W1U**	18
NEW Meursault | **SW7**	-
NEW Soif | **SW11**	-

FRENCH (BISTRO)

Bistrot Bruno Loubet | **EC1M**	26
Brula | **TW1**	26
Comptoir Gascon | **EC1M**	25
Galvin Bistrot | **W1U**	25
Le Café/Marché | **EC1M**	25
Le Vacherin | **W4**	25
Bar Boulud | **SW1X**	24
La Bouchée | **SW7**	24
L'Absinthe | **NW1**	24
Le Boudin Blanc | **W1J**	24
Bibendum Oyster | **SW3**	23
La Poule au Pot | **SW1W**	23
Bistrotheque | **E2**	22
28-50 Wine | **multi.**	22
Chabrot | **SW1X**	21
Mon Plaisir | **WC2H**	21
Grumbles | **SW1V**	19
Patisserie Valerie | **multi.**	19
Aubaine | **multi.**	18
Café Boheme | **W1D**	18
✦ Café Rouge | **multi.**	18
Ebury Wine | **SW1W**	18
Truc Vert | **W1K**	18

FRENCH (BRASSERIE)

Angelus | **W2**	25
Le Colombier | **SW3**	24
Racine | **SW3**	24
NEW Balcon | **SW1Y**	23
Brasserie Blanc | **multi.**	22
✦ Côte | **multi.**	22
Le Café Anglais | **W2**	22
Brass. St. Jacques | **SW1A**	21
Cheyne Walk | **SW3**	21
Kettner's | **W1D**	21
Langan's Brass. | **W1JJ**	21
Chez Gérard | **EC2N**	20
Gazette | **multi.**	20
Pig's Ear | **SW3**	20
La Brasserie | **SW3**	19
NEW Brasserie Zédel | **W1F**	-

GASTROPUB

✦ Harwood Arms | British | **SW6**	28
Anchor/Hope | British | **SE1**	25
Paradise | British | **W10**	25
Princess Victoria | British | **W12**	25
Great Queen St. | British | **WC2B**	24
Palmerston | British | **SE22**	24
Abbeville | British/Euro. | **SW4**	23
Bull & Last | British | **NW5**	23
Duke of Sussex | British/Spanish | **W4**	23
Eagle | Med. | **EC1R**	23
Gun | British | **E14**	23
Sands End | British/Irish | **SW6**	23
Empress | British | **E9**	23
Albion | British | **N1**	22
Cow | British | **W2**	22
Duke/Cambridge | British | **N1**	22
Orange Restaurant | Euro. | **SW1W**	22
Wells | Euro. | **NW3**	22
Abingdon | Euro. | **W8**	21
Anglesea Arms | British | **W6**	21
Enterprise | Eclectic | **SW3**	21
Princess/Shoreditch | British | **EC2A**	21
Thomas Cubitt | British | **SW1W**	21
Waterway | Euro. | **W9**	21
Draft House | Eclectic | **multi.**	20
Fox/Grapes | British | **SW19**	20
Pig's Ear | British/French | **SW3**	20
Warrington | British | **W9**	20

York/Albany | Euro. | **NW1** 20

Admiral Codrington | British/Euro. | **SW3** 19

NEW Devonshire Arms | British | **W4** 19

Builders Arms | British | **SW3** 18

Narrow | British | **E14** 18

Only Running | British | **W1J** 18

GEORGIAN

NEW Colchis | **W2** -

GREEK

Carob Tree | **NW5** 24

Halepi | **W2** 24

Lemonia | **NW1** 21

Real Greek | **multi.** 19

NEW Mazi | **W8** -

HUNGARIAN

Gay Hussar | **W1D** 21

INDIAN

Zayna | **W1H** 28

Z Babur | **SE23** 27

Z Rasoi Vineet | **SW3** 27

NEW Roti Chai | **W1H** 27

Z Amaya | **SW1X** 26

Café Spice | **E1** 26

Chutneys | **NW1** 26

Hot Stuff | **SW8** 26

Star of India | **SW5** 26

Trishna | **W1U** 26

Benares | **W1J** 25

Cinnamon Club | **SW1P** 25

Cinnamon Kitchen | **EC2M** 25

Indian Zing | **W6** 25

Ma Goa | **SW15** 25

Moti Mahal | **WC2B** 25

Red Fort | **W1D** 25

Tamarind | **W1J** 25

Veeraswamy | **W1B** 25

Zaika | **W8** 25

Bombay Palace | **W2** 24

Chor Bizarre | **W1S** 24

Chutney Mary | **SW10** 24

Z Mooli's | **W1D** 24

Rasa | **multi.** 24

Bombay Brass. | **SW7** 23

Dishoom | **WC2H** 23

Mela | **WC2H** 23

Mint Leaf | **multi.** 23

Noor Jahan | **multi.** 23

Painted Heron | **SW10** 23

Punjab | **WC2H** 23

Woodlands | **multi.** 23

Bengal Clipper | **SE1** 22

Dockmaster's | **E14** 22

Gaylord | **W1W** 22

Imli | **W1F** 22

Khan's | **W2** 22

La Porte/Indes | **W1H** 22

Malabar | **W8** 22

Sagar | **multi.** 22

NEW Chakra | **W11** 21

Haandi | **SW7** 21

Chowki | **W1D** 20

Gopal's | **W1D** 19

Malabar Junction | **WC1B** 19

Masala Zone | **multi.** 19

NEW Cinnamon Soho | **W1B** -

Quilon | **SW1E** -

INDONESIAN

Bali Bali | **WC2H** 22

IRISH

Sands End | **SW6** 23

ITALIAN

Z River Café | **W6** 27

Z Zucca | **SE1** 27

Apsleys | **SW1X** 26

Assaggi | **W2** 26

Bocca/Gelupo | **W1D** 26

Locanda Locatelli | **W1H** 26

Mennula | **W1T** 26

Murano | **W1J** 26

Portobello | **W11** 26

Refettorio | **EC4V** 26

Theo Randall | **W1J** 26

Tinello | **SW1W** 26

Vasco & Piero's | **W1F** 26

A Cena | **TW1** 25

Amaranto | **W1J** 25

Brunello | **SW7** 25

Dehesa | **W1F** 25

Enoteca Turi | **SW15** 25

Giovanni's | **WC2N** 25

Harry's Bar | **W1K** 25

L'Anima | **EC2A** 25

Locanda Ottoemezzo | **W8** 25

Osteria Basilico | **W11** 25

Quirinale | **SW1P** 25

Rossopomodoro | **multi.** 25

Scalini | **SW3** 25

Timo | **W8** 25

CUISINES

Restaurant	Area	Rating
Zafferano	SW1X	25
Ziani	SW3	25
500	N19	24
Il Bordello	E1W	24
La Genova	W1K	24
Latium	W1T	24
Little Italy	W1D	24
Mediterraneo	W11	24
Oliveto	SW1W	24
Olivomare	SW1W	24
Opera Tavern	WC2B	24
Pescatori	multi.	24
Princi London	W1F	24
Salt Yard	W1T	24
Tempo	W1J	24
Tentazioni	SE1	24
Trullo	N1	24
2 Veneti	W1U	24
Alba	EC1Y	23
Amerigo Vespucci	E14	23
Antonio's	N1	23
Artigiano	NW3	23
Caraffini	SW1	23
C London	W1K	23
Fifteen	N1	23
Il Convivio	SW1W	23
La Porchetta	multi.	23
Sale e Pepe	SW1X	23
Semplice Rist.	W1S	23
Signor Sassi	SW1X	23
Spuntino	W1D	23
Vapiano	multi.	23
Aglio e Olio	SW10	22
Al Duca	SW1Y	22
Alloro	W1S	22
Cecconi's	W1S	22
Como Lario	SW1W	22
Daphne's	SW3	22
Franco's	SW1Y	22
Il Baretto	W1U	22
Incognito	WC2H	22
Olivo	SW1W	22
Pellicano	SW3	22
Polpo	multi.	22
Sardo	W1T	22
Sartoria	W1S	22
Amico Bio	EC1A	21
Ark	W8	21
Babbo	W1S	21
Cantina/Ponte	SE1	21
Citrus	W1J	21
NEW Downtown Mayfair	W1S	21
Elistano	SW3	21
La Famiglia	SW10	21
Lucio	SW3	21
Orso	WC2E	21
Osteria Antica	SW11	21
Osteria dell'Arancio	SW10	21
Z Pizza Express	multi.	21
Quadrato	E14	21
Red Pepper	W9	21
San Lorenzo	multi.	21
Caldesi	multi.	20
Z Carluccio's	multi.	20
Delfino	W1K	20
Elena's L'Etoile	W1T	20
Il Portico	W8	20
Z Jamie's Italian	multi.	20
NEW Novikov	W1J	20
Prezzo	multi.	20
Santini	SW1W	20
Sardo	NW1	20
Semplice Bar Trattoria	W1C	20
Strada	multi.	20
Z Zizzi	multi.	20
Ask Italian	multi.	19
Buona Sera	multi.	19
Caravaggio	EC3A	19
Da Mario	SW7	19
Made in Italy	multi.	19
Rocca	multi.	19
Ciro's Pizza	SW3	18
Frankie's	multi.	18
Manicomio	multi.	18
Montpeliano	SW7	18
Armani Caffé	SW3	17
NEW Bunga Bunga	SW11	17
Giant Robot	EC1M	17
Riccardo's	SW3	17
NEW Briciole	W1H	–
NEW Cotidie	W1U	–
NEW Mele e Pere	W1F	–
NEW Sette	SW3	–

JAPANESE

(* sushi specialist)

Restaurant	Area	Rating
Z Dinings*	W1H	28
Sushi-Say*	NW2	28
Z Yashin Sushi*	W8	28
Ikeda*	W1K	27
Z Jin Kichi*	NW3	27
Z Nobu London*	W1K	27
Z Umu*	W1J	27
Z Zuma*	SW7	27
Kiku*	W1J	26

Nobu Berkeley*	W1J	26
Roka*	multi.	26
Atari-Ya Sushi Bar*	multi.	25
Café Japan*	NW11	25
Koya	W1D	25
L'Etranger	SW7	25
Sake No Hana*	SW1A	25
Ten Ten Tei*	W1	25
Yoshino*	W1J	25
Abeno	multi.	24
Defune*	W1U	24
Taro*	multi.	24
Tsunami*	multi.	24
Akari	N1	23
Aqua Kyoto*	W1B	23
Bento*	NW1	23
Bincho	multi.	23
Chisou*	multi.	23
Koi*	W8	23
Matsuri*	SW1Y	23
Miyama*	multi.	23
Sakura*	W1S	23
Sumosan*	W1S	23
Tsuru*	multi.	23
Hare & Tortoise*	multi.	22
Kulu Kulu*	multi.	22
Tokyo Diner*	WC2H	22
Wasabi	multi.	22
☑ Wagamama	multi.	21
Benihana	multi.	20
Hi Sushi*	multi.	20
Satsuma*	W1D	20
Feng Sushi*	multi.	19
Itsu*	multi.	19
Yo! Sushi*	multi.	18
Nozomi*	SW3	16
NEW Meursault	SW7	-

JEWISH

Bevis Marks	E1	24
Gaby's	WC2H	24
Reubens	W1U	21
NEW Mishkin's	WC2B	20
Solly's	NW11	20

KOREAN

Asadal*	WC1V	23

KOSHER/ KOSHER-STYLE

Bevis Marks	E1	24
Reubens	W1U	21
Solly's	NW11	20

LEBANESE

Beiteddine	SW1X	25
Ishbilia	SW1X	25
Kenza	EC2M	24
Yalla Yalla	multi.	24
Al Hamra	W1J	23
Fairuz	W1H	23
Maroush	multi.	23
Al Sultan	W1J	22
Al Waha	W2	22
Noura	multi.	22
Comptoir Libanais	multi.	20
Fakhreldine	W1J	19

MALAYSIAN

Champor	SE1	23
Singapore Gdn.	multi.	23

MEDITERRANEAN

☑ French Table	KT6	28
☑ La Petite Maison	W1K	27
☑ Ottolenghi	multi.	26
Carob Tree	NW5	24
Eagle	EC1R	23
Oxo Tower Brass.	SE1	23
NEW Aurelia	W1S	22
Ciao Bella	WC1N	22
Franco's	SW1Y	22
Morton's	W1J	22
Baker & Spice	multi.	21
Del'Aziz	multi.	21
Terroirs	WC2N	21
Union Cafe	W1U	21
Leon	multi.	20
Massimo	SW1N	20
Cafe Med	NW8	19
Cantina Vino.	SE1	19
Rocket	multi.	19
Raoul's	multi.	17
NEW Kitchen 264	SW3	-

MEXICAN

Tortilla	multi.	24
Cantina Laredo	WC2H	23
Lupita	WC2N	23
Taqueria	W11	23
☑ Wahaca	multi.	23
Chilango	multi.	22
Mestizo	NW1	22
Cafe Pacifico	WC2H	20
Crazy Homies	W2	18
El Camion	multi.	17
NEW La Bodega Negra	W1D	-
NEW Shrimpy's	N1C	-

MIDDLE EASTERN

Nopi	**W1B**	25
Gaby's	**WC2H**	24
Solly's	**NW11**	20

MOROCCAN

Kenza	**EC2M**	24
Adams Cafe	**W12**	22
Pasha	**SW7**	21
Momo	**W1B**	20

NOODLE SHOPS

Koya	**W1D**	25
Z Wagamama	**multi.**	21
New Culture Rev.	**multi.**	20

NORTH AFRICAN

Z Morito	**EC1R**	27
Moro	**EC1R**	27
Del'Aziz	**multi.**	21
Souk	**WC2H**	21

PAKISTANI

Zayna	**W1H**	28
Tayyabs	**E1**	26
Lahore Kebab House	**multi.**	25
Salloos	**SW1X**	24
Original Lahore	**multi.**	23

PAN-LATIN

Las Iguanas	**multi.**	22
Floridita	**W1F**	18

PERSIAN

Alounak	**multi.**	24

PERUVIAN

Z Nobu London	**W1K**	27
Nobu Berkeley	**W1J**	26
NEW Ceviche	**W1D**	-
NEW Lima	**W1T**	-

PIZZA

Portobello	**W11**	26
Franco Manca	**multi.**	25
Osteria Basilico	**W11**	25
Rossopomodoro	**SW10**	25
Oliveto	**SW1W**	24
Princi London	**W1F**	24
La Porchetta	**multi.**	23
Z Pizza Express	**multi.**	21
Red Pepper	**W9**	21
Delfino	**W1K**	20
Pizza East	**multi.**	20
Strada	**multi.**	20

Z Zizzi	**multi.**	20
Ask Italian	**multi.**	19
Buona Sera	**multi.**	19
Made in Italy	**multi.**	19
Rocket	**multi.**	19
Ciro's Pizza	**SW3**	18
NEW Bunga Bunga	**SW11**	17
NEW Brooklyn Bite	**SW3**	-

POLISH

Gessler/Daquise	**SW7**	25
Baltic	**SE1**	24

PORTUGUESE

Portal	**EC1M**	26
Eyre Brothers	**EC2A**	24
Z Nando's	**multi.**	21

RUSSIAN

NEW Mari Vanna	**SW1X**	-

SCANDINAVIAN

North Rd.	**EC1M**	27
Verru	**W1U**	24

SCOTTISH

Boisdale	**multi.**	22
Albannach	**WC2N**	21

SEAFOOD

Nautilus Fish	**NW6**	27
Z J. Sheekey	**WC2N**	26
J. Sheekey Oyster	**WC2N**	26
Randall/Aubin	**W1F**	26
Z Scott's	**W1K**	26
Wilton's	**SW1Y**	26
Bentley's	**W1B**	25
Mandarin Kitchen	**W2**	25
North Sea	**WC1H**	25
Poissonnerie/l'Avenue	**SW3**	25
Cape Town Fish	**W1F**	24
Golden Hind	**W1U**	24
Olivomare	**SW1W**	24
Pescatori	**multi.**	24
Rock & Sole	**WC2H**	24
Wright Brothers	**multi.**	24
Bibendum Oyster	**SW3**	23
Caviar House	**W1J**	23
Fish	**SE1**	23
Le Pont/Tour	**SE1**	23
Lutyens	**EC4**	23
Sweetings	**EC4N**	23
Two Brothers Fish	**N3**	23
Wheeler's	**SW1A**	23
Green's	**multi.**	22

Le Suquet	**SW3**	22
Loch Fyne	**multi.**	22
One-O-One	**SW1X**	22
FishWorks	**multi.**	21
Geales	**multi.**	20

SINGAPOREAN

Singapore Gdn.	**multi.**	23

SMALL PLATES

(See also Spanish tapas specialist)

🖪 Dinings	Japanese	**W1H**	28
🖪 Hunan	Chinese	**SW1W**	28
🖪 L'Atelier/Robuchon	French	**WC2H**	28
🖪 Amaya	Indian	**SW1X**	26
Bocca/Gelupo	Italian	**W1D**	26
Brawn	British	**E2**	26
Club Gascon	French	**EC1A**	26
Maze	French	**W1K**	25
Providores	Eclectic	**W1U**	25
Caravan	Euro.	**EC1R**	24
Le Cercle	French	**SW1X**	24
Akari	Japanese	**N1**	23
Bar Battu	Euro.	**EC2V**	23
Cellar Gascon	French	**EC1A**	23
Spuntino	Amer./Italian	**W1D**	23
Imli	Indian	**W1F**	22
Polpo	Italian	**multi.**	22
Riding Hse. Café	Euro.	**W1W**	21
Terroirs	Med.	**WC2N**	21
Fulham/Kens. Wine Rooms	Euro.	**W8**	19
Real Greek	Greek	**multi.**	19
Riccardo's	Tuscan	**SW3**	17
🆕 Tapasia	Asian	**W1D**	-

SOUTH AMERICAN

Sabor	**N1**	25

SPANISH

(* tapas specialist)

🖪 Barrafina*	**W1D**	28
🖪 José*	**SE1**	28
🖪 Morito*	**EC1R**	27
Moro*	**EC1R**	27
Angels & Gypsies*	**SE5**	25
Barrica*	**W1T**	25
Dehesa*	**W1F**	25
Fino*	**W1T**	25
🆕 Pizarro*	**SE1**	25
Brindisa*	**multi.**	24
Cambio/Tercio	**SW5**	24
El Parador*	**NW1**	24
Eyre Brothers	**EC2A**	24

Opera Tavern*	**WC2B**	24
Salt Yard*	**W1T**	24
Camino*	**multi.**	23
🆕 Copita*	**W1F**	23
Iberica*	**multi.**	23
Meson Don Felipe*	**SE1**	23
Aqua Nueva*	**W1B**	22
Barcelona Tapas*	**multi.**	22
El Pirata*	**multi.**	22
Fernandez & Wells	**multi.**	22
Tendido Cero*	**SW5**	22
Cigala*	**WC1N**	21
Tendido Cuatro*	**SW6**	21
Galicia*	**W10**	18
Pix Pintxos*	**multi.**	13
🆕 Donostia*	**W1H**	-

TAIWANESE

Leong's Legend	**multi.**	22

TEX-MEX

Hoxton Square	**N1**	17

THAI

🖪 Pepper Tree	**SW4**	27
Nahm	**SW1X**	26
🖪 Blue Elephant	**SW6**	24
🖪 101 Thai	**W6**	24
Patara	**multi.**	24
Thai Thai	**EC1V**	24
🖪 Busaba Eathai	**multi.**	23
Churchill Arms	**W8**	23
Rosa's	**multi.**	23
Yum Yum	**N16**	23
Esarn Kheaw	**W12**	22
Thai Sq./Soho Thai	**multi.**	22
Sri Nam	**E14**	22
🆕 Suda	**WC2E**	22
Mango Tree	**SW1X**	21
Crazy Bear	**multi.**	20

TUNISIAN

Adams Cafe	**W12**	22

TURKISH

Antepliler	**N1**	25
Kazan	**SW1V**	25
Haz	**multi.**	23
Efes	**W1W**	22
Fora	**multi.**	22
Gallipoli	**N1**	22
Pasha	**N1**	22
Tas	**multi.**	22
Ishtar	**W1U**	21

CUISINES

Özer	**W1B**	_21_
Sofra	**multi.**	_21_

Amico Bio	**EC1A**	_21_
Saf*	**W8**	_21_

VEGETARIAN

(* vegan)

Morgan M	**EC1A**	_28_
Chutneys	**NW1**	_26_
Food/Thought	**WC2H**	_25_
Gate*	**multi.**	_25_
Rasa	**multi.**	_24_
222 Veggie Vegan*	**W14**	_24_
Vanilla Black	**EC4A**	_24_
Woodlands	**multi.**	_23_
Sagar	**multi.**	_22_

VIETNAMESE

Cafe East	**SE16**	_26_
Song Que	**E2**	_26_
Mien Tay	**multi.**	_24_
Banh Mi Bay	**WC1X**	_23_
Viet Hoa	**E2**	_23_
Cây Tre	**multi.**	_22_
Pho	**multi.**	_21_

WEST AFRICAN

805	**SE15**	_24_

Locations

Includes names, cuisines and Food ratings.

Central London

BELGRAVIA

(See map on page 74)

🔁 Petrus	*French*	28
Koffmann's	*French*	27
🔁 Marcus Wareing	*French*	27
🔁 Amaya	*Indian*	26
Apsleys	*Italian*	26
🔁 Mosimann's	*Eclectic*	26
Nahm	*Thai*	26
🔁 Ottolenghi	*Bakery/Med.*	26
Ishbilia	*Lebanese*	25
Zafferano	*Italian*	25
Oliveto	*Italian*	24
Olivomare	*Italian/Seafood*	24
Salloos	*Pakistani*	24
Il Convivio	*Italian*	23
Memories/China	*Chinese*	23
Boisdale	*British/Scottish*	22
Noura	*Lebanese*	22
Palm	*Amer./Chops*	22
Pantechnicon Rooms	*Euro.*	22
Baker & Spice	*Bakery/Med.*	21
Motcombs	*Eclectic*	21
Thomas Cubitt	*British*	21
Santini	*Italian*	20
Jenny Lo's Tea	*Chinese*	19
Patisserie Valerie	*French*	19
Ebury Wine	*Euro./French*	18
Grenadier	*British*	18
NEW Hix Belgravia	*Eclectic*	-

BLOOMSBURY/ FITZROVIA

🔁 Pied à Terre	*French*	27
NEW Dabbous	*Euro.*	26
🔁 Hakkasan	*Chinese*	26
Mennula	*Italian*	26
Roka	*Japanese*	26
Barrica	*Spanish*	25
Fino	*Spanish*	25
North Sea	*Seafood*	25
Abeno	*Japanese*	24
Archipelago	*Eclectic*	24
Latium	*Italian*	24
Pescatori	*Italian/Seafood*	24
Salt Yard	*Italian/Spanish*	24
Tortilla	*Mex.*	24

Tsunami	*Japanese*	24
🔁 Busaba Eathai	*Thai*	23
Bam-Bou	*Asian*	22
Brasserie Blanc	*French*	22
Ciao Bella	*Med.*	22
Efes	*Turkish*	22
Gaylord	*Indian*	22
Hare & Tortoise	*Japanese*	22
Sardo	*Italian*	22
Tas	*Turkish*	22
Cigala	*Spanish*	21
🔁 Nando's	*Portug.*	21
Pho	*Viet.*	21
Ping Pong	*Chinese*	21
Riding Hse. Café	*Euro.*	21
🔁 Wagamama	*Japanese*	21
Black & Blue	*Chops*	20
🔁 Carluccio's	*Italian*	20
Crazy Bear	*Thai*	20
Draft House	*Eclectic*	20
Elena's L'Etoile	*French/Italian*	20
🔁 Zizzi	*Italian*	20
Adam & Eve	*British*	19
Ask Italian	*Italian*	19
Malabar Junction	*Indian*	19
Villandry	*French*	19
Dim T	*Asian*	18
Giraffe	*Eclectic*	18
All Star Lanes	*Amer.*	17
NEW Lima	*Peruvian*	-

CHINATOWN

Haozhan	*Chinese*	25
Plum Valley	*Chinese*	25
Golden Dragon	*Chinese*	24
Empress of Sichuan	*Chinese*	23
Four Seasons	*Chinese*	23
Spice Mkt.	*SE Asian*	23
Imperial China	*Chinese*	22
Leong's Legend	*Taiwanese*	22
Mr. Kong	*Chinese*	22
Tokyo Diner	*Japanese*	22
Harbour City	*Chinese*	21
Joy King Lau	*Chinese*	21
New World	*Chinese*	20
Chuen Cheng Ku	*Chinese*	19
Wong Kei	*Chinese*	19
NEW Wulumuchi	*Chinese*	-

LOCATIONS

COVENT GARDEN

(See map on page 73)

☑ L'Atelier/Robuchon	*French*	28
☑ Hawksmoor	*Chops*	26
☑ J. Sheekey	*Seafood*	26
J. Sheekey Oyster	*Seafood*	26
☑ Clos Maggiore	*French*	25
Food/Thought	*Veg.*	25
Giovanni's	*Italian*	25
Moti Mahal	*Indian*	25
Rossopomodoro	*Italian*	25
☑ Rules	*Chops*	25
Savoy Grill	*British/French*	25
Abeno	*Japanese*	24
Asia de Cuba	*Asian/Cuban*	24
Gaby's	*Jewish/Mideast.*	24
Great Queen St.	*British*	24
☑ Ivy	*British/Euro.*	24
Ladurée	*French*	24
Opera Tavern	*Italian/Spanish*	24
Rock & Sole	*Seafood*	24
☑ Busaba Eathai	*Thai*	23
Cantina Laredo	*Mex.*	23
Dishoom	*Indian*	23
Forge	*Euro.*	23
Indigo	*Euro.*	23
Kopapa	*Eclectic*	23
Lupita	*Mex.*	23
Mela	*Indian*	23
Punjab	*Indian*	23
NEW 10 Cases	*Euro.*	23
Tom's Kitchen	*British*	23
☑ Wahaca	*Mex.*	23
Adam St.	*British*	22
Bill's Produce	*British*	22
Brasserie Blanc	*French*	22
☑ Byron	*Burgers*	22
☑ Côte	*French*	22
Fernandez & Wells	*Spanish*	22
Kulu Kulu	*Japanese*	22
Le Deuxième	*Euro.*	22
Loch Fyne	*Seafood*	22
Polpo	*Italian*	22
Sagar	*Indian/Veg.*	22
Savoy River	*French*	22
Sophie's	*Amer./Chops*	22
NEW Suda	*Thai*	22
Thai Sq./Soho Thai	*Thai*	22
Wasabi	*Japanese*	22
Belgo	*Belgian*	21
NEW Delaunay	*Euro.*	21
☑ Gourmet Burger	*Burgers*	21
Mon Plaisir	*French*	21

☑ Nando's	*Portug.*	21
Orso	*Italian*	21
☑ Pizza Express	*Pizza*	21
Simpson's/Strand	*British*	21
Sofra	*Turkish*	21
Souk	*African*	21
Terroirs	*Med.*	21
☑ Wagamama	*Japanese*	21
☑ Browns	*British*	20
Cafe Pacifico	*Mex.*	20
☑ Carluccio's	*Italian*	20
Christopher's	*Amer./Chops*	20
Crazy Bear	*Thai*	20
Hi Sushi	*Japanese*	20
☑ Jamie's Italian	*Italian*	20
Leon	*Med.*	20
NEW Mishkin's	*Jewish*	20
PJ's B&G	*Amer.*	20
☑ Zizzi	*Italian*	20
Angus Steakhouse	*Chops*	19
Café des Amis	*French*	19
Circus	*Asian*	19
Joe Allen	*Amer.*	19
NEW Leon De Bruxelles	*Belgian*	19
Les Deux	*French*	19
Masala Zone	*Indian*	19
Maxwell's	*Amer.*	19
Patisserie Valerie	*French*	19
Real Greek	*Greek*	19
Smollensky's	*Amer./Chops*	19
Tuttons	*British*	19
☑ Café Rouge	*French*	18
Canteen	*British*	18
Diner	*Amer.*	18
Porters English	*British*	18
Pix Pintxos	*Spanish*	13
NEW Meat Market	*Burgers*	–

HOLBORN

☑ Pearl	*French*	28
Chancery	*Euro.*	25
☑ Gaucho	*Argent./Chops*	25
Vanilla Black	*Veg.*	24
Asadal	*Korean*	23
Banh Mi Bay	*Viet.*	23
La Porchetta	*Italian*	23
Shanghai Blues	*Chinese*	23
Brasserie Blanc	*French*	22
Chilango	*Mex.*	22
Cigalon	*French*	22
28-50 Wine	*French*	22
Belgo	*Belgian*	21
Bountiful Cow	*Chops*	21

LOCATIONS

Patisserie Valerie	*French*	19
Real Greek	*Greek*	19
Aubaine	*French*	18
Canteen	*British*	18
Giraffe	*Eclectic*	18
Wallace	*French*	18
Yo! Sushi	*Japanese*	18
NEW Briciole	*Italian*	-
NEW Cotidie	*Italian*	-
NEW Donostia	*Spanish*	-

MAYFAIR

(See map on page 73)

🛿 Le Gavroche	*French*	28
🛿 Square	*French*	28
🛿 Alain Ducasse	*French*	27
Ikeda	*Japanese*	27
🛿 La Petite Maison	*Med.*	27
🛿 Nobu London	*Japanese*	27
🛿 Umu	*Japanese*	27
Goodman	*Chops*	26
🛿 Gordon Ramsay/Clar.	*Euro.*	26
Greenhouse	*French*	26
🛿 Hakkasan	*Chinese*	26
Hibiscus	*French*	26
Kiku	*Japanese*	26
Murano	*Euro./Italian*	26
Nobu Berkeley	*Japanese*	26
Patterson's	*British*	26
🛿 Scott's	*Seafood*	26
Theo Randall	*Italian*	26
Amaranto	*Italian*	25
Benares	*Indian*	25
NEW Burger & Lobster	*Amer.*	25
Corrigan's Mayfair	*British*	25
NEW Cut/45 Park Ln.	*Amer./Chops*	25
Dorchester	*British*	25
🛿 Espelette	*French*	25
Galvin at Windows	*French*	25
Harry's Bar	*Italian*	25
Hélène Darroze	*French*	25
Hix at the Albemarle	*British*	25
Kai Mayfair	*Chinese*	25
Maze	*French*	25
🛿 Pollen St. Social	*British*	25
Tamarind	*Indian*	25
Veeraswamy	*Indian*	25
Bellamy's	*French*	24
Chor Bizarre	*Indian*	24
Guinea Grill	*Chops*	24
JW Steak	*Amer./Chops*	24
La Genova	*Italian*	24
Le Boudin Blanc	*French*	24

Maze Grill	*Chops*	24
Patara	*Thai*	24
Pescatori	*Italian/Seafood*	24
Princess Garden	*Chinese*	24
Rasa	*Indian/Veg.*	24
Tempo	*Italian*	24
Al Hamra	*Lebanese*	23
NEW Arts Club	*Euro.*	23
Chisou	*Japanese*	23
C London	*Italian*	23
George	*Euro.*	23
Miyama	*Japanese*	23
Sakura	*Japanese*	23
Semplice Rist.	*Italian*	23
🛿 Sketch/Lecture	*Euro.*	23
Sumosan	*Japanese*	23
NEW 34	*Chops*	23
Wild Honey	*British*	23
Alloro	*Italian*	22
Al Sultan	*Lebanese*	22
NEW Alyn Williams	*Euro.*	22
NEW Aurelia	*Med.*	22
Cecconi's	*Italian*	22
China Tang	*Chinese*	22
El Pirata	*Spanish*	22
Flemings Grill	*Euro.*	22
Morton's	*Med.*	22
Noura	*Lebanese*	22
Sartoria	*Italian*	22
🛿 Sketch/Gallery	*Euro.*	22
Thai Sq./Soho Thai	*Thai*	22
Annabel's	*British/French*	21
Babbo	*Italian*	21
NEW Downtown Mayfair	*Italian*	21
Greig's	*Chops*	21
Hush	*Euro.*	21
Langan's Brass.	*British/French*	21
Mark's Club	*British/French*	21
🛿 Sketch/Parlour	*British*	21
Sofra	*Turkish*	21
🛿 Browns	*British*	20
🛿 Carluccio's	*Italian*	20
Delfino	*Italian*	20
Ed's Easy Diner	*Amer.*	20
Mews/Mayfair	*British*	20
NEW Novikov	*Asian/Italian*	20
Prezzo	*Italian*	20
Semplice Bar Trattoria	*Italian*	20
Angus Steakhouse	*Chops*	19
Ask Italian	*Italian*	19
Automat	*Amer.*	19
Patisserie Valerie	*French*	19

Rocket	*Med.*	19	
Aubaine	*French*	18	
Only Running	*British*	18	
Truc Vert	*French*	18	
Yo! Sushi	*Japanese*	18	
Richoux	*British*	16	

PICCADILLY

(See map on page 73)

Bentley's	*British/Seafood*	25
🔁 Gaucho	*Argent./Chops*	25
🔁 Ritz	*British/French*	25
Yoshino	*Japanese*	25
Ladurée	*French*	24
Caviar House	*Seafood*	23
🔁 Wolseley	*Euro.*	23
Citrus	*Italian*	21
Criterion	*Euro.*	21
FishWorks	*Seafood*	21
Benihana	*Japanese*	20
Chowki	*Indian*	20
Ed's Easy Diner	*Amer.*	20
Fortnum's Fountain	*British*	20
Momo	*Moroccan*	20
Prezzo	*Italian*	20
Strada	*Italian*	20
Fakhreldine	*Lebanese*	19
Patisserie Valerie	*French*	19
Aubaine	*French*	18
Hard Rock	*Amer.*	17
Restaurant/Arts	*British*	17
Planet Hollywood	*Amer.*	16
NEW Brasserie Zédel	*French*	-

SOHO

(See map on page 73)

🔁 Barrafina	*Spanish*	28
🔁 Gauthier	*French*	28
🔁 NEW Pitt Cue Co.	*BBQ*	28
🔁 L'Escargot	*French*	27
🔁 Yauatcha	*Chinese*	27
Bocca/Gelupo	*Italian*	26
Randall/Aubin	*British/Seafood*	26
Vasco & Piero's	*Italian*	26
Arbutus	*Euro.*	25
Aurora	*Euro.*	25
NEW Burger & Lobster		25
Dehesa	*Italian/Spanish*	25
Koya	*Japanese*	25
New Mayflower	*Chinese*	25
Nopi	*Asian/Mideast.*	25
Red Fort	*Indian*	25
St. John Hotel Rest.	*British*	25
Ten Ten Tei	*Japanese*	25

Andrew Edmunds	*Euro.*	24
Ba Shan	*Chinese*	24
Brindisa	*Spanish*	24
Cape Town Fish	*Eclectic/Seafood*	24
Giaconda	*Euro.*	24
Little Italy	*Italian*	24
🔁 Mooli's	*Indian*	24
Patara	*Thai*	24
Princi London	*Bakery/Italian*	24
Taro	*Japanese*	24
Wright Brothers	*Seafood*	24
Yalla Yalla	*Lebanese*	24
Yming	*Chinese*	24
Aqua Kyoto	*Japanese*	23
Barshu	*Chinese*	23
Bincho	*Japanese*	23
🔁 Busaba Eathai	*Thai*	23
NEW Copita	*Spanish*	23
Paramount	*Euro.*	23
Rosa's	*Thai*	23
Spuntino	*Amer./Italian*	23
Vinoteca	*Euro.*	23
🔁 Wahaca	*Mex.*	23
Woodlands	*Indian/Veg.*	23
Aqua Nueva	*Spanish*	22
Bali Bali	*Indonesian*	22
Bill's Produce	*British*	22
🔁 Bob Bob Ricard	*British*	22
🔁 Bodeans	*BBQ*	22
Breakfast Club	*British*	22
🔁 Byron	*Burgers*	22
Cây Tre	*Viet.*	22
🔁 Côte	*French*	22
Dean St.	*British*	22
Fernandez & Wells	*Spanish*	22
Hix	*British*	22
Imli	*Indian*	22
Incognico	*French/Italian*	22
Kulu Kulu	*Japanese*	22
Polpo	*Italian*	22
Portrait	*British*	22
Thai Sq./Soho Thai	*Thai*	22
Wasabi	*Japanese*	22
Albannach	*Scottish*	21
Banana Tree	*SE Asian*	21
Gay Hussar	*Hungarian*	21
Kettner's	*French*	21
Pho	*Viet.*	21
Ping Pong	*Chinese*	21
🔁 Pizza Express	*Pizza*	21
Quo Vadis	*British*	21
Soho Hse.	*British*	21

Souk	*African*	21
🏠 Wagamama	*Japanese*	21
Ed's Easy Diner	*Amer.*	20
Hi Sushi	*Japanese*	20
Inamo	*Asian*	20
Leon	*Med.*	20
Satsuma	*Japanese*	20
Angus Steakhouse	*Chops*	19
Balans	*British*	19
Gopal's	*Indian*	19
Le Pain Quot.	*Bakery/Belgian*	19
Made in Italy	*Italian*	19
Masala Zone	*Indian*	19
National Dining Rooms	*British*	19
Patisserie Valerie	*French*	19
Antidote	*French*	18
Café Boheme	*French*	18
Cha Cha Moon	*Chinese*	18
Diner	*Amer.*	18
NEW Ducksoup	*Euro.*	18
Floridita	*Pan-Latin*	18
Giraffe	*Eclectic*	18
Groucho Club	*British*	18
Yo! Sushi	*Japanese*	18
El Camion	*Mex.*	17
Pix Pintxos	*Spanish*	13
NEW Ceviche	*Peruvian*	-
NEW Cinnamon Soho	*Indian*	-
NEW La Bodega Negra	*Mex.*	-
NEW Mele e Pere	*Italian*	-
NEW Tapasia	*Asian*	-
NEW 10 Greek Street	*Euro.*	-

ST. JAMES'S

(See map on page 73)

L'Oranger	*French*	27
Wilton's	*British/Seafood*	26
Sake No Hana	*Japanese*	25
Le Caprice	*British/Euro.*	24
Rowley's	*British*	24
NEW Balcon	*British/French*	23
Brumus	*Euro.*	23
Bumbles	*Euro.*	23
Matsuri	*Japanese*	23
Mint Leaf	*Indian*	23
Wheeler's	*Seafood*	23
Al Duca	*Italian*	22
Franco's	*Italian/Med.*	22
Green's	*British/Seafood*	22
Thai Sq./Soho Thai	*Thai*	22
Avenue	*British*	21
Brass. St. Jacques	*French*	21
Quaglino's	*Euro.*	21
Inamo	*Asian*	20

Inn the Park	*British*	18
Richoux	*British*	16

VICTORIA

Goring	*British*	25
Olivo	*Italian*	22
Mango Tree	*Thai*	21
Prezzo	*Italian*	20
🏠 Zizzi	*Italian*	20
Ask Italian	*Italian*	19
Dim T	*Asian*	18
Quilon	*Indian*	-

WESTMINSTER

Atari-Ya Sushi Bar	*Japanese*	25
Cinnamon Club	*Indian*	25
Quirinale	*Italian*	25
Roux/Parliament	*Euro.*	24
Shepherd's	*British*	23
🏠 Byron	*Burgers*	22
Sagar	*Indian/Veg.*	22
Wasabi	*Japanese*	22
Bank Westminster	*Euro.*	21
English Pig	*British*	20
Massimo	*Med.*	20
Prezzo	*Italian*	20
Angus Steakhouse	*Chops*	19
Yo! Sushi	*Japanese*	18

East/South East London

CANARY WHARF/ DOCKLANDS

Goodman	*Chops*	26
Roka	*Japanese*	26
🏠 Gaucho	*Argent./Chops*	25
Le Relais	*Chops/French*	24
Plateau	*French*	24
Tortilla	*Mex.*	24
Amerigo Vespucci	*Italian*	23
Camino	*Spanish*	23
Gun	*British*	23
Haz	*Turkish*	23
Iberica	*Spanish*	23
Lotus Floating	*Chinese*	23
Royal China	*Chinese*	23
🏠 Wahaca	*Mex.*	23
Boisdale	*British/Scottish*	22
🏠 Byron	*Burgers*	22
Dockmaster's	*Indian*	22
Sri Nam	*Thai*	22
Quadrato	*Italian*	21
🏠 Browns	*British*	20
🏠 Carluccio's	*Italian*	20

✓ Jamie's Italian | *Italian*	20
Leon | *Med.*	20
Rocket | *Med.*	19
Smollensky's | *Amer./Chops*	19
✓ Café Rouge | *French*	18
Canteen | *British*	18

CITY

(See map on page 78)

Café Spice | *Indian*	26
Goodman | *Chops*	26
✓ Hawksmoor | *Chops*	26
Refettorio | *Italian*	26
Cinnamon Kitchen | *Indian*	25
✓ Galvin Chapelle/Cafe | *French*	25
✓ Gaucho | *Argent./Chops*	25
L'Anima | *Italian*	25
Rhodes 24 | *British*	25
Bevis Marks | *British/Jewish*	24
Kenza | *Lebanese/Moroccan*	24
Le Relais | *Chops/French*	24
Tortilla | *Mex.*	24
Alba | *Italian*	23
Bar Battu | *Euro.*	23
Barbecoa | *BBQ*	23
Bonds | *French*	23
Coq d'Argent | *French*	23
Haz | *Turkish*	23
Lutyens | *French*	23
Mint Leaf | *Indian*	23
Miyama | *Japanese*	23
1901 | *British*	23
Sweetings | *Seafood*	23
Tsuru | *Japanese*	23
Barcelona Tapas | *Spanish*	22
✓ Bodeans | *BBQ*	22
Boisdale | *British/Scottish*	22
Brasserie Blanc | *French*	22
Breakfast Club | *British*	22
Chilango | *Mex.*	22
✓ Côte | *French*	22
Don | *Euro.*	22
Fora | *Turkish*	22
Green's | *British/Seafood*	22
Hare & Tortoise | *Japanese*	22
Loch Fyne | *Seafood*	22
Mercer | *British*	22
✓ 1 Lombard | *French*	22
Paternoster Chop | *Chops*	22
Thai Sq./Soho Thai | *Thai*	22
Wasabi | *Japanese*	22
NEW Bread St. Kitchen | *Euro.*	21
Chiswell St. Dining | *British*	21
Imperial City | *Chinese*	21

Marco Pierre White | *Chops*	21
1 Lombard Brass. | *Euro.*	21
Ping Pong | *Chinese*	21
✓ Pizza Express | *Pizza*	21
✓ Wagamama | *Japanese*	21
Benihana | *Japanese*	20
✓ Browns | *British*	20
Chez Gérard | *French*	20
✓ Jamie's Italian | *Italian*	20
Leon | *Med.*	20
Strada | *Italian*	20
Caravaggio | *Italian*	19
Patisserie Valerie | *French*	19
Prism | *British*	19
Rocket | *Med.*	19
Folly | *Euro.*	18
Manicomio | *Italian*	18
Anthologist | *Euro.*	17
Luxe | *British*	17
Northbank | *British*	15
NEW Door | *Chops*	-
NEW Drift | *Euro.*	-

CLERKENWELL/
FARRINGDON

Morgan M | *French/Veg.*	28
✓ Morito | *African/Spanish*	27
Moro | *African/Spanish*	27
North Rd. | *Euro.*	27
Bistrot Bruno Loubet | *French*	26
Club Gascon | *French*	26
Portal | *Portug.*	26
St. John | *British*	26
Comptoir Gascon | *French*	25
✓ Gaucho | *Argent./Chops*	25
Le Café/Marché | *French*	25
Modern Pantry | *Eclectic*	25
Caravan | *Euro.*	24
Hix Oyster | *British/Chops*	24
Bincho | *Japanese*	23
Bleeding Heart | *British/French*	23
Cellar Gascon | *French*	23
Eagle | *Med.*	23
La Porchetta | *Italian*	23
Smiths/Top Fl. | *British*	23
Vinoteca | *Euro.*	23
Cottons | *Carib.*	22
Gail's | *Bakery*	22
Polpo | *Italian*	22
Tas | *Turkish*	22
Amico Bio | *Italian/Veg.*	21
Little Bay | *Euro.*	21
Medcalf | *British*	21

Pho	*Viet.*	21
Smiths/Dining Rm.	*British*	21
🄴 Carluccio's	*Italian*	20
Strada	*Italian*	20
Yo! Sushi	*Japanese*	18
Giant Robot	*Amer./Italian*	17
Dans Le Noir	*Eclectic*	13

GREENWICH/ BLACKHEATH

Chapters All Day	*Euro.*	25
Rivington Grill	*British*	24
🄴 Byron	*Burgers*	22
Las Iguanas	*Pan-Latin*	22
🄴 Nando's	*Portug.*	21
Rodizio Rico	*Brazilian*	21
Old Brewery	*British*	19

MILE END/HACKNEY/ BETHNAL GREEN

Corner Room	*Euro.*	29
Buen Ayre	*Argent.*	26
Viajante	*Eclectic*	26
Empress	*British*	23
A Little/Fancy	*British*	22
Bistrotheque	*French*	22
🄴 Nando's	*Portug.*	21

PECKHAM

805	*African*	24

SHOREDITCH/ HOXTON/ WHITECHAPEL

Brawn	*British/French*	26
🄴 Hawksmoor	*Chops*	26
Song Que	*Viet.*	26
Tayyabs	*Pakistani*	26
Lahore Kebab House	*Pakistani*	25
Rossopomodoro	*Italian*	25
St. John Bread	*British*	25
Eyre Brothers	*Portug./Spanish*	24
Mien Tay	*Viet.*	24
Rivington Grill	*British*	24
Thai Thai	*Thai*	24
Boundary	*British/French*	23
🄴 Busaba Eathai	*Thai*	23
Fifteen	*Italian*	23
🄴 Les Trois Garçons	*French*	23
Rosa's	*Thai*	23
Viet Hoa	*Viet.*	23
Cây Tre	*Viet.*	22
Hoxton Grill	*Amer.*	22

Las Iguanas	*Pan-Latin*	22
Princess/Shoreditch	*British*	21
Leon	*Med.*	20
Pizza East	*Pizza*	20
Great Eastern	*Asian*	19
Real Greek	*Greek*	19
Whitechapel	*Euro.*	19
Canteen	*British*	18
Giraffe	*Eclectic*	18
Diner	*Amer.*	18
All Star Lanes	*Amer.*	17
Hoxton Square	*Tex-Mex*	17
NEW Tramshed	*British*	-

SOUTH BANK/ BOROUGH

Roast	*British*	25
Brindisa	*Spanish*	24
Tortilla	*Mex.*	24
Wright Brothers	*Seafood*	24
Fish	*Seafood*	23
Oxo Tower Brass.	*Asian/Med.*	23
Tsuru	*Japanese*	23
Oxo Tower	*Euro.*	22
Tas	*Turkish*	22
Ping Pong	*Chinese*	21
🄴 Wagamama	*Japanese*	21
Black & Blue	*Chops*	20
Skylon	*Euro.*	20
Tate Modern	*Euro.*	20
Cantina Vino.	*Eclectic/Med.*	19
Feng Sushi	*Japanese*	19
Le Pain Quot.	*Bakery/Belgian*	19
Canteen	*British*	18
Giraffe	*Eclectic*	18

STRATFORD

Franco Manca	*Pizza*	25
Tortilla	*Mex.*	24
🄴 Busaba Eathai	*Thai*	23
Rosa's	*Thai*	23
🄴 Wahaca	*Mex.*	23
Las Iguanas	*Pan-Latin*	22
NEW Cabana	*Brazilian*	21
Pho	*Viet.*	21
Comptoir Libanais	*Lebanese*	20
🄴 Jamie's Italian	*Italian*	20
Balans	*British*	19
Bumpkin	*British*	19
All Star Lanes	*Amer.*	17

TOWER BRIDGE/ WAPPING

🄴 José	*Spanish*	28
🄴 Zucca	*Italian*	27

Magdalen | *Euro.*	26
🅉 Gaucho | *Argent./Chops*	25
NEW Pizarro | *Spanish*	25
Constancia | *Argent./Chops*	24
Il Bordello | *Italian*	24
Tentazioni | *Italian*	24
Butlers Wharf | *Chops*	23
Champor | *Malaysian*	23
Le Pont/Tour | *French/Seafood*	23
Village East | *British*	23
Bengal Clipper | *Indian*	22
Blueprint | *Euro.*	22
Cantina/Ponte | *Italian*	21
Del'Aziz | *African/Med.*	21
Ping Pong | *Chinese*	21
Vivat Bacchus | *Euro.*	21
🅉 Browns | *British*	20
Draft House | *Eclectic*	20
Wapping Food | *Euro.*	20
Ask Italian | *Italian*	19
Dim T | *Asian*	18
Narrow | *British*	18

WATERLOO/
SOUTHWARK/
KENNINGTON/
VAUXHALL

Cafe East | *Viet.*	26
Hot Stuff | *Indian*	26
Anchor/Hope | *British*	25
Baltic | *E Euro.*	24
Meson Don Felipe | *Spanish*	23
R.S.J. | *British*	23
Vapiano | *Italian*	23
Brasserie Blanc | *French*	22
Dragon Castle | *Chinese*	22
Las Iguanas | *Pan-Latin*	22
Tas | *Turkish*	22
Del'Aziz | *African/Med.*	21
Leon | *Med.*	20
Waterloo | *British*	20
Real Greek | *Greek*	19
NEW Gillray's | *Chops*	-

North/
North West London

BELSIZE PARK/
HAMPSTEAD/
KILBURN/
SWISS COTTAGE

Sushi-Say | *Japanese*	28
🅉 Jin Kichi | *Japanese*	27

Nautilus Fish | *Seafood*	27
Atari-Ya Sushi Bar | *Japanese*	25
🅉 Gaucho | *Argent./Chops*	25
Paradise | *British*	25
Artigiano | *Italian*	23
Bradley's | *British/French*	23
Singapore Gdn. | *Malaysian/Singapor.*	23
Woodlands | *Indian/Veg.*	23
Gail's | *Bakery*	22
Wells | *Euro.*	22
Banana Tree | *SE Asian*	21
Del'Aziz | *African/Med.*	21
🅉 Gourmet Burger | *Burgers*	21
Little Bay | *Euro.*	21
🅉 Nando's | *Portug.*	21
XO | *Asian*	21
Old Bull & Bush | *Euro.*	20
Feng Sushi | *Japanese*	19
🅉 Café Rouge | *French*	18
Dim T | *Asian*	18

CAMDEN TOWN/
CHALK FARM/
KENTISH TOWN/
PRIMROSE HILL

Chutneys | *Indian/Veg.*	26
Odette's | *Euro.*	25
Rossopomodoro | *Italian*	25
Carob Tree | *Greek/Med.*	24
El Parador | *Spanish*	24
L'Absinthe | *French*	24
Made/Camden | *Euro.*	24
Bento | *Japanese*	23
Bull & Last | *British*	23
Camden Brass. | *Euro.*	23
La Porchetta | *Italian*	23
Cottons | *Carib.*	22
Haché | *Burgers*	22
Mestizo | *Mex.*	22
Wasabi | *Japanese*	22
Belgo | *Belgian*	21
Lemonia | *Greek*	21
🅉 Nando's | *Portug.*	21
🅉 Wagamama | *Japanese*	21
Ed's Easy Diner | *Amer.*	20
Gilgamesh | *Asian*	20
Hi Sushi | *Japanese*	20
Sardo | *Italian*	20
York/Albany | *Euro.*	20
Feng Sushi | *Japanese*	19
Masala Zone | *Indian*	19
Diner | *Amer.*	18

LOCATIONS

GOLDERS GREEN/ FINCHLEY/HENDON/ MILL HILL

Atari-Ya Sushi Bar	*Japanese*	25
Café Japan	*Japanese*	25
Good Earth	*Chinese*	24
Original Lahore	*Pakistani*	23
Two Brothers Fish	*Seafood*	23
Hi Sushi	*Japanese*	20
Solly's	*Kosher/Mideast.*	20
🅩 Zizzi	*Italian*	20

HIGHGATE/ MUSWELL HILL/ CROUCH END

500	*Italian*	24
La Porchetta	*Italian*	23
🅩 Zizzi	*Italian*	20
Ask Italian	*Italian*	19
🅩 Café Rouge	*French*	18
Dim T	*Asian*	18
Giraffe	*Eclectic*	18

ISLINGTON

🅩 Ottolenghi	*Bakery/Med.*	26
Santa Maria/Garufa	*Argent./Chops*	26
Antepliler	*Turkish*	25
Sabor	*S Amer.*	25
Gate	*Veg./Vegan*	25
Afghan Kitchen	*Afghan*	24
La Fromagerie	*Euro.*	24
Rasa	*Indian/Veg.*	24
Tortilla	*Mex.*	24
Trullo	*Italian*	24
Akari	*Japanese*	23
Almeida	*French*	23
Antonio's	*Italian*	23
Elk in the Woods	*Eclectic*	23
Frederick's	*British/Euro.*	23
La Porchetta	*Italian*	23
Albion	*British*	22
Bill's Produce	*British*	22
Breakfast Club	*British*	22
🅩 Byron	*Burgers*	22
Chilango	*Mex.*	22
Duke/Cambridge	*British*	22
Gallipoli	*Turkish*	22
Pasha	*Turkish*	22
Thai Sq./Soho Thai	*Thai*	22
Wasabi	*Japanese*	22
Banana Tree	*SE Asian*	21

Le Mercury	*French*	21
🅩 Nando's	*Portug.*	21
Rodizio Rico	*Brazilian*	21
🅩 Wagamama	*Japanese*	21
🅩 Browns	*British*	20
🅩 Carluccio's	*Italian*	20
🅩 Jamie's Italian	*Italian*	20
New Culture Rev.	*Chinese*	20
Strada	*Italian*	20
Ask Italian	*Italian*	19
Masala Zone	*Indian*	19
Diner	*Amer.*	18
Giraffe	*Eclectic*	18

KING'S CROSS

Yalla Yalla	*Lebanese*	24
Camino	*Spanish*	23
Rotunda	*British*	23
Le Pain Quot.	*Bakery/Belgian*	19
Gilbert Scott	*British*	18
St. Pancras	*British*	18
NEW Karpo	*Eclectic*	-
NEW Shrimpy's	*Calif./Mex.*	-

ST. JOHN'S WOOD

Oslo Court	*French*	26
L'Aventure	*French*	25
Original Lahore	*Pakistani*	23
Fora	*Turkish*	22
Gail's	*Bakery*	22
Baker & Spice	*Bakery/Med.*	21
Red Pepper	*Italian*	21
Waterway	*Euro.*	21
Warrington	*British*	20
Cafe Med	*Med.*	19
🅩 Café Rouge	*French*	18
Raoul's	*Med.*	17
Richoux	*British*	16
NEW 1 Blenheim Terrace	*British*	-

STOKE NEWINGTON

Rasa	*Indian/Veg.*	24
La Porchetta	*Italian*	23
Yum Yum	*Thai*	23

South/ South West London

BARNES

Annie's	*British*	23
Strada	*Italian*	20
NEW Georgina's	*Euro.*	-
NEW Sonny's Kitchen	*Euro.*	-

BATTERSEA

Santa Maria/Garufa | *Argent./Chops*	26
Mien Tay | *Viet.*	24
Tom Ilic | *Euro.*	24
🇿 Pizza Express | *Pizza*	21
Ransome's | *British/Eclectic*	21
Butcher & Grill | *British*	20
Draft House | *Eclectic*	20
Gazette | *French*	20
NEW Bunga Bunga | *Italian*	17
NEW Soif | *French*	–

BRIXTON/CLAPHAM

Honest Burgers | *Burgers*	27
🇿 Pepper Tree | *Thai*	27
Trinity | *Euro.*	26
Franco Manca | *Pizza*	25
Tsunami | *Japanese*	24
Abbeville | *British*	23
🇿 Bodeans | *BBQ*	22
Gail's | *Bakery*	22
Haché | *Burgers*	22
Wasabi | *Japanese*	22
Banana Tree | *SE Asian*	21
Belgo | *Belgian*	21
Del'Aziz | *African/Med.*	21
🇿 Gourmet Burger | *Burgers*	21
🇿 Nando's | *Portug.*	21
Osteria Antica | *Italian*	21
Draft House | *Eclectic*	20
Strada | *Italian*	20
Buona Sera | *Italian*	19

CAMBERWELL/ DULWICH

🇿 Babur | *Indian*	27
Angels & Gypsies | *Spanish*	25
Palmerston | *British*	24
Barcelona Tapas | *Spanish*	22
Draft House | *Eclectic*	20
Rocca | *Italian*	19
🇿 Café Rouge | *French*	18

CHELSEA

(See map on page 74)

🇿 Gordon Ramsay/68 | *French*	28
🇿 Rasoi Vineet | *Indian*	27
🇿 Gaucho | *Argent./Chops*	25
Medlar | *French*	25
Poissonnerie/l'Avenue | *French/Seafood*	25
Rossopomodoro | *Italian*	25
Scalini | *Italian*	25
Tom Aikens | *French*	25

Ziani | *Italian*	25
🇿 Blue Elephant | *Thai*	24
Chutney Mary | *Indian*	24
Le Cercle | *French*	24
Le Colombier | *French*	24
🇿 Busaba Eathai | *Thai*	23
Caraffini | *Italian*	23
Eight Over Eight | *Asian*	23
Painted Heron | *Indian*	23
Tom's Kitchen | *British*	23
Aglio e Olio | *Italian*	22
🇿 Byron | *Burgers*	22
Daphne's | *Italian*	22
El Gaucho | *Argent./Chops*	22
Haché | *Burgers*	22
Le Suquet | *French/Seafood*	22
Pellicano | *Italian*	22
Sophie's | *Amer./Chops*	22
Baker & Spice | *Bakery/Med.*	21
Big Easy | *Amer.*	21
Cheyne Walk | *French*	21
Elistano | *Italian*	21
Enterprise | *British*	21
La Famiglia | *Italian*	21
Lucio | *Italian*	21
Osteria dell'Arancio | *Italian*	21
🇿 Pizza Express | *Pizza*	21
Benihana | *Japanese*	20
Black & Blue | *Chops*	20
Bluebird | *British*	20
Geales | *Seafood*	20
New Culture Rev. | *Chinese*	20
Pig's Ear | *British/French*	20
PJ's B&G | *Amer.*	20
Admiral Codrington | *British/Euro.*	19
Botanist | *British*	19
Buona Sera | *Italian*	19
Foxtrot Oscar | *British*	19
Itsu | *Japanese*	19
Le Pain Quot. | *Bakery/Belgian*	19
Made in Italy | *Italian*	19
Marco Pierre/King's | *Chops*	19
Patisserie Valerie | *French*	19
Builders Arms | *British*	18
Manicomio | *Italian*	18
Riccardo's | *Italian*	17
Brinkley's | *Eclectic*	16
NEW Brooklyn Bite | *Pizza*	–
NEW Sette | *Italian*	–

EARL'S COURT

222 Veggie Vegan | *Vegan*	24
Troubadour | *Eclectic*	22

Strada	*Italian*	20
Z Zizzi	*Italian*	20
Balans	*British*	19
Masala Zone	*Indian*	19

FULHAM

Z Harwood Arms	*British*	28
Mao Tai	*Asian*	25
Royal China	*Chinese*	23
Sands End	*British/Irish*	23
Z Bodeans	*BBQ*	22
Z Côte	*French*	22
Manson	*British*	22
Del'Aziz	*African/Med.*	21
Z Gourmet Burger	*Burgers*	21
Z Pizza Express	*Pizza*	21
Tendido Cuatro	*Spanish*	21
Z Carluccio's	*Italian*	20
Feng Sushi	*Japanese*	19
Fulham/Kens. Wine Rooms	*Euro.*	19
Masala Zone	*Indian*	19
Frankie's	*Italian*	18
Yo! Sushi	*Japanese*	18
NEW Lowcountry	*Amer.*	-

PIMLICO

Z Hunan	*Chinese*	28
Tinello	*Italian*	26
Kazan	*Turkish*	25
About Thyme	*Euro.*	24
La Poule au Pot	*French*	23
Como Lario	*Italian*	22
Daylesford	*Eclectic*	22
Orange Restaurant	*Euro.*	22
Grumbles	*British/French*	19

PUTNEY/
RICHMOND/
SURBITON/
TWICKENHAM

Z French Table	*French/Med.*	28
Glasshouse	*Euro.*	27
Brula	*French*	26
A Cena	*Italian*	25
Enoteca Turi	*Italian*	25
Z Gaucho	*Argent./Chops*	25
Ma Goa	*Indian*	25
Bingham	*British/Euro.*	24
Petersham Nurseries	*Euro.*	24
Popeseye	*Chops*	24
Petersham	*Euro.*	23
Z Côte	*French*	22
Hare & Tortoise	*Japanese*	22
Las Iguanas	*Pan-Latin*	22

Thai Sq./Soho Thai	*Thai*	22
FishWorks	*Seafood*	21
Z Gourmet Burger	*Burgers*	21
Z Carluccio's	*Italian*	20
Z Jamie's Italian	*Italian*	20

SOUTH KENSINGTON

(See map on page 74)

Star of India	*Indian*	26
Gessler/Daquise	*Polish*	25
L'Etranger	*French/Japanese*	25
Brindisa	*Spanish*	24
Cambio/Tercio	*Spanish*	24
La Bouchée	*French*	24
Patara	*Thai*	24
Bibendum	*French*	23
Bibendum Oyster	*French/Seafood*	23
Bombay Brass.	*Indian*	23
Noor Jahan	*Indian*	23
Z Byron	*Burgers*	22
El Gaucho	*Argent./Chops*	22
Kulu Kulu	*Japanese*	22
Tendido Cero	*Spanish*	22
Thai Sq./Soho Thai	*Thai*	22
Cassis Bistro	*French*	21
Pasha	*Moroccan*	21
Black & Blue	*Chops*	20
Ask Italian	*Italian*	19
Blakes	*Eclectic*	19
Bumpkin	*British*	19
Da Mario	*Italian*	19
La Brasserie	*French*	19
Le Pain Quot.	*Bakery/Belgian*	19
Rocca	*Italian*	19
Aubaine	*French*	18
NEW Dorsia	*Euro.*	-
NEW Kitchen 264	*Med.*	-
NEW Meursault	*French/Japanese*	-

WANDSWORTH/
BALHAM/
WIMBLEDON/
STREATHAM

Z Chez Bruce	*British*	28
Lamberts	*British*	27
Lahore Kebab House	*Pakistani*	25
Light House	*Eclectic*	25
Tortilla	*Mex.*	24
Bill's Produce	*British*	22
Z Gourmet Burger	*Burgers*	21
San Lorenzo	*Italian*	21
Butcher & Grill	*British*	20
Fox/Grapes	*British*	20
Gazette	*French*	20

Strada | *Italian* 20
Le Pain Quot. | *Bakery/Belgian* 19
NEW Lawn Bistro | *Euro.* -

West London

BAYSWATER

Angelus | *French* 25
Goldmine | *Chinese* 25
Mandarin Kitchen | 25
   Chinese/Seafood
Alounak | *Persian* 24
Bombay Palace | *Indian* 24
Halepi | *Greek* 24
Four Seasons | *Chinese* 23
Royal China | *Chinese* 23
Al Waha | *Lebanese* 22
Z Byron | *Burgers* 22
Khan's | *Indian* 22
Le Café Anglais | *French* 22
Banana Tree | *SE Asian* 21
Z Gourmet Burger | *Burgers* 21
Z Nando's | *Portug.* 21
Rodizio Rico | *Brazilian* 21
Masala Zone | *Indian* 19
Z Café Rouge | *French* 18
Yo! Sushi | *Japanese* 18
All Star Lanes | *Amer.* 17

CHISWICK

Z La Trompette | *Euro./French* 28
Charlotte's | *Euro.* 26
Franco Manca | *Pizza* 25
Le Vacherin | *French* 25
Sam's Brass. | *Euro.* 24
Annie's | *British* 23
Chisou | *Japanese* 23
Duke of Sussex | *British/Spanish* 23
Singapore Gdn. | 23
   Malaysian/Singapor.
Z Côte | *French* 22
Gail's | *Bakery* 22
NEW Hedone | *Euro.* 22
High Road Brass. | *Euro.* 22
Z Gourmet Burger | *Burgers* 21
NEW Union Jacks | *British* 20
Z Zizzi | *Italian* 20
NEW Devonshire Arms | *British* 19
Z Café Rouge | *French* 18
Giraffe | *Eclectic* 18

EALING

Charlotte's | *Euro.* 26
Atari-Ya Sushi Bar | *Japanese* 25

Z Côte | *French* 22
Hare & Tortoise | *Japanese* 22

HAMMERSMITH

Z River Café | *Italian* 27
Gate | *Veg./Vegan* 25
Indian Zing | *Indian* 25
Z 101 Thai | *Thai* 24
Tortilla | *Mex.* 24
Sagar | *Indian/Veg.* 22
Wasabi | *Japanese* 22
Raoul's | *Med.* 17

HOLLAND PARK

Belvedere | *British/French* 22
Julie's | *British* 19
Giraffe | *Eclectic* 18

KENSAL RISE

Diner | *Amer.* 18

KENSINGTON

(See map on page 76)
Z Yashin Sushi | *Japanese* 28
Clarke's | *British* 26
Kitchen W8 | *Euro.* 26
Min Jiang | *Chinese* 26
Z Ottolenghi | *Bakery/Med.* 26
Brunello | *Italian* 25
Launceston Pl. | *British* 25
Locanda Ottoemezzo | *Italian* 25
Timo | *Italian* 25
Zaika | *Indian* 25
Babylon | *British* 23
Churchill Arms | *Thai* 23
Koi | *Japanese* 23
Maggie Jones's | *British* 23
Memories/China | *Chinese* 23
Z Byron | *Burgers* 22
Z Côte | *French* 22
Ffiona's | *British* 22
Hare & Tortoise | *Japanese* 22
Abingdon | *Euro.* 21
Ark | *Italian* 21
Z Pizza Express | *Pizza* 21
Saf | *Eclectic/Vegan* 21
Black & Blue | *Chops* 20
Il Portico | *Italian* 20
Kensington Pl. | *British* 20
Prezzo | *Italian* 20
Balans | *British* 19
Feng Sushi | *Japanese* 19
Fulham/Kens. Wine Rooms | *Euro.* 19
Le Pain Quot. | *Bakery/Belgian* 19
Patisserie Valerie | *French* 19

LOCATIONS

Sticky Fingers | *Amer.* 19
Aubaine | *French* 18
Giraffe | *Eclectic* 18

LADBROKE GROVE

Dock Kitchen | *Euro.* 25

NOTTING HILL

(See map on page 76)

🔁 Ledbury | *French* 28
Assaggi | *Italian* 26
Books/Cooks | *Eclectic* 26
🔁 Ottolenghi | *Bakery/Med.* 26
Portobello | *Italian* 26
Hereford Rd. | *British* 25
Osteria Basilico | *Italian* 25
Rossopomodoro | *Italian* 25
Mediterraneo | *Italian* 24
Tom's Deli | *Eclectic* 24
E&O | *Asian* 23
Taqueria | *Mex.* 23
🔁 Côte | *French* 22
Cow | *British* 22
Daylesford | *Eclectic* 22
El Pirata | *Spanish* 22
Gail's | *Bakery* 22
Malabar | *Indian* 22
Notting Hill Brass. | *Euro.* 22
NEW Chakra | *Indian* 21
Ping Pong | *Chinese* 21
🔁 Pizza Express | *Pizza* 21
Geales | *Seafood* 20
Pizza East | *Pizza* 20
Bumpkin | *British* 19
Feng Sushi | *Japanese* 19
Itsu | *Japanese* 19
Le Pain Quot. | *Bakery/Belgian* 19
Lucky 7 | *Amer.* 19
202 | *Euro.* 19
Crazy Homies | *Mex.* 18
Galicia | *Spanish* 18
NEW Granger & Co. | *Australian/Eclectic* 18

El Camion | *Mex.* 17
Raoul's | *Med.* 17
NEW Colchis | *Georgian* -
NEW Mazi | *Greek* -

OLYMPIA

Alounak | *Persian* 24
Popeseye | *Chops* 24

PADDINGTON

Frontline | *British* 24
Pearl Liang | *Chinese* 24
Noor Jahan | *Indian* 23
Yo! Sushi | *Japanese* 18

SHEPHERD'S BUSH

Princess Victoria | *British* 25
🔁 Busaba Eathai | *Thai* 23
🔁 Wahaca | *Mex.* 23
Adams Cafe | *Moroccan/Tunisian* 22
🔁 Byron | *Burgers* 22
Esarn Kheaw | *Thai* 22
Anglesea Arms | *British* 21
Del'Aziz | *African/Med.* 21
Pho | *Viet.* 21
Comptoir Libanais | *Lebanese* 20
🔁 Jamie's Italian | *Italian* 20
Balans | *British* 19
Real Greek | *Greek* 19
🔁 Café Rouge | *French* 18

In the Country

🔁 Waterside Inn | *French* 29
🔁 Le Manoir/Quat | *French* 28
🔁 Fat Duck | *British* 27
Auberge du Lac | *Euro./French* 26
French Horn | *British/French* 25
Hinds Head | *British* 24
Gravetye Manor | *British* 23
Aubergine | *French* 22
Caldesi | *Italian* 20
Cliveden Hse. | *British/French* 20

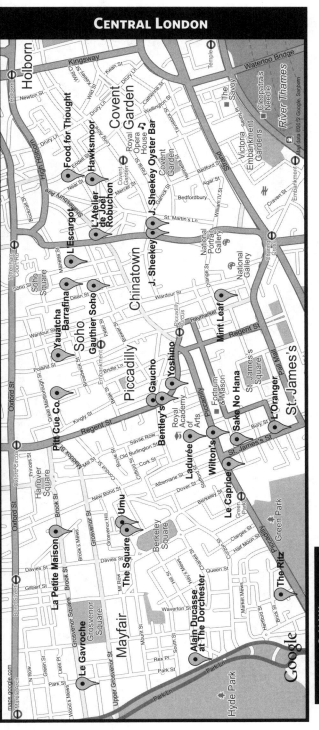

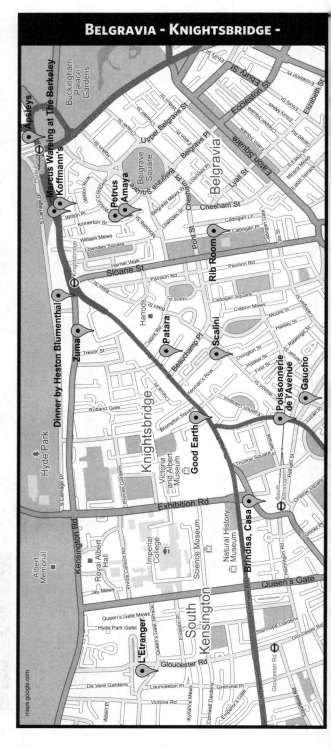

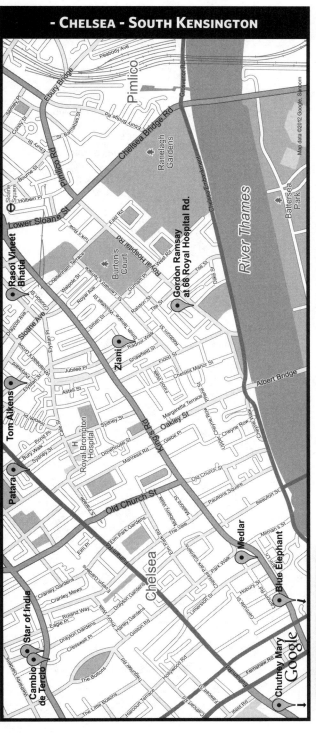

- CHELSEA - SOUTH KENSINGTON

Pimlico

Chelsea Bridge Rd.

Ranelagh Gardens

River Thames

Battersea Park

Map data ©2012 Google, Sanborn

Sloane Square

Lower Sloane St.

Rasoi Vineet Bhatia

Burton's Court

Royal Hospital Rd.

Gordon Ramsay at 68 Royal Hospital Rd.

Albert Bridge

Ziani

Sloane Ave.

Tom Aikens

King's Rd.

Oakley St.

Royal Brompton Hospital

Patara

Old Church St.

Chelsea

Medlar

Blue Elephant

Star of India

Cambio de Tercio

The Boltons

Chutney Mary

Google

MAPS

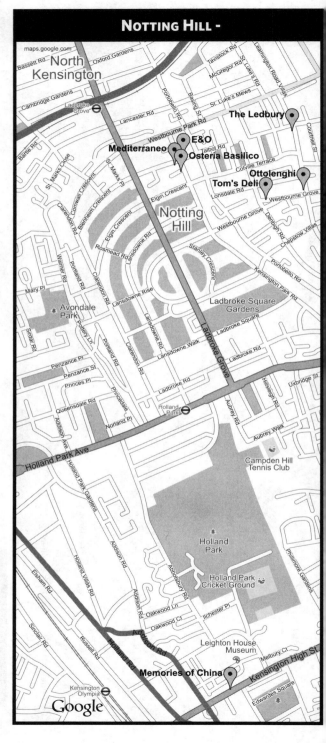

Latest openings, menus, photos and more on plus.google.com/local

- Kensington

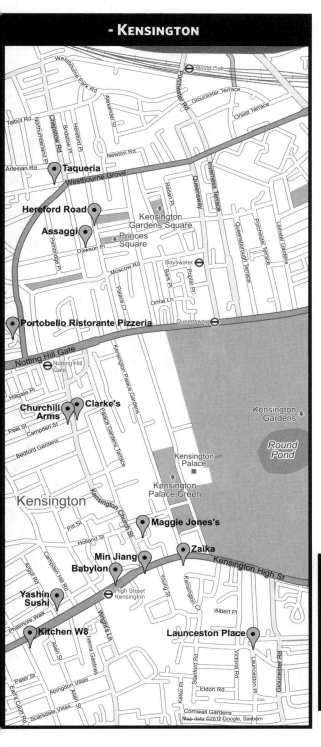

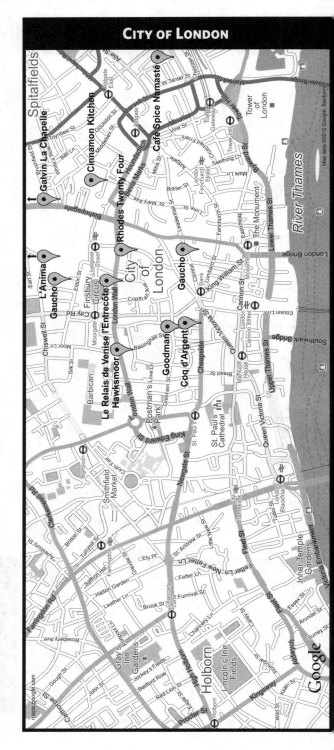

CITY OF LONDON

Spitalfields

Galvin La Chapelle

Cinnamon Kitchen

Café Spice Namasté

Rhodes Twenty Four

Houndsditch

L'Anima

Gaucho

Le Relais de Venise / l'Entrecôte

City of London

Gaucho

Finsbury Circus

London Wall

Hawksmoor

Goodman

Coq d'Argent

Cheapside

Barbican

Postman's Park

St. Paul's Cathedral

Smithfield Market

Newgate St.

Blackfriars

Fleet St.

Inner Temple Gardens

Holborn

Gray's Inn Gardens

Lincoln's Inn Fields

Tower of London

River Thames

Tower Bridge

London Bridge

Southwark Bridge

The Monument

Map data ©2012 Google, Sanborn

maps.google.com

Google

RESTAURANT
DIRECTORY

	FOOD	DECOR	SERVICE	COST

The Abbeville *British*   23 | 19 | 21 | £32

Clapham | 67-69 Abbeville Rd., SW4 9JW | 020-8675-2201 |
www.theabbeville.com

It's "worth veering off the main Clapham track" for the "brilliant"
British fare at this "earthy", "comfy" gastropub on a "quiet, gentrified
street"; with its "charming" vibe, moderate prices and "attentive"
staff, it's a "great local place to eat, drink and hang out", especially
for a "quiet date" or "long, lazy lunch."

Abeno *Japanese*   24 | 17 | 22 | £29

Bloomsbury | 47 Museum St., WC1A 1LY | 020-7405-3211
Abeno Too *Japanese*
Covent Garden | 17-18 Great Newport St., WC2H 7JE |
020-7379-1160
www.abeno.co.uk

The "scrummy" smell of "giant" okonomiyaki (Japanese pancakes with
savoury toppings) "sizzling" on a "hot plate embedded in your table"
"gets your taste buds dancing" at this "spartan", "party-friendly" pair
in Bloomsbury and Covent Garden; "half the fun" is listening to the
"gentle" staffers explain it all, but "be prepared to wash your clothes
after", because those scents stick; P.S. lunch offers "better bang for
your buck" – it's "economiyaki!"

The Abingdon *European*   21 | 19 | 20 | £40

Kensington | 54 Abingdon Rd., W8 6AP | 020-7937-3339 |
www.theabingdon.co.uk

A "cool Kensington crowd" crams into the booths of this "trusted
local" for "consistently decent" Modern European gastropub fare;
"sweet" staff and an "excellent wine list" help keep things "convivial", even when it's "busy", and while it may be "a little overpriced
for a pub, you're paying for the location."

About Thyme 🗷 *European*   24 | 20 | 23 | £36

Pimlico | 82 Wilton Rd., SW1V 1DL | 020-7821-7504 |
www.aboutthyme.co.uk

If you crave "incredible" Modern European dishes, "it's about
time you visited" this "crowd-pleasing" Pimlico "gem"; the "ta-
blecloth atmosphere" upstairs is "upmarket enough for clients",
while downstairs is where you get "the bistro effect" – but wherever you end up, the service is generally "reliable" and the prices
are wholly "reasonable."

A Cena *Italian*   25 | 20 | 22 | £43

Richmond | 418 Richmond Rd., TW1 2EB | 020-8288-0108 |
www.acena.co.uk

"Fab cocktails get things off to a good start" at this "cracking"
neighbourhood eatery over the river from Richmond, where the
experience continues with "delicious" Northern Italian dishes
comprised of "gorgeous" ingredients "handled with much care";
"ever-present owners" ensure "consistent service", so even
though it's a "little expensive" "for regular use", for a "treat", it's
"worth the price."

	FOOD	DECOR	SERVICE	COST

Adam & Eve British
19 | 20 | 16 | £26

Fitzrovia | 77 Wells St., W1T 3QQ | 020-7636-0717 |
www.theadamandevewellsstreet.co.uk

"Plenty of nooks, crannies" and oversized pics of '60s icons like Twiggy make the "interesting decor" the standout at this "lovely", "low-key" Fitzrovia gastropub "where you can hear each other speak"; though the Brit menu is "slightly generic", there are specials that "occasionally surprise", plus everything's "hearty" and reasonably priced.

Adams Cafe ☒ Moroccan/Tunisian
22 | 18 | 23 | £37

Shepherd's Bush | 77 Askew Rd., W12 9AH | 020-8743-0572 |
www.adamscafe.co.uk

The "authentic Moorish ceramic tiles" of this "cafe by day" in Shepherd's Bush are the only clues to its evening alter-ego as a Moroccan-Tunisian bistro offering "super-value" "mix 'n' match" set menus starring "delicious couscous and tagines"; there's "excellent" service too, corresponding to the "relaxed" atmosphere.

Adam Street ☒ British
22 | 21 | 21 | £51

Covent Garden | private club | 9 Adam St., downstairs, WC2N 6AA | 020-7379-8000 | www.adamstreet.co.uk

"Sophisticated yet relaxed" (it is a private club, after all, though anyone can book a table to dine here), this "intimate" subterranean "gem" "hidden away" off The Strand serves up "delicious" Modern British staples; whilst a few penny-pinchers protest that it's "pricey", the "cool" setting (brick walls, vaulted ceilings) and "friendly" vibe lead to many a "lovely evening."

Admiral Codrington British/European
19 | 18 | 19 | £39

Chelsea | 17 Mossop St., SW3 2LY | 020-7581-0005 |
www.theadmiralcodrington.co.uk

Ask the "smiling" servers for recommendations about the "sophisticated", "tempting" Modern British–European menu at this Chelsea gastropub; the atmosphere is always "buzzing", but in summer, the roof literally gets raised thanks to a retractable glass ceiling, much to the delight of the "trendy crowd" filled with "boys named Harry and girls named Philippa."

Afghan Kitchen Ⓜ⇎ Afghan
24 | 16 | 18 | £20

Islington | 35 Islington Green, N1 8DU | 020-7359-8019

"Phenomenal lamb spinach", "homemade bread to-die-for" and other "nourishing grub" offer a "flavourful" introduction to Afghan cuisine at this "cosy", "friendly" Islington joint; "ridiculously cheap" prices, a "table-share policy" and no credit cards lend it the vibe of a "student cafe", but that doesn't stop it from getting "crowded" with all manner of people, so "prepare to queue."

Aglio e Olio ● Italian
22 | 14 | 17 | £32

Chelsea | 194 Fulham Rd., SW10 9PN | 020-7351-0070

The homemade pasta, gnocchi and such are "delizioso", the portions "plentiful" and the prices "reasonable" at this Chelsea Italian, so little wonder "young, glossy" types pile into its "narrow railway carriage"–

like setting for "quick lunches" and "easy weekday dinners"; staff can be "glum" and the acoustics a touch "noisy", but still, somehow "no one wants to leave" (read: there's probably "going to be a wait").

Akari Ⓜ *Japanese*

23 | 19 | 21 | £32

Islington | 196 Essex Rd., N1 8LZ | 020-7226-9943 | www.akarilondon.co.uk

"Buckets of hot noodles, warm salmon rice balls, garlicky greens" and other "wonderful Japanese small plates" make "a welcome change from the usual sushi" at this "affordable" Essex Road izakaya set in a Victorian pub; the tables, which are "a bit close together", are "always packed" – and serviced by "staff whose friendliness would melt the heart" of any Islingtonite.

Ⓩ Alain Ducasse at The Dorchester Ⓢ Ⓜ *French*

27 | 26 | 27 | £112

Mayfair | The Dorchester | 53 Park Ln., W1A 2HJ | 020-7629-8866 | www.alainducasse-dorchester.com

Alain Ducasse's "staggeringly inventive" "use of different textures and flavours" and "amazing attention to detail" yield "exquisite" New French meals at this Dorchester outpost where the "deluxe" experience extends to the "regal" surroundings, "terrific" Gallic-centric wine list and "stellar" staff; in short, it's "worth the arm and leg" charged to sup here, though the prix fixe lunch is "such a bargain, it almost hurts to pay dinner prices."

Alba Ⓩ *Italian*

23 | 20 | 25 | £46

City | 107 Whitecross St., EC1Y 8JH | 020-7588-1798 | www.albarestaurant.com

"Charming", "attentive but never overbearing" staff deliver "excellent" Italian fare at this casual option for a quick meal near the Barbican in the City; what's more, there's a "wonderful list of slightly unusual wines" from Italy, which adds to the wholly "great atmosphere."

Albannach *Scottish*

21 | 21 | 20 | £40

Soho | 66 Trafalgar Sq., WC2N 5DS | 020-7930-0066 | www.albannach.co.uk

"Exiled Scots" missing "shortbread and Irn-Bru" make their way to this antler-bedecked Trafalgar Square dining room for "a dram" from the "extensive whisky list" and a wee haggis from the "fairly priced" menu, all delivered by "well-dressed staff"; a word of warning: the bar below can get "noisy at night" so get a "table upstairs after 7 PM" if you're not in a party mood.

The Albion *British*

22 | 23 | 19 | £30

Islington | 10 Thornhill Rd., N1 1HW | 020-7607-7450 | www.the-albion.co.uk

"Take foreign visitors" to this "chilled" Islington gastropub to "change their view of British cooking", as the traditional menu is not only "well prepared", it lists "options for even the fussiest eater", not to mention a Sunday lunch with "fantastic Yorkshire puds"; what's more, it's a spot for all seasons, with a Georgian bar that's especially "cosy" in winter and a "fantastic beer garden" for "balmy summer evenings."

	FOOD	DECOR	SERVICE	COST

Al Duca 🗷 *Italian* | 22 | 17 | 20 | £40 |

St. James's | 4-5 Duke of York St., SW1Y 6LA | 020-7839-3090 |
www.alduca-restaurant.co.uk

This "charming" terra-cotta–hued St. James's Italian stands out with
an all-day menu that boasts "unmistakably old-world flavour", plus
"interesting wines" and "excellent value for the area"; also of another
time is "personable" service that's "prompt without being rushed."

Al Hamra ❷ *Lebanese* | 23 | 16 | 20 | £38 |

Mayfair | 31-33 Shepherd Mkt., W1J 7PT | 020-7493-1954
Brasserie Al Hamra 🗷 *Lebanese*
Mayfair | 52 Shepherd Mkt., W1J 7QU | 020-7493-1068
www.alhamrarestaurant.co.uk

This "reliable, reasonably priced" Lebanese duo that sits on either
side of Shepherd Market is "always jammed" with diners "grazing"
on "wave after wave" of "mouth-watering" mezze and more, all
washed down with "excellent" wines from the region; if you don't
like "cramped" quarters, go in summer and ask the mostly "pleasant" staff to seat you outside.

A Little of What You Fancy 🅼 *British* | 22 | 19 | 19 | £34 |

Dalston | 464 Kingsland Rd., E8 4AE | 020-7275-0060 |
www.alittleofwhatyoufancy.info

Don't let the "no-frills setting" fool you: fans of this "quirky" "hole-
in-the-wall" that "epitomises the cool Dalston lifestyle" have taken
a fancy to its "delicious" all-day British fare; "variable service" and
prices that belie its "shoestring production values" vex a few, but
overall it's a "welcome little place" that "fits in nicely with what the
local clientele is after."

Alloro 🗷 *Italian* | 22 | 19 | 19 | £56 |

Mayfair | 19-20 Dover St., W1S 4LU | 020-7495-4768 |
www.alloro-restaurant.co.uk

"One of Mayfair's best-kept secrets", this "handy" Italian draws
business types and "special-day" celebrants with a "tremendous wine
list" and "well-executed" fare whose prices equal "nice value" for the
location; "spot-on service" and a "comfortable" setting adorned with
its namesake bay leaf further its reputation as a "sure bet."

All Star Lanes *American* | 17 | 21 | 18 | £25 |

Bloomsbury | Victoria House | Bloomsbury Pl., WC1B 4DA |
020-7025-2676 ❷
NEW **Stratford** | Westfield Stratford City | 2 Stratford Pl., 2nd fl.,
E20 1ET | 020-3167-2434
Shoreditch | Old Truman Brewery | 95 Brick Ln., E1 6QL |
020-7426-9200 ❷
Bayswater | Whiteleys Shopping Ctr. | 6 Porchester Gdns., W2 4DB |
020-7313-8363 ❷
www.allstarlanes.co.uk

"Channel your inner 1950s American teenager" by joining the "stag
parties" and "vintage fiends" who patronise these "nostalgic" bowling
alley–cum–diners; many suggest that "you wouldn't come just for

the food" – mainly "cheesy, calorie-laden" burgers, fries and milk-shakes served "at a glacial pace" by "overworked" though "friendly" staff – but "the funky vibe" and "lethal" cocktails make for a "cracking night out", which ends with an "acceptable" bill.

Almeida ● French   `23` `21` `22` `£41`

Islington | 30 Almeida St., N1 1AD | 020-7354-4777 | www.almeida-restaurant.co.uk

At this "posh" Islington New French "convenient" to the Almeida Theatre, "consistently strong" bistro fare is dished out in a "refined" room; "smooth" service and a "splendid" wine list add to the "winning formula", whilst pre- and post-show menus offer "exceptional value."

Alounak ● Persian   `24` `15` `17` `£28`

Bayswater | 44 Westbourne Grove, W2 5SH | 020-7229-4158
Olympia | 10 Russell Gdns., W14 8EZ | 020-7603-1130

Fans of this "down-to-earth" pair of BYO Persians in Bayswater and Olympia laud the "fresh-out-of-the-oven" bread and "succulent", "cheaper-than-chips" grilled meats; yes, the Iran-themed decor may be nothing special and the waits "annoying", but "huge" portions and "reasonable value" keep them "packed."

Al Sultan ● Lebanese   `22` `16` `19` `£37`

Mayfair | 51-52 Hertford St., W1J 7ST | 020-7408-1155 | www.alsultan.co.uk

"Great smells" herald the "tasty hummus, kibbeh, falafel" and other "excellent mezze" doled out in "hearty portions" at this longtime Mayfair Lebanese; ok, so the "dull, dark" decor is probably in need of a "major uplift", but it's "good value for the food quality", and you can get in and out "quick."

Al Waha Lebanese   `22` `15` `18` `£33`

Bayswater | 75 Westbourne Grove, W2 4UL | 020-7229-0806 | www.alwaharestaurant.com

"Unless you have a Lebanese grandmother tucked away somewhere", this "family-friendly" Bayswater local is the closest you'll get to "fabulous, home-style" fare, with a "multitude of choices for all palates", from "tasty lamb" to "great vegetarian" dishes; the "cramped" setting is "not for a special occasion", but it is "reliable" for "excellent value" and "friendly service."

NEW Alyn Williams at   ∇ `22` `19` `23` `£77`
The Westbury ⑤ European

Mayfair | Westbury Hotel | 37 Conduit St., W1S 2YF | 020-7078-9579 | www.alynwilliams.co.uk

After several years at Marcus Wareing at The Berkeley, "talented" chef Alyn Williams has set up shop in Mayfair's Westbury Hotel, employing "welcoming" staffers to serve "inventive" Modern European cuisine – including an "incredible-value" tasting menu – in what aesthetes deem a "wonderfully decorated" modern room; for oenophiles, there's also an eight-seat wine salon with a specially designed menu.

	FOOD	DECOR	SERVICE	COST

Amaranto ◐ *Italian* — ▽ 25 | 24 | 26 | £65

Mayfair | Four Seasons Hotel London at Park Ln. | Hamilton Pl., Park Ln., W1J 7DR | 020-7319-5206 | www.fourseasons.com

"Outstanding" hospitality sets the tone at this "stylish", "pricey" Italian in Mayfair's recently refurbished Four Seasons Hotel at Park Lane, where "tasty" fare is "well presented" in a "beautiful", scarlet-hued room; there's also a garden dining area ripe for a "summer rendezvous", a "lovely" bar specialising in Italian wines and a lounge serving afternoon tea.

☑ Amaya ◐ *Indian* — 26 | 23 | 22 | £61

Belgravia | 15-19 Halkin Arcade, Motcomb St., SW1X 8JT | 020-7823-1166 | www.amaya.biz

Bringing a "new dimension to Indian cuisine" is this "fashionable" Belgravia hot spot where a "gleaming" open kitchen turns out "new-wave" tapas-style dishes served in a "cool" contemporary setting; once you've secured a "difficult-to-score reservation", prepare to be treated "like a maharani", though penny-pinchers warn that tasting "a bit of everything" can "try your credit-card limit."

Amerigo Vespucci ☒ *Italian* — 23 | 18 | 23 | £45

Canary Wharf | 25 Cabot Sq., E14 4QA | 020-7513-0288 | www.amerigovespucci.co.uk

"Almost a tradition" after 17-plus years in "business-lunch" territory, this "casual" Canary Wharf venue cooks up "excellent" renditions of Italian standards accompanied by a "solid" wine list and solid service, all at the "right price"; P.S. a new alfresco bar should help improve the "average" setting.

Amico Bio ☒ *Italian/Vegetarian* — ▽ 21 | 16 | 18 | £22

Clerkenwell | 44 Cloth Fair, EC1A 7JQ | 020-7600-7778 | www.amicobio.co.uk

Rustic, "small and family-run", this Clerkenwell tratt is London's only "entirely vegetarian" (and organic) Italian eatery; the secret of its "delicious", "constantly changing menu" is "fresh produce from its own farm in Italy", some of which is available for sale in an on-site shop.

Anchor & Hope *British* — 25 | 17 | 20 | £37

Waterloo | 36 The Cut, SE1 8LP | 020-7928-9898

"Fantastic", "reasonably priced" Modern British fare is the stock-in-trade of this Waterloo gastropub; its "comfy" ambience and "friendly, unhurried" service also earn kudos, though impatient types decry "having to queue" for a taste of the ever-changing menu (reservations are taken only for Sunday lunch).

Andrew Edmunds *European* — 24 | 22 | 23 | £44

Soho | 46 Lexington St., W1F 0LW | 020-7437-5708

If you're not "gazing into someone's eyes" across a "small" candlelit table, you'll be "sharing smug smiles with the complete strangers seated inches away from you" at this "snug", "romantic" Soho bistro for foodies in the know; while the Modern Euro menu is "always

| | FOOD | DECOR | SERVICE | COST |

changing", expect "sumptuous", "delicious" "comfort food" that's "not as pricey as you'd think it would be", complemented by "great-value" wines recommended by "friendly, well-informed" staff.

Angels & Gypsies *Spanish*   `25` `22` `23` `£35`

Camberwell | Church Street Hotel | 29-33 Camberwell Church St., SE5 8TR | 020-7703-5984 | www.churchstreethotel.com
While "the name doesn't readily conjure up Spain", the "fresh produce on the counter", whole hams and "tasty", "innovative tapas" do at this "beautifully styled" venue in a Latin-themed Camberwell hotel; "amazing wines by the glass" come at an "attractively fair markup", matching the "not-overpriced" food bill, and "friendly, efficient" staff only "add to the charm."

Angelus *French*   `25` `20` `24` `£52`

Bayswater | 4 Bathurst St., W2 2SD | 020-7402-0083 | www.angelusrestaurant.co.uk
"Expertly prepared" "French classics" "with a twist" (like the "out-of-this-world" foie gras crème brûlée) are complemented by "great wines" at this "cosy" Bayswater brasserie; the "lovely" chandelier-lit surrounds and "excellent" service make it "ideal for couples on a cold winter's night", but be prepared: excepting the "brilliant lunchtime set-menu deal", such "quality" comes at an "expensive" price.

Anglesea Arms *British*   `21` `17` `18` `£31`

Shepherd's Bush | 35 Wingate Rd., W6 0UR | 020-8749-1291 | www.anglesea-arms.com
Though the "edited menu" "varies daily", you can always count on "well-sourced ingredients" and "grub with panache" at this "upscale" (yet affordable) British gastropub in Shepherd's Bush; it works as well for "cosy winter evenings" as it does "outdoor summer lunches with the dogs at your feet", but whatever the season, it's "rammed" on Sundays with a "yummy mummy crowd", so if you're after "a quieter evening", go midweek.

Angus Steakhouse ❷ *Chophouse*   `19` `16` `18` `£34`

Covent Garden | 20 Cranbourn St., WC2H 7AD
Marylebone | 243 Argyll St., W1D 2LU
Mayfair | 24 Haymarket, SW1Y 4DG
Leicester Square | 50 Leicester Sq., WC2H 7LU
Westminster | 10 Woodstock St., W1C 2AD
Westminster | 163 Praed St., W2 1RH
020-7420-6204 | www.angussteakhouse.co.uk
"You get what you expect" at this chophouse chain's "conveniently located" outposts, namely "hearty steaks", ribs and such, plus "friendly" service; however, critics counter it's "for hungry tourists only", warning of "dated" decor and "inflated prices."

Annabel's ❷🅱 *British/French*   `21` `23` `23` `£81`

Mayfair | private club | 44 Berkeley Sq., W1J 5QB | 020-7629-1096 | www.annabels.co.uk
"Ageing rockers with arm candy", "wannabe Kates and Pippas" and those who've been "regulars for 30 years" converge at this "pictur-

esque, dignified" members-only Mayfair "institution" with "money oozing out of its antique paintings and ceilings"; the "expensive" Classic French–Traditional British fare is "reliable" and served in a "regal" manner, but truly, it's the "social show" and the "old-world clubby charm" that's the draw.

Annie's *British*   23 | 23 | 24 | £35

Barnes | 36-38 White Hart Ln., SW13 0PZ | 020-8878-2020
Chiswick | 162 Thames Rd., W4 3QS | 020-8994-6848
www.anniesrestaurant.co.uk

"Belly-busting portions" of "tasty", "non-fancy" Modern British fare make this pair – "by the glorious Thames" in Chiswick and in the "leafy green" depths of Barnes – "fantastic value"; "beautiful", somewhat "bohemian decor" and "personable", "efficient" staff ensure it's a "'home from home' type of local" that's as "comfortable" "for a night out with friends" as it is for brunch.

Antepliler Restaurant *Turkish*   25 | 19 | 20 | £25

Islington | 139 Upper St., N1 1QP | 020-7226-5441 |
www.anteplilerrestaurant.com

"When you can't get to Istanbul", this moderately priced Upper Street spot offers the next best thing in the form of "wonderful Turkish pizzas", "smoky, flavoursome" kebabs, "delicious mezze and never-ending bread and salad"; a few aesthetes complain that "the decor is a bit in your face", but "friendly, attentive service" elevates the experience to "a cut above the usual."

The Anthologist ⊠ *European*   17 | 22 | 17 | £32

City | 58 Gresham St., EC2V 7BB | 0845-468-0101 |
www.theanthologistbar.co.uk

"Buzzy lunch spot by day and happening (read: rammed) bar by night", this City Modern Euro provides "posh pub food" and "yummy cocktails" "without burning a hole in your pocket"; "service could be improved", but "the attention to detail in decor is outstanding" (especially with the "cool art"), so fans who "love the vibe" are often "spilling onto the pavement."

Antidote Wine Bar *French*   ∇ 18 | 19 | 18 | £28

Soho | 12 Newburgh St., W1 7RR | 020-7287-8488 |
www.antidotewinebar.com

Just the antidote "after a long day", this "intimate" bi-level Soho wine bar "for a date or a girls' catch-up session" delivers "tasty" cheese, charcuterie and other French-accented small plates at sensible prices; if you need a hand navigating the selection of organic and bio-dynamic wines from the South of France, "friendly" staff are on hand to "offer up great suggestions."

Antonio's Ristorante *Italian*   23 | 20 | 22 | £31

Islington | Rear of 137 Upper St., N1 1QP | 020-7226-8994 |
www.antoniosristorante.co.uk

When somewhere "off the beaten track" is "packed, even on a Monday night", you know it's something "special" – and this "easy-going Italian" in Islington fits the description, with its "excellent-value" menu of "wonderfully prepared" dishes; another draw is the "engaging, efficient" service, adding to the "warm" ambience; P.S. for a lighter bite with a drink or two, there's a new antipasti bar on the first floor.

Apsleys *Italian*   26 | 26 | 26 | £73
Belgravia | The Lanesborough | Hyde Park Corner, SW1X 7TA | 020-7333-7254 | www.lanesborough.com

"A swirling circle" of staffers makes you "feel spoilt" at this "sedate", "romantic" Italian in The Lanesborough, where "sensational" savouries and "thrilling desserts" "seriously impress", as do the "fantastic wine list" and "exquisite" "ballroom" setting with glass ceilings, "extravagant" chandeliers and "well-spaced tables"; perhaps unsurprisingly, the price of this level of "refinement" is "very expensive", unless you come for the "excellent-value" set lunch.

Aqua Kyoto ⊠ *Japanese*   23 | 26 | 22 | £58
Soho | 240 Regent St., W1B 3BR | 020-7478-0540 | www.aqua-london.com

"London needs more" roof terraces like the "fantastic" one that this Oxford Circus Japanese shares with its neighbour, Aqua Nueva, and the view from the "beautiful" interior is no less "amazing", keeping the place "packed and buzzing" with a "chic crowd" no matter what the weather; furthermore, staff are usually "sweet" as they serve the "expensive" though "delicious sushi."

Aqua Nueva ⊠ *Spanish*   22 | 26 | 19 | £60
Soho | 240 Regent St., W1B 3BR | 020-7478-0540 | www.aqua-london.com

"From the charging bull at the entrance to the thousands of dangling wooden beads", the "stylish" decor of this Oxford Circus Spaniard "impresses", and that's before you've seen the "amazing" views from the roof bar and terrace (open till 4 AM) it shares with its sib, Aqua Kyoto; indeed, "it's all about the atmosphere" here, though there are some "nice" tapas on offer, "overpriced" though they may be (and accompanied by sometimes "snooty" service).

Arbutus *European*   25 | 19 | 23 | £50
Soho | 63-64 Frith St., W1D 3JW | 020-7734-4545 | www.arbutusrestaurant.co.uk

"Thoughtful dishes" made from "imaginative", "robust" ingredients cater for the "sophisticated palate" at this Modern European in Soho, where the "elegant" staff "happily assist in identifying some of the more outré items", all of which come at "a perfectly acceptable price"; some surveyors knock "plain" decor, but everyone loves the wine programme, built on the "brilliant idea" of offering the "extensive" selection by the glass or carafe so you "can try something special without paying over the odds."

Archipelago ⊠ *Eclectic*   24 | 25 | 23 | £46
Fitzrovia | 110 Whitfield St., W1T 5ED | 020-7383-3346 | www.archipelago-restaurant.co.uk

"Tables cluttered with mementos from travels across the world" hint at the "enticing", somewhat "expensive" Eclectic menu featuring "things you usually only see at the zoo" (e.g. crocodile, kangaroo, ostrich) at this "dark, unexpected" spot near Warren Street station in Fitzrovia; it's "perfect for a first date" because there's "heaps to talk about" and you can also "gauge a new partner's sense for adventure" by proposing a round of "snake-infused absinthe shots."

The Ark ⊠ *Italian*

FOOD	DECOR	SERVICE	COST
21	16	19	£38

Kensington | 122 Palace Gardens Terr., W8 4RT | 020-7229-4024 | www.ark-restaurant.com

Though it "doesn't look like much from the outside", this "small", "well-kept Kensington secret" harbours a "comfortable" dining room and "well-executed" Italian menu with "delicious seasonal dishes" and "reasonable prices"; mostly "attentive" service keeps the mood "relaxed", and it's particularly "worth a try" in summer, when "tables on the little terrace" out front are available.

Armani Caffé ⊠ *Italian*

FOOD	DECOR	SERVICE	COST
17	20	17	£44

Knightsbridge | Emporio Armani | 191 Brompton Rd., SW3 1NE | 020-7584-4549

"If the budget doesn't stretch to one of Signor Armani's suits", you can at least eat amongst them at this daytime in-store Italian in Knightsbridge, all "polished black surfaces and mirrors"; but whilst some insist there are "great small bites" to be had, others say "don't expect gourmet" – but do prepare for an "expensive" bill.

Artigiano *Italian*

FOOD	DECOR	SERVICE	COST
23	20	20	£45

Hampstead | 12 Belsize Terr., NW3 4AX | 020-7794-4288 | www.etruscarestaurants.com

Hampstead folks are "happy" to have this light and airy "local" whose Italian menu is "solid", "dependable" and filled with "fantastic" pastas; so even though the prices seem a bit "inflated" to a few, the place remains a "neighbourhood standby", particularly due to "nice staff."

NEW Arts Club *European*

FOOD	DECOR	SERVICE	COST
23	25	21	£59

Mayfair | private club | 40 Dover St., W1S 4NP | 020-7499-8581 | www.theartsclub.co.uk

Since 1896, the likes of Dickens, Liszt and Whistler have been congregating at this "sophisticated" private club in Mayfair, and after an "elegant relaunch" in 2011, it's once again one of the "hottest" spots in town, "teeming with famous faces"; a "tasty", "pricey", fish-heavy Modern European menu, "relaxing" ambience and "friendly" service are further inducements – that is, "if you can get a member to invite you."

Asadal *Korean*

FOOD	DECOR	SERVICE	COST
23	17	20	£32

Holborn | 227 High Holborn, WC1V 7DA | 020-7430-9006 | www.asadal.co.uk

"Melt-in-the-mouth" barbecue "cooked at your table" and "feisty bibimbop" are the stars of the "yummy", affordable Korean menu at this "dark", subterranean spot with "a super-convenient location next to Holborn tube"; what's more, if you're not familiar with the "delightfully different" cuisine, "attentive" staff can guide you.

	FOOD	DECOR	SERVICE	COST

Asia de Cuba ● *Asian/Cuban*
24 | 23 | 20 | £59

Covent Garden | St. Martins Lane Hotel | 45 St. Martin's Ln., WC2N 4HX |
020-7300-5588 | www.stmartinslane.com

"Inventive" Asian-Cuban "dishes that look and taste beautiful" come
in "huge", "made-to-share" portions at "proportionate prices" at
this St. Martins Lane Hotel haunt with "stark" though "sumptuous"
bright-white surrounds; "efficient" staff offer "helpful advice" as
they shuttle "chichi cocktails" to the "fun, young" habitués who keep
the place "buzzing" in the "high decibels."

Ask Italian *Italian*
19 | 17 | 19 | £24

Bloomsbury | 48 Grafton Way, W1T 5DZ | 020-7388-8108
Bloomsbury | 74 Southampton Row, WC1B 4AR | 020-7405-2876
Marylebone | 197 Baker St., NW1 6UY | 020-7486-6027
Marylebone | 56-60 Wigmore St., W1U 2RZ | 020-7224-3484
Mayfair | 121-125 Park St., W1K 7JA | 020-7495-7760
Victoria | 160-162 Victoria St., SW1E 5LB | 020-7630-8228
Tower Bridge | Butlers Wharf Bldg. | 34 Shad Thames, SE1 2YE |
020-7403-4545
Muswell Hill | 43 The Broadway, N10 3HA | 020-8365-2833
Islington | 52 Upper St., N1 0PN | 020-7226-8728
South Kensington | 23-24 Gloucester Arcade, SW7 4SF |
020-7835-0840 ●
www.askitalian.co.uk
Additional locations throughout London

You'll get "exactly what you'd expect" at this Italian chain: "quick,
no-fuss" pizza, "simple pastas" and other "tasty" standards that
appeal to "families with kids", "girls getting together" and other
"budget-minded" people; the settings range from "bright", "light
and airy" to "needs a touch of paint", whilst service is "friendly"
more often than not.

Assaggi ☒ *Italian*
26 | 18 | 24 | £62

Notting Hill | 39 Chepstow Pl., 1st fl., W2 4TS | 020-7792-5501

"Tough-to-get" tables groan with "stunning" Sardinian pastas and
fish at this Notting Hill spot where everyone feels "like part of one
big, noisy Italian family"; the room might be "not much to look at",
but the "pricey" bill is warranted, especially when factoring in the
"superb wine list" and "well-trained" staff; P.S. "the secret" to getting a reservation? – "book your next one on your way out."

Atari-Ya Sushi Bar *Japanese*
25 | 13 | 21 | £28

Westminster | 20 James St., W1U 1EH | 020-7491-1178
Swiss Cottage | 75 Fairfax Rd., NW6 4EE | 020-7328-5338 Ⓜ
Hendon | 31 Vivian Ave., NW4 3UX | 020-8202-2789 Ⓜ
Ealing | 1 Station Parade, W5 3LD | 020-8896-3175 Ⓜ
www.atariya.co.uk

"Why go to the retailer when you can go to the supplier?" ask fans
of this "busy" sushi bar offshoot of a chain of Japanese fishmongers,
where "outstanding" maki, etc. is "handmade in front of you while
you wait"; the "cramped surrounds and Formica tables" don't encourage lingering, but for a "quick, casual bite" or "sensibly priced"
takeaway, it "hits the spot."

	FOOD	DECOR	SERVICE	COST

Aubaine *French*

18 **19** **17** **£33**

Marylebone | Selfridges | 400 Oxford St., 2nd fl., W1A 1AM | 020-7318-3738
NEW **Mayfair** | 31 Dover St., W1S 4ND | 020-7368-0955
Piccadilly | 4 Heddon St., W1B 4BS | 020-7440-2510
South Kensington | 260-262 Brompton Rd., SW3 2AS | 020-7052-0100
Kensington | 37-45 Kensington High St., W8 5ED | 020-7368-0950
www.aubaine.co.uk
These "bright, buzzing" all-day cafes deliver "solid", "standard" French bistro fare to "ladies who lunch", as well as "great people-watching" ("when the sun shines", folks "fight for the outside tables" at some branches); in sum, it's an "efficient and generally pleasant" option, despite the "mediocre service" and that niggling feeling that it's "too expensive for what it is."

Auberge du Lac 🅱🅼 *European/French*

▽ **26** **25** **24** **£68**

Welwyn | Brocket Hall | B653 off A1, Hertfordshire | 01707-368 888 | www.aubergedulac.co.uk
Whether you go for the "great-value midweek treat" prix fixe or splurge on the tasting menu, the Classic French–Modern Euro cuisine of this "friendly" yet "formal" Hertfordshire destination is "an absolute joy"; what's more, "beautiful", "stately" Brocket Hall, the 1760s hunting lodge–turned-hotel where the restaurant resides, is a "romantic" setting for "a weekend break away", even though it doesn't serve on Sundays.

Aubergine at The Compleat Angler *French*

22 **21** **23** **£68**

Marlow | Macdonald Compleat Angler Hotel | Bisham Rd., Buckinghamshire | 01628-405405 | www.auberginerestaurant.co.uk
For a "lovely, quiet meal", Marlow offers this spot with a "beautiful location" "right on the river", where "accommodating", "knowledgeable" staff ferry "great" New French fare; "the selection of wine is impressive" too – nevertheless, a few cost-calculators find the whole experience "slightly overpriced."

NEW Aurelia ⬤ *Mediterranean*

22 **20** **19** **£62**

Mayfair | 13-14 Cork St., W1S 3NS | 020-7409-1370 | www.aurelialondon.co.uk
The "terrific" Mediterranean dishes are meant for sharing at this "stylish" Mayfair newcomer whose "attractive clientele" chooses between a "chic, buzzing" upstairs and a "quieter, more serious" downstairs; "teething issues on the service side" have been reported, but regardless of that, advocates assure that you'll have a "charming" experience – "but at a price."

Aurora *European*

▽ **25** **23** **24** **£51**

Soho | 49 Lexington St., W1F 9AP | 020-7494-0514 | www.aurorasoho.co.uk
Dark red walls and dripping candles in wine bottles make for a "cosy", "romantic" setting at this "charming" Soho Modern European with a dining garden that's "a fantastic bonus" in summertime; "friendly, attentive staff" proffer a "frequently changing" menu of fare that's

not only "quite good", but also "great value" for money, sometimes "difficult to find in the Theatre District."

Automat ◑ *American*　　　　19 | 20 | 18 | £38

Mayfair | 33 Dover St., W1S 4NF | 020-7499-3033 | www.automat-london.com

Its "hipster glory days might be over", but "Mayfair's beautiful people" still say this all-day diner "hits the spot" for "uncomplicated American comfort food" like burgers, fries, pancakes and mac 'n' cheese, despite what a few deem "slightly bonkers pricing"; some reckon service can be "surly", but all "love the decor", both in the "train car" simulacrum with "intimate booths" and the "light, bright and airy" conservatory.

Avenue ◑𝄞 *British*　　　　21 | 20 | 20 | £50

St. James's | 7-9 St. James's St., SW1A 1EE | 020-7321-2111 | www.theavenue-restaurant.co.uk

On St. James's Street, "where there aren't a lot of dining options", this "spacious", "trendy" Modern Brit is "the pick of the litter" for "business dining" – or so say "loud lads on expense accounts" and their guests "from out of town"; indeed, it can get "ridiculously noisy" the later it gets, so good thing there are "smart" staff to keep everything in line.

Babbo 𝄞 *Italian*　　　　21 | 20 | 20 | £70

Mayfair | 39 Albermarle St., W1S 4JQ | 020-3205-1099 | www.babborestaurant.co.uk

"Heart-warming" dishes with "a few surprise twists" and a wine list that's "extensive and expensive" (like the food menu) are the draws at this "warm, quaint" Mayfair Italian; "attentive", "friendly staff" (whose pictures adorn the walls) add to the "relaxed" vibe, "perfect" for a "business lunch" or "first date"; P.S. "nothing to do with the NY spot" of the same name.

🅉 Babur ◑ *Indian*　　　　27 | 22 | 25 | £30

Dulwich | 119 Brockley Rise, SE23 1JP | 020-8291-2400 | www.babur.foodkingdom.com

"Taking Indian food to new heights", this Dulwich destination presents "amazing gourmet" cuisine with "exciting flavour combinations" and "seasonal" specials made with "not-typical" meats (quail, haddock, venison and rabbit have all been spotted); the "classy" exposed-brick digs are home to staff who exhibit real "enthusiasm" as they deliver the fare and "fantastic cocktails", all "great value" – and "worth the journey" from anywhere.

Babylon *British*　　　　23 | 26 | 23 | £62

Kensington | Roof Gdns. | 99 Kensington High St., 7th fl., W8 5SA | 020-7368-3993 | www.roofgardens.com

Set seven floors above Kensington High Street, this "upscale" Sir Richard Branson property presents Modern Brit cuisine that, whilst "excellent", could never "measure up" to the "wonderful setting", including a "stunning" garden boasting "great views" and even flamingos; it's unsurprisingly "a little pricey", but "value" comes via the set lunch – or for a splurge, come Friday or Saturday night, when dinner plus an additional fee buys you access to the private club below.

Baker & Spice   *Bakery/Mediterranean*   21 | 16 | 14 | £26

Belgravia | 54-56 Elizabeth St., SW1W 9PB | 020-7730-5524
St. John's Wood | 20 Clifton Rd., W9 1SU | 020-7289-2499
Chelsea | 47 Denyer St., SW3 2LX | 020-7225-3417
www.bakerandspice.uk.com

"Knockout pastries", "wonderful breads" and "well-prepared salads" are the draws at this "gourmet" Mediterranean bakery/cafe trio; given that service can range from "charming" to "inattentive" to downright "sociopathic", most do takeaway, but whether you dine in or out, be prepared to pay the relatively "stratospheric" prices that earn it the nickname "Baker & Mortgage."

Balans   *British*   19 | 18 | 20 | £30

Soho | 60-62 Old Compton St., W1D 4UG | 020-7439-2183 🕐
NEW Stratford | Westfield Stratford City | 2 Stratford Pl., E20 1EN | 020-8555-5478 🕐
Earl's Court | 239 Old Brompton Rd., SW5 9HP | 020-7244-8838 🕐
Kensington | 187 Kensington High St., W8 6SH | 020-7376-0115 🕐
Shepherd's Bush | Westfield Shopping Ctr. | Ariel Way, lower ground fl., W12 7GA | 020-8600-3320

Balans Café 🕐 *British*

Soho | 34 Old Compton St., W1 4TS | 020-7439-3309
www.balans.co.uk

Whether you're "watching the world and his well-groomed dog go past" at the "cramped, camp" Soho mother-ship cafe (open nearly 24/7) or dining in one of its "jovial" offshoots, you're assured an "entertaining" time at this "reliable" Modern Brit; "cheerful", "efficient" staff deliver everything from all-day breakfasts "guaranteed to beat a hangover" to "wicked cocktails" that'll assuredly give you one, all at "reasonable prices."

NEW Balcon   *British/French*   ∇ 23 | 27 | 24 | £53

St. James's | Sofitel St. James | 8 Pall Mall, SW1Y 5NG | 020-7968-2900 | www.thebalconlondon.com

"Culinary escapism" is available via the "unabashedly luxurious" French brasserie–Modern Brit fare and "elegant, classy" setting at this all-day dining room at the Sofitel St. James, a "stunning conversion" of Brasserie Roux; the "caring" *équipe* includes a "champagne angel" who "can match any food with fabulous fizz", and whilst bills are somewhat "high", they're not as "upmarket" as they could be, plus there's an "excellent-value" pre-theatre menu.

Bali Bali 🕐 *Indonesian*   22 | 17 | 21 | £26

Soho | 150 Shaftesbury Ave., WC2H 8HL | 020-7836-2644 | www.balibalirestaurant.com

A "wide variety" of "tasty" Indonesian dishes including "staples such as beef rendang" come from "friendly" staff at this "unpretentious" spot; its Soho locale and "excellent-value" set menus make it a place to "visit before or after the theatre" or for lunch, whether with a "group" or *à deux*.

	FOOD	DECOR	SERVICE	COST

Baltic *E European*

24 | 22 | 23 | £38

Southwark | 74 Blackfriars Rd., SE1 8HA | 020-7928-1111 |
www.balticrestaurant.co.uk

While mostly Polish, the "hearty" menu at this "bare, white-walled"
Southwark "barn" with a large skylight "hops through the Baltic States
like an Iron Curtain InterRailer", showcasing "scrumptious" "ingredients and preparations you won't see much outside their home na-
tions"; the "buzzy" adjacent cocktail bar stocks "a multitude of
different vodkas" and, while "reasonable prices" seem to come
straight from the Eastern Bloc, fortunately the service is "not surly."

Bam-Bou ◑🅭 *Asian*

22 | 22 | 20 | £47

Bloomsbury | 1 Percy St., W1T 1DB | 020-7323-9130 |
www.bam-bou.co.uk

Set in a three-storey townhouse, this "high-end" Pan-Asian is a
"date-night favourite" amongst the Bloomsbury set, who kick things
off with "great cocktails" in the top-floor bar before moving on to the
"lushly decorated" dining rooms below; "spice combinations ranging from subtle to strong" mean there's something to suit all tastes
(ask "helpful" staff for suggestions), and whilst it's "not the cheapest", most feel it's "a treat worth spending a bit more on."

Banana Tree *SE Asian*

21 | 18 | 19 | £22

NEW **Soho** | 103-109 Wardour St., W1F 0UQ | 020-7479-4790
Hampstead | 237 West End Ln., NW6 1XN | 020-7431-7808
Islington | 412-416 St. John St., EC1V 4NJ | 020-7278-7565
Clapham | 75-79 Battersea Rise, SW11 1HN | 020-7228-2828
Bayswater | 21-23 Westbourne Grove, W2 4UA | 020-7221-4085
www.bananatree.co.uk

"Huge portions" of "big-flavoured" Southeast Asian fare, including
"classics", "imaginative" dishes and the "exceptional" Legendary
Rendang ("legendary for a reason"), come for "very reasonable
prices" at this mini-chain; there's almost "always a queue", but
"sweet" and "speedy" staff keep things moving – nevertheless, the
"long communal tables" tend to be "hectic", so it's "better for
refuelling than romancing."

Banh Mi Bay 🅭 *Vietnamese*

23 | 15 | 19 | £12

Holborn | 6 Theobald's Rd., WC1X 8PN | 020-7831-4079

At lunchtime, Holborn "office workers" reckon it's "worth the wait"
for the "to-die-for" sandwiches, "huge bowls of pho (perfect "on a
cold, wintry day") and other "wonderfully filling" Vietnamese fare
served at this "cheap and cheerful" caff; there's "not a lot of room"
and "not much atmosphere", so most do takeaway, even though
"in-house service is quick."

Bank Westminster & Zander Bar 🅭 *European*

21 | 24 | 20 | £47

Westminster | 45 Buckingham Gate, SW1E 6BS | 020-7630-6644 |
www.bankrestaurants.com

In a "sunlit room with huge windows" framing "spectacular views" of a
"wonderful" courtyard (where you can sit in summer), this Modern

European provides a "pleasant" place for Westminster workers to "entertain clients" over a "good range" of "well-cooked" dishes, all brought by "attentive" staff; post-prandial, many hit the adjacent "lovely bar", which is amongst "the longest in London."

Bar Battu ⊠ *European*   ▽ 23 | 18 | 18 | £32

City | 48 Gresham St., EC2V 7AY | 020-7036-6100 | www.barbattu.com

A "rustic" Modern Euro menu that runs the gamut from "nibbles" to mains is "good enough for the price" at this bare brick–meets–art deco spot that's "injected some life into a dead area of the City, barwise"; the grub, brought by "lovely staff", is complemented by an "interesting wine list" that includes many natural and biodynamic labels.

Barbecoa *BBQ*   23 | 23 | 20 | £54

City | 20 New Change Passage, EC4M 9AG | 020-3005-8555 | www.barbecoa.com

A "meat lover's paradise" sums up this "lively", "unpretentious" City BBQ joint from Jamie Oliver and Adam Perry Lang (the latter of NYC's Daisy May's fame); besides "excellent" ribs, steak and more, it boasts "unsurpassed views" of St. Paul's Cathedral plus "cool, relaxed" service, so most deem it "well worth visiting" even without an "expense account"; P.S. there's an on-site butchery too.

Bar Boulud *French*   24 | 21 | 23 | £55

Knightsbridge | Mandarin Oriental Hyde Park | 66 Knightsbridge, SW1X 7LA | 020-7201-3899 | www.barboulud.com

"Whatever the occasion, it fits" say fans of Daniel Boulud's "busy", "buzzy" bistro in Knightsbridge's Mandarin Oriental, where "beautifully executed" French dishes plus "London's poshest burger" are served in an "informal" yet "glamourous" setting; if a few cite "close tables" and "noise", more are won over by the "knowledgeable" service, "varied" wine list and "reasonable" prices for the quality, especially via the "absolute bargain" set menus.

Barcelona Tapas *Spanish*   22 | 18 | 21 | £38

City | 15 St. Botolph St., EC3A 7DT | 020-7377-5111 ⊠
City | 24 Lime St., EC3M 7HR | 020-7929-2389 ⊠
Dulwich | 481 Lordship Ln., SE22 8JY | 020-8693-5111 ●
www.barcelona-tapas.com

A "massive menu" of "tasty" tapas complemented by an "extensive" list of "brilliant" wines makes this Spanish trio work for anything from a "quick" dinner to a "family get-together"; "generous portions" boost its value, as do the "friendly" staffers, some with just the "right lack of English vocabulary to complete the air of authenticity."

❷ Barrafina *Spanish*   28 | 19 | 23 | £42

Soho | 54 Frith St., W1D 4SL | 020-7813-8016 | www.barrafina.co.uk

"Sublime", "flavour-packed" Spanish tapas, including "perfectly cooked" seafood and "soft, sweet, salty" jamon, explain why fans are "happy" to brave the "inevitable queue" (no booking) and "perch" "shoulder to shoulder" on the two-dozen or so barside seats at this "funky", "buzzy" Soho sister of Fino; everything is cooked "before your eyes" by the "enthusiastic", "knowledgeable" staff, and even if the cost can "creep up", you'll "never regret the bill."

Barrica ⊠ *Spanish* | 25 | 19 | 22 | £37 |

Bloomsbury | 62 Goodge St., W1T 4NE | 020-7436-9448 | www.barrica.co.uk

This Bloomsbury tapas bar is appreciated not only for its "lovely and unusual" small plates and "fabulous" range of Spanish wines and sherries, but also for its "airy", "laid-back atmosphere" and fairly "gentle tabs" (especially in comparison to "pricier neighbours"); add in "knowledgeable" service, and some say it's "right up there with Goodge Street's best."

Barshu *Chinese* | 23 | 16 | 13 | £36 |

Soho | 28 Frith St., W1D 5LF | 020-7287-8822 | www.bar-shu.co.uk

"Like it hot?" – you'll be "blown away" by the "fabulous, fiery" Sichuan fare this traditionally decked-out Soho spot serves up for prices "aiming at high-end"; indeed, the heat is "not for the faint-hearted", though you might be left "cold" by "abrupt" service (to be fair, "some staff are fine").

Ba Shan *Chinese* | 24 | 19 | 17 | £31 |

Soho | 24 Romilly St., W1S 5AH | 020-7287-3266

"If you don't like spice", this Soho Sichuan, an offshoot of Barshu, "probably isn't for you"; however, heat-lovers call it "mecca", cramming into the "small nooks" of the "cosy", traditionally outfitted dining room where "fluctuating" though often "willing" staff ferry fare that's "a world apart" from what you often find in Chinatown – and "worth" the slight "extra cost."

Beiteddine ● *Lebanese* ∇ | 25 | 20 | 25 | £36 |

Knightsbridge | 8 Harriet St., SW1X 9JW | 020-7235-3969 | www.beiteddinerestaurant.com

If you're of Arabic ancestry, this "quiet" Knightsbridge Lebanese's "brilliant" mezze and signature mixed-grill platter might well "remind you of your grandmother's food", and maybe it's even "better"; "excellent" staff who "make you feel welcome" serve the "feast", whose prices seem "cheap" compared to the place's "posher" neighbours.

Belgo *Belgian* | 21 | 17 | 18 | £27 |

Covent Garden | 50 Earlham St., WC2H 9LJ | 020-7813-2233
Holborn | 67 Kingsway, WC2B 6TD | 020-7242-7469
Chalk Farm | 72 Chalk Farm Rd., NW1 8AN | 020-7267-0718
Clapham | 44-48 Clapham High St., SW4 7UR | 020-7720-1118 ●
www.belgo-restaurants.co.uk

"Big pots" of "brilliant moules frites" are the "highlights" of the "hearty" menu at these "raucous" Belgian beer halls, but it's the "mega selection" of "fancy" brews distributed by "helpful staff" "dressed as monks" that "really makes the experience"; small wonder, they're populated by "large parties" of "young" "tourists" who particularly "love the 'beat the clock' deal", in which the time you order is the price you pay – you "can't beat" it!

	FOOD	DECOR	SERVICE	COST

Bellamy's ⊠ *French*
Mayfair | 18 Bruton Pl., W1J 6LY | 020-7491-2727 |
www.bellamysrestaurant.co.uk

24 | 23 | 24 | £62

This "serene", "clublike" Mayfair brasserie and oyster bar serves "reliable, indulgent" Classic French cuisine; it's predictably "expensive", but that's no issue for its "upscale clientele", who also appreciate that "dedicated", "friendly" staff seem to "value" their patronage.

The Belvedere *British/French*
Holland Park | Holland Park | off Abbotsbury Rd., W8 6LU |
020-7602-1238 | www.belvedererestaurant.co.uk

22 | 24 | 23 | £67

Surrounded by "beautiful grounds" with "peacocks screeching", this "romantic", tri-tiered Holland Park "landmark" offers "good people-watching" alongside "well-executed" Modern British–New French fare that "never fails to impress"; "polished service" is a boon, whilst the "wonderful-value" set lunch mitigates the "high-end" prices.

Benares *Indian*
Mayfair | 12 Berkeley Sq., W1J 6BS | 020-7629-8886 |
www.benaresrestaurant.com

25 | 24 | 24 | £65

Chef-owner Atul Kochhar's "refined", "innovative" take on Indian cuisine "leads your taste buds in a dance" at this "sleek", "contemporary" Mayfair dining room with "chichi" clientele and "swanky prices"; "interesting wine pairings" from the "knowledgeable", "reverential" staff only add to the "truly special dining experience", which can also be had in the "lovely bar area."

Bengal Clipper ● *Indian*
Tower Bridge | Cardamom Bldg. | 31 Shad Thames, SE1 2YR |
020-7357-9001 | www.bengalclipper.co.uk

▽ 22 | 17 | 21 | £37

For "reasonably priced" Indian that's often "better than a typical neighbourhood tandoori", fans stop by this site close to Tower Bridge; service is "friendly", however, the setting's "not charming", "despite the nice touch of having a piano player" Tuesday–Saturday evenings.

Benihana *Japanese*
Piccadilly | 37 Sackville St., W1S 3DQ | 020-7494-2525 |
www.benihana.co.uk
City | Grange Hotel St. Paul | 10 Godliman St., EC4V 5AJ |
020-7074-1001 | www.benihanarestaurant.co.uk
Chelsea | 77 King's Rd., SW3 4NX | 020-7376-7799 | www.benihana.co.uk

20 | 16 | 22 | £44

"Tantalising teppanyaki" is "prepared in front of you" by chefs who "love what they do" at this "entertaining" Japanese chain; it's "fantastic for kids" ("the onion volcano trick" "never ceases to delight"), but "theatrics" aside, a number of surveyors feel it's "expensive for what you get", and the "decor's a little dull" too; P.S. "don't wear your best" – the "hibachi leaves a lingering impression."

Bentley's *British/Seafood*
Piccadilly | 11-15 Swallow St., W1B 4DG | 020-7734-4756 |
www.bentleys.org

25 | 22 | 23 | £62

At this "swish" Piccadilly "classic", chef-owner Richard Corrigan prepares an "expansive menu" of "outstanding", "inspired" British seafood – which some quip must come "stuffed with pound notes, accounting for the prices"; service by "old pros" is "exquisite" across the board, but some find the "rather formal" upstairs dining room "slightly staid" and opt to "sit at the bar", slurp "top-quality oysters" and "enjoy the 1920s vibe."

Bento *Japanese*   23 | 14 | 18 | £25
Camden Town | 9 Parkway, NW1 7PG | 020-7482-3990 | www.bentocafe.co.uk

"Local kids" tuck into a "diverse selection" of "wonderful speciality rolls" and "great-value-for-money bento lunch deals" at this Camden sushi spot with an "unassuming environment" (some call it "dull"); "efficient" staff means there's "good service at all times", but there's often a "mad rush" at midday, which you might "avoid" by doing takeaway.

Bevis Marks ☒ *British/Jewish*   ▽ 24 | 23 | 23 | £51
City | 3 Middlesex St., E1 7AA | 020-7247-5474 | www.bevismarkstherestaurant.com

"Delicious" "traditional Jewish dishes" are "spiced up" for "locals", "tourists" and "business" bods at this "gourmet" kosher spot in the City, which also prepares some Modern British fare; by day, a "good atmosphere" pervades, but given the location, it can be "kind of dead in the evening"; P.S. the recent move to new premises may not be reflected in the Decor score, but early visitors rate them as "bigger and more attractive" than before.

Bibendum *French*   23 | 24 | 23 | £64
South Kensington | Michelin Hse. | 81 Fulham Rd., SW3 6RD | 020-7581-5817 | www.bibendum.co.uk

In the "elegant", "high-ceilinged", stained-glass-bedecked "treasure" that is the "famous" Michelin tyre factory, this "see-and-be-seen" "stalwart" in South Kensington "endures" due to "superb" New French fare that leaves fans "feeling stuffed and satisfied", plus "fantastic service" that's "white-glove" but "not stuffy"; sure, the bill "tends to break the bank", but the "moneyed crowd" happily pays it because "a gratifying experience" is virtually guaranteed.

Bibendum Oyster Bar *French/Seafood*   23 | 22 | 21 | £46
South Kensington | Michelin Hse. | 81 Fulham Rd., SW3 6RD | 020-7589-1480 | www.bibendum.co.uk

For a "stylish, elegant" meal of "divine oysters" "paired with a suitable wine" or "a glass of bubbly" in South Kensington, pop into this French bistro with "beautiful art deco tiled mosaics" in the "unique" former Michelin tyre factory; it's "less formal" than Bibendum upstairs, but thankfully, "there's no reduction in service" and a moderate discount in price.

Big Easy *American*   21 | 20 | 19 | £30
Chelsea | 332-334 King's Rd., SW3 5UR | 020-7352-4071 | www.bigeasy.uk.com

"American expats" "craving" a taste of "the Deep South" are rewarded with "awesome" portions of "messy wings", ribs and "other meaty delights" plus "seafood combos with oysters, shrimps and crab claws" at this "friendly", slightly "kitschy" King's Road diner; nightly live bands amp up the "fantastic" atmosphere, while regular "all-you-can-eat" promotions keep costs down, which is why fans keep it "always packed."

Bill's Produce Store *British*   22 | 23 | 18 | £24

Covent Garden | St. Martin's Courtyard | 13 Slingsby Pl., WC2E 9AB | 020-7240-8183
NEW **Soho** | 36-44 Brewer St., W1F 92B | 020-7287-8712
NEW **Islington** | 9 White Lion St., N1 9PD | 020-7713-7272
NEW **Wimbledon** | 20 Hartfield Rd., SW19 3TA | 020-8947-8285
www.bills-website.co.uk

"Produce lines the walls" of this mini-chain of "country shop–style" grocery-cum–tucker houses turning out "yummy", "soulful" Traditional British breakfasts, lunches and dinners; though a few fans fear it's "let down somewhat by slightly inattentive service", "inexpensive" prices make it overall "a great place."

Bincho *Japanese*   23 | 19 | 20 | £34

Soho | 16 Old Compton St., W1D 4TL | 020-7287-9111 ◗
NEW Clerkenwell | 55 Exmouth Mkt., EC1R 4QL | 020-7837-0009
www.bincho.co.uk

A "stylish" crowd crams onto "basic" "wooden benches" to "pick and choose" from a "great variety" of "simple but perfectly grilled" yakitori dishes at this "vibrant" "tapas-style" Japanese duo; "service is fast and efficient", and as for the cost, though "the menu seems reasonably priced" at first, be sure to read "the small print": you "have to order" "at least two" of the same item, so the bill can "easily spiral."

The Bingham *British/European*   24 | 22 | 22 | £61

Richmond | Bingham Hotel | 61-63 Petersham Rd., TW10 6UT | 020-8940-0902 | www.thebingham.co.uk

"Superb", "imaginative" Modern British–European cuisine is complemented by a "huge wine list" at this "idyllic" setting in a "fantastic boutique hotel" on the Richmond riverbank ("wonderful at sunset"); "charming service" is the order of the day, as is an "expensive" bill, though there's a set lunch that's "excellent value"; P.S. afternoon tea boasts "dreamy" treats.

Bistrot Bruno Loubet *French*   26 | 21 | 22 | £53

Clerkenwell | The Zetter | 86-88 Clerkenwell Rd., EC1M 5RJ | 020-7324-4455 | www.bistrotbrunoloubet.com

Bruno Loubet's French bistro fare is "adventurous enough to be interesting" and downright "brilliant" thanks to an "amazing combination of ingredients, flavours and creativity" at the "master" chef's "comeback restaurant" in Clerkenwell's "super-cool" Zetter Hotel; "warm" service from "well-informed" staff abets the "bright and airy" dining room's "laid-back atmosphere", and best of all, it's "priced well for the quality."

	FOOD	DECOR	SERVICE	COST

Bistrotheque *French*
22 | 22 | 18 | £45

Bethnal Green | 23-27 Wadeson St., E2 9DR | 020-8983-7900 |
www.bistrotheque.com

"Anything goes" at this "minimalist New York loft–style" Bethnal Green hangout where a "hipster clientele" of "artists, photographers" and "fashion" types convene over "well-thought-out" French bistro fare; though service is sometimes "surly", it's often "attentive" and "friendly", which helps mollify folks who feel it's "overpriced for what it is"; P.S. a recent revamp, including the closing of the downstairs cabaret, may not be reflected in the Decor score.

Black & Blue *Chophouse*
20 | 18 | 19 | £33

Bloomsbury | 37 Berners St., W1T 3NJ | 020-7436-0451
Marylebone | 90-92 Wigmore St., W1 3RD | 020-7486-1912
Borough | Borough Mkt. | 1-2 Rochester Walk, SE1 9AF |
020-7357-9922
Chelsea | 127 King's Rd., SW3 4PW | 020-7351-1661
South Kensington | 105 Gloucester Rd., SW7 4SS | 020-7244-7666 ◑
Kensington | 215-217 Kensington Church St., W8 7LX | 020-7727-0004
www.blackandbluerestaurants.com

"Stonking sides" accompany "huge, juicy" burgers and "reliable" steaks at this chophouse chain; though somewhat "uninspiring", the environs featuring black leather banquettes and marble tables are "functional" and "comfortable" enough, and service is mostly "quick and polite", so while it might be "nothing to go out of your way for", it's "a good fallback" for an "affordable" meal.

Blakes ◑ *Eclectic*
19 | 21 | 19 | £68

South Kensington | Blakes Hotel | 33 Roland Gdns., SW7 3PF |
020-7370-6701 | www.blakeshotels.com

Its "beautifully stylish" black, "windowless" setting is "as dark as Nosferatu's eyeliner", and that's why this "intimate" South Kensington hotel Eclectic is an "old standby" for "illicit" "rendezvous" and discreet "business meetings"; for some, the "excessive pricing" and slightly "frosty" service don't match up to the setting, but others plead "don't change anything."

Bleeding Heart 🗷 *French*
23 | 21 | 22 | £51

Farringdon | 4 Bleeding Heart Yard, off Greville St., EC1N 8SJ |
020-7242-8238
Bleeding Heart Tavern 🗷 *British*
Farringdon | 19 Greville St., EC1N 8SJ | 020-7242-2056
www.bleedingheart.co.uk

Scattered around a "historic" courtyard in Farringdon, you'll find a choice of "charming" eateries staffed by "passionate" Gauls; for a "special occasion", the "graceful" restaurant "marries romance and elegance" to an "excellent" Modern French menu and an "extensive" wine selection, whilst more casual experiences are offered in a patio-blessed bistro, serving up heartier versions of the same, and a tavern, offering cheaper British fare and "yummy handmade croissants" from 7 AM; whatever chamber you choose, the enamoured reckon this "heart is hard to beat."

Bluebird *British*

FOOD	DECOR	SERVICE	COST
20	22	20	£45

Chelsea | 350 King's Rd., SW3 5UU | 020-7559-1000 |
www.bluebird-restaurant.co.uk

Given its former life as a 1920s garage, this "trendy" Modern Brit is an appropriate "pit stop" for King's Road shoppers to refuel via "delightful" fare in the large first-floor restaurant that boasts "considerable buzz", a glass of wine and a "light" meal on the patio or a treat from the on-site retail shop; the adjacent bar's "vibrant scene" is another aspect that keeps the whole endeavour "popular", despite sometimes "stressed" service and "pricey" costs.

❷ Blue Elephant *Thai*

FOOD	DECOR	SERVICE	COST
24	26	22	£55

Chelsea | The Boulevard, Imperial Wharf, SW6 2UB |
020-7751-3111 | www.blueelephant.com

In its new Imperial Wharf location, this Thai eatery has eschewed its old "tropical rainforest" setting in favour of "sumptuous" surrounds inspired by a Bangkok palace (which may not be reflected in the Decor score); fortunately, the "mouth-watering" dishes and the "legendary" all-you-can-eat Sunday brunch, featuring everything from "seafood cooked in front of you to traditional noodle dishes", remain, as do the mostly "attentive" service and an "expensive" bill ("worth it" for a "treat").

Blueprint Café *European*

FOOD	DECOR	SERVICE	COST
22	22	20	£42

Tower Bridge | Design Museum | 28 Shad Thames, SE1 2YD |
020-7378-7031 | www.blueprintcafe.co.uk

Post-Survey, Mark Jarvis (ex Texture) took over as head chef at the Design Museum's "smart" cafe, and regulars are "interested to see" his updates to the "imaginative" Modern European menu featuring seasonal ingredients and "reasonably priced" prix fixe deals (as it stands, the Food score is outdated); whatever happens, service should remain "charming" and those "huge" windows will still offer "stunning" views of Tower Bridge and the Thames.

❷ Bob Bob Ricard 🅂🅼 *British*

FOOD	DECOR	SERVICE	COST
22	28	24	£55

Soho | 1 Upper James St., W1F 9DF | 020-3145-1000 |
www.bobbobricard.com

"Art deco geeks" "fall in love with the sheer-bonkers luxuriousness" of this "theatrical" Soho dining room that "throws you back to a bygone era of rail travel", with "fantastic", "beautifully uniformed staff" bearing "reliable" "Russian-inspired" Modern Brit "comfort food"; it's generally "fairly priced", but with "dangerously moreish cocktails, bills can soon skyrocket", so be judicious in pressing the 'push for champagne' button in each booth.

Bocca di Lupo *Italian*

FOOD	DECOR	SERVICE	COST
26	20	21	£45

Soho | 12 Archer St., W1D 7BB | 020-7734-2223 |
www.boccadilupo.com

Gelupo *Italian*

Soho | 7 Archer St., W1D 7AU | 020-7287-5555 | www.gelupo.com

"Insanely delicious" regional specialities come in "small or large plates" that "charm and impress" theatregoers at this "buzzy" Soho

Italian; it's "hard to get" one of the "tightly packed" tables – or even a perch at the bar where you can "watch the chefs work their magic" as you sip "fantastic" wine – but it's "always worthwhile", particularly because "prices and portions are excellent for the quality"; P.S. Gelupo, its "sweet" sister across the road, serves "divine gelato."

☒ Bodeans *BBQ*   22 | 17 | 20 | £23

Soho | 10 Poland St., W1F 8PZ | 020-7287-7575
City | 16 Byward St., EC3R 5BA | 020-7488-3883
Clapham | 169 Clapham High St., SW4 7SS | 020-7622-4248
Fulham | 4 Broadway Chambers, SW6 1EP | 020-7610-0440
www.bodeansbbq.com

You'll "carry your stomach out with two hands" after "pigging out" on the "affordable" "monster meat platters" at these "crowded and noisy" BBQ joints; the "decent" American beers on tap and televised U.S. sports appeal to "expats" and "Yankophiles" alike, and "friendly staff" keep things moving "ruthlessly quick."

Boisdale ☒ *British/Scottish*   22 | 22 | 21 | £53

Belgravia | 15 Eccleston St., SW1W 9LX | 020-7730-6922
Canary Wharf | Cabot Pl. W., E14 4QT | 020-7715-5818 ●
City | Swedeland Ct. | 202 Bishopsgate, EC2M 4NR | 020-7283-1763
www.boisdale.co.uk

"Sozzled with the spirit of Scotland", this "post-box-red", tartan-bedecked Belgravia "old boys' club" and its City and Canary Wharf cousins ply fans with "quality" steaks and other "pricey" Traditional British fodder plus a "marvellous" whisky supply; a "renowned" cigar selection (and smokers' terrace), "superb" nightly live jazz and the occasional bagpiper compensate for occasionally "slapdash" service.

Bombay Brasserie ● *Indian*   23 | 23 | 22 | £47

South Kensington | Courtfield Rd., SW7 4QH | 020-7370-4040 | www.bombaybrasserielondon.com

A South Ken "favourite", this "opulent" Indian offers "a last look at the empire in its faded glory", with "reliable" fare in "spacious" digs that can be "a bit hushed during the week"; however, some feel it's slightly "overpriced", notwithstanding the "incredible-value" weekend brunch buffet; P.S. a post-Survey chef change may outdate the Food score.

Bombay Palace ● *Indian*   24 | 19 | 21 | £43

Bayswater | 50 Connaught St., W2 2AA | 020-7723-8855 | www.bombay-palace.co.uk

"Astonishing" flavours abound in the "superb Indian food" prepared at this Bayswater branch of an international chain, where the prices may be a bit "high" for the genre, but they include "attentive", "accommodating" service; post-Survey, the "rich" setting was given a refresh, possibly outdating the Decor score.

Bonds *French*   ▽ 23 | 20 | 18 | £54

City | Threadneedles Hotel | 5 Threadneedle St., EC2R 8AY | 020-7657-8088 | www.theetoncollection.com

Set within a City banking hall–turned–boutique hotel, this spot with high ceilings, white walls, wood and well-spaced tables serves "high-quality" New French fare from dawn till dinner (breakfast only at weekends); "attentive" service is a plus, but it all comes at a "rather expensive" price.

Books for Cooks 🖼️Ⓜ️ *Eclectic*   ▽ 26 | 19 | 22 | £24

Notting Hill | 4 Blenheim Crescent, W11 1NN | 020-7221-1992 | www.booksforcooks.com

Eat surrounded by over 10,000 "wonderful" recipe tomes at this "cosy" Eclectic cafe/test kitchen at the back of a "sweet, slightly scruffy" Notting Hill cookbook store; it's only open for lunch and you have to "get there before they run out" of the usually "excellent" daily changing dishes, which are often crafted by "visiting cooks doing demonstrations" and usually sold for prices that equal "a deal."

The Botanist ⓓ *British*   19 | 19 | 16 | £40

Chelsea | 7 Sloane Sq., SW1W 8EE | 020-7730-0077 | www.thebotanistonsloanesquare.com

Leaving their "Bentleys, Maseratis and other exotic rides" outside, a "hip Chelsea crowd" hangs out at this "light, airy" Sloane Square spot "more for the happening bar" than the adjacent all-day dining room, where breakfast is the "most reliable" option and the rest of the midpriced Modern British offerings are "fine" though "without surprises"; so "come here for the scene", but when it gets busy, "be prepared to be looked over" by the "rushed" staff.

Boundary *British/French*   23 | 23 | 21 | £56

Shoreditch | 2-4 Boundary St., E2 7DD | 020-7729-1051 | www.theboundary.co.uk

"Another successful venture" from Sir Terence Conran, this "stylish" Shoreditch warehouse "attracts cool East London characters" with its "vaulted, cavernous" basement dining room and "strong menu" of "tasty", "expensive" Classic French–Anglo fare served by "polite" staff; other features include a "spectacular" roof terrace, a dozen hotel rooms and, on the ground floor, Albion, a "trendy cafe" popular for Sunday brunch.

Bountiful Cow 🖼️ *Chophouse*   21 | 14 | 16 | £31

Holborn | 51 Eagle St., WC1R 4AP | 020-7404-0200 | www.thebountifulcow.co.uk

"Great-quality" steaks and "big" burgers are "cooked just the way you want" by flamboyant chef-owner Roxy Beaujolais at this chophouse with a virtually "hidden" Holborn location; the service can be "sketchy" and the publike decor is a bit "drab", but the more the "Malbec flows", the less those seem to matter.

Bradley's *British/French*   23 | 18 | 20 | £49

Swiss Cottage | 25 Winchester Rd., NW3 3NR | 020-7722-3457 | www.bradleysnw3.co.uk

"Personable" staff deliver chef-owner Simon Bradley's "solid", "interesting" French-accented Modern British cuisine alongside a "short, well-chosen wine list" at this Swiss Cottage site; if the "small" digs are looking "a little tired", at least the prices are "reasonable" due to the set lunch, dinner and "pre-Hampstead Theatre" menus.

Brasserie Blanc *French*
22 | 21 | 20 | £41

NEW **Bloomsbury** | 8 Charlotte St., W1T 2LS 🏠 Ⓜ
NEW **Covent Garden** | Covent Garden Piazza | 35 The Market, WC2E 8RF | 020-7379-0666
NEW **Holborn** | 119 Chancery Ln., WC2A 1PP | 020-7405-0290
NEW **City** | 1 Watling St., EC4M 9BP | 020-7213-0540 🏠
City | 60 Threadneedle St., EC2R 8HP | 020-7710-9440 🏠
NEW **City** | Trinity Sq., EC3N 4AA | 020-7480-5500 🏠
NEW **Waterloo** | 9 Belvedere Rd., SE1 8YL | 020-7202-8470
www.brasserieblanc.com

For a "reasonably priced" lunch or dinner of "great French food", this informal chain of Raymond Blanc brasseries (part of an ever-expanding nationwide network) fits the bill; also on offer are "excellent" bar scenes and staff who have clearly "been taking lessons in service from the boss."

Brasserie St. Jacques 🏠 *French*
▽ 21 | 21 | 24 | £41

St. James's | 33 St. James's St., SW1A 1HD | 020-7839-1007 | www.brasseriestjacques.co.uk

"Sabre-opened champagne" courtesy of a "larger-than-life" sommelier who "knows his stuff" adds to the "great atmosphere" at this "busy" French brasserie that brings a "little piece of Paris to St. James's"; whether they're there for "pleasure or business", guests promise they'll "be back for more" of the "lovely" "classic" dishes and "*sympathique*" service.

NEW Brasserie Zédel ● *French*
- | - | - | M

Piccadilly | 20 Sherwood St., W1F 7ED | 020-7734-4888 | www.brasseriezedel.com

Francophiles, art deco devotees and fans of gifted restaurateurs Chris Corbin and Jeremy King (The Wolseley, The Delaunay) are captivated in equal measure by this newcomer, a lavishly restored Piccadilly landmark dating back to the early 1900s; the multi-use environs comprise a street-level cafe and bustling below-ground French brasserie, cabaret and cocktail bar, whilst sensible pricing and a few tables saved for walk-ins can be found throughout.

Brawn *British/French*
26 | 21 | 22 | £35

Shoreditch | 49 Columbia Rd., E2 7RG | 020-7729-5692 | www.brawn.co

"Overlooked grapes and ingredients" are celebrated at this "simple, stylish" Shoreditch sib of Terroirs, whose "wonderful" British-French small-plates menu includes an "all-things-pork" section and an "interesting" wine list that highlights natural and biodynamic options; "über-cool" staffers, "super-fair" prices and a "fantastic" set lunch on Sundays complete the picture.

NEW Bread Street Kitchen *European*
21 | 23 | 20 | £46

City | 10 Bread St., EC4M 9AJ | 020-7592-1616 | www.breadstreetkitchen.com

"Floor-to-ceiling windows" and "exposed beams" give this "huge", "airy" City space from Gordon Ramsay an "NYC vibe"; the "safe" Modern European menu offers "all-day dining" options "just right for a client lunch", but even the "strong, fruity" cocktails don't quite dull the sense that you're "paying a lot of bread" for "portions that verge on mean", not to mention variable (though "well-intentioned") service.

Breakfast Club *British*   22 | 20 | 18 | £17

Soho | 33 D'Arblay St., W1F 8EU | 020-7434-2571
City | 12-16 Artillery Ln., E1 7LS | 020-7078-9633
Islington | 31 Camden Passage, N1 8EA | 020-7226-5454
www.thebreakfastclubcafes.com

"Hipsters" cite the "amazing-value" grub at these "funky" cafes specialising in "huge" breakfasts, ranging from "healthy", "delicious" smoothies to "heart-attack-on-a-plate" full Englishes and American-style brunch; "waits at weekends" are the norm both before getting a table and after, when it "often takes a long time to get your food" from "friendly", "good-looking", "tight-jeaned" staff; P.S. in the City, "ask to see 'The Mayor'" for access through a fridge to the secret cocktail bar downstairs.

NEW Briciole *Italian*   - | - | - | M

Marylebone | 20 Homer St., W1H 4NA | 020-7723-0040 |
www.briciole.co.uk

Latium's chef adds a second string to his bow with this unassuming Marylebone Italian, which houses a small deli/cafe for espresso, snacks and takeaway in front and a larger dining room doling out reasonably priced regional small plates in back; the cheery space is fitted with exposed brick and chalkboard menus, lending it an authentic trattoria vibe, plus there's alfresco seating in warm weather.

Brindisa, Tapas *Spanish*   24 | 17 | 19 | £34

Soho | 46 Broadwick St., W1F 7AF | 020-7534-1690
Borough | Borough Mkt. | 18-20 Southwark St., SE1 1TJ |
020-7357-8880

Brindisa, Casa *Spanish*

South Kensington | 7-9 Exhibition Rd., SW7 2HE |
020-7590-0008
www.brindisa.com

"Superb", "simple" tapas, "top-notch" jamón and other Spanish flavours "pack a tasty punch" at these "lively", "super-casual" spots; still, regulars warn that, encouraged by "pleasant" and "knowledge-able" staff and emboldened by "wonderful" wines, it's too "easy to run up an eye-watering bill"; P.S. not all locations take reservations, so "go early, go late, otherwise wait."

Brinkley's ◗ *Eclectic*   16 | 16 | 17 | £44

Chelsea | 47 Hollywood Rd., SW10 9HX | 020-7351-1683 |
www.brinkleys.com

"Push through the bustling bar" of this Chelsea boîte to the "cosy dining area at the back" for "not-bad", "occasionally imaginative" Eclectic eats; it's been around for "30-odd years", so it "must be doing something right", though many reckon it's the "good-value" wine list and the chance that you might "bump into Hugh Grant" that pull in the punters, not what a number of folks calls "poor service."

	FOOD	DECOR	SERVICE	COST

Brompton Bar & Grill *British/European*   19 | 18 | 21 | £44

Knightsbridge | 243 Brompton Rd., SW3 2EP | 020-7589-8005 |
www.bromptonbarandgrill.com

"Charming" staff who "remember their regulars" make even tourists
"feel like locals" at this bright, art-bedecked Knightsbridge brasserie,
where the "solid" British menu with Modern European touches is "a bit
pricey" but leaves most feeling "stuffed and content"; furthermore,
there's a "lively" bar scene fuelled by "awesome absinthe cocktails."

Brompton Quarter Brasserie *Eclectic*   16 | 16 | 15 | £41

Knightsbridge | 223-225 Brompton Rd., SW3 2EJ |
020-7225-2107 | www.bqbrasserie.com

A "perky" atmosphere and a "bright", "well-designed" dining
room make this Eclectic brasserie a "decent" pick for "quick",
"casual" eats at all times of day; the menu offers enough options
to "keep one happy", even if the prices, being "what you'd expect for
Knightsbridge", and the "uneven" service don't.

NEW Brooklyn Bite Ⓜ *Pizza*   - | - | - | M

Chelsea | 342 King's Rd., SW3 5UR | 020-7352-5057 |
www.brooklynbite.com

Pizza comes in New York–sized portions at this affordable King's Road
newcomer where diners settle into red-leather banquettes to tuck
into whole pies, slices and calzones with names like 'Fugetaboutit',
'Bugsy' and 'Packin' Heat'; in the basement, a speakeasy-style lounge
features a copper-topped bar serving up cocktails and, naturally,
bottles of Brooklyn brews.

Ⓩ Browns *British*   20 | 20 | 19 | £37

Covent Garden | 82-84 St. Martin's Ln., WC2N 4AG |
020-7497-5050
Mayfair | 47 Maddox St., W1S 2PG | 020-7491-4565
Canary Wharf | Hertsmere Rd., E14 8JJ | 020-7987-9777
City | 8 Old Jewry, EC2R 8DN | 020-7606-6677 Ⓢ
Tower Bridge | Shad Thames, SE1 2YG | 020-7378-1700 ◖
Islington | 9 Islington Green, N1 8DU | 020-7226-2555
www.browns-restaurants.com

"Grand cafe" decor plus "dependable", "wholesome" Traditional
British fare is a "formula" that "works" for many types of customers at
this national chain; families and "tourists" are fond of the "affordable"
cost, and the pre-theatre crowd appreciates the "efficient" service,
not to mention that they can "almost always" find a free table.

Brula *French*   26 | 21 | 26 | £49

Twickenham | 43 Crown Rd., St. Margaret's, TW1 3EJ |
020-8892-0602 | www.brula.co.uk

A "local favourite" that's "worth a detour" for visitors, this "quaint"
Twickenham bistro is like "going to grandma's . . . if grandma were
French, had an amazing wine cellar" and a talent for cooking "simple" yet "exceptional" fare; lunch, when the "sun streams through
the stained-glass windows" and "attentive" staff proffer a "great-
value" set menu, is particularly "delightful."

	FOOD	DECOR	SERVICE	COST

Brumus *European*
▽ 23 | 23 | 21 | £42

St. James's | Haymarket Hotel | 1 Suffolk Pl., SW1Y 4HX | 020-7470-4007 | www.firmdalehotels.com

At this all-day European in St. James's "funky" Haymarket Hotel, guests and theatregoers enjoy "high-quality cooking" and "great-value set meals"; whilst service is usually "efficient", at peak times you may have to "wait a while", so consider the bar, offering "fine" tapas; P.S. "delicious scones" are the highlights of afternoon tea.

Brunello ● *Italian*
▽ 25 | 22 | 23 | £69

Kensington | Baglioni Hotel | 60 Hyde Park Gate, SW7 5BB | 020-7368-5900 | www.brunellorestaurant.com

"Willing", "accommodating" staff serve "awesome" if "expensive" Italian fare, including some "lovely sauces", and a "great selection of wines" at this Kensington hotel dining room; surveyors find the decor, all black Murano glass chandeliers and velvet chairs, pleasingly "decadent", though in warmer weather, they opt for the "patio overlooking Hyde Park."

Buen Ayre *Argentinean*
26 | 16 | 21 | £39

Hackney | 50 Broadway Mkt., E8 4QJ | 020-7275-9900 | www.buenayre.co.uk

"Massive portions" of "perfectly cooked" Argentinean beef are best "washed down with a hearty Malbec" from the "decent" wine list at this "relaxed", "reasonably priced" *parrilla* in Hackney; despite the "cramped", "brightly lit" quarters, it's "deservedly full" of diners who "take their steak seriously", so "booking is a must."

Builders Arms *British*
18 | 19 | 18 | £30

Chelsea | 13 Britten St., SW3 3TY | 020-7349-9040 | www.geronimo-inns.co.uk

"Fashionable" "locals" looking for an "easy option" in Chelsea come to this "convivial, warm" gastropub for a "pint or two" and "hearty" Traditional Brit dishes; those after a Sunday lunch" know to "arrive early", as it can get busy – and "noisy", especially if rugby is showing.

Bull & Last *British*
23 | 17 | 20 | £41

Kentish Town | 168 Highgate Rd., NW5 1QS | 020-7267-3641 | www.thebullandlast.co.uk

Expect "Scotch eggs to die for" and other "tempting" fare on an "imaginative" seasonal menu at this "high-calibre" Traditional British gastropub with "top-end" prices and "unpretentious" environs opposite the heath in Kentish Town; booking is "essential", especially at weekends when crowds swamp the place and occasionally "strain" the normally "helpful" service (upstairs is "quieter"); P.S. in summer, you can reserve an "awesome picnic hamper" to take away.

Bumbles 🗷 *European*
23 | 15 | 23 | £31

St. James's | 16 Buckingham Palace Rd., SW1W 0QP | 020-7828-2903 | www.bumbles1950.com

First-time visitors say they're "going to become regulars" of this "tiny", unassuming "gem" "near Victoria station", praised for its "generous portions" of "creative", "tasty" European cuisine and "efficient" service "with a smile"; best of all, value-hunters swear that it's "pretty much untouchable" compared to others of its quality.

Bumpkin *British*   19 | 20 | 18 | £38

NEW **Stratford** | Westfield Stratford City | 105-106 The Street, E20 1EN | 020-8221-9900
South Kensington | 102 Old Brompton Rd., SW7 3RD | 020-7341-0802 ●
Notting Hill | 209 Westbourne Park Rd., W11 1EA | 020-7243-9818 ●
www.bumpkinuk.com

"Yummy mummies" take the family to these "cute, rustic" bistros done out in "homey designer-shabby" style for "reliable", "tasty" Modern Brit fare, often with an "organic" bent; if a few are "underwhelmed" due to what they deem "pricey" bills for "ordinary" offerings, most are won over by the "warm ambience" and "laid-back but efficient service."

NEW Bunga Bunga ● 🖼 Ⓜ *Italian*   ▽ 17 | 18 | 14 | £30

Battersea | 37 Battersea Bridge Rd., SW11 3BA | 020-7095-0360 | www.bungabunga-london.com

"Quirky" pictures on the wall and staff who have been spotted wearing "Italian-statue aprons baring all" state the deliberately "cheesy" intentions of this Battersea addition; the pizza is merely "good" and service "leaves much to be desired" – so perhaps it's true that it's "all about the drinks and ambience" here, especially in the Eurovision Room, with karaoke, DJs and a "party any night of the week."

Buona Sera ● *Italian*   19 | 18 | 21 | £26

Clapham | 22-26 Northcote Rd., SW11 1NX | 020-7228-9925
Chelsea | 289A King's Rd., SW3 5EW | 020-7352-8827

"Families" and "groups of girls keen to catch up" populate the "large tables" at these "friendly" Chelsea and Clapham trattorias presenting "solid", "good-value" pizza and Italian "staples"; the settings are "not flashy", though "attentive" service and a "lively" vibe help to "bring the place to life"; P.S. kids love the "novelty of climbing up ladders to dine" at the King's Road branch.

NEW Burger & Lobster 🖼 *American*   25 | 21 | 21 | £32

Mayfair | 29 Clarges St., W1J 7EF | 020-7409-1699
Soho | 36 Dean St., W1D 4PS
www.burgerandlobster.com

There's no menu and just one price at this "converted pub"-turned-American-style eatery in Mayfair, where you order either a "juicy, tasty burger" or "toothsome" lobster (the latter's a "bargain", whether "steamed, char-grilled or in a brioche bun"), paired with "perfectly salted" chips and "crisp" salad; although "chirpy" staff aim to seat you ASAP on a "comfortable couch" or "high stool", there's "no booking", so plan to wait; P.S. the Soho offshoot opened post-Survey.

🗷 Busaba Eathai *Thai*   23 | 20 | 19 | £24

Bloomsbury | 22 Store St., WC1E 7DF | 020-7299-7900
Covent Garden | 44 Floral St., WC2E 9DA | 020-7759-0088
Marylebone | 8-13 Bird St., W1U 1BU | 020-7518-8080

(continued)

Busaba Eathai

Soho | 106-110 Wardour St., W1F 0TR | 020-7255-8686
Soho | 35 Panton St., SW1Y 4EA | 020-7930-0088
NEW **Stratford** | Westfield Stratford City | 2 Stratford Pl., E20 1GL | 020-8221-8989
Shoreditch | 313-319 Old St., EC1V 9LG | 020-7729-0808
NEW **Chelsea** | 358 King's Rd., SW3 5UZ | 020-7349-5488
Shepherd's Bush | Westfield Shopping Ctr. | Ariel Way, lower ground fl., W12 7GA | 020-3249-1919
www.busaba.com

"A bewildering array" of "tasty" "modern Thai food" – including "criminally addictive calamari" – is the draw at this "good-looking", "reasonably priced" chain; there's "generally a queue" outside and "noisy" crowds sitting "cheek by jowl" at the communal tables inside (particularly at the "more touristy locations"), but don't let that "intimidate" you, as service is usually "speedy."

Butcher & Grill *British*   20 | 18 | 19 | £35

Battersea | 39-41 Parkgate Rd., SW11 4NP | 020-7924-3999
Wimbledon | 33 High St., SW19 5BY | 020-8944-8269 **M**
www.thebutcherandgrill.com

With a "butcher at the front and restaurant in the back", "carnivores" are well catered for at this "large", casual Traditional British pair in Wimbledon and Battersea; "generous portions" and "value" prices mean it's "great for families", and as for the quality, while many feel that the "basics" are "done well", others say they "need improvement", just like sometimes "indifferent" service.

Butlers Wharf Chop House *Chophouse*   23 | 20 | 23 | £43

Tower Bridge | Butlers Wharf Bldg. | 36 Shad Thames, SE1 2YE | 020-7403-3403 | www.chophouse.co.uk

"Fabulous" chophouse "classics" like beef with Yorkshire pudding are paired with a "fantastic wine selection" and "formal" though "friendly" service at this all-day venue; with "amazing views" of Tower Bridge (from the alfresco or window tables) thrown in, it's the sort place to "take an out-of-towner and watch their jaw drop" – "even those on a budget", who should check out the "superb-value" bar menu.

Ⓩ Byron *Burgers*   22 | 17 | 20 | £20

Covent Garden | 33-35 Wellington St., WC2E 7BN | 020-7420-9850
Soho | 24-28 Charing Cross Rd., WC2H 0DT | 020-7557-9830
Westminster | 11 Haymarket, SW1Y | 020-7925-0276
Canary Wharf | Cabot Pl. E., E14 4QT | 020-7715-9360
NEW **Greenwich** | Greenwich Promenade, SE10 9HT | 020-8269-0800
Islington | 341 Upper St., N1 0PB | 020-7704-7620
Chelsea | 300 King's Rd., SW3 5UH | 020-7352-6040
South Kensington | 75 Gloucester Rd., SW7 4SS | 020-7244-0700
NEW **Bayswater** | 103 Westbourne Grove, W2 4UW | 020-7243-4226 ◗
Kensington | 222 Kensington High St., W8 7RG | 020-7361-1717

(continued)

(continued)

Byron

Shepherd's Bush | Westfield Shopping Ctr. | Ariel Way, mezzanine, W12 7GF | 020-8743-7755
www.byronhamburgers.com
Additional locations throughout London

"No silly options" are offered at this American-style chain, just a "simple menu" of "finger-licking" "gourmet burgers" and sides ("courgette fries are an absolute must"), all offered for a "fair price"; "every branch has its own individual style", but like the service, they're all "jolly" enough, and while the "kids can't get enough", an "interesting beer selection" means it's also a "grown-up joint for an after-work treat."

NEW Cabana *Brazilian* · 21 | 19 | 20 | £28

Holborn | 7 Central St. Giles Piazza, WC2H 8AB | 020-7632-9630 ●
Stratford | Westfield Stratford City | 5 Chestnut Plaza, Montfitchet Way, E20 1GL | 020-8536-2650
www.cabana-brasil.com

"Something different" comes in the form of "yummy" Brazilian barbecue plus "delish" sides and salads at these "funky", "colourful" skewer-specialists in Holborn and Stratford; service is typically "attentive", prices are relatively "inexpensive" and "tasty" cocktails like caipirinhas "complete the experience."

Café Boheme ● *French* · 18 | 21 | 18 | £35

Soho | 13-17 Old Compton St., W1D 5JQ | 020-7734-0623 |
www.cafeboheme.co.uk

"As atmospheric now as it was 20 years ago", this "buzzing" Soho French bistro presents a "lovely", "cosy" setting of mosaic floors, zinc-topped bar and a patio; open from breakfast until 2.30 AM, it's as "great for a relaxing brunch" as it is for "late drinks" (featuring free live music at the weekend), with "basic" bites that are "never disappointing" and "reasonably priced" to boot.

Café des Amis ● *French* · 19 | 18 | 18 | £35

Covent Garden | 11-14 Hanover Pl., WC2E 9JP | 020-7379-3444 |
www.cafedesamis.co.uk

For a "quick pre-theatre meal" "away from the crowds" of Covent Garden, ticket-holders "heartily recommend" this "relaxed" French "standby", despite a bill that is "perhaps a bit overpriced"; what's more, service is mostly "attentive even when the restaurant is busy" and particularly in the "cosy" downstairs wine bar, where "lighter" fare is offered.

Cafe East ⊟ *Vietnamese* · 26 | 10 | 16 | £17

Southwark | 100 Redriff Rd., SE16 7LH | 020-7252-1212 |
www.cafeeast.foodkingdom.com

"Oh yeah!" fawn fans of the "famous pho" ladled out at this "super-cheap" Southwark Vietnamese where the signature "spicy, complex broth" is augmented by other "simple", "flavoursome" dishes; the "service is a bit surly", the "decor leaves something to be desired" and you can "expect a queue during peak times", but its shortcomings are inconsequential if "the pilgrimage of Vietnamese natives from all over London" is any indication.

Café Japan Ⓜ *Japanese*

| 25 | 14 | 21 | £32 |

Golders Green | 626 Finchley Rd., NW11 7RR | 020-8455-6854

"Large slices" of "cracking sushi and sashimi" are accompanied by "obscure Japanese beers" at this "well-priced" Golders Green cafe where the digs are "modest" and the "welcome" is "warm"; just be sure to "go early or make reservations", because "word is out" amongst "young North Londoners", hence it's "always crowded."

Cafe Med *Mediterranean*

| 19 | 17 | 20 | £36 |

St. John's Wood | 21 Loudoun Rd., NW8 0NB | 020-7625-1222 | www.cafemed.co.uk

When St. John's Wood "locals" "can't be bothered to cook", they turn to this "reliable neighbourhood stalwart" for "tasty" "home-style" Mediterranean meals at the "right price"; highlights of the "casual" setting include "outdoor seating for warm evenings", "a blazing fire" in winter and "helpful staff" the whole year through.

Cafe Pacifico ⬤ *Mexican*

| 20 | 17 | 19 | £28 |

Covent Garden | 5 Langley St., WC2H 9JA | 020-7379-7728 | www.cafepacifico-laperla.com

For nearly 30 years, this "fun, noisy" Covent Garden cantina has been serving up "big portions" of "tasty" Mexican fare at prices that "won't give your wallet a belting"; but it's the "fantastic atmosphere", fuelled by "hot music", a "great choice of tequila" and "prompt" service, that really make it a such a "popular" "hangout."

ⓩ Café Rouge *French*

| 18 | 18 | 17 | £26 |

Covent Garden | 34 Wellington St., WC2E 7BD | 020-7836-0998
Knightsbridge | 27-31 Basil St., SW3 1BB | 020-7584-2345
Canary Wharf | 10 Cabot Sq., E14 4PH | 020-7537-9696
Hampstead | 38-39 High St., NW3 1QE | 020-7435-4240
Highgate | 6-7 S. Grove, N6 6BP | 020-8342-9797
St. John's Wood | 120 St. John's Wood High St., NW8 7SG | 020-7722-8366
Dulwich | 84 Park Hall Rd., SE21 B8W | 020-8766-0070
Bayswater | 151 Whiteleys, Unit 209, W2 4SB | 020-7221-1509
Chiswick | 227-229 Chiswick High Rd., W4 2DW | 020-8742-7447
Shepherd's Bush | 98-100 Shepherd's Bush Rd., W6 7PD | 020-7602-7732
www.caferouge.co.uk
Additional locations throughout London

With "convenient" locations all over the capital and beyond, this all-day chain provides a "useful meeting point for friends and families" ("it's "very child-friendly") seeking "dependable" "basic French bistro food"; opinions about the "retro Parisian chic" settings swing from "warm" to "tired" and service comments range from "friendly" to "indifferent", but few find fault with the prices – you can dine here "without taking out a second mortgage."

	FOOD	DECOR	SERVICE	COST

Café Spice Namasté 🛇 *Indian*

26 | 20 | 24 | £39

City | 16 Prescot St., E1 8AZ | 020-7488-9242 |
www.cafespice.co.uk

Chef-owner Cyrus Todiwala's "exceptional" regional Indian specialties with a "twist", featuring local produce, create a "taste explosion"
at this City venue; yes, it's "pricey", the "quirky" decor "is a bit off-
the-wall" and it's in an "odd location" (east of Tower Hill), but "enthusiastic" staff "who know" about what they're serving help make
it "worth a trip."

Caffe Caldesi 🛇 *Italian*

20 | 17 | 17 | £41

Marylebone | 118 Marylebone Ln., W1U 2QF | 020-7487-0753

Caldesi in Campagna Ⓜ *Italian*

Bray | Old Mill Ln. | 01628-788 500
www.caldesi.com

"Well located" for "the ladies who lunch", this "cosy" Italian "in a
little lane off the main Marylebone drag" specialises in "nicely prepared" Tuscan plates, just like its "joy" of a cousin in Bray; however,
some feel that it "should be better" given the "posh" prices, recom-
mending you stick to "the bar area downstairs, which is supposedly
a bit cheaper than upstairs."

Cambio de Tercio *Spanish*

24 | 18 | 20 | £53

South Kensington | 163 Old Brompton Rd., SW5 0LJ |
020-7244-8970 | www.cambiodetercio.co.uk

"Wonderful", "nontraditional takes on tapas" plus a "delicious" wine
list that includes "more sherries than you could ever dream of" draw
"stylish" diners to the "cosy, dark corners" of this "vibrant" South
Ken Spaniard; what's more, the service is typically "warm" and "efficient", making the "fairly pricey" cost the only thing to criticise.

Camden Brasserie *European*

23 | 19 | 21 | £33

Camden Town | 9-11 Jamestown Rd., NW1 7BW | 020-7482-2114 |
www.camdenbrasserie.co.uk

A "second home" to locals, this "friendly" Camden "landmark"
doles out "reliable" Modern European brasserie fare – including
"huge bowls of frites" – suitable for "quick, easy meals"; some quibble that although "they try with the wallpaper" (resembling shelves
of books), the decor is slightly "lacking", in contrast to the service,
which is "efficient."

Camino *Spanish*

23 | 21 | 20 | £34

Canary Wharf | 28 Westferry Circus, E14 8RR | 020-7239-9077
King's Cross | 3 Varnishers Yard, Regents Quarter, N1 9FD |
020-7841-7331
www.camino.uk.com

Hispanophiles are "surprised" to find these "atmospheric" tapas bars
in King's Cross and Canary Wharf, both "usually packed" with peeps
sampling the "yummy" small plates and "incredible" wines; the "noise
level" is a bit of a "drawback" for some, but most just focus on the
"helpful" service, "decent pricing", "brilliant" weekend brunch and,
at Westferry Circus, "buzzy fun" on the deck in summer.

	FOOD	DECOR	SERVICE	COST

Canteen *British*
18 | 17 | 17 | £28

NEW **Covent Garden** | The Market at Covent Gdn. | 21 Wellington St., WC2E 7DN | 020-7836-8368
Marylebone | 55 Baker St., W1U 8EW | 0845-686-1122
Canary Wharf | Park Pavilion, 40 Canada Sq., E14 5FW | 0845-686-1122
Shoreditch | 2 Crispin Pl., E1 6DW | 0845-686-1122
South Bank | Royal Festival Hall | Belvedere Rd., SE1 8XX | 0845-686-1122
www.canteen.co.uk

A "basic selection" of Traditional British "comfort food and school dinner–style desserts" is dished up in a "modern", "communal" "cafeteria setting with table service" at this "casual" chain; however, a number of respondents "like the idea more" than the experience, citing staff who "vary" ("upbeat" vs. "unfriendly") and the fact that it "seems odd to be paying [relatively speaking] lots for childhood staples."

Cantina del Ponte *Italian*
∇ 21 | 21 | 21 | £44

Tower Bridge | Butlers Wharf Bldg. | 36 Shad Thames, SE1 2YE | 020-7403-5403 | www.cantinadelponte.co.uk

Surveyors find it "hard to criticise" this rustic Thameside Italian, which boasts "terrific views over Tower Bridge" and "a great location, especially in summer when you sit outside"; "on-the-ball" staff serve the "hearty, satisfying" fare, available in "great-value" set menus that help counter allegations that it's a "bit on the expensive side."

Cantina Laredo ● *Mexican*
23 | 20 | 21 | £34

Covent Garden | St. Martin's Courtyard | 10 Upper St. Martin's Ln., WC2H 7PU | 020-7420-0630 | www.cantinalaredo.co.uk

When you need your Mexican fix", this light and bright Covent Garden cantina charges to the rescue with "upmarket, tastefully prepared" dishes starring "excellent guacamole made fresh at the table"; "pricey top-shelf" tequila can bump up the bill, and normally "wonderful service" can go "to pot when it's busy", but neck enough amazing margaritas" and you won't care.

Cantina Vinopolis ⊠ *Eclectic/Mediterranean*
∇ 19 | 23 | 21 | £37

South Bank | Vinopolis Museum | 1 Bank End, SE1 9BU | 020-7940-8333 | www.cantinavinopolis.com

After a "relaxing day" at Bankside wine museum Vinopolis, tipplers "retreat" to the "lovely surroundings" of this Eclectic-Med eatery with vaulted ceilings; the "locally sourced" grub offered up by "accommodating" staff is "delicious" enough (and "good value" if you stick to the set menu), but you really "come here for the wines" – and they "do not disappoint."

Cape Town Fish Market *Eclectic/Seafood*
∇ 24 | 21 | 23 | £32

Soho | 5-6 Argyll St., W1F 7TE | 020-7437-1143 | www.capetownfishmarket.co.uk

If you're angling for "top-quality fish" in "the heart of the West End", this large, slick, neon-lit diner vends a "wide variety" of "wonderful tasting" Eclectic seafood dishes with "South African flair", all brought to table by "friendly" servers; an "extensive sushi" selection comes via conveyor belt at the bar (where "creative cocktails" are crafted) whilst all of the wares are "value for money."

Caraffini ●🛇 *Italian*   23 | 18 | 24 | £46

Chelsea | 61-63 Lower Sloane St., SW1 8DH | 020-7259-0235 | www.caraffini.co.uk

"Long-time repeat customers" are "welcomed" by "charming" staff at this "reliable" Chelsea Italian with "old-world ambience" and a "sunny terrace"; the "delicious", "comforting classics" and "good selection of wines" are all "reasonably priced", guaranteeing that it remains "hard to get into", so "make sure to make reservations."

Caravaggio 🛇 *Italian*   19 | 18 | 19 | £45

City | 107-112 Leadenhall St., EC3A 4DP | 020-7626-6206 | www.etruscarestaurants.com

Set in a high-ceilinged former City banking hall, this upscale Italian gets nods for its "attentive" service, "lovely" food and "great" wine list; it does have critics who pan it for being "old-fashioned" and "ordinary" – however, for a "reliable" "business" meal, most attest that you "won't go wrong."

Caravan *European*   24 | 21 | 19 | £25

Clerkenwell | 11-13 Exmouth Mkt., EC1R 4QD | 020-7833-8115 | www.caravanonexmouth.co.uk

"You'll queue in a sea of flannel shirts" (mostly at weekends) to land a table at this "adorable", "feel-good" cafe in Exmouth Market, where the Modern European menu spans everything from "sterling" house-roasted coffee, "fantastic brunch", "delicious cocktails" and "small bites of heaven" at dinner; service stays "friendly" no matter how "hectic" things get, and prices remain affordable despite how "trendy" the place is.

🄩 Carluccio's Caffè *Italian*   20 | 18 | 19 | £29

Bloomsbury | 1 The Brunswick, WC1N 1AF | 020-7833-4130 ●

Bloomsbury | 8 Market Pl., W1W 8AG | 020-7636-2228 ●

Covent Garden | Garrick St., WC2E 9BH | 020-7836-0990 ●

Marylebone | St. Christopher's Pl., W1U 1AY | 020-7935-5927 ●

Mayfair | Fenwick | 63 New Bond St., downstairs, W1A 3BS | 020-7629-0699

Canary Wharf | Reuters Plaza | 2 Nash Ct., E14 5AJ | 020-7719-1749 ●

Farringdon | 12 W. Smithfield, EC1A 9JR | 020-7329-5904

Islington | 305-307 Upper St., N1 2TU | 020-7359-8167

Fulham | 236 Fulham Rd., SW10 9NB | 020-7376-5960

Putney | Putney Wharf, SW15 2JQ | 020-8789-0591 www.carluccios.com

Additional locations throughout London

"You know what you're getting" at this "bright", "unpretentious" chain of all-day cafes, namely "basic", "quality" Italian eats, "served with a smile" in "family-friendly" atmospheres; an "affordable" bill ensures they're usually "packed to the rafters", thus "noisy", so many surveyors grab takeaway from the on-site deli, which also vends ingredients and dishes to "cook at home" – "a nice touch."

Carob Tree Ⓜ *Greek/Mediterranean*   24 | 17 | 23 | £33
Kentish Town | 15 Highgate Rd., NW5 1QX | 020-7267-9880
"Loyal" Kentish Town locals make it "hard to get a table" at this "bustling", "rustic" Greek-focused Mediterranean featuring "delicious homemade" mezze alongside an "impressive" choice of "first-class" fish in a "smart but austere" space; "attentive", "friendly" service is the norm, and as for the bill, it's usually "reasonable."

Cassis Bistro *French*   21 | 21 | 21 | £54
South Kensington | 232 Brompton Rd., SW3 2BB | 020-7581-1101 | www.cassisbistro.co.uk
"If you're a lady who lunches or you just want to masquerade as one", patronise this "relaxed, elegant", "Mediterranean-chic" South Kensington bistro specialising in "delicious" Provençal plates: though a handful of respondents bemoan "ear-splitting noise" ("turn the music down!"), most of the criticism is lobbed at the "overpriced wine list" – good thing there's "attentive service" to "smooth" things out.

Caviar   23 | 20 | 20 | £73
House & Prunier *Seafood*
Piccadilly | 161 Piccadilly, W1J 9HS | 020-7409-0445 | www.caviar-house.ch
"Luxurious snacks" to "reenergise the soul" is how surveyors describe the caviar-centric seafood proffered at this sleek, glass-fronted Piccadilly spot where "everything is superb", including "attentive service"; it's expectedly "expensive" (and "worth every penny"), so best "let someone take you."

Cây Tre *Vietnamese*   22 | 13 | 15 | £25
Soho | 42-43 Dean St., W1 4PZ | 020-7317-9118 | www.caytresoho.co.uk
Hoxton | 301 Old St., EC1V 9LA | 020-7729-8662 | www.vietnamesekitchen.co.uk
"Exotic, intriguing, mouth-watering tastes" of Vietnam provide "filling" sustenance at this "excellent value" in Hoxton and its newer Soho offshoot; it's "worth the queue" as long as you "focus on the food" rather than the "indifferent, rushed" staff, "lack of decor" and "noisy atmosphere."

Cecconi's ● *Italian*   22 | 22 | 22 | £61
Mayfair | 5 Burlington Gdns., W1S 3EP | 020-7434-1500 | www.cecconis.co.uk
"You'll feel fabulous as you step through the doors" of this all-day Italian "scene" in Mayfair, where the "corner tables with wall-to-wall velvet" are tops for "people-watching" (you'll see "stars", "hedgies, their blond companions" et al.), but the bar where "you don't need a reservation" runs a close second; "old-school" staff are "on top of

everything" as they ferry the fare, which is as "delicious" as it is "expensive" (a contingent calls it "overpriced").

Cellar Gascon ●🗷 *French*   ▽ 23 | 21 | 20 | £56
Farringdon | 59 W. Smithfield, EC1A 9DS | 020-7600-7561 | www.comptoirgascon.com
Southwest-focused New French "nibbles of the highest quality" take centre stage at this "cosy" "informal" "little brother" of Club Gascon (also in Farringdon); things can get "loud" as the place fills up – and people partake in the "wonderful" wine selection – yet the atmosphere remains remarkably "civilised."

NEW Ceviche *Peruvian*   - | - | - | M
Soho | 17 Frith St., W1D 4RG | 020-7292-2040 | www.cevicheuk.com
At this small, lively Soho newcomer, an all-day no-reservations dining bar majors, as the name suggests, in Peru's national dish, marinated seafood; a more extensive yet moderately priced menu highlighting skewers and salads is available at the bookable wooden tables, where you can relax and sample the impressive range of Pisco-based cocktails.

Chabrot *French*   ▽ 21 | 16 | 23 | £49
Knightsbridge | 9 Knightsbridge Green, SW1X 7QL | 020-7225-2238 | www.chabrot.co.uk
At this "tiny" two-storey bistro "just a diamond's throw" from Knightsbridge's multimillion-pound flats, "friendly, professional" staff serve up "traditional" French bistro dishes with "satisfying flavours" and a "wine list to match"; it's "not cheap", but it's "good value" for the well-heeled denizens of the neighbourhood.

Cha Cha Moon *Chinese*   18 | 17 | 15 | £19
Soho | 15-21 Ganton St., W1F 9BN | 020-7297-9800 | www.chachamoon.com
"Squeeze" into a communal table and "watch your noodles being pulled in the open kitchen" at this bamboo-ceilinged Chinese eatery in Soho; though there are complaints of "forgetful" service, most applaud the "tasty", "quickly prepared" grub – which everyone agrees is "a steal for London."

NEW Chakra *Indian*   ▽ 21 | 19 | 19 | £49
Notting Hill | 157-159 Notting Hill Gate, W11 3LF | 020-7229-2115 | www.chakralondon.com
Fans herald this sophisticated Notting Hill newcomer as a "triumph", praising its "light, refreshing" take on Indian cuisine; though the sophisticated setting replete with tufted leather walls and banquettes is matched by upscale pricing, there's still value to be found, namely at the all-you-can-eat weekend lunches.

Champor-Champor 🗷 *Malaysian*   ▽ 23 | 22 | 20 | £47
Tower Bridge | 62-64 Weston St., SE1 3QJ | 020-7403-4600 | www.champor-champor.com
"Flavourful" fusion cuisine is "masterfully prepared" at this "intimate", somewhat "expensive" Malaysian with an "out-of-the-way"

Tower Bridge location and "quirky, eclectic" decor based on souvenirs from far-flung lands; if you can snare it, romantics "highly recommend the candlelit balcony for two", but at any table, "friendly" staff help shape a "memorable" experience.

The Chancery 🅭 *European* ▽ 25 | 20 | 23 | £49

Holborn | 9 Cursitor St., EC4A 1LL | 020-3589-2096 | www.thechancery.co.uk

"Perfect for client entertaining", this "tiny", "lovely" Modern European "hidden" in the Holborn backstreets boasts "formal service" that "runs like a well-oiled machine" as it ferries fare that "impresses with technique and flavour"; tables that are "small and close together" are a bit of a peeve, but "affordable" prix fixes for both lunch and dinner invariably please.

Chapters All Day Dining *European* 25 | 21 | 23 | £46

Blackheath | 43-45 Montpelier Vale, SE3 0TJ | 020-8333-2666 | www.chaptersrestaurants.com

"On a nice day, it's hard to get a better location" than the alfresco area "looking out over the Heath", but the "elegant, modern" interior is its own draw at this all-day Blackheath Modern European where the are is "superb", especially the "cut-above" Josper oven–cooked meats; "it's not the cheapest", but with "personable" service thrown into the mix, fans are "more than happy to pay the price."

Charlotte's Bistro ◑ *European* 26 | 21 | 25 | £44

Chiswick | 6 Turnham Green Terr., W4 1QP | 020-8742-3590
Charlotte's Place ◑ *European*
Ealing | 16 St. Matthew's Rd., W5 3JT | 020-8567-7541
www.charlottes.co.uk

"Beautifully set on the common" in Ealing and by Turnham Green tube, these "gems" provide "fabulous", "seasonal, locally sourced" Modern European cuisine, "fantastic cocktails" and "friendly, knowledgeable" service in "smart" settings; most folks find "great value for money" here, but "if the price seems a little high" to you, there are "cost-conscious" set menus at both lunch and dinner.

Cheyne Walk 21 | 21 | 18 | £61
Brasserie *French*

Chelsea | 50 Cheyne Walk, SW3 5LR | 020-7376-8787 | www.cheynewalkbrasserie.com

"After a pleasant walk through a quiet section of Chelsea", the "airy" dining room of this "neighborhood gem" makes for a "romantic date destination", thanks to river views and an "impressive" French menu that includes "delicious" meats cooked on the "open wood-fired oven" ("you'll smell "plenty of rosemary"); if there's one criticism, it's the "high prices", but at least service is mostly "friendly."

🅭 Chez Bruce *British* 28 | 22 | 27 | £63

Wandsworth | 2 Bellevue Rd., SW17 7EG | 020-8672-0114 | www.chezbruce.co.uk

"A team of top pros" "perfectly present" chef-owner Bruce Poole's "impeccably sourced", "exquisitely executed" dishes – complemented by "a trolley full of delicious, pungent cheeses" and the "brilliant" sommelier's "extensive wine list" – at this "lovely" Modern Brit "overlooking Wandsworth Common"; true, it leaves "a large hole in your pocket", but for a "romantic" "special occasion", it's "worth every penny"; P.S. it's "easier to get a table" and more "reasonably priced" at lunch.

Chez Gérard ⑤ *French*   20 | 19 | 19 | £40

City | 64 Bishopsgate, EC2N 4AW | 020-7588-1200 | www.chezgerard.co.uk

"Solid" French brasserie fare delivered in "pleasant" surroundings sums up this "popular", "convenient" City brasserie; it may be "un-exceptional", with service that swings between "good" and not so, but it "does the job" for a "quick" bite, with "manageable prices" to boot.

Chilango *Mexican*   22 | 17 | 21 | £12

Holborn | 76 Chancery Ln., WC2A 1AA | 020-7430-1231 ⑤
City | 142 Fleet St., EC4A 2BP | 020-7353-6761 ⑤
Islington | 27 Upper St., N1 0PN | 020-7704-2123
www.chilango.co.uk

Even famished folks "struggle to finish the huge burritos" at this "trendy" Mexican chainlet that "hits the spot" for a lunchtime treat or a "post-pub snack" with "well-priced", "design-your-own" options "packed with flavour"; you'll most likely have to "queue" to either dine in the "practical" settings or take away, but don't be daunted – "super-speedy" staff get you in and out "quick."

China Tang ● *Chinese*   22 | 24 | 22 | £71

Mayfair | The Dorchester | 53 Park Ln., W1K 1QA | 020-7629-9988 | www.dorchesterhotel.com

Underneath The Dorchester Hotel, this "exquisite" space evokes a "chic" "private club" in "'20s Shanghai", where "tuxedoed staff" serve "international business types" and their "well-dressed" dates "upscale", "excessively expensive" Cantonese fare; "duck in some manner is a must", but the "dim sum is just as good", as are "divine cocktails" at the "packed bar."

Chisou *Japanese*   23 | 17 | 19 | £42

Knightsbridge | 31 Beauchamp Pl., SW3 1NU | 020-3155-0005
Mayfair | 4 Princes St., W1B 2LE | 020-7629-3931 ⑤
NEW **Chiswick** | 1-4 Barley Mow Passage, W4 4PH | 020-8994-3636
www.chisourestaurant.com

"Deluxe, reliable sushi" is "surprisingly good value" at this "relaxed" Japanese trio with decor that's "nothing memorable" yet sufficiently "functional"; a notable "business-lunch" option, it's also a "busy" dinner destination thanks in part to a "sommelier with a great command of the sake list."

Chiswell Street Dining Rooms ● *British*   ▽ 21 | 23 | 23 | £46

City | 56 Chiswell St., EC1 4SA | 020-7614-0177 | www.chiswellstreetdining.com

The owners of The Botanist and The Gun are behind this "charming" new dining room near the Barbican, with "beautiful" green-and-white decor, "friendly" staff and all-day Modern British fare; it's "good for breakfast", "buzzy at lunchtime" and suitable for "business dinners" too, but a bit "pricey."

Chor Bizarre ● Indian   24 | 23 | 20 | £39

Mayfair | 16 Albemarle St., W1S 4HW | 020-7629-9802 | www.chorbizarre.com

"Flea-market treasures" create an "exotic", "whimsical" environment for "highly spiced", "scrumptious" Indian delicacies at this "cosy" Mayfair offshoot of the New Delhi institution; service can be "slow", but staff are wholly "warm", and thankfully, the whole experience is "not too stressful on the wallet."

Chowki ● Indian   20 | 14 | 16 | £35

Piccadilly | 2-3 Denman St., W1D 7HA | 020-7439-1330 | www.chowki.com

An "unusual variety" of regional Indian fare, doled out in "generous portions", is the mainstay of this "solid", "convenient" Piccadilly stop where "reasonable prices" and late hours attract a post-show crowd, "tourists" and "large drunken groups" crowding the "long communal tables"; but there's "nothing spectacular about the ambience", which is why some diners suggest "go, eat, leave."

Christopher's   20 | 20 | 19 | £43
Covent Garden American/Chophouse

Covent Garden | 18 Wellington St., WC2E 7DD | 020-7240-4222 | www.christophersgrill.com

With "wonderful high ceilings and clubby burgundy walls", this "classic American" chophouse in Covent Garden is a "long-standing" option for "decent" steaks, offered in everything from "pre-theatre meals" to "blow-out three-course Sunday brunches"; surveyors say that service is mostly "efficient" both in the first-floor dining room as well as the "quiet, softly lit" ground-floor bar, which is home to an "extensive cocktail menu."

Chuen   19 | 10 | 14 | £22
Cheng Ku ● Chinese

Chinatown | 17 Wardour St., W1D 6PJ | 020-7437-1398 | www.chuenchengku.co.uk

"Dumplings that look like clouds" and other "delicious dim sum" delivered on trolleys supplement Cantonese specialties like "melt-in-your-mouth crispy duck" at this Chinatown "stalwart"; staff vacillate between "polite" and "curt", and the "scruffy" surroundings look "about 100 years old", but most grievances are forgiven in light of the "modest prices."

Churchill Arms Thai   23 | 20 | 18 | £19

Kensington | 119 Kensington Church St., W8 7LN | 020-7727-4242 | www.fullers.co.uk

With its "old English" "boozer" setting, "decorated with Churchill memorabilia" and "hanging baskets" that "spill over with flowers and foliage", this Kensington pub proffers an "unexpected" menu rife with "scrumptious", "spicy" Thai plates at "economical" prices;

"fast" (and "friendly") staff facilitate the "high turnover" necessary to service all those "standing at the bar" "waiting for a table", so don't expect to linger over your meal.

Chutney Mary ◑ *Indian* 24 | 22 | 22 | £49
Chelsea | 535 King's Rd., SW10 0SZ | 020-7351-3113 | www.chutneymary.com

With "mouth-watering delights" galore, this "posh" King's Road Indian "deserves its reputation" for "zingy", "stylish" dishes served with "aplomb" by "attentive staff"; though it might be "somewhat pricey" for the genre, the consensus is "after all these years" it's still "a delight", especially "dining in the conservatory."

Chutneys ◑ *Indian/Vegetarian* 26 | 18 | 20 | £21
Euston | 124 Drummond St., NW1 2PA | 020-7388-0604 | www.chutneyseuston.co.uk

Carnivores get "converted to veggies" by the "wonderful", "varied" Indian dosas and such at this "cheerful", "hospitable" vegetarian haunt situated in Euston; surveyors say that, while prices are always reasonable, the all-you-can-eat lunch buffet is especially "excellent value" – and dessert's included, so save room to "test as many as possible."

Ciao Bella ◑ *Mediterranean* 22 | 19 | 20 | £27
Bloomsbury | 86-90 Lamb's Conduit St., WC1N 3LZ | 020-7242-4119 | www.ciaobellarestaurant.co.uk

"Always packed-to-the-rafters", this trattoria located in Bloomsbury provides "massive portions" of "yummy" Mediterranean fare served by "fast", "friendly" staff in an "entertaining family atmosphere"; a wine list that "exceeds expectations" and a "resident pianist" that entertains nightly add to the "charm", but its best aspect may be the "not-expensive" bill.

Cigala *Spanish* 21 | 16 | 20 | £38
Bloomsbury | 54 Lamb's Conduit St., WC1N 3LW | 020-7405-1717 | www.cigala.co.uk

If you're planning on indulging in the "lovely tapas" and "hearty" paella at this "hyped" Spanish destination in Bloomsbury , "get there early, as it fills up quickly"; a few can "only afford these prices once in a while", but some "reasonable" varieties can be found amongst the "excellent" wine and brandy selection, plus a "warm welcome" is part of the deal.

Cigalon ☒ *French* ∇ 22 | 23 | 22 | £49
Holborn | 115 Chancery Ln., WC2A 1PP | 020-7242-8373 | www.cigalon.co.uk

"Robust flavours" from Provence abound at this "bright, cheery" and "intimate" venue "in the heart of the legal district" in Holborn, where the "well-executed" fare is complemented by a wine list that also "flies the flag" of the region; with the added advantages of "excellent service", "reasonable" à la carte prices and "bargain" set menus, it's no wonder supporters peg it as "an option for any time and any occasion."

	FOOD	DECOR	SERVICE	COST

Cinnamon Club 🗷 *Indian* — 25 | 25 | 23 | £63

Westminster | Old Westminster Library | 30-32 Great Smith St., SW1P 3BU | 020-7222-2555 | www.cinnamonclub.com

"You'll never want to eat tikka masala again" after you've sampled Vivek Singh's "fragrant", "cutting-edge", "cleverly constructed" modern Indian fare paired with "terrific" wines and presented by "warm, competent staff" at this Westminster venue; unsurprisingly given its location, the "sumptuous", "book-lined" "old-library" setting is "a favourite with politicians" and other types who can handle the "unmentionable" cost; P.S. don't miss the "excellent Asian-inspired" cocktails in the "cool bar downstairs."

Cinnamon Kitchen ◑🗷 *Indian* — 25 | 21 | 21 | £41

City | 9 Devonshire Sq., EC2M 4WY | 020-7626-5000 | www.cinnamon-kitchen.com

Vivek Singh's "modern" "reinterpretations" of Indian cuisine (including a "great vegetarian selection") are dished up by "helpful" staff at Cinnamon Club's "trendy" City offspring, which follows the same "sublime" "formula" as its parent in "more casual", "cosmopolitan" digs; it's a "destination" for everything from "great-value set lunches" to "business" dinners to "late-night cocktails", so "get your cash out and go!"

NEW Cinnamon Soho 🗷 *Indian* — - | - | - | M

Soho | 5 Kingly St., W1B 5PF | 020-7437-1664 | www.cinnamonsoho.com

Building on the success of his Cinnamon Club and Cinnamon Kitchen, chef Vivek Singh's latest outpost is a more relaxed affair, offering a midpriced modern Indian menu of shareable plates that cheekily play to the British palate (e.g. roganjosh shepherd's pie, Punjabi-style fish and masala chips); the chic, bi-level Soho space features dark-wood walls sliced with neon orange lighting, plus alfresco tables on pedestrian-friendly Kingly Street.

Circus 🗷Ⓜ *Asian* — 19 | 25 | 20 | £46

Covent Garden | 27-29 Endell St., WC2H 9BA | 020-7420-9300 | www.circus-london.co.uk

"Fire-eating acrobats in sequins" "prance down the long table" and "voluptuous lovelies gyrate in hoops mere feet from you" at this "quirky" "opulent Tom Dixon–designed" Covent Garden "cabaret" where a team of "great" staffers deliver Pan-Asian plates; the "food is good, but definitely not the main event", which is why some deem it "pricey for what you get" – notwithstanding the "awesome cocktails."

Ciro's Pizza Pomodoro ◑ *Italian* — ∇ 18 | 17 | 20 | £31

Knightsbridge | 51 Beauchamp Pl., SW3 1NY | 020-7589-1278 | www.pomodoro.co.uk

It's all about the "great live music" and "enviably cool crowd" at this "buzzing" Knightsbridge Italian plastered with photos of celebs who have stopped by; it's "not the place for gourmet food", though the pizzas are usually "good" (so too the service) and "reasonably priced" to boot.

Citrus *Italian*

▽ | 21 | 19 | 19 | £41

Piccadilly | Park Lane Hotel | 112 Piccadilly, W1J 7BX | 020-7290-7364 | www.citrusrestaurant.co.uk

"Decent", "fancy" Italian cuisine is served in an "informal" atmosphere at this Piccadilly hotel dining room with a "convenient" location "across from Green Park"; what's more, it's "surprisingly affordable" given the "posh minimalist decor" featuring black-and-white-portraiture wallpaper by Fornasetti, "brilliant" alfresco seating and "above-average" service.

Clarke's *British*

26 | 18 | 23 | £63

Kensington | 124 Kensington Church St., W8 4BH | 020-7221-9225 | www.sallyclarke.com

"Wonderfully selected" "farm-to-table" ingredients are whipped into "complex flavours" at this "relaxed", "reliable" Kensington Modern Brit "star" where chef-owner Sally Clarke usually "can be seen behind the stoves"; also to be found in the bi-level setting are "understated elegance" in the decor, "efficient" staff and a "decent wine list", adding up to a "sophisticated" experience whose "loyal following" feels is "worth every pound – and you'll spend lots of them."

Cliveden House Restaurant *British/French*

▽ | 20 | 26 | 24 | £75

Taplow | Cliveden Country House Hotel | 1 Taplow Rd., SL6 0JF | 01628-668 561 | www.clivedenhouse.co.uk

Fans of stately homes are "charmed" by this Berkshire destination's and its "decadent" main dining room, the Terrace, serving "lovely", pricey British-French fare amidst "ironed table linens" and "beautiful" views of the gardens; there's also a "spectacular" afternoon tea and, in the Duke of Westminster's onetime stables, the Club Room, with booths built into the old stalls and the same "excellent service."

C London ● *Italian*

23 | 21 | 23 | £74

Mayfair | 23-25 Davies St., W1K 3DE | 020-7399-0500 | www.crestaurant.co.uk

"The paparazzi outside" this "famous" Davies Street Italian confirm that it's still a "hotspot" for "people-watching" a "diverse" "parade" of "hedge-fund managers", "*X Factor*" contestants and the like; the "smart", "vibrant" setting boasts "a lot of character" and "charming" staff, and as for the fare, it "pleases" – as it should for being so "extravagantly priced."

❷ Clos Maggiore *French*

25 | 27 | 24 | £58

Covent Garden | 33 King St., WC2E 8JD | 020-7379-9696 | www.closmaggiore.com

"Escape from the world" to the "magical" flower-filled conservatory – or to a "romantic" table near a fireplace – at this Covent Garden "find" that pairs "wonderful" New French cuisine with a "comprehensive wine list" and "cosseting" service; it's the sort of "special-occasion" place for which "you need to book far in advance" – and pay a "pricey" bill, so to "really get your money's worth", try the amazing pre-theatre deal."

Club Gascon 🅱 *French*

FOOD	DECOR	SERVICE	COST
26	22	24	£72

Farringdon | 57 W. Smithfield, EC1A 9DS | 020-7796-0600 | www.clubgascon.com

"Exquisite foie gras" in many permutations, "even the desserts", is the star of the "wonderful", "innovative" Southwest French, small plates-focused menu at this "formidable", "formal" Smithfield site from chef-owner Pascal Aussignac; "attentive service", "old-school" marble-and-wood environs and an "excellent selection of niche-y wines" are part of the package – just "be prepared to pay well for it" all.

🆕 Colchis ❶ *Georgian*

FOOD	DECOR	SERVICE	COST
-	-	-	E

Notting Hill | 39 Chepstow Pl., W2 4TS | 020-7221-7620 | www.colchisrestaurant.co.uk

Named after a medieval state on the Black Sea, this Notting Hill newcomer offers Georgian cuisine backed by a 150-strong international wine list; filling the former pub space below Assaggi, the stylish, wood-floored digs include an entrance bar with high stools, leather banquettes and striking wall-mounted wine display.

Como Lario ❶ *Italian*

FOOD	DECOR	SERVICE	COST
22	16	23	£52

Pimlico | 18-22 Holbein Pl., SW1W 8NL | 020-7730-2954 | www.comolario.co.uk

"Jovial staff" clearly "want you to enjoy yourself" at this perennially "packed", 40-plus-year-old Pimlico place pairing "excellent" Northern Italian eats with "drinkable house wine"; whilst somewhat "cramped", the "cheery atmosphere" makes it a "keeper" for an "informal" "evening with friends", though it is a bit pricey.

Comptoir Gascon 🅱🅼 *French*

FOOD	DECOR	SERVICE	COST
25	19	20	£44

Farringdon | 63 Charterhouse St., EC1M 6HJ | 020-7608-0851 | www.comptoirgascon.com

"All the imagination" and "excellent taste" of Club Gascon is offered at "a better price" at this "lovely little" French "bistro relative", also in Farringdon; "simply decorated with tables tightly packed", the "intimate" setting benefits from "charming" staff who are as "knowledgeable" about chef Pascal Aussignac's fare as they are the "great" wine selection, making it all in all "a real joy to eat here."

Comptoir Libanais *Lebanese*

FOOD	DECOR	SERVICE	COST
20	17	15	£20

Marylebone | 65 Wigmore St., W1U 1PZ | 020-7935-1110
Stratford | Westfield Stratford City | 2 Stratford Pl., E20 1EN | 020-8811-2222
Shepherd's Bush | Westfield Shopping Ctr. | Ariel Way, balcony, W12 7GE | 020-8811-2222
www.lecomptoir.co.uk

"Groaning plates of mezze" and other "delicious" Lebanese staples are "washed down with mint tea or fresh smoothies" at this "funky" chain; though the "colourful" decor strikes some as "Formica heaven" and the "slow" service can be "a letdown", shoppers seeking "respite" – financial and otherwise – deem it "terrific."

	FOOD	DECOR	SERVICE	COST

Constancia *Argentinean/Chophouse*   ▽ 24 | 20 | 21 | £36

Tower Bridge | 52 Tanner St., SE1 3PH | 020-7234-0676 |
www.constancia.co.uk

"As soon as you walk in, you start salivating at the smell of the char
coal grill" at this "cosy" chophouse near Tower Bridge, where "atten
tive" staff deliver "fabulous Argentinean steaks", "great sides" and
"superb" South American wines; the "laid-back" setting is as "right
for a romantic dinner" as it is "comfortable for big groups", and best
of all, it "knocks the spots off some" of its "pricier" competitors.

NEW Copita ☒ *Spanish*   ▽ 23 | 21 | 20 | £30

Soho | 26 D'Arblay St., W1F 8EP | 020-7287-7797 |
www.copita.co.uk

"Clever combinations", "excellent ingredients" and "strong punches
of flavour" abound in the "varied" Spanish tapas at this "loud"
Soho sib of Barrica that's "appropriately priced" for being so "ca
sual"; you can't book for the "small seating area", so the "cool"
clientele passes waiting time at the bar with a glass of wine or sherry
from the "simple, good" list.

Coq d'Argent *French*   23 | 23 | 21 | £59

City | 1 Poultry, EC2R 8EJ | 020-7395-5000 |
www.coqdargent.co.uk

From early morning until night, this "rooftop hub" is "packed" with
"City high fliers" "expensing" "reliable", "well-presented" Classic
French fare and quaffing "excellent" cocktails whilst taking in
"smashing views"; it may seem "a bit pricey" for those without busi
ness accounts, but the package includes "professional service", a
"gorgeous" garden terrace and, during Saturday dinners and Sunday
lunches, live jazz.

Corner Room *European*   ▽ 29 | 25 | 25 | £33

Bethnal Green | Town Hall Hotel | Patriot Sq., E2 9NF |
020-7871-0460 | www.townhallhotel.com

"Inspiring", "delicious" European dishes with "inventive" "flair"
leave diners "in awe" of chef Nuno Mendes at this "small", "informal" venture in the same Bethnal Green hotel as his Viajante; it's
"off the beaten path" for many, and the "no-reservations policy"
at dinner (lunch is bookable) irks some, but with such "thoughtful"
service and "economical prices", fans conclude it's "well worth the
detour and the wait."

Corrigan's Mayfair *British*   25 | 23 | 25 | £74

Mayfair | Grosvenor Hse. | 28 Upper Grosvenor St., W1K 7EH |
020-7499-9943 | www.corrigansmayfair.com

"Business" types and "special-night-out" celebrants converge on
Richard Corrigan's "gentleman's club"–like Modern Brit in the
Grosvenor House for "solicitous" service from "white-suited" staffers;
"beautifully prepared", "decadent" "gastronomic delights" com
prise the bill of fare, but they come at "frightening" prices that may
compel you to "take the bus home when you get the bill"; P.S. "the
chef's table private dining package is particularly excellent."

	FOOD	DECOR	SERVICE	COST

▣ Côte *French*

FOOD 22 | DECOR 19 | SERVICE 21 | COST £31

Covent Garden | 17-21 Tavistock St., WC2E 7PA |
020-7379-9991
Covent Garden | 50-51 St. Martin's Ln., WC2N 4EA |
020-7379-9747
Soho | 124-126 Wardour St., W1F 0TY | 020-7287-9280
City | 26 Ludgate Hill, EC4M 7DR | 020-7236-4399
Fulham | 45-47 Parsons Green Ln., SW6 4HH | 020-7736-8444
Richmond | 24 Hill St., TW9 1TW | 020-8948-5971
Chiswick | 50-54 Turnham Green Terr., W4 1QP |
020-8747-6788
Ealing | 9-10 The Green, High St., W5 5DA | 020-8579-3115
Kensington | 47 Kensington Ct., W8 5DA | 020-7938-4147
Notting Hill | 98 Westbourne Grove, W2 5RU | 020-7792-3298
www.cote-restaurants.co.uk

"Interesting and varied" French fare and "good wines" "impress" at this "solid bistro chain" that's "amazingly consistent" across multiple "convenient" locations; "accommodating" staff shimmy around the "simple but effective" digs whose "buzzing environment" and "staggeringly low prices" (including "early-bird" specials and lunch deals) ensure they remain "so popular."

NEW Cotidie ◑ *Italian*

- | - | - | E

Marylebone | 50 Marylebone High St., W1U 5HN | 020-7258-9878 |
www.cotidierestaurant.com

The name translates to 'everyday', but the prices may be a little more 'once in a while' at this Marylebone arrival where the daily changing menu comes courtesy of Italian celebrity chef Bruno Barbieri; the interior sports elegant dark-grey colours, sultry lighting and a snack-and-cocktail bar, called Barbieri, wrapped in bulbous glass orbs.

Cottons *Caribbean*

22 | 21 | 22 | £28

Clerkenwell | 70 Exmouth Mkt., EC1R 4QP | 020-7833-3332 |
www.cottons-restaurant.co.uk
Camden Town | 55 Chalk Farm Rd., NW1 8AN | 020-7485-8388 |
www.cottonscamden.co.uk

If you're "feeling homesick for the islands", this "family-friendly" pair in Clerkenwell and Camden takes you back via "yummy" Caribbean dishes with "a modern twist" plus a "fantastic selection of rums"; "great prices" keep it "crowded", and for those who've been saddled with "slow service" (it's "prompt" only sometimes), regulars suggest you tune into the "laid-back" island vibe of the bar.

The Cow *British*

∇ 22 | 15 | 17 | £33

Notting Hill | 89 Westbourne Park Rd., W2 5QH | 020-7221-0021 |
www.thecowlondon.co.uk

"Push past the crowds" of hip Notting Hillers at this "cultish" pub to find a "small upstairs dining room" serving "well-prepared" Modern British fare that "changes daily depending on what fresh meats are available" ("everything from steak to squirrel to pigeon"); some feel that the "food may be an afterthought" downstairs (where the menu is "smaller"), so they fill up via the "great beer selection."

	FOOD	DECOR	SERVICE	COST

Crazy Bear *Thai* | 20 | 24 | 19 | £53

Fitzrovia | private club | 26-28 Whitfield St., W1T 2RG | 020-7631-0088
Covent Garden | private club | 17 Mercer St., WC2H 9QJ |
020-7520-5450 🗷
www.crazybeargroup.co.uk

With all the "opulence" of an "over-the-top Dubai hotel", the
"baroque-meets-Gothic" decor of this "loungey" Covent Garden and
Fitzrovia Thai duo "impresses" "first dates" and "out-of-towners"
(check out the "awesome", "trippy" bathrooms); it's "a bit on the
pricey side" and service is "inconsistent" (though often "helpful"),
but the menu's "great variety" is appreciated, with both "traditional"
and "adventurous dishes", plus "nibbles and creative drinks."

Crazy Homies *Mexican* | 18 | 18 | 14 | £29

Notting Hill | 125-127 Westbourne Park Rd., W2 5QL |
020-7727-6771 | www.crazyhomieslondon.co.uk

A "hipster" crowd frequents this "tiny", "kitsch" Notting Hill
"dive", which offers up "filling" Mexican fare backed by a "loud"
soundtrack; but the main draw is the "rocking range" of tequilas and
"wicked" margaritas that "knock your socks off" – it's certainly not
prices that some deem "too high for what it is" or staff who can
be "downright rude."

Criterion Restaurant ● *European* | 21 | 27 | 21 | £52

Piccadilly | 224 Piccadilly, W1J 9HP | 020-7930-0488 |
www.criterionrestaurant.com

"The sheer opulence of the gold mosaic ceilings" and marble walls is
"reason enough to visit" this "sumptuous" neo-Byzantine Piccadilly
"haven"; and though the "magical" surroundings are "not quite
matched" by the Modern European dishes, they're "alright" nonetheless, and "well presented" by "polite" staff – but "on the expensive
side", so consider opting for the "bargain" pre-theatre menu.

NEW Cut at | 25 | 22 | 22 | £93
45 Park Lane *American/Chophouse*

Mayfair | 45 Park Ln. | 45 Park Ln., W1K 1PN | 020-7493-4554 |
www.45parklane.com

"Some of the finest steaks in London" are being "cooked to perfection" at this Wolfgang Puck chophouse in a Mayfair hotel, where the
"imported American meat" "comes with all the trimmings", via "attentive" service and amidst an "unusual" '80s rock soundtrack; just
a few folks find the "corridorlike setting" "uninspiring", but for the
most part, everyone "loves everything about this restaurant" – except perhaps the "staggeringly expensive" prices.

NEW Dabbous ●🗷Ⓜ *European* | 26 | 18 | 24 | £52

Fitzrovia | 39 Whitfield St., W1T 2SF | 020-7323-1544 |
www.dabbous.co.uk

"Passionate", "perfectionist" chef Ollie Dabbous' "creative", "beautifully plated" Modern European dishes "surprise" and "excite" at his
"informal", "industrial-style" Fitzrovia venture employing "welcoming" staff; some surveyors are "dubious" about the "small" portions,

but most feel in every other respect, it "lives up to the hype", particularly the tasting menu, a "dream and a total bargain" to boot; P.S. "fantastic cocktails" are poured in the downstairs bar.

	FOOD	DECOR	SERVICE	COST

Da Mario ● *Italian*
∇ | 19 | 16 | 21 | £27

South Kensington | 15 Gloucester Rd., SW7 4PP | 020-7584-9078 | www.damario.co.uk

"Italian waiters" are an "authentic" touch at this "cheap and cheerful" South Ken trattoria that's been serving "solid" "classics" like thin-crust pizza since 1972; there are "always balloons for the kids", so "families" love it, though it's also fit for a "casual" meal "before the Albert Hall", and as it's open till 11.30 PM, you can even swing by after.

Dans Le Noir ⊠ *Eclectic*
∇ | 13 | 18 | 26 | £41

Clerkenwell | 30-31 Clerkenwell Green, EC1R 0DU | 020-7253-1100 | www.danslenoir.com

The "novelty value" draws "curiosity"-seekers to this "unique" Clerkenwell "experience" where, in "pitch black", "very loud" surrounds, diners are seated just "inches from strangers" and served Eclectic dishes by "efficient" blind staff; it can be "(excuse the pun) an eye-opening experience", but because "the food is almost an afterthought", some leave feeling "slightly ripped off."

Daphne's ● *Italian*
22 | 20 | 22 | £57

Chelsea | 112 Draycott Ave., SW3 3AE | 020-7589-4257 | www.daphnes-restaurant.co.uk

Twenty years on, this "smart", "stylish" Chelsea "must" with "charming service" remains "ground zero for ladies who lunch" and "famous" folks; indeed, whilst the "upmarket" Italian fare is "reliable", it "isn't the point here" – you're paying "expensive" prices for the "buzzy" atmosphere and "great people-watching" (try for "a table near the windows").

Daylesford Organic Café *Eclectic*
22 | 20 | 17 | £29

Pimlico | Daylesford Organic Store | 44 Pimlico Rd., SW1W 8LP | 020-7881-8060

Notting Hill | 208-212 Westbourne Grove, W11 2RH | 020-7313-8050 www.daylesfordorganic.com

"Divine", "straight-from-the-farm" produce fills the "healthy" Eclectic fare presented (often in a "slow" manner) at this pair of "glamourous" all-day cafes in Notting Hill and Pimlico; they're "jam packed" at weekends, when "yummy mummies" and "beautiful Europeans" "browse" the organic groceries at the adjacent shop before settling in for "virtuous" bits of "heaven" – and "the prices reflect the altitude."

Dean Street Townhouse ● *British*
22 | 24 | 20 | £48

Soho | Dean Street Townhse. | 69-71 Dean St., W1D 3SE | 020-7434-1775 | www.deanstreettownhouse.com

"Sophisticated", "clubby" environs complete with velvet chairs – augmented by a "hot bar" and terrace made for "people-watching" – are the milieus of "solid", "simple" British fare that many find "fairly priced" at this all-day Soho hotel dining room; "classy" staff are "welcoming and attentive" to the "celeb", "advertising and media"–

heavy crowd, however, there are reports that, "if you're a nobody", the service can slip to "so-so."

Defune *Japanese*   24 | 15 | 20 | £71

Marylebone | 34 George St., W1U 7DP | 020-7935-8311
"Elegant" preparations of "superb sushi" will "blow you away", as will the "super-expensive" prices at this "quiet", "understated" Marylebone Japanese; don't come "looking for atmosphere", but do feel free to "stay all night", because it's "easy to secure a table" and the servers "won't throw you out."

Dehesa *Italian/Spanish*   25 | 20 | 23 | £43

Soho | 25 Ganton St., W1F 9BP | 020-7494-4170 | www.dehesa.co.uk
"Graze" your way through "inventive", "seasonal" Spanish-Italian tapas and "outstanding charcuterie" at this "slick", "lively-verging-on-noisy" Salt Yard sibling "close to Carnaby Street" in Soho; it's quite "small", but staff do their best to be "speedy" – setting an example for fans who "could spend hours" at one of the "shared tables", getting carried away by the "fabulous wine list."

NEW The Delaunay ● *European*   21 | 26 | 24 | £52

Covent Garden | 55 Aldwych, WC2B 4BB | 020-7499-8558 |
www.thedelaunay.com
"Those wonderful folks who brought you The Wolseley" have "hit the target once again" with this "pricey" Covent Garden newcomer that feels "like stepping into the grandest part of the Titanic", where a "comforting" menu of "tasty" Modern Euro "classics" ("textbook schnitzels", "splendid sausages") is served; "open all day for all sorts of meals", all ferried by "spot-on" staff, the "palpable hit" has created "buzz from day one", so it's no surprise that tables are "difficult to get."

Del'Aziz *African/Mediterranean*   21 | 22 | 18 | £27

Tower Bridge | Bermondsey Sq. | 11 Bermondsey Sq., SE1 3UN | 020-7407-2991
Southwark | Blue Fin Bldg. | 5 Canvey St., SE1 9AN | 020-7633-0033
Swiss Cottage | Swiss Cottage Leisure Ctr. | Adelaide Rd., NW3 3NF | 020-7586-3338
NEW Clapham | 55-57 The Pavement, SW4 0JQ | 020-7498-9128
Fulham | 24-32 Vanston Pl., W6 1AX | 020-7386-0086
Shepherd's Bush | Westfield Shopping Ctr. | Ariel Way, W12 7GB | 020-8740-0666 ●
www.delaziz.co.uk
"Massive" meringues and "decadent cakes" lure you into these "atmospheric" all-day deli/cafes, where the "reasonably priced" Med-North African menu includes "hearty breakfasts", "tasty" "mezze lunches" and "something for everyone" at all times; it's just a pity about the "hit-and-miss" service, sometimes "attentive", often "slow"; P.S. many branches offer belly dancing on certain nights.

Delfino ⊠ *Italian*   20 | 15 | 19 | £42

Mayfair | 121 Mount St., W1K 3NW | 020-7499-1256 | www.finos.co.uk
It's a "basic proposition", but for "filling" Italian eats and "awesome pizza" at prices that, for Mayfair anyway, are "reasonable", this trat-

toria in a Victorian building ticks a lot of boxes; though the "tight" setting is "always busy", staff manage to make you "feel loved", even if you're just doing takeaway.

NEW Devonshire Arms *British*

FOOD	DECOR	SERVICE	COST
19	20	18	£30

Chiswick | 126 Devonshire Rd., W4 2JJ | 020-8742-2302
Pot pies, Sunday roasts and other "comforting" British dishes are doled out by "friendly" folks for affordable rates at this "decent" Chiswick gastropub; other lures include a "good choice of draft beers" and wines, "courteous" staff and, on sunny days, outdoor seating.

Dim T *Asian*

FOOD	DECOR	SERVICE	COST
18	16	18	£26

Bloomsbury | 32 Charlotte St., W1T 2NQ | 020-7637-1122
Victoria | 56-62 Wilton Rd., SW1V 1DE | 020-7834-0507
Tower Bridge | 2 More London Pl., Tooley St., SE1 2DB | 020-7403-7000
Hampstead | 3 Heath St., NW3 6TP | 020-7435-0024
Highgate | 1 Hampstead Ln., N6 4RS | 020-8340-8800
www.dimt.co.uk
"Groups" find "something for everyone" at this "informal" chain known for a "mix of Asian cuisines" and "great dim sum"; "friendly staff" and "modern" digs are further pluses, but the "reasonable prices" are really what make it "worth a visit."

The Diner *American*

FOOD	DECOR	SERVICE	COST
18	19	16	£19

NEW Covent Garden | 190 Shaftesbury Ave., WC2H 8JL | 020-3551-5225 ◖
Soho | 18 Ganton St., W1F 7BU | 020-7287-8962 ◖
Shoreditch | 128-130 Curtain Rd., EC2A 3AQ | 020-7729-4452 ◖
Camden Town | 2 Jamestown Rd., NW1 7BY | 020-7485-5223
Islington | 21 Essex Rd., N1 2SA | 020-7226-4533
Kensal Rise | 64-66 Chamberlayne Rd., NW10 3JJ | 020-8968-9033
www.goodlifediner.com
A "feel-good destination" for "family get-togethers" or "hungover Sundays", this "value" chain "captures the feel and decor of a proper American diner", with "standard" "comfort food" and "thick milk-shakes" that "hit the spot if you're in need of a touch of gluttony"; if "hipster staff seem to forget they're at work sometimes", maybe they're just in sympathy with the "laid-back atmosphere."

◪ Dinings ▨ *Japanese*

FOOD	DECOR	SERVICE	COST
28	13	21	£61

Marylebone | 22 Harcourt St., W1H 4HH | 020-7723-0666 | www.dinings.co.uk
"You want to cry, they're so good" assure acolytes of the "breathtak-ing" Japanese tapas and "stunning" sushi "exquisitely presented" by "professional" staff at this Marylebone "shoebox"; though it's "ex-pensive" and the "clinical" decor "leaves a lot to be desired", fans hope to "keep it a secret", as it's already "tough to get a table."

◪ Dinner by Heston Blumenthal *British*

FOOD	DECOR	SERVICE	COST
26	24	25	£92

Knightsbridge | Mandarin Oriental Hyde Park | 66 Knightsbridge, SW1X 7LA | 020-7201-3833 | www.dinnerbyheston.com
"Genius" chef Heston Blumenthal "reinterprets" "historic British recipes" with "mind-blowing" results at this "elegant" "adventure" in

the Mandarin Oriental, where meals start with the "legendary meat fruit", end with "amazing" tipsy cake (made with "pineapples slowly roasting on a spit" in the glass-walled kitchen) and come via "enthusiastic", "informed" service; yes, the "cost is substantial, but odd as it may be to say, it's good value" considering "you won't get this experience anywhere else"; P.S. the lunch prix fixe is a "stunning" bargain.

Dishoom *Indian* | 23 | 23 | 20 | £26 |

Covent Garden | St. Martin's Courtyard | 12 Upper St. Martin's Ln., WC2H 9FB | 020-7420-9320 | www.dishoom.com
Plastered with "family snaps", the "vibrant", "quirky and kitschy decor" of this all-day "Bombay cafe" near Covent Garden is the perfect complement to its "different", "yummy Indian street food"; while the "no-reservations policy is a nuisance", "charming service" and "economical prices" keep it "busy" and "buzzing."

Dock Kitchen *European* | 25 | 23 | 24 | £46 |

Ladbroke Grove | Wharf Bldg., Portobello Dock | 344 Ladbroke Grove, W10 5AH | 020-8962-1610 | www.dockkitchen.co.uk
In the "immaculate open kitchen" of this "beautifully appointed" venue atop the Tom Dixon showroom on the canal in Ladbroke Grove, "risk-taking" chef-owner Stevie Parle creates Modern Euro fare showcasing "innovative flavour combinations and a dedication to seasonality", all delivered by "attentive", "friendly staff"; some moan that it's "a bit pricey", but still, it's "cheaper" than Parle's alma mater, the River Cafe.

Dockmaster's House ⊠ *Indian* | ∇ 22 | 23 | 19 | £35 |

Canary Wharf | 1 Hertsmere Rd., E14 8JJ | 020-7345-0345 | www.dockmastershouse.com
Set in a "superb", "imposing" Georgian Canary Wharf building that was a 19th-century customs house, this venue offers a "refreshingly different take on Indian cuisine" – and the results are "fantastic"; staff are mostly "accommodating" and the prices are reasonable, so it's just a "shame it's a bit out of the way" for many.

The Don ⊠ *European* | 22 | 22 | 22 | £53 |

City | The Courtyard | 20 St. Swithins Ln., EC4N 8AD | 020-7626-2606 | www.thedonrestaurant.co.uk
Whether it's the "sophisticated" main dining room with its "monumental paintings" or the "noisier downstairs" with its "vaulted ceilings" and cheaper prices, this "charming" City Modern European in the circa-1798 Sandeman's port warehouse is a "discreet" option that's "good for business or pleasure"; "skilful cooking" and "understated elegance" are evident in the fare, which is delivered via "reliable" service and enhanced by an array of "excellent" sherries and wines.

NEW Donostia Ⓜ *Spanish* | - | - | - | M |

Marylebone | 10 Seymour Pl., W1H 7ND | 020-3620-1845 | www.donostia.co.uk
Ex-Barrafina chef Tomasz Baranski brings midpriced, Basque-inspired tapas to Marble Arch, complementing them with unusual regional wines; the space is almost Scandinavian in its simplicity, with an open kitchen and barstool seating that allows for a full view of the action.

	FOOD	DECOR	SERVICE	COST

NEW The Door ⓧ *Chophouse* — | — | — | E

City | 33 Cornhill, EC3V 3ND | 020-7929-1378 |
www.thedoor-group.com

Steaks from the Argentine Pampas, Midwest America, Chile and
Australia, along with oysters from an estuary in Essex, are the main-
stays of the classy chophouse menu at this bi-level City newcomer;
the glossy, clubby digs feature handsome curved windows and a silver
corniced ceiling, and prices lean toward expensive.

Dorchester - The Grill *British*   25 | 24 | 26 | £77

Mayfair | The Dorchester | 53 Park Ln., W1K 1QA | 020-7629-8888 |
www.dorchesterhotel.com

"Formal" yet "not stuffy", this "fantastic" all-day grill in The
Dorchester pairs a "civilised", "clubby" setting of Scottish murals
and tartan with "terrific" Modern British fare, plus "superb" "traditional" Sunday lunches starring "roast beef carved at table"; it's "quite
expensive", but "considering what you get" – including "welcoming",
"exact" service – it's really "not badly priced", whether for "business"
or a "special treat."

NEW Dorsia ⓧ Ⓜ *European* — | — | — | E

South Kensington | private club | 3 Cromwell Rd., SW7 2HR |
020-7590-4630 | www.thedorsia.co.uk

Located in a luxe townhouse, this South Kensington entry dishes up
high-class Modern European classics – think old favourites like lobster
bisque, and grilled Dover sole – in a refined first-floor dining room;
the flashier onyx bar is a decadent space to sample cocktails like the
'Bateman', a reference to the novel *American Psycho,* which inspired
the restaurant's name.

NEW Downtown Mayfair ● *Italian*   21 | 22 | 21 | £73

Mayfair | 15 New Burlington Pl., W1S 2HX | 020-3056-1001 |
www.downtownmayfair.com

Like its "trendy" cousin, C London, this new off–Savile Row Italian is
a "place to be seen" in Mayfair – indeed, there's "wonderful people-
watching" in the warm setting adorned with walnut, leather and
chandeliers; and similar to the Davies Street original, the service is
"attentive" and the fare is usually "great", though cost-calculators
suspect you pay "three times more" than the usual for it.

Draft House *Eclectic*   20 | 21 | 20 | £24

NEW Fitzrovia | 43 Goodge St., W1T 1TA ⓧ Ⓜ
Tower Bridge | 206-208 Tower Bridge Rd., SE1 2UP |
020-7378-9995 | www.drafthouse.co.uk
Battersea | 74-76 Battersea Bridge Rd., SW11 3HE |
020-7228-6482 | www.drafthouse.co.uk
Clapham | 94 Northcote Rd., SW11 6QW | 020-7924-1814 |
www.drafthouse.co.uk
NEW Dulwich | 21 Lordship Ln., SE22 8EW | 020-8299-3511

"Worth it for the beer selection alone", these "informal", "convivial"
gastropubs also house a "small" menu of "well-executed" Eclectic
eats, including a choice of "rhyming burgers" (yolk, poke and smoke –

and "they're all good"); there's a "decent Sunday lunch" too, plus "great service" and affordable prices every day.

Dragon Castle *Chinese*   ▽ 22 | 13 | 14 | £27
Kennington | 100 Walworth Rd., SE17 1JL | 020-7277-3388 | www.dragoncastle.eu

A "wide range" of Cantonese delicacies including "fabulous dim sum" is doled out in "generous" portions at this "large" "culinary oasis" "a five-minute walk from Elephant & Castle station"; service can be "comically brusque", but bills cause such a "little dent to the wallet", "it's worth just ignoring the staff and tucking right in."

NEW The Drift *European*   - | - | - | M
City | Heron Tower | 110 Bishopsgate, EC2 4AY | 0845-468-0103 | www.thedriftbar.co.uk

A kaleidoscope of bustling bars, loungey nooks and casual dining areas sums up this huge, glass-wrapped sibling of The Anthologist and The Folly on the ground floor of a flashy new City skyscraper; served all day, the midpriced Modern European menu meanders from grazing snacks to hearty grills, supported by reasonably priced wines and punchy cocktails.

NEW Ducksoup *European*   ▽ 18 | 15 | 16 | £38
Soho | 41 Dean St., W1D 4PY | 020-7287-4599 | www.ducksoupsoho.co.uk

A daily changing menu of "small" yet "hearty" European plates and a "focus on natural wines" get "trendy" types "queuing" for this "no-reservations" Soho space; however, some find it "hard to see past the things that irritate" them, namely "small", "stripped-back" digs and occasionally "not-helpful staff", leading them to deem it "overpriced."

Duke of Cambridge *British*   22 | 18 | 19 | £26
Islington | 30 St. Peter's St., N1 8JT | 020-7359-3066 | www.sloeberry.co.uk

"Even if you don't care" that this "comfortable", rustic Islington "classic" bills itself as Britain's first and only certified organic gastropub, you'll appreciate the "terrific" Modern British fare, not to mention the "reasonable prices"; it's the sort of place where staff "recognise you on a return visit" – no wonder the crowd seems so "friendly."

Duke of Sussex *British/Spanish*   23 | 20 | 21 | £27
Chiswick | 75 S. Parade, W4 5LF | 020-8742-8801 | www.thedukeofsussex.co.uk

"Classic British dishes" with "great twists" and "hearty" Spanish tapas make this "inviting" Chiswick gastropub with art deco chandeliers a bit different than most; "helpful staff" wait on "locals" enjoying a "romantic night" out, a "lazy" lunch or a warm-weather repast in the "large beer garden at the back" ("great if you're with the kids"), whilst delivering "excellent value" at all times.

The Eagle *Mediterranean*   23 | 15 | 16 | £26
Clerkenwell | 159 Farringdon Rd., EC1R 3AL | 020-7837-1353

The "original" gastropub, and "still one of the best, at least in terms of food", this "rambunctious" Clerkenwell boozer presents "hearty", "superb-quality" Med fare with Iberian influences; "thankfully, the decor and service aren't what set the trend", though "watching the chefs do their magic" in the open kitchen is "fun."

E&O *Asian*   23 | 20 | 19 | £50

Notting Hill | 14 Blenheim Crescent, W11 1NN | 020-7229-5454 | www.rickerrestaurants.com

"Creative" Pan-Asian dishes "delight the palate" at this "smooth" Notting Hill "scene" that's "buzzy all day" (thanks in part to the "bargain" lunch deal) and flat-out "noisy at night" when "beautiful people" and the "occasional star" flood the "trendy bar" for "wonderful cocktails"; service is "young" and "upbeat", and as for the cost, it's "slightly pricey, but money well spent."

Ebury Wine Bar &   18 | 18 | 19 | £41
Restaurant *European/French*

Belgravia | 139 Ebury St., SW1W 9QU | 020-7730-5447 | www.eburywinebar.co.uk

Since 1959, the "caring staff" employed at this "lively", "cosy" wine bar and bistro "close to Victoria Station" in Belgravia have been keeping "after-work" crowds happy with an "excellent wine list" that "caters for all tastes"; some feel the "emphasis" is more oenological than culinary, but the French-heavy Modern Euro eats are "nifty and relatively thrifty", plus they give you something else to linger over whilst studying the "funny satirical paintings" that decorate the place.

Ed's Easy Diner *American*   20 | 21 | 21 | £19

Mayfair | Sedley Pl. | 14 Woodstock St., W1C 2AG | 020-7493-9916

Piccadilly | London Trocadero Ctr. | 19 Rupert St., W1D 7PA | 020-7287-1951

Soho | 12 Moor St., W1D 5NG | 020-7434-4439 ◑

Euston | The Piazza | Euston Station, NW1 2DY | 020-7388-6967 www.edseasydiner.co.uk

"Ravenous" "tourists and teens" scoff "standard diner fare" like burgers, chili dogs and fries plus "amazing milkshakes" that are "meals in themselves" at this "kitsch", "'50s-style" "slice of Americana"; "friendly staff" skirt round digs bedecked with chrome, neon, red-vinyl counter stools, "loads of memorabilia" and "jukeboxes", and though to some it's all "a little cheesy", at least the prices are appropriately "fair."

Efes 2 Turkish Restaurant ◑ *Turkish*   22 | 17 | 22 | £37

Bloomsbury | 175-177 Great Portland St., W1W 5PJ | 020-7436-0600 | www.efes2.co.uk

Efes Restaurant ◑⊠ *Turkish*

Bloomsbury | 80-82 Great Titchfield St., W1W 7QT | 020-7636-1953 | www.efesrestaurant.co.uk

"Succulent" lamb kebabs and other "wonderful" grill-heavy Turkish fare come in "good portions" and for "the right price" at this "reliable" pair of separately owned Bloomsbury spots; as a result, the traditionally outfitted digs are "always crowded" with punters who appreciate the staff's "charm" and, in Great Portland Street, those of the nightly belly dancer.

	FOOD	DECOR	SERVICE	COST

805 ◗ *African* — 24 | 19 | 21 | £27

Peckham | 805 Old Kent Rd., SE15 1NX | 020-7639-0808 |
www.805restaurant.com

The Old Kent Road might not strike you as the best "place to go to reminisce about" Africa, or even to get your "first taste" of its cuisine, but that it is, thanks to this light, airy, "peaceful environment" that plates "marvellous" renditions of West African fare; affordable prices for "large portions" are further incentives, as is the "good" service.

Eight Over Eight *Asian* — 23 | 22 | 21 | £51

Chelsea | 392 King's Rd., SW3 5UZ | 020-7349-9934 |
www.rickerrestaurants.com

"Sophisticated" types inhabit this "cool" minimalist E&O sister located "in the heart of Chelsea", where a "vibrant menu" of "tasty" Pan-Asian "bites" is complemented by "delicious cocktails"; it's "not the cheapest" of destinations, but at least it's "predictable" (in a good way), with "attentive, welcoming service" and a "buzzing" atmosphere virtually guaranteed.

El Camion *Mexican* — ∇ 17 | 17 | 17 | £24

Soho | 25-27 Brewer St., W1F 0RR | 020-7734-7711
Notting Hill | 272 Portobello Rd., W10 5TY | 020-8960-8556
www.elcamion.co.uk

When you just want "a few cervezas and a quesadilla", these colourful Mexicans in Portobello Road and Soho are "cheap" albeit "generic" options; expect "disappointing" service and a "tourist"-heavy crowd, except in the "buzzy" "speakeasy-style basement" below the Brewer Street branch, where the cocktails are "a real strong point."

Elena's L'Etoile ⊠ *French/Italian* — 20 | 18 | 18 | £48

Bloomsbury | 30 Charlotte St., W1T 2NG | 020-7636-1496 |
www.elenasletoile.co.uk

"From the moment you enter to the moment you leave, the whole experience is joy" aver advocates of this "charming" Charlotte Street "page from the past", whipping up "decent" "old-school" Franco-Italian fare; though modernists moan that it "feels rather tired" for being so "pricey", for most, the "slightly worn" scarlet-hued decor and "venerable staff only add to its timeless quality."

El Gaucho *Argentinean/Chophouse* — 22 | 19 | 20 | £46

Chelsea | Chelsea Farmers Mkt. | 125 Sydney St., SW3 6NR |
020-7376-8514
South Kensington | 30 Old Brompton Rd., SW7 3DL |
020-7584-8999 ◗
www.elgaucho.co.uk

"Sizzling", "reliable" steaks shipped from the Pampas are accompanied by a "good selection of wines" and "lovely cocktails" at these "casual", "well-run" Argentinean chophouses in Chelsea and South Ken, both decked out in "over-the-top" "cowboy decor", the latter dinner-only during the week; though it's a bit "pricey", the portions are "large", which causes hungry types to exclaim that they "cannot wait to go back."

	FOOD	DECOR	SERVICE	COST

Elistano *Italian* ▽ 21 | 16 | 20 | £41
Chelsea | 25-27 Elystan St., SW3 3NT | 020-7584-5248 |
www.elistano.com
"Lovely, especially in summer" when pavement tables are available,
this sleek, modern Italian is a "recommended meeting place" in
Chelsea; pizzas, pastas and other "simple" dishes do a "great" job of
staving off hunger, and it's reasonably priced for the location.

Elk in the Woods *Eclectic* 23 | 23 | 20 | £27
Islington | 39 Camden Passage, N1 8EA | 020-7226-3535 |
www.the-elk-in-the-woods.co.uk
"Seriously cool wallpaper", antlers and mirrors comprise the "quirky",
"eccentric" and somehow "soothing decor" at this "informal" cafe/
pub "tucked in Camden Passage", whilst "big, tasty" dishes fill the
affordable all-day Eclectic menu; "relaxed" staff provide the "friendly
service" – no wonder it's "always on the right side of busy."

El Parador *Spanish* ▽ 24 | 13 | 19 | £28
Camden Town | 245 Eversholt St., NW1 1BA | 020-7387-2789 |
www.elparadorlondon.com
There's a "folksy feel" to this Camden Spaniard in "a storefront setting", where the "brilliant", "reasonably priced" tapas menu "changes
frequently yet always seems to leave your favourite dish available",
a boon for "repeat visitors"; if some find the decor a bit "uninspiring",
they concede that the back garden offers a "great escape."

El Pirata ●☒ *Spanish* 22 | 18 | 20 | £41
Mayfair | 5-6 Down St., W1J 7AQ | 020-7491-3810
El Pirata Detapas *Spanish*
Notting Hill | 115 Westbourne Grove, W2 4UP | 020-7727-5000
www.elpiratadetapas.co.uk
"On a dull winter day", you can practically "feel the Spanish sun
on your back" at this pair in Notting Hill and Mayfair, "traditional
wooden" settings where "friendly" staff serve a "great selection of
tasty tapas"; sure, it can be a bit "crowded" and "noisy", but with
such "great value", especially via the fixed price menus, most just
say "bravo"; P.S. "if you can't get a table", sit at the "well-stocked" bar.

The Empress *British* 23 | 20 | 21 | £38
Hackney | 130 Lauriston Rd., E9 7LH | 020-8533-5123 |
www.theempressofindia.com
Just outside of "leafy Victoria Park", this "reliable" 19th-century
Hackney gastropub delivers "fantastic" Modern British dishes from a
chef who "clearly cares about quality and presentation"; everything's
"served promptly" to the "well-spaced tables" by "friendly staff", and
as you'd expect from a boozer, there's a "good beer selection" too.

Empress of Sichuan *Chinese* 23 | 17 | 17 | £31
Chinatown | 6 Lisle St., WC2H 7BG | 020-7734-8128 |
www.restaurantprivilege.com
"Spicy-as-you-like Sichuan cooking" is the speciality of this "yummy"
Chinatown spot; some confess to being "put off" by the "mediocre"

service and "average" surrounds, especially those for whom the bill "ended up being a little more expensive" than they "would have liked", but on the plus side, the portions are "ample."

English Pig 🗷 *British* ▽ 20 | 15 | 16 | £39

Westminster | 4 Millbank, SW1P 3JA | 020-7600-9707 | www.theenglishpig.co.uk

"Piggy heaven" squeal hog-hounds about this "original concept" whose Modern British menu, "concentrating on all the bits of the pig", stars "melt-in-the-mouth 21-hour roast pork belly", augmented with "creative desserts and delicious drinks"; a recent move to Westminster may not be reflected in the Decor score, but those who found the "pictures of pigs all over the wall" "a bit disturbing" should know that they made the trip.

Enoteca Turi 🗷 *Italian* 25 | 18 | 23 | £52

Putney | 28 Putney High St., SW15 1SQ | 020-8785-4449 | www.enotecaturi.com

"Superb", "modern" takes on Italian classics are matched by a "large but not intimidating wine list" at this spot "over the bridge in Putney", where "professional", "friendly service" makes up for decor that some deem "a little dated"; so, despite "pricey" costs, there's "value for money" here, thus locals would "would rather keep it a secret."

The Enterprise *British* 21 | 22 | 22 | £40

Chelsea | 35 Walton St., SW3 2HU | 020-7584-3148 | www.theenterprise.co.uk

"One of the most convivial" spots in Chelsea, this "fancy local" is often "tourist free" but "always busy with investment/Sloane Ranger types" and other "wealthy people" enjoying "haute" (read: "not cheap") Modern British gastropub grub and some "unique specials"; bookings are only taken for weekday lunches, so if you come for dinner, "arrive early or have a few drinks at the bar" while you wait.

Esarn Kheaw *Thai* ▽ 22 | 10 | 15 | £25

Shepherd's Bush | 314 Uxbridge Rd., W12 7LJ | 020-8743-8930 | www.esarnkheaw.co.uk

"Rich and delicious" Thai tastes are available for "reasonable prices" at this Shepherd's Bush venue; the gold-and-green surroundings are "rather tired", the service can be a little "weird" and it's "off the beaten track" for many, but that "doesn't seem to deter people" – some even say it's "worth travelling to."

🗷 Espelette *French* 25 | 27 | 28 | £66

Mayfair | The Connaught | Carlos Pl., W1K 2AL | 020-7107-8861 | www.the-connaught.co.uk

Watch the goings on in "fashionable Mount Street" whilst "fantastic" staff ferry chef Hélène Darroze's "delightful, refined" Classic French cuisine at this "stunning" glass conservatory in The Connaught; devotees "could eat here every night and every day" (starting with breakfast), but the "ethereal afternoon tea is the highlight", so "take gran, charm her – and let her pay" the "rather expensive" bill.

	FOOD	DECOR	SERVICE	COST

Eyre Brothers 🗷 *Portuguese/Spanish* | 24 | 20 | 21 | £46

Shoreditch | 70 Leonard St., EC2A 4QX | 020-7613-5346 |
www.eyrebrothers.co.uk

Fortunately it's "rustic Spanish and Portuguese" plates (including
Ibérico ham that "has to be tasted to be believed") that are "bold
and have attitude", not the "approachable" staffers, at this "classy"
"low-lit" "dark-wood" dining room in a Shoreditch backstreet; it can
be "a touch pricey", so for something a bit cheaper, go for tapas at
the bar, home to a wine list that is "an Iberian education" in itself.

Fairuz ● *Lebanese* | 23 | 13 | 19 | £32

Marylebone | 3 Blandford St., W1H 3DA | 020-7486-8108 |
www.fairuz.uk.com

"Big portions" of "tasty" Lebanese eats fill the "small" handmade
tables at this "cosy" Marylebone eatery with no frills in the decor
department; habitués appreciate that they're "never rushed" by
"polite" staff, but they're most impressed by the "excellent value."

Fakhreldine ● *Lebanese* | 19 | 20 | 18 | £48

Piccadilly | 85 Piccadilly, 1st fl., W1J 7NB | 020-7493-3424 |
www.fakhreldine.co.uk

"Perfectly decent" Lebanese fare is delivered by "quick, helpful"
servers at this modern, minimalist "staple on Piccadilly", with "great
views over Green Park" and belly dancers at weekends; quite a few
folks feel it's "overpriced for what it is" ("small portions"), but you're
"paying for the history" (it's been around more than 30 years), the
"exclusive address" and to dine amongst the "beautiful people."

🗷 Fat Duck 🗷🅼 *British* | 27 | 23 | 27 | £225

Bray | High St., Berkshire | 01628-580 333 | www.thefatduck.co.uk
In this "tiny", "understated" cottage in "sleepy" Bray (about an hour
from London), chef Heston Blumenthal's "fantastic experiments" with
Modern British cuisine border on "performance art"; indeed, "seeing,
smelling and hearing the dishes is as much a part of the experience
as tasting them" (they taste "terrific"), not to mention the "theatrical" presentation of the tasting menu by a "consummate" "cast"; a
wine list composed of "hard-to-find labels" is another "sublime"
feature, enhancing "an experience of a lifetime that's worth the trek",
"the pain of trying to get a reservation" and the very "high price."

Feng Sushi *Japanese* | 19 | 14 | 17 | £30

Borough | 13 Stoney St., SE1 9AD | 020-7407-8744
South Bank | Royal Festival Hall | Unit 9 Festival Terr., Belvedere Rd.,
SE1 8XX | 020-7261-0001
NEW **Hampstead** | 280 West End Ln., NW6 1LJ | 020-7435-1833
Chalk Farm | 1 Adelaide Rd., NW3 3QE | 020-7483-2929
Fulham | 218 Fulham Rd., SW10 9NB | 020-7795-1900
Kensington | 24 Kensington Church St., W8 4EP | 020-7937-7927
Notting Hill | 101 Notting Hill Gate, W11 3JZ | 020-7727-1123
www.fengsushi.co.uk

The eco-conscious "commend" this "functional" midrange sushi
chainlet for the "emphasis it puts on sustainably sourced fish",

available in "attractively presented" "basics" as well as some "interesting" dishes that "change seasonally"; though "friendly", service can be "not the speediest", and with "no atmosphere" taken into consideration, it's perhaps "better suited to takeaway."

Fernandez & Wells *Spanish*   22 | 20 | 21 | £25

NEW **Covent Garden** | Somerset Hse. | The Strand, WC2R 1LA | 020-7420-9408
Soho | 16 St. Anne's Court, W1F 0BF | 020-7494-4242 🛇
Soho | 43 Lexington St., W1F 9AL | 020-7734-1546
Soho | 73 Beak St., W1F 9SR | 020-7287-8124
www.fernandezandwells.com
"Superb coffee" and "brilliant" wines wash down "fantastic" sandwiches, "beautiful cheeses and meats" and "lovely" cakes at these "informal", Spanish-style cafe/tapas bars; the Soho branches are a bit "small", there's more space at Somerset House and all benefit from "charming" staff, "relaxed" atmospheres and reasonable prices.

Ffiona's Ⓜ *British*   22 | 18 | 23 | £38

Kensington | 51 Kensington Church St., W8 4BA | 020-7937-4152 | www.ffionas.com
"Long-standing regulars" head for this "quirky", "cosy" Kensington bistro for "ffabulous" Traditional British "comfort food" that's "reasonably priced"; after a recent revamp, it's lighter and brighter (and now offers an Anglo-American brunch), but as always, the "star attraction" is "one-of-a-kind" owner Ffiona Reid-Owen, who delivers a "warm welcome" and "guides you to the best dishes of the day."

Fifteen *Italian*   23 | 20 | 21 | £53

Hoxton | 15 Westland Pl., N1 7LP | 020-3375-1515 | www.fifteen.net
"Fill your stomach" and "feed your soul" at Jamie Oliver's "comfortable" Hoxton Italian eatery, which trains underprivileged youths for a career in the restaurant industry; certain surveyors call the bill "higher than expected", but with "varied, tasty" cooking, "great" wine pairings, "effervescent" service and "palpable energy", both in the "casual" upstairs trattoria and "more intimate" downstairs, most conclude it's "well worth the price."

Fifth Floor *European*   22 | 19 | 20 | £52

Knightsbridge | Harvey Nichols | 109-125 Knightsbridge, 5th fl., SW1X 7RJ | 020-7235-5250 | www.harveynichols.com
"Take a break at Harvey Nicks" at this "real pleasure", a "modern" dining room where "well-made", "expensive" Modern European eats are served by "delightful staff" who also have at hand an "excellent selection of wines"; fans feel it's the most "calm and elegant" option in the famed department store, so if you're after "buzz", go for a "champagne cocktail at the adjacent bar."

Fifth Floor Cafe *European*   19 | 15 | 16 | £35

Knightsbridge | Harvey Nichols | 109-125 Knightsbridge, 5th fl., SW1X 7RJ | 020-7823-1839 | www.harveynichols.com
A lower-priced "alternative" to the "fine-dining" Fifth Floor next door, this "hip", "light and airy" Harvey Nicks "pit stop" provides shoppers

	FOOD	DECOR	SERVICE	COST

with "yummy" Modern European snacks and mains; you can escape the "hustle and bustle" of the "noisy" atmosphere (it sits next to the food hall) on the small but "lovely outdoor terrace", but wherever you sit, expect service that regulars "wish was better."

Fino ●☒ *Spanish* 25 | 21 | 22 | £55

Fitzrovia | 33 Charlotte St., W1T 1RR | 020-7813-8010 | www.finorestaurant.com

"Phenomenal" "upscale tapas" as well as "more-substantial" "full-flavoured" Spanish dishes are "elegantly presented" with "friendly flair" at this "boisterous", "glamourous underground" locale on Charlotte Street; when it comes to drinks, the "exceptional" Iberian wine list intrigues, but it's the "array of sherries" that "bewilders" – just watch out, as everything quickly "adds up to a fine bill" (however, it's "worth it").

Fish *Seafood* 23 | 17 | 19 | £35

Borough | Borough Mkt. | Cathedral St., SE1 9AL | 020-7407-3803 | www.fishkitchen.com

"If the fish were any fresher, it would be flapping about on the plate" muse supporters of this "light and airy" Borough Market spot where the "great array" of "professionally prepared" piscatorial delights comes via "friendly" service; a few find the "hubbub" "too noisy" and the cost "too expensive for what it is", so they stick to the takeaway stand outside for "super delish" fish 'n' chips.

FishWorks *Seafood* 21 | 16 | 18 | £38

Marylebone | 89 Marylebone High St., W1U 4QW | 020-7935-9796
Piccadilly | 7-9 Swallow St., W1B 4DE | 020-7734-5813
Richmond | 13-19 The Square, TW9 1EA | 020-8948-5965
www.fishworks.co.uk

The premise of this seafood trio is "simple": you pick your catch from the on-site fishmonger's "great range", and it's cooked "as you like", with "tasty" results; sticklers for value say "it's more expensive than one expects" given the "no-frills" environment and "hit-and-miss" service, but for many, it's a "reasonable restaurant" all around.

500 *Italian* 24 | 18 | 21 | £31

Highgate | 782 Holloway Rd., N19 3JH | 020-7272-3406 | www.500restaurant.co.uk

"Wonderful", "well-sourced" Italian cuisine with "seasonal menu changes" – not to mention "attentive service" and "great value" – make this "tiny, family-run" trattoria "a must-try" in Archway, not far from Highgate; despite the "unpromising" location, "word has spread far", so "book ahead" or risk being "disappointed."

Flemings Grill *European* ▽ 22 | 20 | 23 | £60

Mayfair | Flemings Hotel | 7-12 Half Moon St., W1J 7BH | 020-7499-0000 | www.flemings-mayfair.co.uk

"Under the radar" in a Mayfair hotel set in six Georgian townhouses, this plush, dark "hideaway" delivers "expensive", "quality" Modern European fare to those in the know; indeed, it's "often uncrowded" (and "quiet"), which can make it feel like you have staff who "really seem to care that you're having a great time" all to yourself; P.S. there's a value-priced pre-theatre prix fixe.

Floridita ●🗷Ⓜ *Pan-Latin*   18 | 21 | 18 | £52
Soho | 100 Wardour St., W1F 0TN | 020-7314-4000 |
www.floriditalondon.com

"Tremendous energy" pulses through this Cuban-themed subterranean Soho nightspot where "amazing dancers" come to salsa to "loud" nightly DJs and live bands; the Pan-Latin dishes may be a bit of "an afterthought", but they're "fine", albeit somewhat "overpriced" considering their "small size", the "slightly lacking service" and the requisite music charge at the tables (hence, some just stick to "excellent cocktails" at the bar).

The Folly *European*   18 | 25 | 16 | £24
City | 41 Gracechurch St., EC3V 0BT | 0845-468-0102 |
www.thefollybar.co.uk

There's a "wicked", "happening atmosphere" at this "quirky" all-day City venue, a combination deli, flower shop, "buzzing" bar and mid-priced restaurant serving "better-than-average" Modern European eats; it's sometimes "let down by slow service", but with "large tables to suit large groups" and private areas too, it's "good for sociable" meals "with friends."

Food for Thought ⇗ *Vegetarian*   25 | 13 | 19 | £12
Covent Garden | 31 Neal St., WC2H 9PR | 020-7836-9072 |
www.foodforthought-london.co.uk

Even "meat fanatics" find themselves "delighted" by this "legendary" Covent Garden vegetarian that's been serving up "generous portions" of "creative", "earthy" fare since 1974; the "quirky nooks and crannies" of the "small" basement setting are quite "cramped", but that's made up for by "lovely" service, pricing that's "as cheap as it gets" and the feeling that you "come away distinctly healthier."

Fora *Turkish*   22 | 19 | 22 | £25
City | 34-36 Houndsditch, EC3A 7DB | 020-7626-2222 🗷
St. John's Wood | 11 Circus Rd., NW8 6NX | 020-7586-9889
www.forarestaurants.co.uk

Post-Survey, this "reasonably priced" St. John's Wood Turk with a modern red-and-white color scheme split from the Sofra franchise and joined forces with a similarly themed, fancily decorated City site; so while all scores are probably outdated, word is the "interesting selection" of "delicious" Med eats is only slightly different, while the "lovely" decor and "pleasant staff" are the "same."

The Forge ● *European*   23 | 21 | 22 | £41
Covent Garden | 14 Garrick St., WC2E 9BJ | 020-7379-1432 |
www.theforgerestaurant.co.uk

The "wide-ranging menu makes choosing a time-consuming process" at this "reliable" Covent Garden Modern European where service is "accommodating"; with its "charming", exposed-brick dining room upstairs and "lovely bar downstairs", it "fits for all age groups" – and it's a notably "outstanding option for before or after theatre."

	FOOD	DECOR	SERVICE	COST

Fortnum's Fountain *British*

20 | **20** | **20** | **£35**

Piccadilly | Fortnum & Mason | 181 Piccadilly, W1A 1ER |
020-5602-5694 | www.fortnumandmason.com

"Tourists" and shoppers seeking an "oasis from the fray of Piccadilly"
retire to this "serene", "light and airy" all-day cafe in Fortnum &
Mason, where staff with "old-style manners" bring "reliable, well-
prepared" British fare, "excellent" "traditional high tea" and "wonderful ice cream sundaes" in the first-floor Parlour; in short, it's just
"like when granny took you there for a special treat", and "there's no
quibble about the cost – it's affordable."

Four Seasons Chinese ● *Chinese*

23 | **12** | **16** | **£28**

Chinatown | 12 Gerrard St., W1D 5PR | 020-7494-0870
Chinatown | 23 Wardour St., W1D 6PW | 020-7287-9995
Bayswater | 84 Queensway, W2 3RL | 020-7229-4320
www.fs-restaurants.co.uk

"No matter what time you get" to this "venerable institution" with
branches in Queensway and Chinatown, there's "always a queue"
"down the street" because, for many, it's "the go-to place" for "sublime", "value-for-money" Cantonese fare, specifically what may be
"the best roast duck in the world"; so "who cares" that there's "zero
atmosphere" and "service takes nonchalance to a whole new level"?

Fox & Grapes *British*

20 | **20** | **20** | **£34**

Wimbledon | 9 Camp Rd., SW19 4UN | 020-8619-1300 |
www.foxandgrapeswimbledon.co.uk

"With such headlining pedigree" (Hibiscus' Claude Bosi is executive
chef), Wimbledon diners "expect great things" of this "typical"-
looking gastropub in the middle of the Common; lucky for them, the
Modern Brit fare is "hearty" and "high-quality", with "courteous"
service and reasonable prices that make the place "just right" for a
"casual" meal, as well as a "standby for a drink."

Foxtrot Oscar *British*

19 | **17** | **20** | **£45**

Chelsea | 79 Royal Hospital Rd., SW3 4HN | 020-7352-4448 |
www.gordonramsay.com

"Improved since its early days", this "unpretentious" Chelsea venue
from the Gordon Ramsay stable serves "tasty" Traditional British
"schoolboy" fare in a "compact" (some say "cramped") setting overseen by "smiley", "attentive" staff; it may be a "tad pricey" for a bistro,
but still, it's much cheaper than the celeb chef's nearby flagship.

Franco Manca *Pizza*

25 | **15** | **19** | **£15**

NEW Stratford | Westfield Shopping City | 2 Stratford Pl., E20 1ES |
020-8522-6669
Brixton | 4 Market Row, SW9 8LD | 020-7738-3021
Chiswick | 144 Chiswick High Rd., W4 1PU | 020-8747-4822
www.francomanca.co.uk

"It's all about the top-quality ingredients" at this trio of "basic" but "vibrant" Neapolitan-style pizzerias where "chewy yet crispy" sourdough
crusts are topped with "incredible" sauce and "interesting toppings",
then sold for an "unbeatable price"; there's "nearly always a queue"

that's "usually huge" ("no reservations", except for Chiswick), but "efficient" staff do their best to mitigate the "worth-it" waits.

Franco's ☒ *Italian/Mediterranean* `22` `20` `22` `£53`

St. James's | 61 Jermyn St., SW1Y 6LX | 020-7499-2211 | www.francoslondon.com

"Reliable" Italian-Mediterranean fare is served from breakfast to dinner at this "sophisticated" St. James's spot whose "bright" 1940s-inspired interior is always "buzzy", whether with the "lunchtime high-finance crowd" or the "pre-theatre" and "media-types" who meander in later; service is generally "friendly and attentive" – just what you'd expect given the "big price tag."

Frankie's *Italian* `18` `18` `20` `£35`

Knightsbridge | 3 Yeoman's Row, SW3 2AL | 020-7590-9999 | www.frankies-knightsbridge.org
Fulham | Chelsea Football Club Complex | Stamford Bridge, Fulham Rd., SW6 1HS | 020-7957-8298 | www.frankies-chelsea.org

Many punters praise chef Marco Pierre White and jockey Frankie Dettori's duo at Stamford Bridge ("wide-screen TVs showing football") and in Knightsbridge ("glitter balls hanging from the ceiling") for "friendly" service and "quality", "reasonably priced" Italian dishes; others however, finding everything "just adequate", suggest that it "up its game" – with a "bit of sparkle and effort, it could be really quite good."

Frederick's ◗☒ *British/European* `23` `22` `22` `£50`

Islington | 106 Camden Passage, N1 8EG | 020-7359-2888 | www.fredericks.co.uk

During the day it's strictly "business", while at night, "romantics" drink at the "buzzy" bar before retiring to the "smart" dining room, "beautiful conservatory" or, in summer, "attractive garden" at this "pleasant" Islington haunt where the Modern British–European fare is "well executed" and served with "class"; but unless you nab a "great-value" lunch or pre-theatre prix fixe, the prices are "expensive" – though "worth it."

French Horn *British/French* `25` `26` `24` `£65`

Sonning | French Horn Hotel | Sonning-on-Thames | 01189-692 204 | www.thefrenchhorn.co.uk

"For special occasions" or a weekend lunch out of town, this "cosy, oldy-worldy" dining room in a 17th-century coaching inn with "superb views" "overlooking the river at Sonning" is "worth the trip"; the "classic" Franco-Brit fare is "excellent", plus it comes with "plenty of attention" from staff, and intriguing wines – even if you don't want any, do "take a look at the list" and its vintages from the '40s commanding four-figure sums.

☑ French Table Ⓜ *French/Mediterranean* `28` `23` `25` `£51`

Surbiton | 85 Maple Rd., KT6 4AW | 020-8399-2365 | www.thefrenchtable.co.uk

Chef-owners Eric and Sarah Guignard's "smart", "bright" Surbiton "gem" is "no longer a secret", as evidenced by the foodies who flock from all over for the "imaginative", "fantastic" French-Mediterranean cuisine; "knowledgeable", "friendly" staff and prices that, whilst "expensive", are ultimately "good value" for the overall "quality" are two more reasons it's "worth the trek" from Central London.

Frontline 🅱 *British* ▽ | 24 | 22 | 21 | £37 |

Paddington | 13 Norfolk Pl., W2 1QJ | 020-7479-8960 | www.frontlineclub.com

"Foreign war correspondents" on their "way to Heathrow" join civvies at this "cosy, comfortable", "high-ceilinged" Traditional British dining room that's decorated with "striking" photography and located underneath the private Paddington club of the same name; "delicious", "reasonably priced" dishes formed from organic ingredients give a good send-off, as do "obliging" staff.

Gaby's ● *Jewish/Mideastern* | 24 | 15 | 21 | £15 |

Covent Garden | 30 Charing Cross Rd., WC2H 0DB | 020-7836-4233

"Fantastic falafel and hummus, proper salt beef sandwiches" and other similarly "comforting" Jewish–Middle Eastern grub have been served since 1965 at this "gem of the West End" near Leicester Square; and although "the decor's never been up to much", "the service keeps you coming back" for "a quick bite before the theatre or cinema" or simply when you're "hungry" and "skint"; P.S. this is an "institution under threat" of redevelopment, so before you go, check to make sure it hasn't relocated.

Gail's *Bakery* | 22 | 16 | 17 | £17 |

Clerkenwell | 33-35 Exmouth Mkt., EC1R 4QL | 020-7713-6550
Hampstead | 64 Hampstead High St., NW3 1QH | 020-7794-5700
Kilburn | 75 Salusbury Rd., NW6 6NH | 020-7625-0068
St. John's Wood | 5 Circus Rd., NW8 6NX | 020-7722-0983
Clapham | 64 Northcote Rd., SW11 6QL | 020-7924-6330
Chiswick | 282-284 Chiswick High Rd., W4 1PA | 020-8995-2266
Notting Hill | 138 Portobello Rd., W11 2DZ | 020-7460-0766
www.gailsbread.co.uk

Fans are "addicted" to the "scrumptious cakes" and "mouth-watering savouries" at this all-day bakery/cafe chain, despite the feeling that they're a relatively "expensive indulgence"; though service is often "friendly", it can also be "indifferent", so entertain yourself by squeezing into the "tight communal tables" and listening to the "amazing conversations" of the "daily crush of mums" (with "babies") who keep it "crowded."

Galicia ●Ⓜ *Spanish* ▽ | 18 | 14 | 17 | £28 |

Notting Hill | 323 Portobello Rd., W10 5SY | 020-8969-3539

"Swirling ceiling fans, bright-yellow walls", "Galician waiters" and a "wide choice" of *bueno* tapas make it feel like Northern Spain and not Notting Hill at this "cheerful" spot; ok, so it's "nothing to write home about", but "if you're in the neighbourhood", you'll probably have a "fun evening out" here, and a "well-priced" one at that.

	FOOD	DECOR	SERVICE	COST

Gallipoli *Turkish*
22 | **21** | **21** | **£25**

Islington | 102 Upper St., N1 1QN | 020-7359-0630
Islington | 107 Upper St., N1 1QN | 020-7226-5333
Islington | 120 Upper St., N1 1QP | 020-7359-1578
www.cafegallipoli.com

"There's something to be said" for a place that has three locations on the same street – such is the case with this Islington provider of "tasty Turkish" eats at "incredibly reasonable prices"; though each branch offers "varying casualness", all are "lovely", "cluttered and noisy", with "efficient" staff who are "anxious to please" as they "stuff you in like sardines."

Galvin at Windows *French*
25 | **25** | **25** | **£68**

Mayfair | London Hilton on Park Ln. | 22 Park Ln., 28th fl., W1K 1BE | 020-7208-4021 | www.galvinatwindows.com

"Celebrate" something "special" with "spectacular" views ("ask for a table by a window"), "opulent" decor and "fantastic, gourmet" New French fare at chef-owner Chris Galvin's "destination" on the 28th floor of the Hilton Park Lane; "splendid" staff can suggest "brilliant wine pairings" from the "excellent" list, and whilst prices are "expensive", they're "not as extreme as you would expect from such a top-quality place"; P.S. "the lunchtime set menu is amazing value."

Galvin Bistrot de Luxe *French*
25 | **22** | **23** | **£56**

Marylebone | 66 Baker St., W1U 7DJ | 020-7935-4007 | www.galvinrestaurants.com

Brothers Chris and Jeff Galvin's "classy Parisian bistro" on Baker Street serves "sensible portions" of "rich" "French classics", which are "executed with a skilled hand" and distributed by "well-trained staff" in wood-panelled environs dotted with "comfortable" leather banquettes; though costs are "a bit expensive", they're actually "reasonably priced" for the "high standards maintained", especially if you go for the set lunch "deal" and suss out the "good-value bins" on the "excellent wine list."

☑ Galvin La Chapelle *French*
25 | **26** | **24** | **£62**

City | St. Botolph's Hall | 35 Spital Sq., E1 6DY | 020-7299-0400

Galvin Cafe a Vin *French*
City | 35 Spital Sq., E1 6DY | 020-7299-0404
www.galvinrestaurants.com

In a "divine" Victorian former school chapel on Spital Square, gourmets come to "worship" chefs/brothers Chris and Jeff Galvin's "truly sublime" "gourmet" New French dishes, including the "conversation-ceasing" signature Dorset crab lasagna; "charming staff", for whom "nothing is too much trouble", cosset the congregation, which tilts toward a "corporate clientele" expensing the "expensive" (but "worth every pound") bills; P.S. "reasonable prices" and a more casual atmosphere are available in the "superb" adjacent cafe.

The Gate ☒ *Vegetarian/Vegan*
25 | **18** | **22** | **£35**

NEW **Islington** | 370 St. John St., EC1V 4NN | 020-7278-5483 | www.thegaterestaurants.com **Ⓜ**

(continued)

The Gate

Hammersmith | 51 Queen Caroline St., W6 9QL | 020-8748-6932 | www.thegate.tv

"Knowledgeable" staff are "happy to serve you at your own pace" at this "reasonably priced" Hammersmith haunt ("up the wooden stairs" in a former artist's studio), where "creative", "well-presented" vegetarian and vegan dishes leave guests "begging for more"; just know that tables are "close together", so it "can feel like you're eavesdropping" on the trendy, "bohemian" types who frequent it; P.S. a new branch opened post-Survey in Islington.

⊠ Gaucho *Argentinean/Chophouse* | 25 | 22 | 22 | £57 |

Holborn | 125-126 Chancery Ln., WC2A 1PU | 020-7242-7727 ⊠
Piccadilly | 25 Swallow St., W1B 4QR | 020-7734-4040 ◖
Canary Wharf | 29 Westferry Circus, E14 8RR | 020-7987-9494
City | 1 Bell Inn Yard, EC3V 0BL | 020-7626-5180 ⊠
City | 5 Finsbury Ave., EC2M 2PG | 020-7256-6877 ⊠
Farringdon | 93 Charterhouse St., EC1M 6HL | 020-7490-1676 ⊠
Tower Bridge | 2 More London Riverside, SE1 2AP | 020-7407-5222
Hampstead | 64 Heath St., NW3 1DN | 020-7431-8222
Chelsea | 89 Sloane Ave., SW3 3DX | 020-7584-9901
Richmond | The Towpath, TW10 6UJ | 020-8948-4030
www.gauchorestaurants.com
Additional locations throughout London

It's "carnivore heaven" at this "dark", "sexy" chophouse chain whose "chic" "cowhide decor" sets the stage for "amazing" Argentinean steaks, complemented by "excellent sides" and a "wonderful selection of Malbecs"; with a "lively atmosphere" and "solicitous" staff as added boons, it's little surprise that supporters say they "would eat here every week" – if they "could afford" the "pricey" bill.

⊠ Gauthier Soho ⊠ *French* | 28 | 24 | 25 | £60 |

Soho | 21 Romilly St., W1D 5AF | 020-7494-3111 | www.gauthiersoho.co.uk

"An amazing sensory experience" awaits in this "charming, elegant" Soho townhouse where chef-owner Alexis Gauthier's "extraordinary" New French fare is ferried by "professional, cosseting" staff in "several small rooms" spread "over three floors"; "delightful" suggestions from a "wine-pairing genius" will "blow you away", whilst the tasting menu will "leave you on a high" – and best of all, everything comes at a comparatively "great price", particularly the "unbelievable-bargain" lunch and pre-theatre prix fixes.

Gay Hussar ⊠ *Hungarian* | 21 | 20 | 22 | £39 |

Soho | 2 Greek St., W1D 4NB | 020-7437-0973 | www.gayhussar.co.uk

"Steeped in fascinating heritage", this "atmospheric" Soho spot from 1953 presents "glorious" pictures of "patrons past" as a backdrop for "solid", "old-school" Hungarian meals like "hearty goulash" and other "filling" fare (perfect for "winter") washed down with Bull's Blood wine; indeed, you'll eat "extremely well for relatively little", and you'll get "friendly service" in the bargain.

	FOOD	DECOR	SERVICE	COST

Gaylord *Indian*

22 | 18 | 20 | £42

Fitzrovia | 79-81 Mortimer St., W1W 7SJ | 020-7580-3615 | www.gaylordlondon.com

"Imaginative cuisine from the subcontinent" is what's on offer at this "solid", long-time Fitzrovia Indian eatery whose "interesting variety includes lots of fish"; it's "always busy", but "generously spaced" tables in the "traditionally decorated" dining room means it never feels cramped, whilst "friendly staff" ensure everyone is comfortable.

Gazette *French*

20 | 21 | 19 | £31

Battersea | 79 Sherwood Ct., Chatfield Rd., SW11 3UY | 020-7223-0999
Balham | 100 Balham High Rd., SW12 9AA | 020-8772-1232
www.gazettebrasserie.co.uk

"Locals count themselves lucky" to have this pair of brasseries decked out in "typically French" fashion "on their doorstep", as the "classic" cuisine is "delightful" and "good value for money" too; "sweet" service helps to keep it a "lovely place to chill out", whether in the "romantic" interior, on the "nice" patio in Battersea or on the pavement in Balham.

Geales *Seafood*

20 | 14 | 18 | £31

Chelsea | 1 Cale St., SW3 3QT | 020-7965-0555
Notting Hill | 2 Farmer St., W8 7SN | 020-7727-7528
www.geales.com

"Serious about fish 'n' chips, 'n' good at it too" affirm champions of these "poshed-up" chippies in Notting Hill (since 1939) and Chelsea (a relatively recent arrival), where the "delectable" seafood and sides are "fairly priced" and served alongside "some pleasant wines"; service can be "accommodating", whilst the "classic black-and-white settings" are definitely "a bit snug", though "welcoming" nonetheless.

George ⊠ *European*

23 | 23 | 24 | £71

Mayfair | private club | 87-88 Mount St., W1K 2SR | 020-7491-4433 | www.georgeclub.com

"George delivers a first-class product at breakfast, lunch and dinner" say members of this "well-run" private club in Mayfair, which employs "discreet, thoughtful" staff to proffer its Modern European menu; affiliates choose the Hockney-bedecked dining room, the high-energy downstairs bar or the patio ("don't mind the traffic noise"), all reportedly "worth every pound" – and many are needed.

NEW Georgina's *European*

- | - | - | M

Barnes | 56 Barnes High St., SW13 9LF | 020-8166-5559 | www.georginasrestaurants.com

Locally known financial bigwig Nicola Horlick is at the helm of this all-day Barnes arrival, and she's got consulting chef Adam Byatt (Trinity) to design the Modern European menu, which ranges from big, bold salads and pastas to tempting deli treats; the whimsical white- and pastel-hued, triangulated space includes a teeny terrace for alfresco dining, and the prices are moderate.

	FOOD	DECOR	SERVICE	COST

Gessler at Daquise *Polish*

▽ 25 | 19 | 25 | £34

South Kensington | 20 Thurloe St., SW7 2LT | 020-7589-6117 |
www.gessleratdaquise.co.uk

"If there's such a thing as Nouvelle Polish", it can be found at this
South Ken "legend", now operated by a Warsaw-based restaurant
group "putting its best foot forward in London" with "huge portions"
of "succulent" cuisine; contrary to the fare, the art deco dining room
is an "amazing anachronism" "mostly unchanged" since its 1947 debut, and the service is "traditional" too, with toque-sporting chefs
"bringing the food to your table."

Giaconda Dining Room *European*

▽ 24 | 14 | 18 | £42

Soho | 9 Denmark St., WC2H 8LS | 020-7240-3334 |
www.giacondadining.com

The "no-man's-land between Covent Garden and Oxford Street"
harbours this Soho "secret", a "compact", "modest setting"–cum–
"fine-dining experience" with an "excellent husband-and-wife team"
at the helm and "complex", "imaginative" Modern European fare on
the menu; what's more, it's "good value for money", particularly when
factoring in the "great" wine list that includes a "decent selection of
half bottles"; P.S. it was scheduled to close in late-July and reopen
sometime later with double the space.

Giant Robot ❶ *American/Italian*

▽ 17 | 23 | 18 | £26

Clerkenwell | 45-47 Clerkenwell Rd., EC1M 5RS | 020-7065-6810 |
www.gntrbt.com

"High on style" with "not a robot in sight", this "fantastic"-looking,
bare-brick Clerkenwell hangout presents a "tasty, different" and
affordable American-Italian menu on which "meatballs and sliders
feature heavily"; even pickier palates who find the fare only "so-so"
say "go for cocktails" made by "friendly" mixologists at the bar.

Gilbert Scott *British*

18 | 24 | 19 | £63

King's Cross | St. Pancras Renaissance Hotel | Euston Rd., NW1 2AR |
020-7278-3888 | www.thegilbertscott.co.uk

Soaring "gilded" ceilings, pillars and "lovely Victorian" details prove
a "magnificent" backdrop for chef Marcus Wareing's "fascinating"
Traditional British "classics brought up to date" at this St. Pancras
Renaissance Hotel restaurant, named after the 1873 building's ar-
chitect; "attentive" staff offer "sensible" advice, but some feel "the
food does not merit the high prices" – though tipplers recommend
that you should "definitely visit" the bar for "a glass of champagne"
and "elegance beyond belief."

Gilgamesh ❶ *Asian*

20 | 24 | 17 | £50

Camden Town | Stables Mkt. | Chalk Farm Rd., NW1 8AH |
020-7482-5757 | www.gilgameshbar.com

In this "cavernous" setting in Camden's Stables Market, "fantastic",
"opulent decor" featuring "stunning woodwork" sets the scene for
the "different" Pan-Asian creations of chef Ian Pengelley – which
fans find "tasty" but others feel "fall short" considering the "amazing atmosphere" and "pricey" cost; some take issue with "variable

staff" too, yet it's still a magnet for "dates" and "large groups", enticed in part by the "memorable" cocktails.

NEW Gillray's *Chophouse*

- | - | - | E

Waterloo | Marriott Hotel County Hall | Westminster Bridge Rd., SE1 7PB | 020-7902-8000 | www.gillrays.com

Perched near Waterloo station, this pricey new chophouse at the Marriott Hotel County Hall specialises in choice cuts from Hereford cattle reared on the Duke of Devonshire's sprawling Yorkshire estate; the high-ceilinged dining room and gin-centric bar have been given a plush, very English look (chesterfield sofas, chandeliers) to match expansive riverside views highlighting the London Eye and Parliament.

Giovanni's ●🅱 *Italian*

▽ 25 | 22 | 23 | £37

Covent Garden | 10 Goodwin's Ct., WC2N 4LL | 020-7240-2877 | www.giovannislondon.com

The owner "makes you feel like a member of the family", whilst his "friendly", "attentive staff" deliver "wonderful" "old-school" Italian at this "jewel" from 1952 in a "tricky-to-find" corner of Covent Garden; open until 11.30 PM, it's "the perfect after-theatre dinner spot."

Giraffe *Eclectic*

18 | 17 | 19 | £22

Bloomsbury | 19-21 Brunswick Ctr., WC1N 1AF | 020-7812-1336
Marylebone | 6-8 Blandford St., W1U 4AU | 020-7935-2333
Soho | 11 Frith St., W1D 4RB | 020-7494-3491
Shoreditch | Old Spitalfields Mkt. | Crispin St., E1 6HQ | 020-3116-2000
South Bank | Royal Festival Hall | Belvedere Rd., Riverside Level 1, SE1 8XX | 020-7928-2004
Muswell Hill | 348 Muswell Hill Broadway, N10 1DJ | 020-8883-4463
Islington | 29-31 Essex Rd., N1 2SA | 020-7359-5999
Chiswick | 270 Chiswick High Rd., W4 1PD | 020-8995-2100
Holland Park | 120 Holland Park Ave., W11 4UA | 020-7229-8567
Kensington | 7 Kensington High St., W8 5NP | 020-7938-1221
www.giraffe.net
Additional locations throughout London

Like staff who always "have a smile", you must be "family-friendly" to brave this "busy", "funky" all-day cafe chain that's a "go-to" for "yummy mummies, faddy daddies" and their sometimes "screaming" offspring; ok, the Eclectic offerings, including a few "healthy options", are "nothing to get excited about", but the "reasonable prices" sure are, as is the "quick service."

The Glasshouse *European*

27 | 22 | 25 | £58

Richmond | 14 Station Parade, TW9 3PZ | 020-8940-6777 | www.glasshouserestaurant.co.uk

"Ideal for a special night out" or simply after a "visit to Kew Gardens", this "unpretentious" but "refined" Richmond sister of La Trompette produces "assured", "competitively priced" Modern European "cooking of the highest standards", with a menu that changes seasonally; "polished service", an "accomplished wine list" and a "light, sophisticated atmosphere" all cement its "first-class" reputation; P.S. dinner is prix fixe only.

	FOOD	DECOR	SERVICE	COST

Golden Dragon ◐ *Chinese* — 24 | 16 | 17 | £31

Chinatown | 28-29 Gerrard St., W1D 6JW | 020-7734-1073

"Massive portions" of "tasty" dim sum and other "reliable" Chinese fare is the "cheap" deal at this "traditional" Chinatown establishment with a "wide-ranging menu" and "hectic" "school-canteen" atmospherics; there's plenty of room for "family parties" in the "spacious" environs, but this is "not a restaurant where you're encouraged to stay" – in fact, it seems like "not-chummy" staff "can't wait" to "send you packing."

Golden Hind ⓩ *Seafood* — 24 | 11 | 19 | £18

Marylebone | 73 Marylebone Ln., W1U 2PN | 020-7486-3644

"Don't be put off" by the "nondescript" decor of this 99-year-old fryer in Marylebone, as many reckon it's "the golden standard for fish 'n' chips in London", served in "generous portions" and complete with "all the trimmings"; staff are "courteous" and "quick" in equal measure, and whilst the bill is "reasonably priced", the BYO policy (there's a wine shop around the corner) "helps keep the cost down" even further.

Goldmine ◐ *Chinese* — ▽ 25 | 9 | 15 | £33

Bayswater | 102 Queensway, W2 3RR | 020-7792-8331

"If you can bear the crowds" of "large groups" that frequent this Queensway Chinese, you'll be rewarded with its "amazing" signature roast duck, the star amongst "a fairly standard range" of "more-than-acceptable" Cantonese dishes; you'll also have to endure "sometimes surly service" and no-frills decor, but you won't need to spend much money.

The Good Earth *Chinese* — 24 | 20 | 22 | £45

Mill Hill | 143-145 The Broadway, NW7 4RN | 020-8959-7011
Knightsbridge | 233 Brompton Rd., SW3 2EP | 020-7584-3658
www.goodearthgroup.co.uk

"Artfully cooked" dishes, some of which "you won't get elsewhere", "arrive promptly" from "professional" servers who "make you feel looked after" at this "reliable" Chinese duo in Knightsbridge and Mill Hill; sure, it's "a little expensive", but the fact that they've "been there forever" must be a good sign.

Goodman ⓩ *Chophouse* — 26 | 21 | 24 | £60

Mayfair | 26 Maddox St., W1S 1QH | 020-7499-3776
NEW Canary Wharf | Discovery Dock E. | 3 S. Quay, E14 9RU | 020-7531-0300
City | 11 Old Jewry, EC2R 8DU | 020-7600-8220
www.goodmanrestaurants.com

"Three words: awesome, awesome, awesome" say fans of the "well-cooked" American, Irish and Scottish steaks served up alongside "to-die-for" sides and an "extensive matching wine list" at this trio of "smart, masculine" (and "on the noisy side") chophouses; though "quite expensive", it's "worth the money" considering the "high standards" maintained, which extend to "superb" staff who "take the time to explain" the "huge choice" on offer.

Gopal's of Soho ● *Indian*   ▽ 19 | 12 | 20 | £30

Soho | 12 Bateman St., W1D 4AH | 020-7434-0840 |
www.gopalsofsoho.co.uk

"You may not be surprised, but you won't be disappointed" at this "reasonably priced", "old reliable" Indian in Soho; many folks "prefer takeaway", perhaps because they find the environs "a bit tired", but those who opt to eat in are catered for by "ever-so-polite" staff; P.S. late hours make it an "after-theatre" go-to.

☑ Gordon Ramsay at Claridge's *European* 26 | 26 | 26 | £98

Mayfair | Claridge's | 45 Brook St., W1K 4HR | 020-7499-0099 |
www.gordonramsay.com

Gordon Ramsay presents "eating as theatre" at this "dignified" "fine-dining" room at Claridge's, where an "impeccable" "cast of thousands" performs "synchronised" delivery of chef Luke Rayment's "exquisite" Modern European cuisine amidst an "opulent" art deco mise-en-scène; the "brilliant culinary experience" comes complete with plenty of "bells and whistles", an "excellent wine list" on an iPad and "exorbitant" bills that are "worth it" for such "memorable style and panache"; P.S. the lunch prix fixe is "a bargain."

☑ Gordon Ramsay at   28 | 25 | 28 | £122
68 Royal Hospital Rd. ☒ *French*

Chelsea | 68 Royal Hospital Rd., SW3 4HP | 020-7352-4441 |
www.gordonramsay.com

Even those who find Gordon Ramsay "hard to digest personally" "can't fault" his "superb" Chelsea flagship where "admirable" chef Clare Smyth's New French menu boasts "a rare depth and sophistication of flavour" plus "lots of little surprise elements", all of which come via "friendly, precise" service; it's doubly "outstanding" with pairings from the "extensive wine list" (a "brilliant sommelier makes navigating it less daunting") – but the expense is "eye-popping", so "for all the splendour and half the price, go at lunchtime."

Goring Dining Room *British*   25 | 26 | 27 | £74

Victoria | Goring Hotel | 15 Beeston Pl., SW1 0JW | 020-7396-9000 |
www.goringhotel.co.uk

"Prepare to be pampered" at this "outstanding hotel dining room" "a stone's throw from Buckingham Palace", where "long-standing staffers" deliver "superb Traditional British cuisine" and "excellently curated" wines; the "classic setting" is a "model of elegant restraint", though "not as stuffy as you might think", as evidenced by the "freeform" Swarovski chandeliers; in sum, it's the "quintessential high-end experience", complete with a royally "pricey" bill.

☑ Gourmet Burger Kitchen *Burgers*   21 | 15 | 17 | £17

Covent Garden | 13-14 Maiden Ln., WC2E 7NE | 020-7240-9617
Hampstead | 200 Haverstock Hill, NW3 2AG | 020-7443-5335
Hampstead | 331 West End Ln., NW6 1RS | 020-7794-5455
Clapham | 44 Northcote Rd., SW11 1NZ | 020-7228-3309
Fulham | 49 Fulham Broadway, SW6 1AE | 020-7381-4242
Putney | 333 Putney Bridge Rd., SW15 2PG | 020-8789-1199

(continued)

Gourmet Burger Kitchen

Richmond | 15-17 Hill Rise, TW10 6UQ | 020-8940-5440
Wimbledon | 88 The Broadway, SW19 1RH | 020-8540-3300
Bayswater | 50 Westbourne Grove, W2 5SH | 020-7243-4344
Chiswick | 131 Chiswick High Rd., W4 2ED | 020-8995-4548
www.gbk.co.uk
Additional locations throughout London

"Burger fiends" cite this counter-serve, "cafeteria-style" chain's "epic" patties, "from meat to veg to bunless", with an "excellent range of toppings", "chunky chips" and "fantastic", "enormous milkshakes"; bills are "affordable", but to drive them down even further, "sign up" for the many "special offers."

NEW Granger & Co. *Australian/Eclectic* | 18 | 17 | 14 | £37 |

Notting Hill | 175 Westbourne Grove, W11 2SB | 020-7229-9111 | www.grangerandco.com

Australian celeb chef "Bill Granger brings Sydney to Notting Hill" in the form of this pastel-hued, airy "new 'it' place" where the "original" Eclectic dishes with "great Aussie style" are doled out in "generous portions" ("breakfast here is staggeringly good"); early reports suggest "haphazard" service and "perpetual queues" ("no reservations"), but that doesn't prevent curious foodies from braving "long waits" for one of the "jam-packed" tables.

Gravetye Manor Restaurant *British* | ▽ 23 | 25 | 23 | £77 |

East Grinstead | Gravetye Manor | Vowels Ln. | 01342-810-567 | www.gravetyemanor.co.uk

An over 400-year-old Gothic manor and its "beautiful", historically pertinent gardens form the "picturesque setting" of this Sussex hotel eatery whose "traditional" oak-panelled dining room offers "excellent" Modern British fare and "impeccable service"; the atmosphere "could not be more romantic", so "save your pennies", "drink too much" from the impressive wine list and "spend the night."

Grazing Goat *British* | 21 | 20 | 20 | £39 |

Marylebone | Public House & Hotel | 6 New Quebec St., W1 7RQ | 020-7724-7243 | www.thegrazinggoat.co.uk

In the "no-man's land" between Edgware Road and Oxford Street, this "relaxed" (though occasionally "noisy") all-day country-house-style gastropub with eight hotel rooms above offers "tasty" Traditional Brit "classics" to mostly "younger patrons"; "decent wines" and "friendly staff" add to surveyors' "satisfaction", and the prices are "ok" too.

Great Eastern Dining Room ●⊠ *Asian* | 19 | 17 | 13 | £40 |

Shoreditch | 54-56 Great Eastern St., EC2A 3QR | 020-7613-4545 | www.rickerrestaurants.com

Though its decor may be "getting a bit knackered", this "old-school" Shoreditch nightspot is still "a safe choice" for a "champagne-fuelled evening" with "a bunch of friends" or "a date" accompanied by "stylish" Pan-Asian plates and "funky music courtesy of a DJ"; too bad service can be "sloppy", but at least the bartenders do "a bang-up job."

| | FOOD | DECOR | SERVICE | COST |

Great Queen Street *British*
24 | 16 | 21 | £35

Covent Garden | 32 Great Queen St., WC2B 5AA | 020-7242-0622
"Stonking", "gutsy" Modern Brit fare "highlighting local ingredients" "never fails to wow" at this "bustling", "homey", "dark-wood" gastro-pub, an Anchor & Hope sibling "a short stroll" from Covent Garden theatres; there's a separate bar downstairs that's "reminiscent of an old-fashioned gentleman's club", whilst "friendly, informed service" and "good value" are found throughout.

The Greenhouse ⊠ *French*
26 | 26 | 26 | £88

Mayfair | 27 Hay's Mews, W1J 5NY | 020-7499-3331 |
www.greenhouserestaurant.co.uk
Offering "a moment of calm and luxury", this "discreet" New French down a "magical garden path" in a "chic corner of Mayfair" "makes you feel special" with "graceful" staff orchestrating an "amazing gastronomic experience"; it all "comes at a price" of course, but devotees insist "it doesn't get much better than this" for "celebrating a special occasion"; P.S. the "extensive wine list is perhaps one of the best in London."

Green's Restaurant & Oyster Bar ⊠ *British/Seafood*
22 | 20 | 23 | £59

St. James's | 36 Duke St., SW1Y 6DF | 020-7930-4566
City | 14 Cornhill, EC3V 3ND | 020-7220-6300
www.greens.org.uk
Conjuring up the feel of a "gentleman's club" with mahogany panelling, leather banquettes and "impeccable service", this "dependable" St. James's venue and its City cousin offer a "quintessential old-school" Traditional British experience as well as "splendid seafood" that's "not painful to the purse" ("for the quality"); the setting's "general hush" is ideal for "private conversation", a boon for "business lunching", whilst the bar might be a bit livelier, with its martinis and oysters that "never fail."

Greig's ● *Chophouse*
∇ 21 | 20 | 21 | £43

Mayfair | 26 Bruton Pl., W1J 6NG | 020-7629-5613 |
www.greigs.com
"Huge" "dependable" steaks are served up by staff who "care about making you welcome" at this chophouse with "old-fashioned" wood panelling, stained glass and a "superb" location "near Berkeley Square"; however, critics find it too "expensive" for being what they deem simply "average."

Grenadier *British*
18 | 22 | 19 | £34

Belgravia | 18 Wilton Row, SW1X 7NR | 020-7235-3074
"Loaded with military memorabilia", corresponding to its past as the Duke of Wellington's Grenadiers' mess, this "tiny" pub "hidden" in a Belgravia mews draws many "tourists" and some "locals" ("whose Aston Martins and Bentleys line" the nearby streets) for its "great beef Wellington" and other "reasonably priced" Traditional British dishes; "charming staff" add to its reputation as a "great place", "even if for just a pint" or a Bloody Mary at the pewter bar.

	FOOD	DECOR	SERVICE	COST

Groucho Club *British*
FOOD 18 | DECOR 18 | SERVICE 20 | COST £50

Soho | private club | 45 Dean St., W1D 4QB | 020-7439-4685 |
www.thegrouchoclub.com

Members of this "exclusive" Soho private club say "don't expect the debauchery that made the place famous", but do count on "expensive", "well-cooked" Modern Brit fare served alongside a "good wine list" in a brasserie, dining room and several bar areas; so even if it's "not in its heyday", it's "still cool" – and "more about seeing and being seen" amongst "showbiz" types than anything else.

Grumbles *British/French*
▽ 19 | 16 | 21 | £29

Pimlico | 35 Churton St., SW1V 2LT | 020-7834-0149 |
www.grumblesrestaurant.co.uk

"Friendly" staff provide "lovely service" at this "charming", "unpretentious" "little" Pimlico bistro where "noisy" crowds "squash" in for "tasty, hearty" Traditional British fare that's "French in style"; bargain-hunters recommend you "stick to the fixed-price menu and drink the house wine", but even if you go à la carte, count on "excellent value."

Guinea Grill ⊠ *Chophouse*
24 | 19 | 21 | £55

Mayfair | 30 Bruton Pl., W1J 6NL | 020-7499-1210 | www.theguinea.co.uk

"Old-school in the best sense", this "darkly lit" chophouse behind a same-named pub in a "charming" Mayfair mews has "been around forever" (1953), plying locals and their "foreign guests" with "luscious", "cooked-to-perfection steaks" and "wonderful" savoury pies; the prices are a tad "crazy" and seating is a bit "cramped", but much is forgiven thanks to staff who "make you feel that you are welcome."

The Gun *British*
23 | 22 | 21 | £42

Canary Wharf | 27 Coldharbour, E14 9NS | 020-7515-5222 |
www.thegundocklands.com

"Cosy up inside by the log fire in winter" and enjoy Thames views from the "wonderful terrace" in summer at this "old-world" Canary Wharf "escape" offering "reliable" Modern British gastropub fare (including "an incredible Sunday roast"), plus a "solid wine list" and "friendly service"; despite being "a little pricey", "romantics" are drawn in droves, so "you definitely need to reserve a table at busy times."

Haandi *Indian*
21 | 16 | 20 | £33

Knightsbridge | 7 Cheval Pl., SW7 1EW | 020-7823-7373 |
www.haandi-restaurants.com

"On a quiet side street steps from Harrods", this "pleasant" yellow basement might be "overlooked because of its hard-to-find entrance", but those who spot it discover "tasty", sometimes "unusual" North Indian specials, prepared in a glass-fronted kitchen and served in "friendly" fashion; it's "not fancy", but then neither are the prices; P.S. it's part of a small chain with locations in Kampala and Nairobi.

Haché *Burgers*
22 | 18 | 19 | £23

Camden Town | 24 Inverness St., NW1 7HJ | 020-7485-9100
NEW **Clapham** | 153 Clapham High St., SW4 7SS | 020-7738-8760

(continued)

(continued)

Haché

Chelsea | 329-331 Fulham Rd., SW10 9QL | 020-7823-3515
www.hacheburgers.com

"A vast selection" of "juicy, flavoursome" patties made from "every possible ingredient" (beef, lamb, chicken, veggies and more) "satiate burger cravings" at this "welcoming" trio that also doles out "nicely presented" sides; "fairy lights" lend "soul" to the setting, whilst "informative, friendly" servers and "reasonable prices" help to keep the vibe "relaxed."

Z Hakkasan ● Chinese

| 26 | 26 | 21 | £67 |

Fitzrovia | 8 Hanway Pl., W1T 1HD | 020-7927-7000
Mayfair | 17 Bruton St., W1J 6QB | 020-7907-1888
www.hakkasan.com

"Dark, sexy" and "sleek", these "raucous" Fitzrovia and Mayfair haunts are likened to a "James Bond villain's hideaway" – but there's nothing dastardly on the menu, just "incredible, inventive" Cantonese dishes and "divine cocktails" from the "ultracool bar"; however, many find the "table turning" (there's "a strict two hour time limit") by the otherwise "polished, young staff" a bit "aggressive", which is doubly "annoying" considering the "exaggerated" prices.

Halepi ● Greek

| 24 | 15 | 21 | £38 |

Bayswater | 18 Leinster Terr., W2 3ET | 020-7262-1070 | www.halepi.co.uk

"My big fat Greek favourite!" exclaim "regulars" who "delight" in the "huge portions" of "affordable", "lip-smacking" Hellenic fare served in "efficient" fashion at this "buzzing, informal" Bayswater "stalwart"; the interior "could do with a little smartening up" and it's "so cramped that sardines would be upset", but even so, that's "part of the charm."

Haozhan ● Chinese

| 25 | 16 | 20 | £31 |

Chinatown | 8 Gerrard St., W1D 5PJ | 020-7434-3838 |
www.haozhan.co.uk

"Exotic twists" abound on the "well-executed" Chinese menu, which includes a number of "destination dishes" and prices that are a "fraction of the cost" of some other "high-end" competitors, at this minimalist Chinatown "find"; the "service may not be as sophisticated as the food", but it "means well", and it's "swift" to boot.

Harbour City ● Chinese

| ▽ 21 | 14 | 15 | £24 |

Chinatown | 46 Gerrard St., W1D 5QH | 020-7439-7859

"Delicious" dim sum and other "quality" dishes take diners "back to the days of the old Chinatown" at this Cantonese spot where it's all about "no fuss, good food"; there might be "not much space between the tables and chairs" and service is merely "ok", yet all three of its "pleasant" floors are almost always "busy."

Hard Rock Cafe ● American

| 17 | 22 | 19 | £33 |

Piccadilly | 150 Old Park Ln., W1K 1QZ | 020-7629-0382 |
www.hardrock.com

It may be a bit "cheesy", but the "awesome" "rock 'n' roll memorabilia", "loud music" and "lively atmosphere" make this Piccadilly original of the international chain "worth a visit" – or so say the "crowds" of "teenagers and tourists" "waiting outside"; the burgers and other American eats may be "generic", but they're "tasty" enough, plus they come in "large" portions, via "friendly service" and with a bill that "isn't too overpriced."

Hare & Tortoise *Japanese*   22 | 16 | 16 | £24

Bloomsbury | 11-13 Brunswick Ctr., WC1N 1AF | 020-7278-9799
City | 90 New Bridge St., EC4V 6JJ | 020-7651-0266 🖂
Putney | 296-298 Upper Richmond Rd., SW15 6TH | 020-8394-7666
Ealing | 38-39 Haven Green, W5 2NX | 020-8810-7066
Kensington | 373 Kensington High St., W14 8QZ | 020-7603-8887
www.hareandtortoise.co.uk

"Shockingly decent prices" have "students" and "shoppers" flocking to this chain of "canteens" offering a "great choice" of "delicious" Japanese dishes, including "huge" noodle bowls and "solid" sushi; the "service can be curt" and the decor "a bit clinical", yet it remains a "'reliable" choice for an "easy", "quick and convenient" meal.

Harry's Bar ●🖂 *Italian*   25 | 24 | 25 | £82

Mayfair | private club | 26 S. Audley St., W1K 2PD |
020-7408-0844 | www.harrysbar.co.uk

"The chauffeur-driven Bentleys waiting outside" tell you all you need to know about "the rich and famous" clientele who are members of this "beautiful" private club in Mayfair, where "personalised service" conveys "excellent Italian-influenced cuisine"; by all means "beg, borrow, steal or bribe your way in", just make sure "someone else is paying" – it's so "wildly expensive", there must be "gold in the food."

🖸 Harwood Arms *British*   28 | 21 | 23 | £43

Fulham | Walham Grove, SW6 1QP | 020-7386-1847 |
www.harwoodarms.com

You'll "never be able to eat shop-bought Scotch eggs again" after sampling the "triumphant" versions whipped up at this "next-level" Fulham gastropub where the entire Modern British menu is "phenomenal", especially the "to-die-for game dishes", all at prices so "reasonable" you can "bring the whole family along"; "friendly" staff work the "rustic, airy" digs, which are "deservedly popular" – and downright "packed" "when Chelsea is playing" (always "book ahead").

🖸 Hawksmoor *Chophouse*   26 | 21 | 23 | £58

Covent Garden | 11 Langley St., WC2H 9JG | 020-7856-2154
NEW **City** | Guildhall | 10 Basinghall St., EC2V 5BQ | 020-7397-8120 🖂
Shoreditch | 157 Commercial St., E1 6BJ | 020-7246-4850
www.thehawksmoor.com

"Massive", "oozingly succulent steaks" come seemingly "straight from heaven" at these "classy", "atmospheric" chophouses "buzzing" with "carnivores" who wash down the manna with "imaginative", "seriously sexy cocktails" mixed by bartenders who, like the rest of the "brilliant" staff, are "at the top of their game"; the "dark", "old-school", "masculine" interiors inevitably attract "gentlemen dressed in suits", the type with "buoyant wallets" that can handle the "expensive" bill.

				FOOD	DECOR	SERVICE	COST

Haz ● *Turkish*
23 | 20 | 22 | £28

City | 112 Houndsditch, EC3A 7BD | 020-7623-8180 ☒
City | 34 Foster Ln., EC2V 6HD | 020-7515-9467
City | 6 Mincing Ln., EC3M 3BD | 020-7929-3173
City | 9 Cutler St., E1 7DJ | 020-7929-7923
www.hazrestaurant.co.uk

Hazev Canary Wharf ● *Turkish*
Canary Wharf | Discovery Dock W. | 2 S. Quay, E14 9RT |
020-7515-9467 | www.hazev.com

"Fantastic", "tender" char-grilled meats are the highlights of these "reliable" Turkish delights scattered around the City and Canary Wharf, but even vegetarians think they're "divine"; though the settings are "a bit noisy", that's because they're so "popular" (particularly at lunchtime), with "lovely" decor, "helpful", "quick service" and "reasonable prices" as further enticements.

NEW Hedone ☒Ⓜ *European*
22 | 20 | 21 | £72

Chiswick | 301-303 Chiswick High Rd., W4 4HH | 020-8747-0377 |
www.hedonerestaurant.com

"London needs more people like" Mikael Jonsson, the "discerning" Swedish chef-owner who prepares "fascinating", "adventurous" Modern Euro fare at this "welcome addition" to Chiswick, with bare-brick walls, an open kitchen and a ceiling decorated with caveman-style images; even those who think the fare is "not quite there yet" are optimistic about its "real promise", if not the "expensive" bill.

Hélène Darroze
at the Connaught ☒Ⓜ *French*
25 | 26 | 25 | £117

Mayfair | Connaught | Carlos Pl., W1K 2AL | 020-7107-8880 |
www.the-connaught.co.uk

"Like a fine Savile Row suit", this "superb" Hélène Darroze experience at The Connaught "will spoil you completely for much else" with its "exquisite", "refined" Classic French cuisine and "polished, attentive" service; factor in a wood-panelled, "lap-of-luxury" setting that's "one of the loveliest in London", and no wonder most insist that it "actually feels worth" the "bank-breaking" expense; P.S. for "excellent value", choose the three-course set lunch.

Hereford Road *British*
25 | 19 | 22 | £47

Notting Hill | 3 Hereford Rd., W2 4AB | 020-7727-1144 |
www.herefordroad.org

The "exquisitely sourced", "market-driven" dishes "make you proud to be British" at this "fantastic" Notting Hill "gem" whose "surprising" menu majors in meat and offal; the space, a former Victorian butcher's shop, and the service are both described as "über-hip", whilst the prices are portrayed as both "expensive" and "great value."

Hibiscus ☒ *French*
26 | 22 | 26 | £81

Mayfair | 29 Maddox St., W1S 2PA | 020-7629-2999 |
www.hibiscusrestaurant.co.uk

"Life-changing" gasp admirers of the "ingenious" "experimental style" chef Claude Bosi employs in his "magnificent" New French fare, which is "beautifully presented" by "fantastic", "formal" staff at this "swish", "quiet" Mayfair destination; for a "bargain", come at lunch and order the "excellent" set menu, but to be "bowled over", get the "amazing" dinnertime tasting menu with wine pairings – it's "worth sacrificing your retirement savings" for.

High Road Brasserie *European*

| 22 | 22 | 19 | £43 |

Chiswick | High Road Hse. | 162-166 Chiswick High Rd., W4 1PR | 020-8742-7474 | www.highroadhouse.co.uk

To the delight of "Nappyland" trendies, "you don't have to be a member to enjoy" this "lovely, bright" and "efficient" Modern European brasserie underneath Nick Jones' Chiswick hotel and private club; in fact, they say they could eat the "reliable", "frequently changing" fare "every night and still want to come in for lunch", which along with the "reasonable prices", explains why it's "always packed."

The Hinds Head *British*

| 24 | 21 | 22 | £49 |

Bray | High St., Berkshire | 01628-626 151 | www.hindsheadbray.co.uk

"More affordable, down-to-earth" and easier to book than The Fat Duck, this "historic", "atmospheric" Bray pub offers chef Heston Blumenthal's "brilliant" "modern interpretations" of Traditional British fare, which feature "obsessive attention to detail" and "plenty of unexpected twists"; service "checks every box, from the moment you enter to the gracious farewell", which only adds to an already "amazing" lunch" or "great evening out."

Hi Sushi *Japanese*

| 20 | 18 | 17 | £27 |

Covent Garden | 27 Catherine St., WC2B 5JS | 020-7836-9398 | www.hisushi.net
Soho | 40 Frith St., W1D 5LN | 020-7734-9688
Camden Town | 28 Jamestown Rd., NW1 7BY | 020-7482-7088 | www.hisushi.net
Finchley | 830 High Rd., N12 9RA | 020-8446-9808 | www.restaurantprivilege.com
Golders Green | 628 Finchley Rd., NW11 7RR | 020-8201-8585 | www.hisushi.net

"A great selection" of "fresh and delicious" Japanese fare is "quickly delivered" at this local chain with "pleasant" decor; but it's "fantastic value for money" that's the real draw, with "big portions" (e.g. ramen bowls that are "Godzilla-sized"), "bargain bento boxes" and an "all-you-can-eat sushi" option.

Hix *British*

| 22 | 19 | 20 | £54 |

Soho | 66-70 Brewer St., W1F 9UT | 020-7292-3518 | www.hixsoho.co.uk

Chef-owner Mark Hix's "trendy" Soho destination turns out Modern British cuisine that is sometimes "simple", sometimes "daring", always "bang-on" and "rather expensive"; "service is easy and knowing", whilst the "slick", "contemporary art"–bedecked setting can be rather "noisy" – but that sort of "bustling" atmosphere appeals to its "hipster" habitués, especially the "cool downstairs bar", a "late-night" "scene unto itself" complete with "mad-scientist barmen and great alchemic cocktails."

Hix at the Albemarle *British*

| 25 | 25 | 24 | £61 |

Mayfair | Brown's Hotel | 30-34 Albemarle St., W1S 4BP |
020-7518-4004 | www.thealbemarlerestaurant.com

Artwork by Tracey Emin, Michael Landy, Bridget Riley and more give
this "traditional" Brown's Hotel dining room a "fantastic" "contemporary twist", though the "quality" victuals from the Hix stable are
"classic British" (they're "expensive" too); "polished" staff glide
between the "well-spaced" tables (hurrah, "you can hear" your
companions!) as they make the "beautiful mix of Euros and South
Americans" "feel very well looked after."

NEW Hix Belgravia *Eclectic*

| - | - | - | E |

Belgravia | Belgraves Hotel | Pont St., SW1X 9EJ | 020-3189-4850 |
www.hixbelgravia.co.uk

Eschewing its siblings' trademark functional look, this venue from
Mark Hix is set in a bright, grey-hued corner berth of the new boutique Belgraves Hotel; in the same vein, the chef has put aside his
signature British culinary style in favor of an urbane, upscale all-day
Eclectic menu that reflects his world travels; meanwhile, a second
branch of Mark's Bar re-creates everything cocktail fans enjoy about
the Soho original.

Hix Oyster & Chop House *British/Chophouse*

| 24 | 21 | 23 | £52 |

Farringdon | 36-37 Greenhill's Rents, EC1M 6BN | 020-7017-1930 |
www.hixoysterandchophouse.co.uk

When "the decor's so simple", "the place must have a lot of confidence in its food", and that confidence is not misplaced at Mark Hix's
Traditional Brit set in a former Smithfield sausage factory, where
"hearty portions" of "wonderful" chophouse classics are offered
alongside "delicious seafood" ("on the expensive side" but "reasonable for the location"); it's "always full", so if you "drop in without a
reservation", see if "intelligent staff" can seat you at the bar, home
to "impressive" wines.

Honest Burgers *Burgers*

| ▽ 27 | 19 | 21 | £14 |

Brixton | Brixton Village Market | 12 Brixton Vill., SW9 8PR |
020-7733-7963 | www.honestburgers.co.uk

"Tucked away in Brixton Village Market", this "delightful find" griddles
up "simply fantastic", "affordable" burgers made of dry-aged beef
from The Ginger Pig butchers alongside veggie options and upmarket
sides like "excellent" rosemary salt chips and fennel slaw; with only
30 tables, the slightly "scruffy" converted-garage setting "can be a
bit crowded", though "friendly staff" turn tables fast (no bookings).

Hot Stuff *Indian*

| ▽ 26 | 11 | 25 | £17 |

Vauxhall | 19 Wilcox Rd., SW8 2XA | 020-7720-1480 |
www.eathotstuff.com

Trusting foodies feel the Indian fare made at this spot "tucked away" in
a Vauxhall side street is so universally "fragrant and richly flavoured",
they "don't even look at the menu", instead asking the "lovely staff" to
"bring what they recommend"; the already "superb value" is bolstered

by BYOB (there's a "handy" wine shop next door) if they can "fit you in" the "tiny premises", whilst "takeaway is brilliant" if they can't.

Hoxton Grill ● _American_   22 | 20 | 21 | £35

Hoxton | Hoxton Hotel | 81 Great Eastern St., EC2A 3HU | 020-7739-9111 | www.hoxtongrill.com

"Good-value" all-day American fare featuring "amazing" steaks and "solid" "comfort food" (wings, burgers) is dished out all day by "friendly" staffers to punters who pack the red-leather banquettes at this "lovely", "cosy", bare-brick diner in Hoxton Hotel; at night, it's a "trendy" destination where the "post-work crowd" can down "great martinis" until 2 AM, and it's a notable brunch spot too, thanks in part to "cracking Bloody Marys."

Hoxton Square ● _Tex-Mex_   17 | 19 | 16 | £30

Hoxton | 2-4 Hoxton Sq., N1 6NU | 020-7613-0709 | www.hoxtonsquarebar.com

"Hip" Hoxton residents go to this "cool" Tex-Mex–themed bar and restaurant with "plenty of space to spread out" and "people-watch" while listening to live bands or DJs and quaffing "good drinks"; the "food isn't amazing, but the atmosphere makes up for it", and for just a reasonably priced, "quick bite", it's "decent."

☑ Hunan ☒ _Chinese_   28 | 13 | 22 | £57

Pimlico | 51 Pimlico Rd., SW1W 8NE | 020-7730-5712 | www.hunanlondon.com

"Surrender yourself to the whim of the chef" and his "welcoming" son, because at this "unusual" Pimlico Chinese, "you don't choose", you just tell them "what you don't want" before they send "a relentless parade of genuinely exciting", "unusually spiced" Hunan small plates "until you wave the white flag"; oenophiles cite the "strong wine list", while aesthetes don't mind that the "1980s" "atmosphere is not impressive", fearing that "at some point they will update the decor" and "double the prices."

Hush ☒ _European_   21 | 20 | 21 | £47

NEW **Holborn** | 95-97 High Holborn, WC1V 6LF | 020-7242-4580 | www.hushbrasseries.com Ⓜ
Mayfair | 8 Lancashire Ct., W1S 1EY | 020-7659-1500 | www.hush.co.uk

"When the wife is shopping on Bond Street", "jet-setting hedge funders" make their way to this virtually "hidden" brasserie (with a similar new Holborn offshoot) for "solid" Modern Euro fare – "affordable" for Mayfair – or just a cocktail in the "plush" first-floor bar; service "strikes the balance between warm and formal" whether inside or out in the "cobbled" courtyard, just "lovely in the summer."

Iberica _Spanish_   23 | 21 | 21 | £43

Marylebone | 195 Great Portland St., W1W 5PS | 020-7636-8650 ●
Canary Wharf | 12 Cabot Sq., E14 4QQ | 020-7636-8650
www.ibericalondon.co.uk

Like the "handsome" staff, the "wonderful" tapas are "the stuff of fantasy" at this pair of "lively, modern", "upmarket" Spaniards in

Marylebone and Canary Wharf, where both "old standards" and more "unusual" options are "lovingly prepared"; in fact, there are "so many tempting" dishes, not to mention "stunning" wines and "excellent" sherries, the bill can "easily become expensive" – though some find the value "incredible" regardless.

Ikeda ⊠ Japanese | ∇ 27 | 14 | 23 | £72 |

Mayfair | 30 Brook St., W1K 5DJ | 020-7629-2730 | www.ikedarestaurant.co.uk

"Wow, wow, wow" exclaim fans who claim you could "order anything on the menu" and "be happy" at this small but "spectacular" Mayfair Japanese presenting both sushi and hot dishes; despite decor that "probably hasn't changed since it opened", most find the "very expensive" costs justified because there's always a "surprise" to be found – and kimono-clad waitresses to intrigue.

Il Baretto Italian | 22 | 18 | 19 | £53 |

Marylebone | 43 Blandford St., W1U 7HF | 020-7486-7340 | www.ilbaretto.co.uk

"Lively basement dining" is the deal at this spot "next to Baker Street" tube, where "reliable Italian" fare comes in "pleasant" surrounds via "variable" service (though regulars rate it "mostly good"); a number of surveyors say "the bill turns out to be a little more expensive than you expected", though there's some "great value" to be found, namely in the pizzas; P.S. the "cosy ground-floor bar" is its own draw.

Il Bordello Italian | 24 | 19 | 24 | £34 |

Wapping | 81 Wapping High St., E1W 2YN | 020-7481-9950

Even those who "don't live close" to this Wapping site say it's worth "hailing a cab" for wood-fired pizzas that "taste like they do in Naples" and other Italian standards served in portions designed "to fatten you up", and for "reasonable prices"; add in "experienced", "good-humoured" staff who make everyone "feel special", and you understand why "it's always packed."

Il Convivio ⊠ Italian | 23 | 21 | 21 | £49 |

Belgravia | 143 Ebury St., SW1W 9QN | 020-7730-4099 | www.etruscarestaurants.com

"Beautifully presented" pastas that are "delicious down to the last detail" and an extensive wine list make this Belgravia Italian a "reliable" (if "pricey") choice; the "welcoming" service and "cosy", "civilised" vibe inside a Georgian house are fitting for a "romantic meal", while the set-price menu is "sensible" for a "quiet business lunch."

Il Portico ⊠ Italian | 20 | 16 | 24 | £46 |

Kensington | 277 Kensington High St., W8 6NA | 020-7602-6262 | www.ilportico.co.uk

Even "fussy" folks approve of this "old-fashioned", "family-run" Italian in Kensington, which has been dishing up "decent portions" of regional eats "cooked with heart and soul" since the '60s; it's "kid-friendly" too, with "gracious" staff who treat guests "like regulars", compensating for "crowded, cramped" conditions (indeed, "booking is essential").

	FOOD	DECOR	SERVICE	COST

Imli *Indian*
22 | 17 | 19 | £29

Soho | 167-169 Wardour St., W1F 8WR | 020-7287-4243 | www.imli.co.uk

"A lovely alternative to a full-on heavy Indian meal", the "huge spread" of "tasty" "tapas-style" plates at this colourful, "modern" Soho cafe is "perfect for large groups" or "catching a snack" after shopping on nearby Oxford Street; if some feel its "overpriced" considering the "mean" portions, others find the cost "reasonable", especially when factoring in "polite" service.

Imperial China ● *Chinese*
22 | 19 | 19 | £36

Chinatown | 25 Lisle St., WC2H 7BA | 020-7734-3388 | www.imperial-china.co.uk

Hop across a footbridge to this "elegant" "oasis of calm in frantic Chinatown" to feast on "generous helpings" of "moreish" dim sum and a "wide choice" of Cantonese mains whose "price is fair considering the quality"; though a few complain of "long queues", "helpful, efficient" staff keep things moving.

Imperial City ⌧ *Chinese*
∇ 21 | 20 | 21 | £45

City | Royal Exchange, EC3V 3LL | 020-7626-3437 | www.orientalrestaurantgroup.co.uk

With its dramatic arched dining room and "great location" in the basement of the Royal Exchange, this "pricey" Chinese is an "old favourite" amongst the City crowd, especially for "business lunches"; what's more, the "wonderful, spicy" aromatic duck and other "tasty" dishes are matched by equally commendable service.

Inamo ● *Asian*
20 | 23 | 18 | £41

Soho | 134-136 Wardour St., W1F 8ZP | 020-7851-7051 | www.inamo-restaurant.com
St. James's | 4-12 Regent St., SW1Y 4PE | 020-7484-0500 | www.inamo-stjames.com

Order via your "innovative" "computerised table" then play "clever" video games whilst you wait for the "tasty" Asian fusion dishes to be delivered (usually "quickly") at these "funky", "kitschy" spots in Soho and St. James's; however, many say the "novelty wears off" when the "minuscule" portions arrive, followed by a "substantial" bill – but perhaps it's "worth the experience" "at least once."

Incognico ⌧ *French/Italian*
22 | 20 | 22 | £47

Soho | 117 Shaftesbury Ave., WC2H 8AD | 020-7836-8866 | www.incognico.com

"Reliable" French-Italian fare, an "interesting wine list" and "smart surroundings" make this "casual" Soho spot a welcome option; "attentive" but "unobtrusive" staff "get you out on time for the show", and "special deals" can help keep the tab "reasonable."

Indian Zing *Indian*
25 | 20 | 22 | £40

Hammersmith | 236 King St., W6 0RF | 020-8748-5959 | www.indianzing.co.uk

"Modern takes on traditional Indian food" bring "real pizzazz" to this "relaxed", upscale "gem" "tucked away" in Hammersmith, a white-tablecloth affair with a "strong wine list" and prices that are only slightly "expensive"; "charming", "attentive" staff are another reason fans feel it's "worth a trip" from afar, particularly for the "fabulous lunch deal."

Indigo *European*

23 | 23 | 23 | £45

Covent Garden | One Aldwych Hotel | 1 Aldwych, WC2B 4RH | 020-7300-0400 | www.onealdwych.com

Whether you stop by for the "excellent" weekend brunch or a "pre-theatre dinner", you'll find "pleasant" staff at this "comfortable", "contemporary" Modern European overlooking the "beautiful lobby bar" in Covent Garden's One Aldwych Hotel – and it's "not too expensive for the location"; most say that the "noise level is manageable", arguing it adds to the "brilliant atmosphere", whilst those who find it "overwhelming" recommend a seat a little further back.

Inn the Park *British*

18 | 19 | 16 | £45

St. James's | St. James's Park | St. James's Park, SW1A 2BJ | 020-7451-9999 | www.innthepark.com

A "charming" location with "great views all around" gets "tourists" to "pack" this minimalist wooden pavilion in the centre of St. James's Park, especially "during the summer" when the "terrace is wonderful"; as for the Traditional British menu, critics call it a touch "overpriced" (exacerbated by "nothing-special" service), though it does offer "healthy, delicious choices", "fab cocktails" and afternoon tea that's "a must."

Ishbilia ● *Lebanese*

25 | 16 | 20 | £38

Belgravia | 9 William St., SW1X 9HL | 020-7235-7788 | www.ishbilia.com

Ignore the "dull surroundings" of this Belgravia Lebanese and focus on the "beautiful plate of fresh vegetables" set on each table, a harbinger of the "excellent", "beautifully presented" fare yet to come; service is "proficient", but its best aspect is probably the prices – "compared to other nearby options", it's "a real bargain."

Ishtar ● *Turkish*

21 | 17 | 20 | £29

Marylebone | 10-12 Crawford St., W1U 6AZ | 020-7224-2446 | www.ishtarrestaurant.com

"After shopping on Marylebone High Street", fuel up on "fantastic" charcoal-cooked fare at this "busy" Turk boasting "affordable" prices and a "warm welcome" from "helpful" staff; simple chandeliers and red drapes in the "casual" quarters provide the backdrop for "stunning" live music and belly dancing that make for "a complete evening out" at the weekend, though it's "generally a fun place to be" at any time.

Itsu *Japanese*

19 | 15 | 16 | £23

Chelsea | 118 Draycott Ave., SW3 3AE | 020-7590-2400
Notting Hill | 100 Notting Hill Gate, W11 3QA | 020-7229-4016
www.itsu.com

"Conveyor belt sushi" and other Japanese options that "help you keep an eye on your caloric intake" "without compromising on taste" are what's on offer at these "fun", "funky" Chelsea and Notting Hill haunts, ull-service versions of the same-named "quick" takeaway shops around the city; service is so-so and it's easy to "rack up one heck of a bill without realising it", but "if you're sick of eating bread at lunch-ime", it's an "addictive" alternative.

☑ The Ivy ❶ *British/European* `24` `23` `24` `£70`

Covent Garden | 1-5 West St., WC2H 9NQ | 020-7836-4751 | www.the-ivy.co.uk

For a "special occasion" laced with "class" and "elegance", "book well in advance" at this "iconic" Covent Garden "'in' place" where "attentive but unobtrusive" staff serve "consistent-as-they-come" Modern British–Euro dishes to a "trendy" crowd; as for the cost, whilst the well-heeled call it "reasonable for such a famous venue", others quip "even the Queen couldn't afford to eat here more than once a month"; P.S. "the real A-listers are in the private club upstairs."

☑ Jamie's Italian *Italian* `20` `20` `19` `£34`

Covent Garden | St. Martin's Courtyard | 11 Upper St. Martin's Ln., WC2H 9FB | 020-3326-6390 ❶

NEW Stratford | Westfield Stratford City | 2 Stratford Pl., E20 1EN | 020-3535-8063

Canary Wharf | 2 Churchill Pl., E14 5RB | 020-3002-5252

City | 38 Threadneedle St., EC2R 8AY | 020-3005-9445 🗷

NEW Islington | North Retail Angel Bldg. | 403 St. John St., EC1V 4AB | 020-3435-9915

Kingston | 19-23 High St., KT1 1LL | 020-8912-0110

Shepherd's Bush | Westfield Shopping Ctr. | Ariel Way, W12 7GB | 020-8090-9070

www.jamieoliver.com

Jamie Oliver "doesn't disappoint" at his "rustic" Italian chain where everything from "sharing starters" to "heavenly desserts" and the "huge bowls of steaming pasta" in between is "clever, tasty and high quality"; the celeb chef's trademark "chirpiness infuses the service" and the prices are "affordable", both of which help to make the "long waits for a table" (no bookings taken in many situations) and "loud, crowded" atmosphere a bit more bearable.

☑ Jenny Lo's Tea House 🗷🗢 *Chinese* `19` `9` `16` `£17`

Belgravia | 14 Eccleston St., SW1W 9LT | 020-7259-0399 | www.jennylo.co.uk

Travellers "near Victoria Station" seeking "fast food that doesn't come in a bun or with chips" head to this "cracking" Chinese cafe for "a filling bowl of steaming noodles" or other "quick, quality" dishes; yes, it's a bit of a "charm-free environment" (and "some of the staff fall into this category" too), but it's "reliable for takeaway", with "bargain basement prices" to boot.

☑ Jin Kichi Ⓜ *Japanese* `27` `13` `19` `£42`

Hampstead | 73 Heath St., NW3 6UG | 020-7794-6158 | www.jinkichi.com

Known for "divine" yakatori from a robata bar as well as "high-quality sushi", this "well-priced" Japanese is "a local hero" to Hampsteaders; as it's "always full", bookings are "essential" in the "small", "sparse" and "cramped" setting, and while some wish they "could savour it" for longer (there's a two-hour peak time limit on tables), all in all, it "never disappoints."

	FOOD	DECOR	SERVICE	COST

Joe Allen ◐ *American* `19` `19` `20` £40

Covent Garden | 13 Exeter St., WC2E 7DT | 020-7836-0651 | www.joeallen.co.uk

A "stalwart of theatre darlings" ("lawks, how those luvvies can screech sometimes") thanks to its late hours and "handy" Covent Garden location, this "too-busy cellar" plastered with show posters offers "good-value", "appetising" American eats (try the "not-so-secret" off-menu burger) served by "friendly servers"; those who claim that, menuwise, "the world has moved on" may be missing the point: "you don't go for the food – it's an experience."

☑ José *Spanish* `28` `21` `25` £36

Tower Bridge | 104 Bermondsey St., SE1 3UB | 020-7403-4902 | www.josepizarro.com

Reminiscent of "tapas bars in Seville", this "tiny" Bermondsey Street "haven" is "always full to bursting" with people who "don't mind waiting" (no reservations) for chef-owner José Pizarro's "glorious", "vibrant" Spanish menu on which standards like "melt-in-the-mouth croquettes" are supplemented by an "ever-changing blackboard of specials"; factor in the "well-matched" wine list and "charming" staff who have "the patience of saints", and it's easy to see how you could "go in for a quick sherry and not leave for six hours."

Joy King Lau ◐ *Chinese* `21` `11` `17` £24

Chinatown | 3 Leicester St., WC2H 7BL | 020-7437-1133 | www.joykinglau.com

Feel the "joy" of "dim sum goodness" at this "reliable", four-storey Cantonese "standby", a destination for Chinatown locals who like the "extensive", "cheap" menu (there's dinner too) and "prompt" service; just ignore the "no-frills" ambience, and you'll find "great value."

☑ J. Sheekey ◐ *Seafood* `26` `22` `24` £62

Covent Garden | 28-32 St. Martin's Ct., WC2N 4AL | 020-7240-2565 | www.j-sheekey.co.uk

"Point to the menu with your eyes closed", because you "can't choose badly" at this "clubby", "old-school" seafood spot "around the corner from Leicester Square tube", where the "marvellous" meals come from staff who seem "telepathic"; the "bit-cramped" "warren of rooms" is "always busy" with a "cosmopolitan crowd", but for "unparalleled" "stargazing", go "post-theatre" when the clientele reflects the "pictures of famous customers on the wall"; P.S. "book well ahead" and prepare for "high prices" (they're "worth it").

J. Sheekey Oyster Bar ◐ *Seafood* `26` `23` `24` £48

Covent Garden | 33-34 St. Martin's Ct., WC2N 4AL | 020-7240-2565 | www.j-sheekey.co.uk

If its "big sister" "next door is fully booked", or you're after a more "casual" (yet still "sophisticated") "bite pre- or post-theatre", try this "stylish", "intimate" Covent Gardener serving "sampler" portions of J. Sheekey's "fabulous seafood" plus "incredible oysters" at a U-shaped bar; "smart" staff service surroundings that can feel "a bit squashed", though few mind being in such close proximity to the "theatrical luvvies" who frequently drop in.

Julie's *British*　　　　　　　▽ 19 | 23 | 19 | £51

Holland Park | 135 Portland Rd., W11 4LW | 020-7229-8331 | www.juliesrestaurant.com

The "perfect spot for a romantic dinner", this "pretty" Holland Park stalwart with a maze of "multiple rooms" (including an indoor garden-style area) has been "pleasing" both locals and the jet set since 1969; though critics feel the "expensive" Modern British menu "hasn't evolved", the multinational wine list, "special atmosphere" and "likelihood of seeing someone famous" compensate; P.S. an on-site crèche sits well with parents seeking a "chilled-pace" Sunday lunch.

JW Steakhouse *American/Chophouse*　　24 | 20 | 23 | £56

Mayfair | Grosvenor Hse. | 86 Park Ln., W1K 7TL | 020-7399-8460 | www.jwsteakhouse.co.uk

"A little bit of the USA" comes to Mayfair via this "spacious" chophouse in the Grosvenor House hotel that "gets most of the details right", offering "excellent" steaks ("amazing" cheesecake too) in "doggy bag"-worthy portions; service earns good marks as well, and even those hoping for more "buzz" say that overall it "lives up to expectations" (and prices).

Kai Mayfair *Chinese*　　　　　25 | 22 | 23 | £66

Mayfair | 65 S. Audley St., W1K 2QU | 020-7493-8988 | www.kaimayfair.co.uk

"Each meal is an event" at this Mayfair "gourmet Chinese" offering "exquisite" fare distinguished by "unique presentations" and "inventive" twists; an "impressive wine list", "knowledgeable" staff and "chic" but "cosy" setting add to its appeal – just "be prepared to pay for such quality" (or try the set lunch menu).

NEW Karpo *Eclectic*　　　　　– | – | – | E

King's Cross | Megaro Hotel | 23-27 Euston Rd., NW1 2SD | 020-7843-2221 | www.karpo.co.uk

At this earthy, tri-tiered addition in the boutique Megaro Hotel across the road from King's Cross and St. Pancras, an Eclectic menu flits from simple larder dishes to bolder, pricier creations of varied international pedigree; brunch plates, a quality cheese board and afternoon pastries endorse its all-day credentials for train travellers.

Kazan *Turkish*　　　　　　　25 | 21 | 22 | £32

Pimlico | 93-94 Wilton Rd., SW1V 1DW | 020-7233-7100 | www.kazan-restaurant.com

"Traditional with a modern hint" is one take on this "beautiful" Pimlico Turk offering "well-prepared Ottoman fare", including "mouthwatering" mezze and many choices for "lamb lovers"; add "accommodating", "never-rushed" service plus "good-value" prices, and it's touted as a true "Turkish delight" near Victoria Station.

	FOOD	DECOR	SERVICE	COST

Kensington Place *British* | 20 | 17 | 19 | £49 |

Kensington | 201-209 Kensington Church St., W8 7LX |
020-7727-3184 | www.kensingtonplace-restaurant.co.uk

After a "much-needed refurb", this "airy", big-windowed Notting
Hill Gate institution has a "new spring in its step", with "fresh, bright"
decor to go with its "dependable" Modern British menu, including
"lovely" fish from its next-door market; fans also laud its "friendly"
service and "value for money", but the "young crowd" that keeps it
"bustling" can make it "noisy" too.

The Kensington Wine Rooms *European* | 19 | 17 | 19 | £38 |

Kensington | 127-129 Kensington Church St., W8 7LP |
020-7727-8142

The Fulham Wine Rooms *European*

Fulham | 871-873 Fulham Rd., SW6 5HP | 020-7042-9440
www.greatwinesbytheglass.com

This sleek Kensington and Fulham wine bar/restaurant duo pleases
both sippers and nibblers with its "inspired" list of bottles, "fab by-
the-glass selection" (dispensed by Enomatic machines) and "unfussy"
Modern European small plates; a "polite" staff and "fair prices"
(which extend to the "amazingly good-value classes and tastings")
help make it "a real find."

Kenza ⊠ *Lebanese/Moroccan* | ▽ 24 | 26 | 21 | £40 |

City | 10 Devonshire Sq., EC2M 4YP | 020-7929-5533 |
www.kenza-restaurant.com

"Watch belly dancers boogie" at this "decadent" Lebanese-Moroccan
basement in the City, where "carved wooden walls" add to an "exotic
environment", "lovely for a romantic assignation"; the fare is "a bit
pricey" though "high quality", and whilst service can be sometimes
"forgetful", it doesn't detract from the "fantastic atmosphere."

Kettner's *French* | 21 | 22 | 21 | £44 |

Soho | 29 Romilly St., W1D 5HP | 020-7734-6112 |
www.kettners.com

A "lovely, wonky building" houses this "legendary" 1867 brasserie
whose "dark-wood panelling" and "tasteful private dining rooms"
provide a "grown-up", "old Soho" backdrop for "satisfying" French
classics at "reasonable prices"; service has "charm", and whilst "the
Champagne Bar is the main attraction" for those wishing to "see and
be seen", it's all "memorable", especially "when the pianist is playing" (Tuesdays–Saturdays).

Khan's ● *Indian* | 22 | 15 | 18 | £22 |

Bayswater | 13-15 Westbourne Grove, W2 4UA | 020-7727-5420 |
www.khansrestaurant.com

"Don't expect delicate china" at this "no-frills" Bayswater "oldie"
"packed" with diners craving a taste of "what Indians eat at home":
"delicious", "hearty" dishes to "dream about"; service is "variable",
and some find the "no-alcohol" policy "annoying", but "try the mango
lassie" and "be charmed" by the "authentic" experience – not to
mention the "cheap" prices.

	FOOD	DECOR	SERVICE	COST

Kiku *Japanese*
26 | 15 | 21 | £53

Mayfair | 17 Half Moon St., W1J 7BE | 020-7499-4208 | www.kikurestaurant.co.uk

"Marvel at the intense flavours" and "great diversity" at this Japanese destination located in Mayfair, where "friendly" staff "guide your journey", from "top-class sushi" to tempura to shabu-shabu; "basic decor" means the "atmosphere could be better", but "bargain" set lunches earn cheers, whilst the "high standard" makes "pricey" dinners "worth it."

NEW Kitchen 264 @
- | - | - | M

The Collection *Mediterranean*

South Kensington | The Collection | 264 Brompton Rd., SW3 2AS | 020-7225-1212 | www.the-collection.co.uk

A glossy top-to-tail revamp by new owners has revitalised The Collection, a long-standing South Ken establishment where a trendy, evocative lounge is overlooked by an airy, uncluttered mezzanine dining room; respected Israeli chef Oded Oren is behind the edited, mostly moderately priced Mediterranean menu, while the wine list is augmented by signature cocktails and a major-league champagne selection that includes jeroboams.

Kitchen W8 *European*
26 | 20 | 22 | £55

Kensington | 11-13 Abingdon Rd., W8 6AH | 020-7937-0120 | www.kitchenw8.com

"Fresh ingredients" are "put together with creative flair" at this "consistently impressive" Modern European in Kensington that's co-owned by mega chef Philip Howard; with its modern looks, "relaxed, informal" ambience and "attentive" service, it "retains that 'neighbourhood' feel" even as its rep grows, and given the quality, it's a "great value", especially the "bargain" set lunch and no-corkage-fee Sunday evenings.

Koffmann's *French*
27 | 23 | 26 | £65

Belgravia | The Berkeley | Wilton Pl., SW1X 7RL | 020-7235-1010 | www.the-berkeley.co.uk

"Legendary" chef Pierre Koffman "reminds us what great French food is all about" at this "elegant", "comfortable" dining room in Belgravia's Berkeley Hotel, offering "refined" takes on classic dishes, including a "life-changing" stuffed pig's trotter; "superb service" and a "clever wine list" are more reasons why it "exceeds expectations every time", and if cost is a concern, try the "amazing-value" set lunch.

Koi *Japanese*
∇ **23 | 19 | 20 | £53**

Kensington | 1 Palace Gate, W8 5LS | 020-7581-8778

To admirers, this Kensington Japanese destination "feels like a special night out" thanks to its "solid" selection of fare, "nicely designed" setting (complete with low tables) and "beautiful" crowd, and if it's "on the pricey side", at least "you get what you pay for"; a dissenting faction sees it differently ("average", "limited" selection), but they're outvoted.

	FOOD	DECOR	SERVICE	COST

Kopapa *Eclectic*

23 | **16** | **19** | **£32**

Covent Garden | 32-34 Monmouth St., WC2H 9HA | 020-7240-6076 | www.kopapa.co.uk

"Don't be fooled by the cafelike appearance" of this "casual", all-day eatery in Covent Garden: chef Peter Gordon's "artistic", "inventive" Eclectic menu of small and large plates is generally "on point" and "always interesting, even when it near-misses"; views on cost vary ("good value" vs. "a bit high for what you get") and it can be "noisy" with "slow" service, but most simply "love" it.

Koya *Japanese*

25 | **17** | **18** | **£20**

Soho | 49 Frith St., W1D 4SG | 020-7434-4463 | www.koya.co.uk

Even what is, more often than not, a "30-minute wait to get in" (no booking) doesn't deter fans of this "cosy", simple Soho Japanese specialising in "divine" udon noodles "in many forms" and also offering other "delicious" dishes (some "hard to find in London"); with "big shared tables" and "rapid" service, it's "not fancy", but then neither are the prices.

Kulu Kulu Sushi ⊠ *Japanese*

22 | **11** | **17** | **£21**

Covent Garden | 51-53 Shelton St., WC2H 9JU | 020-7240-5687
Soho | 76 Brewer St., W1F 9TX | 020-7734-7316
South Kensington | 39 Thurloe Pl., SW7 2HP | 020-7589-2225

"They keep it simple and the standard high" at this "bare-bones" Japanese conveyor-belt threesome, which rolls out a "great selection" of "fresh", "no-frills" sushi and other cooked dishes that are "usually worth trying"; cost-calculators conclude that "cheap prices sooth any ruffled culinary feathers", while "courteous service" gets the thumbs-up.

NEW La Bodega Negra ❶ *Mexican*

- | **-** | **-** | **M**

Soho | 16 Moor St., W1D 5NH | 020-7758-4100
Soho | 9 Old Compton St., W1D 5JF | 020-7758-4100
www.labodeganegra.com

The prolific restaurateur behind Eight Over Eight, E&O et al. has teamed up with a veteran of the New York nightclub scene to create these multifaceted, moderately priced Mexican arrivals in Soho; an entrance on Old Compton Street leads to a stylish, evening-only basement restaurant/bar, whilst on Moor Street resides a chilled lunch-and-dinner cafe and taqueria.

La Bouchée *French*

24 | **19** | **21** | **£38**

South Kensington | 56 Old Brompton Rd., SW7 3DY | 020-7589-1929

"In a part of town that needs more no-fuss" restaurants, this "quaint, cosy" neighbourhood bistro located in South Kensington fits the bill, with "old-school", "delicious" "French country food" that's "done right" and "superb for the price"; if there's one criticism, regulars say it's that the environment seems "a bit old and dark", but "friendly" service and "interesting people-watching" make amends.

	FOOD	DECOR	SERVICE	COST

La Brasserie ◑ *French*

FOOD 19 | DECOR 20 | SERVICE 18 | COST £42

South Kensington | 272 Brompton Rd., SW3 2AW | 020-7581-3089 |
www.labrasserielondon.com

"Don't change it" plead devotees of this all-day South Ken "institution", a "family" "staple for brunch, coffee or an easy dinner" featuring "good-value", "satisfying" French eats with "English twists";
furthermore, "lovely staff" and a "true brasserie feel" with pleasing
"buzz" ensure a "fun atmosphere."

L'Absinthe Ⓜ *French*

▽ FOOD 24 | DECOR 19 | SERVICE 23 | COST £40

Primrose Hill | 40 Chalcot Rd., NW1 8LS | 020-7483-4848 |
www.labsinthe.co.uk

"Cosy" surrounds "transport you to a smart cafe in rural France", but
what really sets this Primrose Hill bistro apart is its "passionate" staff
who "make you feel seriously welcome" as they present the "tasty"
French "comfort food"; what's more, it's "good value", especially the
"sensibly priced wines", available from the attached shop.

Ladurée *French*

FOOD 24 | DECOR 20 | SERVICE 18 | COST £30

Covent Garden | Covent Garden Piazza | The Market, WC2E 8RA |
020-7240-0706
Knightsbridge | Harrods | 87-135 Brompton Rd., ground fl., SW1X 7XL |
020-3155-0111
Piccadilly | 71-72 Burlington Arcade, W1J 0QX |
020-7491-9155
www.laduree.fr

"Fairy-tale macarons" are "dangerously close to being addictive" at
this "expensive-but-worth-it" French cafe/patisserie, a "must visit" in
Harrods, an "exquisite jewel box" in Burlington Arcade and "a girlie
place" with a balcony overlooking the piazza in Covent Garden; while
you're there, you might also pick up an "artistically created main",
but be prepared for "long queues" born of "slow service."

La Famiglia ◑ *Italian*

FOOD 21 | DECOR 17 | SERVICE 21 | COST £46

Chelsea | 7 Langton St., SW10 0JL | 020-7351-0761 |
www.lafamiglia.co.uk

"Inviting", "old-world service" and a "hearty" menu that "delivers
quality every time" make this "lively neighbourhood" Chelsea Italian
"beyond family-friendly", despite prices that are "not cheap"; being
so "popular", the "homey" interior "can be noisy", just like the large,
covered year-round rear garden.

La Fromagerie Café *European*

FOOD 24 | DECOR 18 | SERVICE 16 | COST £26

Marylebone | 2-6 Moxon St., W1U 4EW | 020-7935-0341
Islington | 30 Highbury Park, N5 2AA | 020-7359-7440
www.lafromagerie.co.uk

"Bagging" a wooden bench for the "fabulous", "rustic" Modern Euro
"lunchy things" at this "cramped" cafe/deli in Marylebone is "pretty
darn challenging", but what has "cheese lovers in rapture" is the
"state-of-the-art" "temperature-controlled cheese room", with its
"impressive selection" for tasting and "to take home"; the Islington
sib "only has six seats, so best head there off-peak."

	FOOD	DECOR	SERVICE	COST

La Genova ⓩ *Italian* — 24 | 19 | 25 | £49

Mayfair | 32 N. Audley St., W1K 6ZG | 020-7629-5916 | www.lagenovarestaurant.com

It may look "fairly inconspicuous" from outside, but step into this Mayfair Italian and you're "transported back" to the old country thanks to its "simple" but "excellent" "traditional" cusine (special praise goes to the "fresh pasta") and "attentive" staff led by a "memorable" host/owner; maybe the decor "could be better", but the ambience is "warm" and prices are "extremely reasonable", at least for this neighbourhood.

Lahore Kebab House *Pakistani* — 25 | 11 | 18 | £20

Whitechapel | 2-10 Umberston St., E1 1PY | 020-7481-9737 ◑
Streatham | 668 Streatham High Rd., SW16 3QL | 020-8679-9980
www.lahore-kebabhouse.com

"Expect long queues to get in" this "cracking" Whitechapel BYO with a "loud, large and laddish" Streatham sibling, both specialising in "amazing" Pakistani cooking featuring "excellent grilled meats" and plenty of "hot and spicy" dishes; many surveyors say the "crude", "cafeterialike" environments "need updating", though the "cheap-as-chips" prices and "fast, efficient service" can remain just as they are.

Lamberts Ⓜ *British* — ▽ 27 | 24 | 26 | £40

Balham | 2 Station Parade, Balham High Rd., SW12 9AZ | 020-8675-2233 | www.lambertsrestaurant.com

"Striking the perfect balance between sumptuous and homely", with "elegant" environs and a "warm welcome" from "fantastic" staff, this "absolute treat" in Balham produces "expertly cooked" "seasonal Modern British cuisine"; best of all, it's "remarkable value", hence "a popular place for all and sundry."

Langan's Bistro ⓩ *British/French* — 21 | 21 | 21 | £49

Marylebone | 26 Devonshire St., W1G 6PH | 020-7935-4531 | www.langansrestaurants.co.uk

"Comfortable and well-furnished" with "great art", this "time-capsule institution" located in Marylebone is "just the place for that discreet supper or extended lunch" of "high-quality" Traditional British–French "comfort food"; service is "charming", and whilst prices skew toward the top end for a bistro, there's plenty of "affordability" on the wine list.

Langan's Brasserie *British/French* — 21 | 20 | 21 | £56

Mayfair | Stratton Hse. | Stratton St., W1JJ 8LB | 020-7491-8822 | www.langansrestaurants.co.uk

"Despite all the new kids on the block", this "epitome of an English brasserie" near Green Park has "been around forever" but is still "buzzing" thanks to "dependable" Traditional British–French cooking and "unstuffy" service that "makes everyone feel welcome"; some critics find it "slightly pricey", but in all other respects, it "should never change."

	FOOD	DECOR	SERVICE	COST

L'Anima 🔲 *Italian*   25 | 21 | 21 | £65

City | 1 Snowden St., EC2A 2DQ | 020-7422-7000 | www.lanima.co.uk

"Always full of people in suits", this "polished", "sophisticated" spot near Liverpool Street Station lures the "business" set with a "gutsy", "assured" regional Italian menu served by "efficient" staffers; the white "minimalist" setting is debatable ("ethereal" for some, too "clinical" for others), whilst the price point is flat-out "expensive" – notwithstanding the "good"-value set lunch.

🔲 La Petite Maison *Mediterranean*   27 | 22 | 23 | £68

Mayfair | 54 Brooks Mews, W1K 4EG | 020-7495-4774 | www.lpmlondon.co.uk

"The crush, the crowded tables, the celebs" – there's a "hectic" scene at this "glamourously cosseted world of hedgies" and "bejewelled" diners in "chic" Mayfair premises, but there's also a "top-class" Mediterranean menu featuring "exquisitely simple and delicious" fare ("dish-sharing" encouraged), plus "excellent" service; given all that, the price is just a "minor downside" since it "hits the mark every time."

La Porchetta Pizzeria *Italian*   23 | 17 | 20 | £23

Holborn | 33 Boswell St., WC1 3BP | 020-7242-2434 🔲
Clerkenwell | 84-86 Rosebery Ave., EC1R 4QY | 020-7837-6060
Camden Town | 74-77 Chalk Farm Rd., NW1 8AN | 020-7267-6822
Muswell Hill | 265 Muswell Hill Broadway, N10 1DE | 020-8883-1500 ◑
Islington | 141-142 Upper St., N1 1QY | 020-7288-2488
Stoke Newington | 147 Stroud Green Rd., N4 3PZ | 020-7281-2892
www.laporchetta.net

"Giant" thin-crust pizzas and other "tasty" Italian fare served in "generous portions" at painless prices equal "solid value" at these "vibrant" standbys; a "fun", "informal" atmosphere, "child-friendly" attitude and "jovial" (if "not always the best") service further boost their appeal, but be prepared for some "noisy" birthday celebrations.

La Porte des Indes *Indian*   22 | 26 | 20 | £49

Marylebone | 32 Bryanston St., W1H 7EG | 020-7224-0055 | www.laportedesindes.com

"The interior designer deserves a medal" for the "exotic", "over-the-top" setting (complete with waterfall, palm trees and more) at this "huge", "upscale" Marble Arch Indian that provides a "fab" backdrop for "groups celebrating this and that"; the "interesting, French-influenced" fare is a "cut above" the norm, and though service "could be tightened up a bit", it's "charming", so all in all it's "worth a visit."

La Poule au Pot *French*   23 | 21 | 21 | £51

Pimlico | 231 Ebury St., SW1W 8UT | 020-7730-7763 | www.pouleaupot.co.uk

"Unbeatable for a date", this "been-there-forever" Pimlico Green French bistro oozes Gallic "charm" with its "ancient farmhouse decor" and "sumptuous" dishes like *magnifique* coq au vin; what's "cosy" to some feels a bit "cramped" to others and service can be "spotty", but given the "smashing wine selection" you may not notice; P.S. "no better place" in summer than the "wonderful terrace."

	FOOD	DECOR	SERVICE	COST

Las Iguanas *Pan-Latin*

22 | 21 | 21 | £28

NEW Stratford | Stratford City | 2 Stratford Pl., E20 1ET | 020-8522-4445
Greenwich | O2 Arena | Peninsula Sq., SE10 0DS | 020-8312-8680
Shoreditch | 1 Horner Sq., E1 6AA | 020-7426-0876
Southwark | Royal Festival Hall | Belvedere Rd., SE1 8XX | 020-7620-1328
NEW Kingston | The Malthouse | 25-29 High St., KT1 1LL | 020-8546-2245 ◗
www.iguanas.co.uk

Expect a "happy", "lively atmosphere" at this burgeoning Pan-Latin chain with a handful of "prime locations" in London (and many more outside the capital); "good-quality" cooking and "excellent cocktails" keep it "heaving with people" at weekends, whilst staff are surprisingly "quick" "considering how jostled they are"; P.S. "special promotions" abet its "great-value" reputation.

◪ L'Atelier de Joël Robuchon *French*

28 | 25 | 26 | £84

Covent Garden | 13-15 West St., WC2H 9NE | 020-7010-8600 | www.joelrobuchon.co.uk

At Joël Robuchon's "sensational" Theatreland "classic", guests are still "astonished" by his *fantastique* New French small (well, "tiny") plates, presented by "commendable" staff in the "sparkling" red-lacquer L'Atelier or the "sophisticated" dinner-only La Cuisine; the "stratospheric prices" are "out of reach" for many, but lunch and pre-theatre set menus are "unbeatable gastronomy for money!"; P.S. the "upstairs bar is one of the best-kept secrets in London."

Latium ◪ *Italian*

24 | 18 | 25 | £50

Fitzrovia | 21 Berners St., W1T 3LP | 020-7323-9123 | www.latiumrestaurant.com

There's a "passion for pasta" evident at this "inventive" Italian in Fitzrovia, a "hidden gem" where regulars say the "ravioli is the thing to get"; though some feel the decor is somewhat "dull", "smart" service that makes everyone "feel welcome", an "extensive" wine list and "comparatively moderate prices" distract.

◪ La Trompette *European/French*

28 | 21 | 25 | £59

Chiswick | 5-7 Devonshire Rd., W4 2EU | 020-8747-1836 | www.latrompette.co.uk

The "stunning" Modern Euro–New French menu "evolves with the seasons and the chef's interests" at this culinary "mecca", a relative of Chez Bruce that makes locals "feel lucky to live in Chiswick"; "for what one gets", i.e. "sheer quality", it's "amazing value" (the "classy wine list" boasts "prices that are exceptionally low for the calibre"), and whilst some bemoan that "tables are quite close together", the environs are otherwise "pleasant", with "near-perfect service" as well

Launceston Place *British*

25 | 23 | 25 | £65

Kensington | 1 Launceston Pl., W8 5RL | 020-7937-6912 | www.launcestonplace-restaurant.co.uk

"Whether it be for business or a celebration", loyalists tout this "intimate" "hideaway" in a "crisp" Kensington "converted townhouse" where "imaginative", "beautifully prepared" Modern British dishes are "wonderfully presented" in a "coolly sophisticated atmosphere"; the prix fixe–only menu may be on the "high end of the price scale", but "wonderful added extras" and "superb service" add value.

L'Autre Pied *European* | 25 | 19 | 23 | £58 |

Marylebone | 5-7 Blandford St., W1U 3DB | 020-7486-9696 | www.lautrepied.co.uk

"Flavours and textures work in perfect harmony" to "shake taste buds awake" at Pied à Terre's "unassuming" (and "cheaper") Marylebone sibling where the "technically clever" Modern European menu showcases "culinary skills that outstrip the price"; some are irked by what they call "cramped", "bland" quarters, but "super-efficient" staffers and "exquisite" wine pairings help to propel it to "top class."

L'Aventure ⌧ *French* ∇ | 25 | 16 | 22 | £49 |

St. John's Wood | 3 Blenheim Terr., NW8 0EH | 020-7624-6232 | www.laventure.co.uk

It's "been around forever", yet this "charming", circa-1979 St. John's Wood bistro remains "worth a visit" for "delicious" French fare that's "great value"; "excellent" servers "treat you like family (in a good way)", but be warned, the "tiny" dimensions mean "you might play footsie with the wrong neighbour" – unless you nab a spot on the patio in summer.

NEW Lawn Bistro *European* | - | - | - | M |

Wimbledon | 67 High St., SW19 5EE | 020-8947-8278 | www.thelawnbistro.co.uk

An ex-chef from La Trompette is behind this upmarket addition to Wimbledon Village offering moderately priced Modern European prix fixe menus; sleek and modern enough for a casual adult tête-à-tête during the week, the atmosphere and service are quite kid-friendly come weekends.

Le Boudin Blanc *French* | 24 | 19 | 21 | £49 |

Mayfair | Shepherd Mkt. | 5 Trebeck St., W1J 7LT | 020-7499-3292 | www.boudinblanc.co.uk

"As French as you can get", this "lively" Shepherd Market "throw-back" supplies "rustic country" "classics" and a "varied wine list" in a "charming" setting equipped with "mismatched furniture" and mostly "friendly" service; though critics cite somewhat "expensive" prices and "tightly packed" tables, most say it's "worth it" for an experience that's the "real deal."

Le Café Anglais *French* | 22 | 21 | 21 | £57 |

Bayswater | Whiteleys Shopping Ctr. | 8 Porchester Gdns., W2 4DB | 020-7221-1415 | www.lecafeanglais.co.uk

"Clever", "well-prepared" French fare is served amidst "great big windows, swish banquettes" and "lovely art deco" decor suggesting a "vintage ocean liner" at chef-owner Rowley Leigh's "airy" brasserie atop Whiteleys shopping centre on Queensway; adding to the "pleasurable experience" are "friendly", "efficient" staff, "fairly priced" wines and a "contented buzz" from the customers.

	FOOD	DECOR	SERVICE	COST

Le Café du Marché ● ◐ ⊠ *French* — 25 | 23 | 23 | £50

Farringdon | 22 Charterhouse Sq., EC1M 6AH | 020-7608-1609 | www.cafedumarche.co.uk

"Tops for many years and keeping it up", this "charming" Smithfield "gem" "more than justifies its reputation" for "memorable" French bistro cuisine; furthermore, the "comfortable armchair"–like atmosphere (the piano playing is a "nice touch") and "superb" service inspire "lots of bonhomie" whilst still staying "sharp enough for business lunches" and dinners.

Le Caprice ● *British/European* — 24 | 22 | 24 | £66

St. James's | Arlington Hse. | Arlington St., SW1A 1RJ | 020-7629-2239 | www.le-caprice.co.uk

"You'll feel like a star" (and you may be sitting amongst some real ones) at this "buzzy" St. James's "stalwart", a long-time "people-watching" paradise where "spot-on" staff ferry "fabulous" Modern British–Euro fare to a "moneyed crowd" (who can easily pay the "expensive" bill); as for the "recent refurbishment" of the "legendary" art deco decor, regulars declare it "a success", especially since the ambience is just as "marvellous" as ever.

Le Cercle ⊠ Ⓜ *French* — 24 | 22 | 23 | £57

Chelsea | 1 Wilbraham Pl., SW1X 9AE | 020-7901-9999 | www.lecercle.co.uk

"Smashing" small plates fill out the "upmarket" menu at this Club Gascon offshoot near Sloane Square, where chef Pascal Aussignac's "carefully prepared" New and Southwestern French dishes can be paired with "interesting regional wines"; the below-ground location "may not be to everyone's taste", but the "excellent" service and "cosy" mood ("not too loud and not too quiet") garner universal praise.

Le Colombier *French* — 24 | 20 | 23 | £57

Chelsea | 145 Dovehouse St., SW3 6LB | 020-7351-1155 | www.le-colombier-restaurant.co.uk

Reminiscent of dining in "Burgundy" and oozing "lots of charm", this "classic" French brasserie in Chelsea provides "simple", "old-school" dishes "made to perfection" and accompanied by a "comprehensive" wine list; "friendly" staff service the crowd of "refined locals", who appreciate pricing that's "surprisingly reasonable for its location."

☑ The Ledbury *French* — 28 | 25 | 28 | £88

Notting Hill | 127 Ledbury Rd., W11 2AQ | 020-7792-9090 | www.theledbury.com

An "elaborate unveiling of dishes is followed by admiring coos" for chef Brett Graham's "glorious", "off-the-chart"-"innovative" New French cuisine at this "tranquil" Notting Hill "destination" with an "attractive" setting and a "relaxed" attitude; amongst "professional", "genial" staff is a "knowledgeable sommelier" who provides "unerring, unusual" "matching wines" from the "world-class" list, bolstering the feeling that the "eye-watering" "cost is justified" (for "excellent value", "lunch is the time to go").

	FOOD	DECOR	SERVICE	COST

Le Deuxième ● *European* | 22 | 19 | 21 | £44 |

Covent Garden | 65 Long Acre, WC2E 9JH | 020-7379-0033 |
www.ledeuxieme.com

"Mouth-watering" Modern European fare, "pleasant staff" and an "extensive wine list" are all boons, but the real blessing of this "smart" venue is that it's "reasonably priced for Covent Garden"; "business friendly" by day, it's known as a "handy" option pre- or post-theatre, so those looking for a quieter, less "cramped" repast opt for the "tranquil period" when the curtain's up.

⊠ Le Gavroche ⊠ *French* | 28 | 25 | 28 | £103 |

Mayfair | 43 Upper Brook St., W1K 7QR | 020-7408-0881 |
www.le-gavroche.co.uk

For "grown-up dining at its best", try this "venerable culinary palace" nestled in a Mayfair basement, where chef Michel Roux Jr.'s "mind-blowing" "traditional haute" French cooking comes via "sublime" service; granted, a meal may cost the "down payment on a small car", and some feel the "sedate", jackets-required setting could use more "zest", but most agree it's "outstanding in every sense of the word"; P.S. the set lunch is "excellent value."

⊠ Le Manoir
aux Quat'Saisons *French* | 28 | 27 | 27 | £122 |

Great Milton | Le Manoir aux Quat'Saisons Hotel | Church Rd. |
01844-278 881 | www.manoir.com

The "stunning" grounds of this "magical" Oxfordshire hotel/restaurant would be "worth the trip" alone, but chef-owner Raymond Blanc ups the ante with "to-die-for" New French cuisine and "faultless" service that's the "pinnacle of graciousness"; "luxury lovers" don't mind the "expensive" prices – indeed, they recommend you "sell the family silver" and "stay the night" for the full "once-in-a-lifetime experience"; P.S. it's over an hour's drive from London, but a "short helicopter flight" – "yes, they have a helipad."

Le Mercury ● *French* | 21 | 19 | 21 | £26 |

Islington | 140 Upper St., N1 1QY | 020-7354-4088 |
www.lemercury.co.uk

Offering "old-school charm on the cheap", this "buzzing", "candlelit" New French destination in Islington, spread over three floors of a Victorian building, is "usually fully booked, and for good reason"; the "chilled-out feel", "spot-on" service and "simple", "nicely done" cuisine make it a "great standby", especially before or after a show at the nearby Almeida Theatre.

Lemonia ● *Greek* | 21 | 17 | 21 | £35 |

Primrose Hill | 89 Regent's Park Rd., NW1 8UY | 020-7586-7454
The "perfect neighbourhood taverna" sums up this Primrose Hill Greek that "still gets it right after all these years" thanks to "simple", "reliably good" food, "friendly" service from a "longtime staff" and a "convivial" "local vibe", complete with occasional "celeb-spotting"; yes, it can be "noisy" and "packed" ("book ahead"), but "terrific value" is the payoff.

Leon *Mediterranean*
20 | 17 | 18 | £14

Covent Garden | 73-76 The Strand, WC2R 0DE | 020-7240-3070
Marylebone | 275 Regent St., W1B 2HB | 020-7495-1514
Soho | 35 Great Marlborough St., W1F 7JE | 020-7437-5280
Soho | 36-38 Old Compton St., W1D 4TT | 020-7434-1200
Canary Wharf | Cabot P. W., promenade, E14 4QS | 020-7719-6200
City | 12 Ludgate Circus, EC4M 7LQ | 020-7489-1580 🛗
City | 86 Cannon St., EC4N 6HT | 020-7623-9699 🛗
Shoreditch | 3 Crispin Pl., E1 6DW | 020-7247-4369
Southwark | Blue Fin Bldg. | 7 Canvey St., SE1 9AN | 020-7620-0035
www.leonrestaurants.co.uk

"This is what fast(er) food should be" declare fans of this eat-in/take-away chain, a "shining light" that dishes up "flavourful", "healthy"-minded Med fare in "casual" settings with a "funky" touch; it can be "a struggle to find a seat" at peak hours, but service is "friendly" and prices "affordable", making it a "go-to" for many.

🆕 Leon De Bruxelles *Belgian*
19 | 18 | 18 | £41

Covent Garden | 24 Cambridge Circus, WC2H 8AA | 020-7836-3500 |
www.leon-de-bruxelles.co.uk

Musseling into London's limited ranks of Belgian eateries, this Cambridge Circus offshoot of a Brussels-born chain provides "large portions" of "consistent" moules frites and other fare, accompanied by "all varieties" of beer; leather banquettes, marble tables, "courteous" service and moderate prices complete the picture.

Leong's Legend *Taiwanese*
22 | 17 | 14 | £24

Chinatown | 26-27 Lisle St., WC2H 7BA | 020-7734-3380 |
www.restaurantprivilege.com
Chinatown | 4 Macclesfield St., W1 6AX | 020-7287-0288 |
www.leongslegend.com

"Those who know their Taiwanese food" frequent this Chinatown duo offering "unusual dim sum", "proper soup dumplings" and other "flavoursome", "authentic" fare; service can vary from "friendly" to "brusque", but the "dark" decor is "decent" and prices are "cheap" enough that you can "test" a lot of dishes without fiscal fear.

Le Pain Quotidien *Bakery/Belgian*
19 | 17 | 17 | £21

Holborn | 174 High Holborn, WC1V 7AA | 020-7486-6154
Marylebone | 72-75 Marylebone High St., W1 5JU | 020-7486-6154
Soho | 18 Great Marlborough St., W1F 7HS | 020-7486-6154
South Bank | Royal Festival Hall | Belvedere Rd., Festival Terr., SE1 8XX |
020-7486-6154
King's Cross | St. Pancras Int'l | 81 Euston Rd., NW1 2QL | 020-7486-6154
Chelsea | 201-203 King's Rd., SW3 5ED | 020-7486-6154
South Kensington | 15-17 Exhibition Rd., SW7 2HE | 020-7486-6154
Wimbledon | 4-5 High St., SW19 5DX | 020-7486-6154
Kensington | 9 Young St., W8 5EH | 020-7486-6154
Notting Hill | 81-85 Notting Hill Gate, W11 3JS | 020-7486-6154
www.lepainquotidien.co.uk
Additional locations throughout London

The "casual", "farmhouse" feel and "quality" eats make these "reliable" Belgian bakery/cafe outposts of the international chain "perfect for chilling out" over a menu running the gamut from "wholesome" soups and salads to "gorgeous" breads and pastries; "lots of choices" and "decent value" compensate for the "shared tables" and "hit-or-miss" service.

Le Pont de la Tour *French/Seafood*

| 23 | 22 | 21 | £57 |

Tower Bridge | Butlers Wharf Bldg. | 36 Shad Thames, SE1 2YE | 020-7403-8403 | www.lepontdelatour.co.uk

"Breathtaking views" of Tower Bridge and the City skyline from the river terrace provide "the wow factor" at this Classic French eatery, a "romantic setting for an anniversary or secret tryst"; inside, a "buzzing bar" leads to an "elegant" art deco–inspired dining room where "excellent", seafood-centric fare ("pricey but worth it") comes by way of "attentive service" and alongside a "fabulous" wine selection.

Le Relais de Venise

| 24 | 18 | 20 | £34 |

l'Entrecôte *Chophouse/French*

Marylebone | 120 Marylebone Ln., W1U 2QG | 020-7486-0878

NEW **Canary Wharf** | 18-20 Mackenzie Walk, E14 4PH | 020-3475-3331

City | 5 Throgmorton St., EC2N 2AD | 020-7638-6325 ⊠ www.relaisdevenise.com

Only "one option" is offered at this beloved spot with "semi-cramped quarters" in Marylebone, with a "more comfortable City counterpart" and a new Canary Wharf branch: "satisfying" steak frites with "secret green sauce", "bookended by walnut salad and tart"; no bookings yield sometimes "painful waiting times", but "a queue outside doesn't deter" devotees, because "ruthlessly efficient" staff get you "in and out in an hour" and the prices are "more than reasonable."

🔽 L'Escargot ● ⊠ *French*

| 27 | 25 | 24 | £63 |

Soho | 48 Greek St., W1D 4EF | 020-7439-7474 | www.lescargotrestaurant.co.uk

"Dine amongst Chagalls, Miros" and mirrors at this longtime "Soho haunt" with "outstanding" Classic French cuisine, a "slightly formal but very welcoming" atmosphere and "exemplary" service; if some cite "expense-account" pricing, others say it delivers real "value" (especially via the set menu options).

Les Deux Salons *French*

| 19 | 21 | 18 | £47 |

Covent Garden | 40-42 William IV St., WC2N 4DD | 020-7420-2050 | www.lesdeuxsalons.co.uk

"Looking the part" of a "grand, old-school cafe", this "bustling" bi-level sib of Arbutus and Wild Honey by Trafalgar Square is "worth a visit" for its "hearty", "well-executed" French fare with some "witty retakes on well-loved favourites", plus a "wonderful wine list"; if sceptics claim it's "nothing wow-worthy", with "hit-and-miss" service, "serious theatregoers" call it an "oasis" thanks to the "amazing-value" pre-show prix fixe.

❷ Les Trois Garçons 🛇 French

	FOOD	DECOR	SERVICE	COST
	23	27	22	£61

Shoreditch | 1 Club Row, E1 6JX | 020-7613-1924 |
www.lestroisgarcons.com
"Eccentric and memorable", this Shoreditch Classic French set in a
Victorian-era pub dazzles with its "opulent", "original" decor – complete with "evening bags hanging from the ceiling" and taxidermy on
the walls – and if the food isn't quite as impressive, it's nevertheless
"done well"; maybe service can vary and prices aren't cheap, but it
makes for a "truly unique" experience.

Le Suquet ➊ French/Seafood

	FOOD	DECOR	SERVICE	COST
	22	17	22	£57

Chelsea | 104 Draycott Ave., SW3 3AE | 020-7581-1785 |
www.lesuquet.co.uk
Soon to complete its fourth decade of service, this "warm and welcoming" Chelsea French presents the same "simple" package "year
after year", namely "outstandingly fresh", "deftly prepared" seafood
(a "plateau de fruits de mer is a must"); sure, the setting's a bit "old-
fashioned" and the prices are a little "expensive", but most deem it
a "delight", with extra praise for "friendly" staff.

L'Etranger French/Japanese

	FOOD	DECOR	SERVICE	COST
	25	18	23	£60

South Kensington | 36 Gloucester Rd., SW7 4QT | 020-7584-1118 |
www.etranger.co.uk
"Adventurous", "beautifully presented" dishes featuring a "well-
orchestrated" mix of French and Japanese flavours (sashimi and
maki too) are backed by an "extensive" wine list and "attentive" service at this South Ken local; it's not cheap and some find it "nothing
special to look at", but the fact that it's "crowded" says a lot.

Le Vacherin French

	FOOD	DECOR	SERVICE	COST
	25	23	22	£54

Chiswick | 76-77 S. Parade, W4 5LF | 020-8742-2121 |
www.levacherin.com
"Can't be faulted" say fans of the "reliable" French cooking matched
with a "fantastic Parisian atmosphere" at this "charming", "quiet" bistro a smidge "off the main track" in Chiswick; "unobtrusive service"
and a "fab wine list" bolster the feeling that, though prices are a "bit
on the expensive side", "what you get is definitely worth paying for."

Light House Eclectic

	FOOD	DECOR	SERVICE	COST
	25	21	24	£42

Wimbledon | 75-77 Ridgway, SW19 4ST | 020-8944-6338 |
www.lighthousewimbledon.com
"A great little find in Wimbledon Village", this "underrated" "local
stalwart" offers an "interesting, keenly priced" Eclectic menu and
generally "spot-on" service that's "quick to correct any concerns";
maybe the "minimalist" setting could use "a designer's touch" and
some detect "no wow factor", but most leave "pleased."

NEW Lima 🛇 Peruvian

	FOOD	DECOR	SERVICE	COST
	-	-	-	E

Fitzrovia | 31 Rathbone Pl., W1T 1JH | 020-3002-2640 |
www.limalondon.com
Standing out amongst London's influx of Peruvian eateries, this
Fitzrovia newcomer is under the auspices of a well-regarded restau-

rateur from Lima, who evokes his flagship eatery with similarly eco-sensitive culinary offerings filled with ingredients rarely seen on menus around town (e.g. Amazon citrus, boniato and cochayuyo); the focus is more on the plate than the decor, though the setting does feel upscale, as do the prices.

Little Bay ● *European*   21 | 19 | 21 | £21

Farringdon | 171 Farringdon Rd., EC1R 3AL | 020-7278-1234
Kilburn | 228 Belsize Rd., NW6 4BT | 020-7372-4699 ⊟
www.little-bay.co.uk

"Quirky", "cool" decor – with "candles in wine bottles and snug balcony tables" in Kilburn and Roman-Greek touches in Farringdon – sets the stage for an "imaginative" Modern Euro menu whose quality is "way greater" than the "dirt-cheap" prices might suggest at this "unassuming" duo; add in a "lovely team", and fans ask "what more could you want?"

Little Italy ● *Italian*   24 | 21 | 22 | £45

Soho | 21 Frith St., W1D 4RN | 020-7734-4737 | www.littleitalysoho.co.uk
"For a quick bite after work or before a show", or a "romantic meal if you can get tucked away upstairs", this Italian in Soho fits the bill with "excellent" grub that's "relatively basic" though "not cheap"; the later it gets, the more "loud" and clublike it becomes – that is, "you can dance" to "fantastic music" until the "wee small" hours (4 AM).

Locanda Locatelli *Italian*   26 | 22 | 24 | £71

Marylebone | Hyatt Regency London - The Churchill | 8 Seymour St., W1H 7JZ | 020-7935-9088 | www.locandalocatelli.com
Fans feel "incredibly lucky to dine" at this Marylebone minimalist, where "master" chef Giorgio Locatelli uses "a light touch and high-quality ingredients" to turn out "exquisite" dishes – with "prices to match"; "excellent" service comes with "a sense of humour", whilst the "exciting wine list" includes "a great grappa selection."

Locanda Ottoemezzo ⊠ *Italian*   ∇ 25 | 17 | 21 | £53

Kensington | 2-4 Thackeray St., W8 5ET | 020-7937-2200 |
www.locandaottoemezzo.co.uk
Though "more expensive than it looks" – with "quirky wooden benches, plastic chairs" and "cool movie decor" paying "tribute" to Fellini's *8 ½* – this "intimate" Kensington Italian "doesn't disappoint" thanks to dishes that are "as excellent as the service"; P.S. "upstairs next to the window is recommended."

Loch Fyne *Seafood*   22 | 18 | 19 | £36

Covent Garden | 2-4 Catherine St., WC2B 5JS | 020-7240-4999
City | Leadenhall Mkt. | 77-78 Gracechurch St., EC3V 0AS |
020-7929-8380 ⊠
www.lochfyne.com
"Fish lovers" say that these "buzzy" outposts of the national chain "never fail" for "simply presented" seafood at "fair prices" – even if the setting is as "colourless as your office canteen" and service is "variable"; Covent Garden is "good before the theatre", whilst the business-oriented City venue is unsurprisingly "popular at lunchtime."

	FOOD	DECOR	SERVICE	COST

L'Oranger 🔲 *French*   27 | 24 | 25 | £68

St. James's | 5 St. James's St., SW1A 1EF | 020-7839-3774 |
www.loranger.co.uk
Centrally located in St. James's, this "French restaurant for grown-ups"
is "a good place for a date night or a business meeting" amongst the
"upper crust"; suitably, the "exquisite presentations", "sublime service" and "superb atmosphere" come with a posh price tag.

Lotus Floating Restaurant *Chinese*   23 | 20 | 21 | £29

Canary Wharf | 9 Oakland Quay, E14 9EA | 020-7515-6445 |
www.lotusfloating.co.uk
With a location that "takes some finding" "in the heart of the docks" at
Canary Wharf, this Chinese is "a great place for a special occasion",
serving "fantastic" dim sum lunches and dinners that hail from all
across the Middle Kingdom; "lovely decor", including authentic Asian
prints, and "chatty" staff add to the "superb experience."

NEW Lowcountry ● *American*   - | - | - | M

Fulham | 4 Fulham High St., SW6 3LQ | 020-7736-7002 |
www.lowcountry.co.uk
Distinctively spiced wings, gumbo, crabs and other specialities of the
American Low Country – i.e. the coastal regions of South Carolina
and Georgia – come courtesy of a St. Louis chef at this big, brash and
affordable Fulham newcomer; the orange-hued setting features an
open kitchen with counter seating and a large terrace with its own
smokehouse, plus there's a special 'family area' for kids.

Lucio *Italian*   21 | 18 | 20 | £54

Chelsea | 257-259 Fulham Rd., SW3 6HY | 020-7823-3007 |
www.luciorestaurant.com
Owner Lucio Altana is the "perfect host" at his "romantic" namesake Chelsea Italian, a "happy find" for "quality" fare; though some
wish for "more menu creativity" and find the "wine list on the pricey
side", it remains a "popular" "neighbourhood choice", thanks in part
to "charming service" and an "excellent-value lunch."

Lucky 7 *American*   19 | 17 | 13 | £24

Notting Hill | 127 Westbourne Park Rd., W2 5QL | 020-7727-6771 |
www.lucky7london.com
When you want to "soothe that Sunday morning hangover" or "stuff
your face like a real American", this "classic '50s diner" in Notting
Hill fits the bill with "fabulous burgers, fries and super milkshakes";
the "authentic vibe" extends to staff who "could try harder" – and
may "make you share" booth seating with another party.

Lupita *Mexican*   23 | 19 | 20 | £24

Covent Garden | 13-15 Villiers St., WC2N 6ND | 020-7930-5355 |
www.lupita.co.uk
"A tasty take on Mexico City cuisine", this "vibrant", "tight" space
brings "big portions" of tacos and other "cheap and cheerful street
food" to Charing Cross; a "great lunch stop", it's also "brill after
work", because the "highly recommended" margaritas have a "kick."

	FOOD	DECOR	SERVICE	COST

Lutyens Restaurant, Bar & Cellar Rooms 🗷 *French*

| 23 | 21 | 22 | £60 |

City | 85 Fleet St., EC4 1AE | 020-7583-8385 |
www.lutyens-restaurant.com

"Lots of suits" populate the "starched white tables" at Sir Terence
Conran's Fleet Street bistro, where "pleasant" staff oversee a "well-
prepared", pricey New French menu and "decent wine list"; open all
day, the "formal" environment transitions from "a convenient breakfast spot" to working lunch mecca to "buzzy" bar – perhaps because
"there isn't that much competition nearby."

The Luxe ❶ *British*

| 17 | 18 | 17 | £34 |

City | 109 Commercial St., E1 6BG | 020-7101-1751 | www.theluxe.co.uk

"Fun for a casual lunch", breakfast, dinner or "a quick drink after
work", this "noisy" Spitalfields Market site from John Torode offers
a "cool" ground-floor bar and "fancy restaurant" above, where
"pleasant" Modern Brit dishes come from an open kitchen; although
some find the service "lax", there's "good value" here, plus you "can
sit outside" in the summer or see live bands at the weekend.

Made in Camden *European*

| ▽ 24 | 18 | 21 | £28 |

Camden Town | The Roundhouse | Chalk Farm Rd., NW1 8EH |
020-7424-8495 | www.madeincamden.com

The distinctive "colour and atmosphere of Camden" is evident in
every corner of this "enjoyable" eatery, whose "delicious" Modern
Euro menu lists "traditional dishes alongside more unusual offerings", all of which are "reasonably priced"; "friendly, efficient service" is another reason advocates "adore" it, and given its location
attached to the Roundhouse performing-arts centre, it's especially
"ideal for pre-theatre."

Made in Italy ❶ *Italian*

| 19 | 16 | 16 | £29 |

Marylebone | 50 James St., W1U 1HB | 020-7224-0182
Soho | 14 Old Compton St., W1D 4TH | 020-0011-1214
Chelsea | 249 King's Rd., SW3 5EL | 020-7352-1880
www.madeinitalygroup.co.uk

"Young, pretty people" come in "groups" to this King's Road Italian
"neighbourhood spot", because its "satisfying" "thin-crust pizza" is
sold by the meter, making it "made to share"; although the "haphazard" service "could be better" and "tables are tight", it all comes at
"a reasonable price"; P.S. the consensus is the Marylebone and Soho
offshoots are a "notch below the original on all fronts."

Magdalen 🗷 *European*

| 26 | 20 | 24 | £53 |

Tower Bridge | 152 Tooley St., SE1 2TU | 020-7403-1342 |
www.magdalenrestaurant.co.uk

"Imaginative", "ever-changing" Modern European cuisine is "cooked
with craft and heart" to "stunning" effect at this "easy-to-find secret"
near Tower Bridge Road; factor in "gracious", "unrushed service", a
"carefully selected wine list" and prices that are "high without being
exorbitant", and no wonder surveyors call it a "place to impress";
P.S. the set lunch menu is "a steal."

Maggie Jones's *British*

| 23 | 24 | 23 | £37 |

Kensington | 6 Old Court Pl., W8 4PL | 020-7937-6462 |
www.maggie-jones.co.uk

If you're hankering for authentic British fare, check out this Kensington "comfort-food" haven where "wholesome", "generous portions" come for "reasonable prices"; "quirky" "farmhouse decor" with "wonderful booths and ancient candles spewing wax" creates a "rustic", "country feel", and though a few find it all too "retro", most deem it a "warm", "welcoming" place for a "quiet" meal, and it's "romantic to boot."

Ma Goa *Indian*

| 25 | 17 | 22 | £32 |

Putney | 242-244 Upper Richmond Rd., SW15 6TG |
020-8780-1767 | www.ma-goa.com

Putney punters "swing by" for a "quick, cheap meal" at this "family-owned and -operated" Indian specialising in "interesting, delicious Goan food" ("the pork vindaloo is particularly brilliant") served by "accommodating staff"; the "good value" extends from the two-courses-for-£10 menu to the "terrific" Sunday buffet.

Malabar ● *Indian*

| 22 | 18 | 22 | £34 |

Notting Hill | 27 Uxbridge St., W8 7TQ | 020-7727-8800 |
www.malabar-restaurant.co.uk

"Wonderful smokey flavour from the charcoal oven" is instilled in the "nicely spiced" Indian dishes "served quickly" by "friendly staff" at this "simple contemporary setting" in a "pretty Notting Hill back street"; it's "always full of the local set", but even people from out of the area say they "definitely would go back", particularly because it's "good value for money."

Malabar Junction *Indian*

| ▽ 19 | 17 | 17 | £28 |

Bloomsbury | 107 Great Russell St., WC1B 3NA | 020-7580-5230 |
www.malabarjunction.com

In an atriumlike "room full of light and greenery", this Bloomsbury spot majors on "impressive" South Indian dishes from "chefs who are proud of their work"; surveyors who appreciate that they're "not rushed" mark it as "one to repeat", particularly for lunch when there's a prix fixe "deal."

Mandalay *Burmese*

| ▽ 25 | 15 | 23 | £18 |

Marylebone | 444 Edgware Rd., W2 1EG | 020-7258-3696 |
www.mandalayway.com

It may have "bright lights", "no decor" and "not much atmosphere" to speak off, but this Edgware Road option is, in fact, a "gem", producing "mind-blowing" Burmese food and offering it at "non-London-like prices"; "friendly, helpful service" is another reason it's "well worth a visit if you're keen to try something different."

Mandarin Kitchen ● *Chinese/Seafood*

| 25 | 16 | 20 | £40 |

Bayswater | 14-16 Queensway, W2 3RX | 020-7727-9012

"Even with a reservation", diners can expect to "queue out the door" for the "famous", "fantastic" lobster noodles at this "temple to the crustacean gods", a recently revamped "nightclub look-alike" in

	FOOD	DECOR	SERVICE	COST

Bayswater; foodies feel that the quality of other items on the Chinese menu "varies", but the "price is right" across the board, whilst the "service is decent."

Mango Tree *Thai*
21 20 18 £48

Victoria | 46 Grosvenor Pl., SW1X 7EQ | 020-7823-1888 | www.mangotree.org.uk

Whilst Victoria businesspeople deem it "a place to bring a client for lunch", in the evening, this "hip", "massive" Thai site becomes "way beyond buzzy" (indeed, "you'd think you were standing on a Heathrow runway"); whatever the hour, the culinary offerings are "decent" and comparatively "expensive" and the service swings between "attentive" and "nonexistent" – cocktails, on the other hand, are generally "brilliant."

Manicomio *Italian*
18 15 17 £44

City | Gutter Ln., EC2V 8AS | 020-7726-5010 🖼
Chelsea | 85 Duke of York Sq., SW3 4LY | 020-7730-3366 www.manicomio.co.uk

Expect "reliable" cooking at this Chelsea Italian, where you can "watch the world go by" from the "sunny terrace", or its City offspring, an "oasis around St. Paul's"; though word is the "service is not as attentive as it should be", somehow they can "get you in, fed and out in an hour", making it a "solid" option for a "getaway lunch"; P.S. it also offers "classy takeaway."

Manson *British*
▽ 22 23 21 £45

Fulham | 676 Fulham Rd., SW6 5SA | 020-7384-9559 | www.mansonrestaurant.co.uk

"Extremely good" British fare, "quick, polite" service and a "warm", "relaxed atmosphere" make this brasserie a "find" in Fulham; a few respondents cite the "uninteresting wine list", but that's a quibble considering the whole is as "good on a Friday night" as it is "fabulous" for lunch, especially weekdays when a "value" prix fixe is offered.

Mao Tai ❶ *Asian*
▽ 25 22 23 £50

Fulham | 58 New King's Rd., SW6 4LS | 020-7731-2520 | www.maotai.co.uk

It's "a treat to eat" at this sleek, "stylish", spacious Fulham venue whose "pricey" Pan-Asian menu offers "lots of choice", including dim sum; staff who "know what they're doing" also oversee the "extensive" selection of wines and "amazing cocktails", the latter alone "worth going for."

Marco Pierre White's King's Rd. Steakhouse *Chophouse*
19 15 19 £55

Chelsea | 386 King's Rd., SW3 5UZ | 020-7351-9997 | www.kingsroadsteakhouseandgrill.com

"Always a lovely experience" sums up supporters' take on this "casual" King's Road chophouse delivering "great" (though "pricey") fare and "efficient service"; however, critics claim it's "a letdown", due in part to its "unlikely" decor: "all white", possibly in deference to its namesake celebrity-chef owner.

	FOOD	DECOR	SERVICE	COST

Marco Pierre White
Steak & Alehouse *Chophouse*

| 21 | 20 | 18 | £53 |

City | East India House | 109-117 Middlesex St., E1 7JF | 020-7247-5050 | www.mpwsteakandalehouse.org

While advocates deem the fare at this "relaxed, posh" City chophouse "yummy", others accuse the eponymous celeb chef of "obviously trading off his name" with "mediocre" dishes; what's more, it's "expensive for what it is", but at least the service is "pleasant" more than it's "disappointing."

⊠ Marcus Wareing
at The Berkeley ⊠ *French*

| 27 | 25 | 27 | £110 |

Belgravia | The Berkeley | Wilton Pl., SW1X 7RL | 020-7235-1200 | www.marcus-wareing.com

Marcus Wareing's "splendid" culinary "twists" produce "mind-blowing" dishes at this "elegant", "hushed" New French dining room at Belgravia's Berkeley Hotel, where "impeccable, professional" staff maneuver amongst "tables spaced well apart"; it's best to be "on expenses", not least to get the best out of the "extensive wine list" (and "awesome" pairing suggestions from the sommelier), but even on your own budget, it's "worth the splurge" for a "special occasion"; P.S. "the set lunch is a bargain."

NEW Mari Vanna ● *Russian*

| - | - | - | E |

Knightsbridge | 116 Knightsbridge, SW1X 7PJ | 020-7225-3122 | www.marivanna.ru

After Moscow, St. Petersburg and NYC, Knightsbridge is the latest locale for this mini-chain named after a mythical Russian hostess who entertained locals with her culinary creations; complementing the expensive menu, which exudes strong Armenian, Georgian and Uzbekistani influences, is a cosy setting replete with tiny dolls, trinkets and a decorative Pechka stove.

Mark's Club ●⊠ *British/French*

| ▽ 21 | 27 | 28 | £92 |

Mayfair | private club | 46 Charles St., W1J 5EJ | 020-7499-2936 | www.marksclub.co.uk

If you "get an invitation" to this private Mayfair club, take it and revel in its "old English" country house look, "superb" service and "very exclusive air"; the "classic" British-Franco cooking is "great", and as for the prices, members sniff "if you have to ask how much it costs, you can't afford to eat here."

Maroush ● *Lebanese*

| 23 | 16 | 20 | £30 |

Knightsbridge | 38 Beauchamp Pl., SW3 1NU | 020-7581-5434
Marylebone | 1-3 Connaught St., W2 2BH | 020-7262-0222
Marylebone | 21 Edgware Rd., W2 2JE | 020-7723-0773
Marylebone | 4 Vere St., W1G 0DG | 020-7493-5050
Marylebone | 68 Edgware Rd., W2 2JE | 020-7224-9339
www.maroush.com

"Whether it be a quick bite or a sit-down dinner", this "affordable" quintet around Marylebone and Knightsbridge is "tried and tested" for "hearty" portions of "tasty", "satisfying" Lebanese "staples"; it's a particular draw for those who "don't mind noise" and "bright", "gaudy" decor but do appreciate a "party scene", which the "efficient servers" oversee with aplomb, right up until the early morning closing time.

Masala Zone Indian   19 | 17 | 19 | £23

Covent Garden | 48 Floral St., WC2E 9DA | 020-7379-0101
Soho | 9 Marshall St., W1F 7ER | 020-7287-9966
Camden Town | 25 Parkway, NW1 7PG | 020-7267-4422
Islington | 80 Upper St., N1 0NU | 020-7359-3399
Earl's Court | 147 Earl's Court Rd., SW5 9RQ | 020-7373-0220
Fulham | 583 Fulham Rd., SW6 5UA | 020-7386-5500
Bayswater | 75 Bishop's Bridge Rd., W2 6BG | 020-7221-0055
www.masalazone.com

For "fab Thalis" and other "solid-as-a-rock" Indian "street food", try these "bustling" "budget standbys" that make "no apologies for upping the spice levels"; although "it's a chain and feels like it", with "no-frills" decor, the "smiley service" smoothes any ruffled feathers.

Massimo ☒ Mediterranean   20 | 24 | 19 | £78

Westminster | Corinthia Hotel London | 10 Northumberland Ave., SW1N 5BY | 020-7998-0555 | www.massimo-restaurant.co.uk
The "wow factor" comes from the "stunning" decor of this upscale Italian in the Corinthia Hotel near Trafalgar Square, with "high ceilings", grand pillars and spherical brass-and-glass chandeliers; but diners are divided over every other aspect – some praise the "superb" fish-centric Med dishes and the "caring" service, whilst others baulk at "steep prices" for "fashionista portions" and "attitude" from some staffers; P.S. there's also a "fantastic champagne selection."

Matsuri Japanese   23 | 19 | 23 | £63

St. James's | 15 Bury St., SW1Y 6AL | 020-7839-1101 | www.matsuri-restaurant.com
For a "high-end Tokyo" experience in St. James's, try this basement Japanese with a bar and table grills where chefs "put on a show" as they prepare a "delectable selection of sushi and teppanyaki"; the "decor is a bit dated, but ok" for what it is, whilst the "pricey" costs are lower at lunch, thanks to "great-value bento boxes."

Maxwell's ● American   19 | 19 | 20 | £31

Covent Garden | 8 James St., WC2E 8BH | 020-7836-0303 | www.maxwells.co.uk
If you "need a quick bite in Covent Garden" before "heading off to the theatre" and don't mind somewhere "manic" and "touristy", this "diner-style" venue is "well worth the money" for "safe" hamburgers and other American eats plus "great cocktails"; what's more, service usually remains "polite" and "attentive", even though "it gets so crowded", particularly during the daily happy hour.

Maze French   25 | 23 | 24 | £75

Mayfair | Marriott Grosvenor Sq. | 10-13 Grosvenor Sq., W1K 6JP | 020-7107-0000 | www.gordonramsay.com
"Buzzing all the time", this "beautiful, modern" Gordon Ramsay French venue in the Marriott Grosvenor Square specialises in "cre-

ative" "little bites" that "blend" in "Asian influences" to "wonderful" effect; "polite", "flexible" service and a "big", "interesting wine list" ("on an iPad") are more reasons why it's "worthwhile", but beware, as the cost "increases dramatically" if "you need a lot" of food.

Maze Grill *Chophouse* | 24 | 21 | 23 | £56 |

Mayfair | Marriott Grosvenor Sq. | 10-13 Grosvenor Sq., W1K 6JP | 020-7495-2211 | www.gordonramsay.com

"If Maze is too high for your budget or you're not dressed for the occasion", then head for this "lively" all-day chophouse sib next door in the Marriott Grosvenor Square, where the decor is "more casual", it's easier to "grab a table" and prices are "cheaper" (though still "rather expensive"); thankfully, Gordon Ramsay's menu, highlighting "premium cuts of meat" and "sides big enough to share", is equally "excellent", just like "well-trained staff."

NEW Mazi *Greek* | - | - | - | M |

Notting Hill | 12-14 Hillgate St., W8 7SR | 020-7229-3794

Holidays in the Hellenic islands are conjured by the whitewashed walls, blue shutters and grapevine-sheltered garden at this Notting Hill spot whose faithfully Greek offerings include innovative twists, such as starters served in modish Kilner jars and feta served tempura style, plus seasonings grown in an on-site herb patch; sharing plates keep prices down, and a deli section sells fare to take home.

NEW Meat Liquor ●🅱 *Burgers* | 24 | 18 | 15 | £22 |

Marylebone | 74 Welbeck St., W1G 0BA | 020-7224-4239 | www.meatliquor.com

"Trashy in all the right ways", this "ultratrendy" Marylebone haunt slings "awesome", "greasy", "American-style" burgers, "to-die-for fries", "amazing fried pickles" and other "naughty" nibbles that are "not for the faint-hearted" – just like the setting, whose "grungy" "black walls covered in graffiti" and "creepy pictures" resemble "something out of *The Texas Chainsaw Massacre*"; "it's a no-bookings place", so expect "unbelievable queues", and once inside, count on service that "needs some work", "stiff cocktails" and "good value."

NEW Meat Market *Burgers* | - | - | - | I |

Covent Garden | Jubilee Market Hall | Tavistock St., WC2E 8BE | 020-7240-4852 | www.themeatmarket.co.uk

Tucked away above Jubilee Market, the less-chichi part of Covent Garden, this inexpensive spin-off of Meat Liquor doles out the same messy American-style burgers, hot dogs, Southern-inspired sides and grown-up desserts like Jägermeister-spiked ice cream and whisky-based shakes; the digs are similarly loud and hip, with kitsch '50s signs, but here the focus is takeaway, as seating is minimal.

Medcalf *British* | ▽ | 21 | 20 | 18 | £41 |

Clerkenwell | 40 Exmouth Mkt., EC1R 4QE | 020-7833-3533 | www.medcalfbar.co.uk

"Casually trendy", as "befits" its Exmouth Market location, this "gorgeously decorated" former butcher's shop (dating back to the

early 1900s) presents a "simple, well-done" Modern British menu;
"friendly service" is another aspect that makes it "a lovely treat" –
but good luck "trying to get in without booking."

Mediterraneo ● *Italian*   24 | 17 | 21 | £41

Notting Hill | 37 Kensington Park Rd., W11 2EU | 020-7792-3131 |
www.mediterraneo-restaurant.co.uk

"If you're in Notting Hill, don't miss" this cousin of Osteria
Basilico "up the street", doling out "amazing pastas" and other
"notable" Italian eats that are "great value"; the "warm", rustic
setting is always "vibrant" with "noisy" "hordes" "jostling" to get
a "cramped" table, so "make sure you book" and try to forgive service if it feels "rushed."

Medlar *French*   25 | 16 | 23 | £56

Chelsea | 438 King's Rd., SW10 0LJ | 020-7349-1900 |
www.medlarrestaurant.co.uk

"Eat like nobility" at this "brilliant" Chelsea spot from two Chez
Bruce protégés whose "inventive" New French menu of "fragrant
creations" (with influences from all over Europe) "fully deserves the
hype"; whilst some take issue with the "austere" setting, "top-notch
service", an "attractive wine selection" and "a cheese board to rival
restaurants in France" make amends, as does the "fantastic value";
P.S. "plead for a window table."

Mela ● *Indian*   23 | 18 | 20 | £32

Covent Garden | 152-156 Shaftesbury Ave., WC2H 8HL |
020-7836-8635 | www.melarestaurant.co.uk

"Delightful staff" "make you feel like you're a regular" at this "convivial" Covent Garden Indian where the "variety of creative dishes" on
a "terrific", "ever-changing" menu satisfies "those wanting something a bit classier than Brick Lane"; what's more, it's "incredible
value", especially for pre-theatre dining, when you can be "in and
out in less than an hour."

NEW Mele e Pere 🅩 *Italian*   - | - | - | E

Soho | 46 Brewer St., W1F 9TF | 020-7096-2096 |
www.meleepere.co.uk

A protégé of the Wild Honey and Arbutus crew is the co-owning
chef of this idiosyncratic Soho trattoria where pricey Italian cuisine
combines tradition with daring; beyond an intricate window display
of colourful Murano glass fruit (hence the name 'apples and pears')
is a brightly lit, unpretentious basement bedecked with chunky
wooden tables and chairs.

Memories of China *Chinese*   23 | 20 | 19 | £60

Belgravia | 65-69 Ebury St., SW1W 0NZ | 020-7730-7734
Kensington | 353 Kensington High St., W8 6NW |
020-7603-6951
www.memories-of-china.co.uk

Long-time regulars and a "just-as-enthusiastic younger following"
call this "fancy" Belgravia Chinese and its lower-profile Kensington
offshoot a "reliable choice" for "ample portions" of "high-quality"

Cantonese and Mandarin dishes; although the bill can be "pricey", the eatery is "recommended" for its "accessible" menu as well as its generally "competent service."

Mennula *Italian*

FOOD	DECOR	SERVICE	COST
26	20	23	£50

Fitzrovia | 10 Charlotte St., W1T 2LT | 020-7636-2833 |
www.mennula.com

The "passionate" chef "clearly loves what he does", that is preparing "exquisite" seasonal Sicilian specialities at this "delightful find" in Fitzrovia; even though prices are "high" and the "retro" setting is "cramped", a "lovely wine" list and "attentive service" "full of sunny warmth" more than "make up for" it.

The Mercer 🅢 *British*

FOOD	DECOR	SERVICE	COST
▽ 22	21	21	£49

City | 34 Threadneedle St., EC2R 8AY | 020-7628-0001 |
www.themercer.co.uk

"Worth trying" for its Traditional British "food to savour" – not to mention "tasteful, elegant surroundings" and "helpful service" – this "well-kept secret" in a former Threadneedle Street banking hall is a "great place" for a "business" breakfast, lunch or dinner; what's more, it's "reasonably priced given the location."

Meson
Don Felipe 🅢 *Spanish*

FOOD	DECOR	SERVICE	COST
▽ 23	16	16	£29

Waterloo | 53 The Cut, SE1 8LF | 020-7928-3237 |
www.mesondonfelipe.com

Now that this "tightly packed" Waterloo haunt is "better known", you should "book a table or be prepared to queue" for its "excellent" Spanish tapas and mains, backed up by an "extensive wine list"; even though the "staff could smile a bit more", the "decor's cheery" and the location "great for before the Old or Young Vic."

Mestizo *Mexican*

FOOD	DECOR	SERVICE	COST
22	20	21	£31

Camden Town | 103 Hampstead Rd., NW1 3EL | 020-7387-4064 |
www.mestizomx.com

"You'll feel like you're walking into Mexico" at this "lively little haven" in Camden Town with a "mind-boggling array of tequilas" and an "extensive" "bargain" menu (check out the all-you-can-eat options) that "doesn't conform to stereotypical offerings", all delivered by way of "helpful" service; just remember that "booking in the evening is essential", as it gets rather "busy", especially at the "heaving bar downstairs."

🆕 Meursault ⬤ *French/Japanese*

FOOD	DECOR	SERVICE	COST
-	-	-	E

South Kensington | L'Etranger | 36 Gloucester Rd., SW7 4QT |
020-7823-9291 | www.meursaultlondon.co.uk

L'Etranger on Gloucester Road in South Kensington has revamped its basement nightclub into this classy, colourful addition, an evening-only destination whose high-end French menu is laced with Japanese influences; a robust oenological theme is evident from the 1,600-strong list and lavish wine cabinets, including one dedicated to its namesake, whilst a somewhat small bar serves complex molecular cocktails.

	FOOD	DECOR	SERVICE	COST

Mews of Mayfair *British*
20 | 20 | 17 | £47

Mayfair | 10-11 Lancashire Ct., New Bond St., W1S 1EY |
020-7518-9388 | www.mewsofmayfair.com

"A good spot to hide away", this discreet Modern Brit down a cobbled Mayfair street serves "expensive", "sophisticated" fare ("could
be more generous with portions") and an "extensive wine list" via
service that's at times "slow" though usually "well meaning"; addi-
tionally, there's a glossy lounge, a bar, a "quirky private dining room"
and a patio.

Mien Tay *Vietnamese*
24 | 9 | 16 | £20

Shoreditch | 122 Kingsland Rd., E2 8DP | 020-7729-3074
Battersea | 180 Lavender Hill, SW11 5TQ | 020-7350-0721
www.mientay.co.uk

"Superb" Vietnamese "street food" keeps this duo in Battersea and
Shoreditch "always packed", despite what critics call "basic", somewhat "uncomfortable" settings and service that can be "less than
friendly"; indeed, it boasts "hordes" of admirers who bring their own
booze and toast the "phenomenal value."

Min Jiang *Chinese*
26 | 25 | 23 | £55

Kensington | Royal Garden Hotel | 2-24 Kensington High St., 10th fl.,
W8 4PT | 020-7937-8000 | www.minjiang.co.uk

"Wow" views of Kensington Palace and Gardens from the Royal
Garden Hotel's 10th-floor dining room are complemented by
"outstanding" Beijing duck ("don't say Peking!"), "higher-end"
dim sum and other "succulent" dishes at this "pricey" Chinese;
"attentive service" and a "popular rendezvous" bar with "decent
cocktails" are "bonuses."

Mint Leaf *Indian*
23 | 22 | 22 | £50

St. James's | Suffolk Pl., SW1Y 4HX | 020-7930-9020 |
www.mintleafrestaurant.com ◐

City | 12 Angel Ct., EC2R 7HB | 020-7600-0992 |
www.mintleaflounge.com 🔄

"Modern", "fancy", often "stunning" Indian dishes are the métier of
this pair where "bit-high" prices also get you access to "polished
service" and "delicious", "unusual cocktails"; the "dark", "loud"
St. James's basement is a "slick", "disco"-like setting with DJ-
driven "dancing in the bar" at weekends, whilst the lighter, loungey
City offshoot offers an "upmarket", "relaxing atmosphere" plus a
champagne bar on the mezzanine.

NEW Mishkin's ◐ *Jewish*
20 | 20 | 18 | £25

Covent Garden | 25 Catherine St., WC2B 5JS | 020-7240-2078 |
www.mishkins.co.uk

"Tasty" non-kosher, "NY-style" Jewish deli "favourites" make this
midpriced "great addition" from the team behind Polpo et al. something "different" for Covent Garden; service can often seem "dis-
tracted", but the "brilliant atmosphere" (red booths, brick walls)
and "dangerously good" cocktail list ("a shrine to gin") are boons
to what fans dub a "gutsy" endeavor.

	FOOD	DECOR	SERVICE	COST

Miyama *Japanese*　23 | 14 | 20 | £48

Mayfair | 38 Clarges St., W1 7EN | 020-7493-3807 |
www.miyama.co.uk
City | 17 Godliman St., EC4V 5BD | 020-7489-1937 |
www.miyamarestaurant.co.uk 🗷

"Look beyond the dated decor" of this "unpretentious" Japanese duo
in Mayfair and the City and you'll find an "amazingly broad range" of
"superb" sushi, teppanyaki and noodles; what's more, it all comes
with "attentive service" and "without costing an arm and a leg", especially if you choose the "fantastic-value set menus", offered at both
lunch and dinner.

Modern Pantry *Eclectic*　25 | 22 | 24 | £40

Clerkenwell | 47-48 St. John's Sq., EC1V 4JJ | 020-7553-9210 |
www.themodernpantry.co.uk

The "clever", "inventive" Eclectic cuisine "draws on all corners of
the globe" to create "amazing flavours" with "just enough quirk"
at this "stylishly minimal" Clerkenwell endeavour with a "bright"
all-day cafe ("great" for alfresco meals) and "elegant" upstairs
dining room (for a "grown-up treat"); wholly "lovely" service and
an "excellent wine list" further "enchant the locals", as does
the "lovely brunch."

Momo ◐ *Moroccan*　20 | 24 | 18 | £50

Piccadilly | 25 Heddon St., W1B 4BH | 020-7434-4040 |
www.momoresto.com

"Exotic", "buzzy" and "unique", this Piccadilly hangout presents "well-
executed" Moroccan eats backed by "great North African wines", all
at "high-end" prices; "so-so service" can be a letdown, but it's "great
for group eating", especially in the "lush outside space", "a home
away from home in the summer."

Mon Plaisir ◐🗷 *French*　21 | 18 | 19 | £36

Covent Garden | 21 Monmouth St., WC2H 9DD | 020-7836-7243 |
www.monplaisir.co.uk

"*Toujours un plaisir*" rave Francophiles of this over-70-year-old
Covent Garden "institution" where a "rabbit warren" of "charming", "cheek-by-jowl" rooms plays host to "dependable" French
bistro staples, plus an "excellent cheese trolley" and "reasonably
priced wines"; service can be "a little offhand", but it's often
"fine", helping to make the place perpetually "useful for pre- and
post-theatre suppers."

Montpeliano ◐ *Italian*　18 | 16 | 20 | £53

Knightsbridge | 13 Montpelier St., SW7 1HQ | 020-7589-0032 |
www.montpelianorestaurant.com

"Still going strong" after nearly 40 years, this Italian eatery located
in Knightsbridge boasts a "pleasant" sky-lighted-conservatory feel
that makes it a staple for "nights out with friends or birthday
dinners"; so even though there's a widespread belief that it's "overpriced" for being merely "average", most conclude that it's "worth it
for the ambience."

	FOOD	DECOR	SERVICE	COST

☑ Mooli's *Indian*   24 | 15 | 22 | £9

Soho | 50 Frith St., W1D 4SQ | 020-7494-9075 | www.moolis.com
"Not so much a restaurant as a place to grab a quick bite", this "zingy,
loveable Soho cafe" doles out "tasty" rotis with "a great choice of
fillings" and other "flavourful" Indian street food, and it's so "cheap",
it's been voted London's No. 1 Best Buy; what's more, it's "fast",
making it "a perfect lunch spot or pre-bar pit stop with friends."

Morgan M ☒ *French/Vegetarian*   ▽ 28 | 19 | 24 | £61

Farringdon | 50 Long Ln., EC1A 9EJ | 020-7609-3560 | www.morganm.com
"Stupendous" New French cuisine comes from "a craftsman who
cares" about "careful, complex assemblies of flavours" at this
vegetarian-friendly venue opposite Smithfield Market (relocated
from Islington); indeed, the pricey fare "more than makes up for the
lack of visual excitement" in the "quiet", green-hued environment,
as does the "spot-on" service.

☑ Morito *African/Spanish*   27 | 18 | 21 | £26

Clerkenwell | 32 Exmouth Mkt., EC1R 4QE | 020-7278-7007
For "delicious", "perfectly seasoned" tapas that share the Spanish–
North African "flavours of its illustrious neighbour" in Exmouth
Market, this "buzzing" "younger sibling" of Moro is "worth a visit of
its own", despite the "tiny", "spartan" space where other diners are
"are all but sharing your seat"; "smiling service" is part of the deal,
as are the "well-chosen" wines and "stonking" "good value."

Moro *African/Spanish*   27 | 20 | 25 | £44

Clerkenwell | 34-36 Exmouth Mkt., EC1R 4QE | 020-7833-8336 |
www.moro.co.uk
"Innovative year after year", this "casual" Exmouth Market "classic"
"never rests on its reputation", as it melds Spanish and North African
traditions into "sublime", "pricey" tapas and other "inventive" dishes
presented by "cheerful staff proud of what they're serving"; although
"it's almost impossible" to get into the "sparse" setting whose noise
is at times "deafening", it "never fails to seduce."

Morton's ☒ *Mediterranean*   ▽ 22 | 22 | 23 | £70

Mayfair | private club | 28 Berkeley Sq., W1J 6EN |
020-7499-0363 | www.mortonsclub.com
There's "no sign of a recession" at this private club comprising a
"beautiful", "top-end" Mediterranean restaurant with "attractive
modern art" and a "stunning view over Berkeley Square", a "relaxed,
vibrant" ground-floor bar and an "energetic" basement "nightclub
that's one of the 'in' spots in modern London"; "first-class service all
round" and a "private living room for meetings or parties" are boons
to its rarified clientele and their guests.

☑ Mosimann's ☒ *Eclectic*   26 | 27 | 27 | £83

Belgravia | private club | The Belfry | 11 W. Halkin St., SW1X 8JL |
020-7235-9625 | www.mosimann.com
"Luxurious without being over the top" and with a "private member-
ship to keep it discreet", this "sophisticated" venue in a former

Belgravia church offers chef Anton Mosimann's "refined" Eclectic dishes and "top-class" service; it's "understandably expensive", but for a "special treat", it's "doesn't get much better" – if you can get in.

Motcombs *Eclectic*   21 | 17 | 21 | £49

Belgravia | 26 Motcomb St., SW1X 8JU | 020-7235-6382 | www.motcombs.co.uk

A "lively crowd" of "locals and visiting Europeans" create the "noisy", "convivial" atmosphere at this "comfy, casual" "hangout" in Belgravia, comprising an "old-fashioned" (some say "scruffy") ground-floor brasserie, cosy basement and "fantastic" "outdoor scene" on the pavement; "charming, efficient" staff serve somewhat "predictable" Eclectic eats that, whilst "not cheap", are "well prepared."

Moti Mahal ⊠ *Indian*   25 | 20 | 21 | £45

Covent Garden | 45 Great Queen St., WC2B 5AA | 020-7240-9329 | www.motimahal-uk.com

"Respecting the diversity and richness of Indian food", this "busy, buzzy" Covent Garden eatery "rewards" diners with a "thoughtful" menu laced with "succulent, fragrant" dishes; tables are on the "crammed" side and it's a "tad expensive, but there are deals to be had", and the "friendly service" keeps things ticking, making it a handy "pre/post-theatre location."

Mr. Chow ● *Chinese*   21 | 20 | 21 | £61

Knightsbridge | 151 Knightsbridge, SW1X 7PA | 020-7589-7347 | www.mrchow.com

"The original low-key power restaurant", this Knightsbridge pillar of an international Chinese mini-chain has been "always packed" and peppered with "celebrities" since the 1960s, thanks in large part to staff who "know the meaning of good service"; even if the "novelty has faded" for some, many still stop by for the "well-prepared" "traditional" Mandarin dishes, for which it's wise to be armed with "an expense account" ("lunch is the better bet").

Mr. Kong ● *Chinese*   22 | 11 | 18 | £24

Chinatown | 21 Lisle St., WC2H 7BA | 020-7437-7341 | www.mrkongrestaurant.com

"Quality and reliability" characterise the "generous plates" of "delightful" Cantonese fare at this Chinatown "staple" whose menu stars "amazing duck" and a "tremendous variety" of vegetarian options; sure, there's "no atmosphere", but with "nice service" thrown into the mix, it's a "great place to spend a little for a feast" – very little; P.S. it's open until the wee small hours.

Murano ⊠ *European/Italian*   26 | 22 | 25 | £84

Mayfair | 20 Queen St., W1J 5PR | 020-7495-1127 | www.muranolondon.com

"Exciting", "intricate" Modern European cooking with a "zesty" "Italian accent" comes from chef Angela Hartnett's kitchen at this Mayfair "gold standard"; though a few folks deem the decor "bland", most call it a "lovely" "atmosphere of class and sophistication", coupled with expectedly "meticulous service" and "grown-up prices";

	FOOD	DECOR	SERVICE	COST

P.S. for "value", choose the "fantastic" set lunch, and for "dazzle", try the "wonderful tasting menu."

Nahm *Thai* 　　　　　　　　　26 | 18 | 25 | £63

Belgravia | The Halkin | 5 Halkin St., SW1X 7DJ | 020-7333-1234 | www.nahm.como.bz

If you crave "classy Thai food" that's "off the scale in terms of authenticity and flavour", "you're in for a treat" at chef David Thompson's "small" dining room in Belgravia's boutique Halkin Hotel; despite "excellent wines", the somewhat "uninspiring" decor means it may not be the place for romance, but with such "polite, professional service" and "expensive" prices, it works for a "business situation."

❷ Nando's *Portuguese* 　　　　21 | 18 | 18 | £17

Bloomsbury | 57-59 Goodge St., W1 1TH | 020-7637-0708
Covent Garden | 66-68 Chandos Pl., WC2N 4HG | 020-7836-4719 ◑
Marylebone | 113 Baker St., W1U 6RS | 020-3075-1044 ◑
Blackheath | 16 Lee High Rd., SE13 5LQ | 020-8463-0119
Bethnal Green | 366 Bethnal Green Rd., E2 0AH |
020-7729-5783
Hampstead | 252-254 West End Ln., NW6 1LU |
020-7794-1331 ◑
Camden Town | 57-58 Chalk Farm Rd., NW1 8AN | 020-7424-9040 ◑
Islington | 324 Upper St., N1 2XQ | 020-7288-0254 ◑
Brixton | 59-63 Clapham High St., SW4 7TG | 020-7622-1475
Bayswater | 63 Westbourne Grove, W2 4UA | 020-7313-9506 ◑
www.nandos.co.uk
Additional locations throughout London

A "cool selection of sauces" ranging from "wimp to extreme" means the flame-grilled peri-peri chicken "suits every taste" at this "casual", "colourful" Portuguese chain; service can be "uneven", but it's mostly "rapid" and "friendly", and the prices are "inexpensive" too, making it an "all-around crowd-pleaser"; P.S. there are "non-chicken things too."

The Narrow *British* 　　　　　18 | 18 | 16 | £40

Wapping | 44 Narrow St., E14 8DP | 020-7592-7950 |
www.gordonramsay.com

For many, it's "a bit of a hike" to this "cosy" Gordon Ramsay gastropub on a "big bend in the Thames" in Wapping, but it's "worth the adventure" for "straight-up" Traditional British grub that "does not disappoint", despite "a few extra quid on the prices for the location" (and famous owner); "trendier-than-need-to-be staff" sometimes "struggle to keep up", but if you snare a window seat, you can "wind away" any waits whilst taking in the "great views."

National Dining Rooms *British* 　∇ 19 | 19 | 16 | £42

Soho | National Gallery, Sainsbury Wing | Trafalgar Sq., WC2N 5DN |
020-7747-2525 | www.thenationaldiningrooms.co.uk

"Lovely views" of Trafalgar Square are afforded from this "oasis" in the National Gallery whose "quality" Modern British menu is "reasonably priced considering the location"; some "communal tables" make it an "easy way to dine alone", either for late-morning "grazing", lunch and, on Fridays when it's open until 8.30 PM, dinner.

	FOOD	DECOR	SERVICE	COST

Nautilus Fish 🗷⍨ *Seafood* ▽ 27 | 12 | 24 | £17

Hampstead | 27-29 Fortune Green Rd., NW6 1DU | 020-7435-2532
Perhaps the "best fish 'n' chips in North London" is found at this stalwart, making it "worth the walk from West Hampstead tube"; affordable prices and "family-friendly service" are further incentives, and if "basic decor" is a deterrent, the "takeaway quality" is equally "high."

New Culture Revolution *Chinese* 20 | 12 | 17 | £20

Islington | 42 Duncan St., N1 8BW | 020-7833-9083
Chelsea | 305 King's Rd., SW3 5EP | 020-7352-9281 |
www.newculturerevolution.co.uk
"Purify your soul" with "big bowls of comforting warm noodles" and other "healthy", "heartwarming" Mandarin dishes at this "reliable" duo in Chelsea and Islington; the "bland", "basic setting" means many "don't want to linger here", but "efficient", "polite service" and "amazing value" keep most coming back for more.

New Mayflower ● *Chinese* 25 | 15 | 19 | £26

Soho | 68-70 Shaftesbury Ave., W1D 6LY | 020-7734-9207
Despite a "lack of space" and "dated" look, this Soho Chinese is "worth going to again and again" to sample its complete line of "amazing" dishes, particularly the seafood; if occasionally "abrupt service" grates, all is forgiven when the affordable bill is presented.

New World ● *Chinese* 20 | 13 | 15 | £25

Chinatown | 1 Gerrard Pl., W1D 5PA | 020-7434-2508
Expect "a never-ending stream" of "traditional dim sum delivered on trolleys" at this "cavernous", "shabby" Chinatown venue where all of the Cantonese eats, including the more "exotic dishes", are a "safe bet", and "well priced" too; "speedy service" makes it "a good choice even at busy times", such as the "exciting Sunday lunch."

1901 *British* 23 | 21 | 20 | £51

City | Andaz Liverpool St. | 40 Liverpool St., EC2M 7QN |
020-7618-7000 | www.andazdining.com
At this "buzzing, huge hall of a place" set in the City's Andaz Liverpool Street Hotel, the "excellent", sometimes "inspired" Modern British fare competes with "beautiful" decor flourishes such as a stained-glass dome; service gets mixed reports ("attentive" vs. "needs to improve"), but most agree it's a "proper" choice for everything from a "quick" "work lunch" to a "special occasion."

Nobu Berkeley St. ● *Japanese* 26 | 22 | 21 | £79

Mayfair | 15 Berkeley St., W1J 8DY | 020-7290-9222 |
www.noburestaurants.com
"Off the charts for watching the young, rich and famous", this "upbeat" Berkeley Square "destination" (sibling of the Park Lane flagship) serves Nobu Matsuhisa's "terrific" Japanese-Peruvian - "inventions", including the "to-die-for" signature black cod; a "swish" setting featuring a "contemporary" upstairs dining room and a "fabulous" downstairs bar, service that runs the gamut from "warm" to "haughty" and "high prices" complete the picture.

	FOOD	DECOR	SERVICE	COST

☑ Nobu London *Japanese* | 27 | 21 | 22 | £83 |

Mayfair | Metropolitan Hotel | 19 Old Park Ln., W1K 1LB |
020-7447-4747 | www.noburestaurants.com

"People-watching foodies" have both penchants sated at this "chic"
Old Park Lane landmark thanks to Nobu Matsuhisa's "wonderful",
"creative" Japanese-Peruvian dishes and the "beautiful" crowd ("more
low-key" than Berkeley Square); some find the service "underwhelm-
ing" and the decor too "minimalist" considering the "very expensive"
prices, but for the most part, the experience "never fails" to please.

Noor Jahan *Indian* | 23 | 13 | 20 | £33 |

South Kensington | 2 Bina Gdns., SW5 0LA | 020-7373-6522
Paddington | 26 Sussex Pl., W2 2TH | 020-7402-2332
www.noorjahanrestaurants.co.uk

"When you're in an Indian food mood" in Paddington or South Ken and
don't mind "simple decor", check out these "trusted places for your
favourite curry"; "courteous staff" and "great value" ("for the areas")
are other pluses, so no surprise "it's often full" ("better book").

Nopi *Asian/Mideastern* | 25 | 22 | 22 | £54 |

Soho | 21-22 Warwick St., W1B 5NE | 020-7494-9584 |
www.nopi-restaurant.com

It's a good thing there's "something for everyone" on the "intriguing",
"innovative" all-day Pan-Asian–Middle Eastern menu at this Soho
offshoot of Ottolenghi, because the "dishes are made for sharing";
however, the "small portions" lead quite a few surveyors to deem it
"overpriced", despite the added benefits of "accommodating" staff
and "gorgeous" digs decked out in "lots of gold and white."

Northbank ☑ *British* | ∇ 15 | 20 | 16 | £49 |

City | 1 Paul's Walk, EC4V 3QH | 020-7329-9299 |
www.northbankrestaurant.com

A "fantastic position" on the north bank of the Thames with "terrific" "views of the Tate Modern" plus "nice booths for an intimate
dinner or bigger tables for groups" earn points for this Modern Brit
in the City; however, it falls short for a few respondents who find the
"no-fuss" fare "overpriced" and some staff "flippant."

North Road ☑ *European* | 27 | 23 | 23 | £61 |

Clerkenwell | 69-73 St. John St., EC1M 4AN | 020-3217-0033 |
www.northroadrestaurant.co.uk

An "exciting", sometimes "avant garde" "adventure" is on offer at
this "friendly" Scandinavian-inspired Modern Euro venue where the
plates are "full of colours" and the decor is "minimal"; it's a bit pricey
and "out of the way" if you're not near Clerkenwell, but it's "well
worth" it, especially if you opt for the "spectacular tasting menu."

North Sea ☑ *Seafood* | 25 | 15 | 22 | £23 |

Bloomsbury | 7-8 Leigh St., WC1H 9EW | 020-7387-5892 |
www.northseafishrestaurant.co.uk

"For a seaside taste in the big city", try this Bloomsbury spot offering
"big portions" of "marvelous fish 'n' chips" et al. with "excellent" sides

like mushy peas; what's more, service is "friendly" and prices are "reasonable" whether taking out or dining in the "no-frills" setting.

Notting Hill Brasserie Ⓜ *European*
22 | 21 | 20 | £57
Notting Hill | 92 Kensington Park Rd., W11 2PN | 020-7229-4481 ▮
www.nottinghillbrasserie.com

As "comfortable and unpretentious" as a brasserie should be, this "vibrant" Notting Hill stalwart pairs "tantalising", sometimes "unusual" Modern European fare with "fab cocktails", all served by "accommodating staff" and "priced in line with the overall quality"; "lovely" nightly jazz and the "perfect distance between tables" makes it appealing "for low-key special occasions."

Noura *Lebanese*
22 | 18 | 20 | £43
Belgravia | 16 Hobart Pl., SW1W 0HH | 020-7235-9444 ◑
Knightsbridge | 12 William St., SW1X 9HL | 020-7235-5900
Mayfair | 16 Curzon St., W1J 5HP | 020-7495-1050 ◑
www.noura.co.uk

"Large" portions of "delicious Lebanese" cuisine with "all the trimmings" – "fit for vegans or carnivores" – come via "friendly, fast" service at this "welcoming" West End trio; prices are "a bit expensive" for the genre, but they also get you "smart" decor and an "out of-this-world" wine selection.

NEW Novikov ◑ *Asian/Italian*
20 | 20 | 20 | £70
Mayfair | 50 Berkeley St., W1J 8HA | 020-7399-4330 |
www.novikovrestaurant.co.uk

Prolific Russian restaurateur Arkady Novikov's first London foray is this "buzzy", tri-tiered Mayfair behemoth comprised of an Asian dining room featuring granite walls, natural wood and a "beautiful market stall", a "lovely, light" Italian eatery with suede-clad walls and a "great", dark lounge with deep sofas and a chill musical beat; meanwhile, "wonderful" cooking, "attentive" service and a "pricey" bill can be found throughout.

Nozomi ◑ *Japanese*
16 | 16 | 16 | £72
Knightsbridge | 15 Beauchamp Pl., SW3 1NQ | 020-7838-1500 |
www.nozomi.co.uk

The "coolest of the cool" come to this "trendy" Knightsbridge spot serving sushi and other Japanese small plates; however, "disco" decor, "loud" DJ-driven music and fare that's "overpriced" for being of merely "adequate" quality mean it's "probably a place to visit for atmosphere rather than food."

Odette's *European*
25 | 23 | 25 | £63
Primrose Hill | 130 Regent's Park Rd., NW1 8XL | 020-7586-8569 ▮
www.odettesprimrosehill.com

"Beautifully cooked" Modern European dishes are offered in a "romantic", "intimate" setting with "efficient service" and a "massive wine list" at this "old-time" Primrose Hill haunt; if some of the regular prices are "expensive", "rock-bottom" lunch and early-bird specials make it "easy to give it a try", with dining in the garden an especially "enjoyable" experience in summertime.

	FOOD	DECOR	SERVICE	COST

Odin's ⊠ *British/French* `21` `24` `23` `£59`
Marylebone | 27 Devonshire St., W1G 6PL | 020-7935-7296 |
www.langansrestaurants.co.uk

"If you like art galleries", this "old-school restaurant" in Marylebone
(dating back to the 1960s) has "walls packed with great charm", including "19th-century paintings" plus some Hockneys; "though never
a knockout", the "reliable" Franco-British cuisine has a "modern
touch", and is presented by "non-intrusive service" with "starchy
napkins" in a "pleasant, gentle ambience."

Old Brewery *British* ▽ `19` `24` `18` `£27`
Greenwich | Pepys Bldg. | Old Royal Naval College, SE10 9LW |
020-3327-1280 | www.oldbrewerygreenwich.com

"Have a pint or two of Meantime Ale right where they make it", that
is this "fabulous" Greenwich microbrewery whose "interesting brews"
are incorporated into many of the "unpretentious", midpriced Modern
British dishes; the "historic" setting – dominated by eight 1,000-litre
copper vats and augmented by a "funky" bar – feels like a "family-
friendly cafe" by day and more of a proper "restaurant by night."

Old Bull & Bush *European* `20` `20` `19` `£32`
Hampstead | North End Rd., NW3 7HE | 020-8905-5456 |
www.thebullandbush.co.uk

With its "great location just off the Heath" and "pleasant" service, this
midpriced Modern Euro is "always full" with Hampstead locals enjoying "tasty victuals", especially the "famous Sunday roast"; combining a "cosy" bar and "more formal" restaurant, the "family venue"
also boasts "log fires" in winter and an outdoor terrace in summer.

Oliveto *Italian* `24` `14` `18` `£34`
Belgravia | 49 Elizabeth St., SW1W 9PP | 020-7730-0074 |
www.olivorestaurants.com

"It doesn't look much from outside", but this Italian is actually a "little
jewel" serving "delicious, unusual" Sardinian bites and "divine thin-
crust pizzas", all "reasonably priced for Belgravia"; despite "high noise
levels" and service that can swing from "friendly" to "brusque", it's
"harder to score a table here than at Olivo" (its nearby sib).

Olivo *Italian* `22` `15` `21` `£39`
Victoria | 21 Eccleston St., SW1W 9LX | 020-7730-2505 |
www.olivorestaurants.com

"Deservedly popular and not that pricey", this "cosy" Victoria Italian
pairs pastas to "dream about" and other "superb", seafood-centric
Sardinian fare with "excellent service"; loyalists who "make a point to
go there" assess that its "down-to-earth", "adult" vibe is "a bit of a ref-
uge by comparison" to its younger sib, Oliveto, though "not less busy."

Olivomare *Italian/Seafood* `24` `17` `21` `£51`
Belgravia | 10 Lower Belgrave St., SW1W 0LJ | 020-7730-9022 |
www.olivorestaurants.com

"Belgravia cognoscenti" feast on "imaginative", "wonderful seafood" with "Sardinian flavour" at this "modern" "cousin to Olivo and

	FOOD	DECOR	SERVICE	COST

Oliveto", where service is a "balance of friendly and professional" and the bill is "pricey without being expensive"; if it's "too bad about the incredible noise levels" – and what some find "bizarre" environs, with its all-white "modern" decor broken up by a fish mural – most usually welcome "an excuse for a return visit."

NEW One Blenheim Terrace Ⓜ British — | — | — | M

St. John's Wood | 1 Blenheim Terr., NW8 0EH | 020-7372-1722 | www.oneblenheimterrace.co.uk

Retro with a 21st-century twist sums up the approach at this new local in St. John's Wood, the debut effort of an Ivy alum who's offering unique spins on British classics; the relaxed setting also mixes tradition (white tablecloths) with modern touches (sleek leather chairs), whilst the prices swing from moderate to expensive.

❷ 1 Lombard Street Ⓢ French   22 | 22 | 22 | £58

City | 1 Lombard St., EC3V 9AA | 020-7929-6611 | www.1lombardstreet.com

"Bankers, lawyers" and other "suits" are "well taken care of" by "slick" staff at this "bright, airy" "power spot" behind the same-named City brasserie in a former banking hall; to eat are "beautifully presented", "dependable" New French dishes, which are available with a "wide choice of wines" and priced for "expense accounts."

1 Lombard Street   21 | 21 | 20 | £46
Brasserie Ⓢ European

City | 1 Lombard St., EC3V 9AA | 020-7929-6611 | www.1lombardstreet.com

Sharing the same "interesting architecture" as its swankier, same-named sib, this "busy, buzzy" Modern European in a former City banking hall is "the more affordable option", with a "better-than-average" menu that "has everything you want"; whether you come for breakfast, lunch or dinner, expect "fast service" and a crowd "awash" in "bankers, brokers and financiers."

One-O-One French/Seafood   22 | 18 | 22 | £70

Knightsbridge | Sheraton Park Tower | 101 Knightsbridge, SW1X 7RN | 020-7290-7101 | www.oneoonerestaurant.com

"Tucked away" in Knightsbridge's Sheraton Park Tower, this New French seafooder showcases "fresh fish" prepared in "imaginative ways" and served by "charming" staff; some are less charmed by the setting ("soulless"), but for admirers who "love pretty much everything about it except the price", there's always the "excellent-value" prix fixe lunch.

108 Marylebone Lane British   21 | 20 | 21 | £44

Marylebone | Marylebone Hotel | 108 Marylebone Ln., W1U 2QE | 020-7969-3900 | www.one08.co.uk

With "prompt" service from "attentive" staff and a "safe" Traditional British menu, this "inviting", "tastefully decorated" bi-level bistro inside a Marylebone hotel is a "decent-value" "standby" if you're in the area; what's more, it's also "a convenient place for after-work" "cocktails and nibbles."

☑ 101 Thai Kitchen *Thai* | 24 | 20 | 22 | £38 |

Hammersmith | 352 King St., W6 0RX | 020-8746-6888 |
www.101thaikitchen.com

"Thai me down here anytime" declare devotees of this Hammersmith
"hole-in-the-wall" serving "curries made with care" and other "exel-
lent" dishes for "reasonable" prices; though some wish they could
"keep it secret", it's "always packed with locals" enjoying the "fab"
service and "simple", "stylish" surrounds.

Only Running Footman *British*   ▽ | 18 | 17 | 19 | £37 |

Mayfair | 5 Charles St., W1J 5DF | 020-7499-2988 |
www.therunningfootman.biz

"In an area packed with expensive eateries", this traditional Mayfair
boozer stands out for its "reasonable" roster of "interesting" British
gastropub fare, served by "efficient" staff; expect "hedgies happily"
indulging in the "roaring" ground-floor bar and more "upscale" upstairs dining room – "both are worth a visit."

Opera Tavern ● *Italian/Spanish* | 24 | 20 | 22 | £42 |

Covent Garden | 23 Catherine St., WC2B 5JS | 020-7836-3680 |
www.operatavern.co.uk

The latest "brilliant extension for the Dehesa/Salt Yard group" is this
Covent Garden hit starring "sumptuous" Spanish-Italian tapas and
grilled items exhibiting both "flair and subtlety"; "wonderful wines",
"accommodating" service and "good atmosphere" – whether in the
downstairs bar or chandeliered upstairs dining room – are further as-
sets, so even if costs can "run up", it's a "welcome addition."

Orange Restaurant ● *European* | 22 | 22 | 20 | £49 |

Pimlico | The Orange | 37-39 Pimlico Rd., SW1W 8NE |
020-7881-9844 | www.theorange.co.uk

This "bustling" Pimlico sibling of Thomas Cubitt offers "something for
everyone" on its Modern European "comfort-food" menu, including
"good pizza"; both the ground-floor pub and "beautifully decorated",
fireplace-equipped upstairs room boast "country home–style decor"
and a "friendly" ambience, and though prices aren't cheap, fans deem
them "good value for London"; P.S. it's part of a small hotel.

Original Lahore ● *Pakastani*   ▽ | 23 | 13 | 18 | £22 |

Hendon | 148-150 Brent St., NW4 2DR | 020-8203-6904
St. John's Wood | 2-4 Gateforth St., NW8 8EH | 020-723-0808
www.originallahore.com

"Amazing kebabs and naan" are just some of the "tasty" dishes sold
for "excellent prices" at this "friendly" pair of Pakistanis in Hendon
and St. John's Wood; the decor may be "getting tired", but that doesn't
deter devotees who could "go here every day."

Orrery *French* | 24 | 22 | 24 | £64 |

Marylebone | 55 Marylebone High St., W1U 5RB | 020-7616-8000 |
www.orreryrestaurant.co.uk

"Good-humoured" staff are "committed to making you feel at home"
at this "discreetly located" Marylebone New French where "exqui-

	FOOD	DECOR	SERVICE	COST

site", "beautifully presented" dishes (including an "exceptional" cheese board) and "serious" wines are "worth the price" for a "special night out" or "fabulous" Sunday lunch; "large, lovely windows" overlooking St. Marylebone Church plus a rooftop terrace enhance the "chic", "comfortable" atmosphere.

Orso ◐ *Italian* 21 | 18 | 21 | £44

Covent Garden | 27 Wellington St., WC2E 7DB | 020-7240-5269 | www.orsorestaurant.co.uk

"Understated" and "underground", this "quirky" Italian "hideaway on the edge of Covent Garden" is "reliable" for "decent-value" fare (including "terrific" pizzas and pastas) served by "agreeable staff"; though "perhaps it needs some redecorating", late hours make it a "great post-theatre spot", where diners are often "rewarded" with "glimpses of celebrities."

Oslo Court ⊠ *French* 26 | 19 | 26 | £54

St. John's Wood | Charlbert St., off Prince Albert Rd., NW8 7EN | 020-7722-8795

A "loving" tribute to a "bygone age", this bit of "ultimate kitsch" (decked out in "flamingo"-"pink chintz") in St. John's Wood is "unbeatable for a special treat", with "rich", "expertly prepared" French classics from a "menu as long as *Great Expectations*"; yes, it's "on the pricey side", but "generous" portions ensure "you won't come away hungry", plus there's "lots of schmoozing" from "attentive, friendly" staff (insiders say the "dessert waiter is worth the dining experience alone").

Osteria Antica Bologna *Italian* ∇ 21 | 18 | 19 | £40

Clapham | 23 Northcote Rd., SW11 1NG | 020-7978-4771 | www.osteria.co.uk

Day-trippers returning to London "ease back in with great pleasure" at this "twee" trattoria a stone's throw from Clapham Junction station, where a Boot-based wine list complements "generous portions" of "classic pasta dishes" and other "reliable", moderately priced Italian fare; solid service and charming decor, with touches of dark wood and wrought iron, make it an "ideal" local pit stop.

Osteria Basilico ◐ *Italian* 25 | 18 | 20 | £39

Notting Hill | 29 Kensington Park Rd., W11 2EU | 020-7727-9957 | www.osteriabasilico.co.uk

"It's not easy to get a reservation, but once there, you're one of the family" at this "vibrant" Notting Hill Italian with a "cosy", "rustic" look and "heartwarming" regional "comfort food" (including "thin, crispy" pizzas and "yummy pastas") at "great prices"; though "the dining room is a little cramped", aficionados consider it a "local failsafe" when they want to "stay awhile, imbibe and relax."

Osteria dell'Arancio *Italian* 21 | 17 | 23 | £51

Chelsea | 383 King's Rd., SW10 0LP | 020-7349-8111 | www.osteriadellarancio.co.uk

"Slightly off the beaten track" on the "cusp of Chelsea and World's End" sits this "quirky", colourful bi-level Italian where "enthusiastic" staff proffer a "strong" menu and a "good choice of wines by the glass"; what's more, the prices "fit the budget" for most, making for an overall "comfortable dining experience."

❸ Ottolenghi   *Bakery/Mediterranean*   26 | 19 | 20 | £32

Belgravia | 13 Motcomb St., SW1X 8LB | 020-7823-2707
Islington | 287 Upper St., N1 2TZ | 020-7288-1454
Kensington | 1 Holland St., W8 4NA | 020-7937-0003
Notting Hill | 63 Ledbury Rd., W11 2AD | 020-7727-1121
www.ottolenghi.co.uk

"Scrumptious desserts" "piled high" in the windows tempt at this "lively" cafe/bakery chain, but what really causes "queues out the door" is the "spectacular choice" of "robust" Mediterranean dishes like "phenomenal" salads), which are served "mainly at communal tables" by "amicable" staff in "white minimalist" environs; quite a few folks find it "pricey for what it is", but even more say it's "worth it" because "passion is evident in the whole package"; P.S. Kensington is takeaway only.

Oxo Tower   *European*   22 | 25 | 22 | £72

South Bank | Oxo Tower Wharf | Barge House St., 8th fl., SE1 9PH | 020-7803-3888 | www.harveynichols.com

"If you want to impress someone", the "panoramic views" of the Thames from the eighth floor of this "posh" South Bank Modern Euro "destination" make for an "unforgettable experience"; the "trendy" are is "enjoyable" too, and staff are usually "attentive", all adding to an "overall positive experience – if your pockets are full of cash."

Oxo Tower Brasserie   *Asian/Mediterranean*   23 | 23 | 21 | £52

South Bank | Oxo Tower Wharf | Barge House St., 8th fl., SE1 9PH | 020-7803-3888 | www.harveynichols.com

This "funky", glass-wrapped perch on the Oxo Tower's eighth floor presents the same "spectacular" skyline view as its next-door sibling, but features a "less pricey" menu of "tasty", "inventive" Med and Pan-Asian victuals and "incredible cocktails" delivered by "helpful" staff; nightly jazz is "an extra perk", and though the "buzzy" atmosphere sometimes verges on "deafening", revelers "can't get enough of the place."

Özer Restaurant & Bar   *Turkish*   21 | 20 | 20 | £35

Marylebone | 5 Langham Pl., W1B 3DG | 020-7323-0505 | www.ozerrestaurant.com

"Amazing" lamb tagine and other "upmarket" Turkish dishes are a "steal for the money" at this "friendly" Oxford Circus "gem" where there's "loads of choice" (including an extensive wine list); "off the beaten path but well worth it", the "cosy", "modern" space is supplemented by a patio suitable for "watching the world go by."

Painted Heron   *Indian*   23 | 20 | 21 | £47

Chelsea | 112 Cheyne Walk, SW10 0DJ | 020-7351-5232 | www.thepaintedheron.com

"One of Chelsea's best-kept secrets", this Indian "hideout" along the Thames serves "traditional curries with a modern twist", using "unique ingredients like venison and pheasant" for a "satisfying" if "pricey" meal; what's more, "charming" service and sophisticated, modern decor make it "a good date spot."

The Palm *American/Chophouse*   22 | 21 | 22 | £63

Belgravia | 1 Pont St., SW1X 9EJ | 020-7201-0710 | www.thepalm.com
"Proper porterhouses" and other "juicy" cuts are "cooked to perfection" and teamed with "enormous sides" at this Belgravia link of the "quintessential American steakhouse" chain, where "efficient" staff "give good recommendations on both food and wine"; "wonderful murals of favoured patrons" jazz up the digs, and whilst some scorn the "lofty prices", most "would go again."

The Palmerston *British*   ▽ 24 | 20 | 21 | £32

Dulwich | 91 Lordship Ln., SE22 8EP | 020-8693-1629 | www.thepalmerston.net
"Whether you want a quiet dinner with a loved one, a laugh with friends or to impress the in-laws", this "gorgeous" Dulwich gastropub is a "reliable" option, with Modern British fare that's "superbly cooked" and "fantastic value" to boot; other enticements include "friendly staff", two fireplaces and works by "local artists" on the walls.

Pantechnicon Rooms *European*   22 | 21 | 22 | £43

Belgravia | 10 Motcomb St., SW1X 8LA | 020-7730-6074 | www.thepantechnicon.com
The "owners have the formula just right" at this "swanky" Cubitt House outpost in Belgravia, where "tasty", "reasonably priced" Modern European eats and "friendly" service make it a "big family hit", especially for a "fantastic Sunday lunch"; from casual eats in the "noisy" ground-floor pub and leisurely patio dining to a "more formal" meal in the"charming" upstairs dining room (complete with a "blazing fireplace"), it's an all-around "delightful experience."

Paradise by way of Kensal Green ● *British* ▽ 25 | 25 | 23 | £38

Kilburn | 19 Kilburn Ln., W10 4AE | 020-8969-0098 | www.theparadise.co.uk
The "playful name" hints at the "laid-back vibe" and "cool crowd" of "fashionistas" at this "gorgeous" Kilburn hangout, "one of the pillars of the Gastro Revolution", with a "fairly priced", "wholesome" Modern British menu and "warm, welcoming" staff; what's more, it boasts a "beautiful" roof terrace and doubles as a "party venue" that's "open late" for "boozing", dancing and karaoke, plus live music at weekends

Paramount ● *European*   23 | 25 | 20 | £76

Soho | Centre Point | 101-103 New Oxford St., 32nd fl., WC1A 1DD | 020-7420-2900 | www.paramount.uk.net
"You feel you're in an exclusive place when they whisk you up in the lift" to this "wow destination" on the 32nd floor of Soho's Centre Point, whose "contemporary" setting with "amazing 360-degree views of London" put it "in high demand"; whilst prices are "expensive", the Modern Euro fare is "delicious", and though sometimes "slow" service is a "turnoff", the "superb wine list" and "cool bar" make amends.

	FOOD	DECOR	SERVICE	COST

Pasha *Turkish*
∇ 22 | 17 | 23 | £31

Islington | 301 Upper St., N1 2TU | 020-7226-1454 |
www.pashaislington.co.uk

"Tasty, high-class Turkish" fare proves quite "popular" in Islington at
this "comfortable" eatery decked out in "contemporary, sophisticated decor"; what's more, "prices are low for what you get", namely
"generous portions" and "helpful" service.

Pasha ● *Moroccan*
∇ 21 | 21 | 19 | £48

South Kensington | 1 Gloucester Rd., SW7 4PP | 020-7589-7969

"Feel transported to North Africa when you step into" this South
Kensington venue where the "solid, expensive" Moroccan menu
boasts the likes of "winter-warming tagines" and the "lavish" setting
is studded with private alcoves; staff who are mostly "charming" abet
its rep as "a great place to make a night of things", especially if you
like belly dancers, who take the floor Thursday–Saturday evenings.

Patara *Thai*
24 | 20 | 21 | £41

Knightsbridge | 9 Beauchamp Pl., SW3 1NQ | 020-7581-8820
Mayfair | 3-7 Maddox St., W1S 2QB | 020-7499-6008
Soho | 15 Greek St., W1D 4DP | 020-7437-1071
South Kensington | 181 Fulham Rd., SW3 6JN | 020-7351-5692
www.patarauk.com

"For a cosy rendezvous, larger get-together" or just "something low-
key and immediate", this "stylish" foursome fits the bill with "well-
executed", "modern upmarket Thai" dishes; "efficient" service and
"great lunch specials" are added enticements, and though it's "priced
just above the norm", enthusiasts declare it "well worth it."

Paternoster Chop House *Chophouse*
22 | 18 | 19 | £48

City | Warwick Ct., Paternoster Sq., EC4M 7DX | 020-7029-9400 |
www.paternosterchophouse.co.uk

The 'beast of the day' on the menu means it's "always an interesting
experience for meat lovers" at this "friendly", rustic City chophouse
where all of the dishes are "enjoyable"; the "pleasant setup" features
an open kitchen where "you can see the food as it's cooked" plus an
alfresco terrace in the "beautiful surrounds" near St. Paul's Cathedral.

Patisserie Valerie *French*
19 | 15 | 15 | £20

Belgravia | 17 Motcomb St., SW1X 8LB | 020-7245-6161
Covent Garden | 15 Bedford St., WC2E 9HE | 020-7379-6428
Covent Garden | 80 Long Acre, WC2E 9NG | 020-7240-5592
Marylebone | 105 Marylebone High St., W1U 4RS | 020-7935-6240
Mayfair | 15 Great Cumberland Pl., W1H 7AS | 020-7724-8542
Piccadilly | 162 Piccadilly, W1J 9EF | 020-7491-1717
Soho | 44 Old Compton St., W1D 4TY | 020-7437-3466
City | Pavillion Bldg. | 37 Brushfield St., E1 6AA | 020-7247-4906
Chelsea | 81 Duke of York Sq., SW3 4LY | 020-7730-7094
Kensington | 27 Kensington Church St., W8 4LL | 020-7937-9574
www.patisserie-valerie.co.uk
Additional locations throughout London

"The temptation to say 'I'll have one of everything' is high" for anyone
with a penchant for "decadent" cakes and "mouth-watering" pastries

at this "busy" chain of "old-world" bistros-cum–coffee shops where the "affordable" French menu also lists "light savoury snacks"; "simple surroundings" and service that "varies widely" depending on location doesn't deter regulars who admit the "guilty pleasure" is "hard to walk past once you've tried it."

Patterson's ⓩ *British*

| | | | 26 | 21 | 23 | £57 |

Mayfair | 4 Mill St., W1S 2AX | 020-7499-1308 |
www.pattersonsrestaurant.co.uk

The chef-owner is "in the kitchen and it shows" in the "appealing", "top-notch" cooking (available in "terrific value" prix fixes) at this Mayfair Modern Brit, an "oasis two steps from the Regent Street madness"; the "intimate" setting with creamy marble walls and dark-leather seating proves "perfect for a romantic dinner", abetted by "professional" service and a "wine list that covers all bases."

☑ Pearl *French*

| | | | 28 | 25 | 25 | £65 |

Holborn | Renaissance Chancery Court Hotel | 252 High Holborn, WC1V 7EN | 020-7829-7000 | www.pearl-restaurant.com

Believers say "bravo" to "incredible chef" Jun Tanaka's "beautifully crafted and presented" dishes resembling "pieces of art" at this "stunning" Holborn hotel New French adorned with pearl chandeliers and elegant expanses of walnut; "sensibly priced for a restaurant of this calibre", with a "spectacular wine list" and "impeccable" service, it's a "wow" venue that provides a "special" experience, especially if "you want to impress somebody."

Pearl Liang *Chinese*

| | | | 24 | 18 | 17 | £37 |

Paddington | 8 Sheldon Sq., W2 6EZ | 020-7289-7000 |
www.pearlliang.co.uk

"Despite being in the middle of nowhere" ("bring your GPS"), this Paddington Chinese is "always packed" thanks to its "lip-smackingly good" Peking duck, "fantastic selection" of dim sum and other "delicious", "diverse" dishes offered alongside an "interesting cocktail menu"; "prices are on the high side" considering sometimes "spotty" service, but they match the "fancy ambience" bedecked with "grand" bright-pink furnishings.

Pellicano *Italian*

| | | | ▽ 22 | 17 | 20 | £45 |

Chelsea | 19-21 Elystan St., SW3 3NT | 020-7589-3718 |
www.pellicanorestaurant.co.uk

A "posh clientele" inhabits this intimate Chelsea trattoria, a blue-hued, family-owned stalwart praised for its "Sardinian specialities" and "great fixed-price lunch"; in sum, it's a "good local" for a leisurely meal, notably in summer when a smattering of outdoor tables under a bright-blue awning beckons.

☑ Pepper Tree *Thai*

| | | | 27 | 18 | 23 | £17 |

Clapham | 19 Clapham Common S., SW4 7AB | 020-7622-1758 |
www.thepeppertree.co.uk

"Be prepared to be cosy with fellow diners" at this "cheap and cheerful" Clapham Thai where guests gather around communal tables for "delicious" dishes; though there's often a "queue at busy times",

| | FOOD | DECOR | SERVICE | COST |

"knowledgeable waiters" supply "quick and easy service"; P.S. the "movie and a meal" deal with Clapham Picture House is a "bargain."

Pescatori 🗷 *Italian/Seafood* `24` `20` `23` `£45`

Fitzrovia | 57 Charlotte St., W1T 4PD | 020-7580-3289
Mayfair | 11 Dover St., W1S 4LH | 020-7493-2652
www.pescatori.co.uk

"You can be sure of a warm welcome" at this "quiet" Italian seafood duo in Fitzrovia and Mayfair, whose "enjoyable" fare "fits the bill" for something "not too stuffy or formal", whether a "business lunch" or an "after-work meal"; though cost-calculators suspect the "pricing is high for what you get", they're mollified by the "great-value set menus"; P.S. "go alfresco" via the summertime terrace seating.

The Petersham *European* `23` `22` `23` `£61`

Richmond | Petersham Hotel | Nightingale Ln., TW10 6UZ |
020-8940-7471 | www.petershamhotel.co.uk

A "fabulous vista down the Thames" is afforded from this "dignified" dining room in a "historic hotel" "on the slopes of Richmond Hill", where the kitchen turns out "well-prepared" Modern European cuisine; although "high prices" deter some, "friendly, nonintrusive service", an "extensive" wine list and "ample parking" encourage revisits.

Petersham Nurseries Café 🅼 *European* `24` `21` `20` `£48`

Richmond | Petersham Nurseries | Church Ln., TW10 7AG |
020-8940-5230 | www.petershamnurseries.com

The "eccentricities" of this "charming", "welcoming", "completely original" Modern European eatery in a Richmond greenhouse include "flimsy wooden benches", a "dirt floor" and "cows mooing in the distance"; post-Survey saw the arrival of a respected Australian chef, and though his new menu remains pricey, it now boasts many Eastern Mediterranean inspirations, outdating the Food score.

🗷 Petrus 🗷 *French* `28` `26` `27` `£103`

Belgravia | 1 Kinnerton St., SW1X 8EA | 020-7592-1609 |
www.gordonramsay.com

Hats off to Gordon Ramsay for his "elegant", "cosseting" Belgravia venue where surveyors "appreciate the charms the kitchen has to offer" in "exhilarating" New French dishes ("high priced but worth it") along with a "stunning" cheese selection; add in staff who are relaxed but 100% professional – including a "sommelier who certainly knows" the "amazing" wines stored in a central glass-encased room – and small wonder advocates say it's a "must-visit" for "a date or just to pamper yourself."

Pho *Vietnamese* `21` `15` `18` `£20`

Fitzrovia | 3 Great Titchfield St., W1W 8AX |
020-7436-0111 🗷
Soho | 163-165 Wardour St., W1F 8WN | 020-7434-3938
Stratford | Westfield Stratford City | 2 Stratford Pl., balcony, E20 1ES |
020-8555-5737
Farringdon | 86 St. John St., EC1M 4EH | 020-7253-7624 🗷

(continued)

(continued)

Pho

Shepherd's Bush | Westfield Shopping Ctr. | Ariel Way, balcony, W12 7GE |
07824-662320

www.phocafe.co.uk

"When only pho will do" – for example, when you need "the perfect
hangover cure" – this "buzzing" Vietnamese "street food" chain delivers "piping-hot", "deeply flavoured" broth and "nice firm noodles"
in "massive portions"; whilst the "no-frills" decor "leaves a lot to be
desired" and service is "hit-and-miss", everything comes "quick" and
"at a great price" too.

Phoenix Palace ◑ *Chinese*   23 | 18 | 19 | £30

Marylebone | 5-9 Glentworth St., NW1 5PG | 020-7486-3515 |
www.phoenixpalace.co.uk

"Good-value" dim sum and "big dishes" (including some "esoteric"
offerings) "rarely disappoint" at this "large and buzzing" Marylebone
Cantonese venue; service is often "charming", but it's the "grand"
"blinged-out Chinese palace" decor, awash in "gold and red", that
elevates it to an "exciting experience."

🖬 Pied à Terre 🗷 *French*   27 | 23 | 26 | £94

Fitzrovia | 34 Charlotte St., W1T 2NH | 020-7636-1178 |
www.pied-a-terre.co.uk

Once past the "unassuming entrance", "prepare to be coddled" at
this "elegant" Fitzrovia "jewel box" where "professional" staff seem
to "read minds" as they deliver the "sublime", "work-of-art" New
French dishes, which are supported by "splendid" wines; prices
are "very expensive" indeed, but "for that special treat", they're
"worth every penny" – though you could save a few by opting for
the "incredible-value prix fixe lunch."

Pig's Ear *British/French*   20 | 17 | 14 | £36

Chelsea | 35 Old Church St., SW3 5BS | 020-7352-2908 |
www.thepigsear.info

There's "lots of quaint local flavour" to soak up at this "buzzing gastropub" on a "charming Chelsea backstreet", where "interesting"
Traditional British and French brasserie fare comes at moderate prices;
service varies "depending on the night and the staff" say regulars
who prefer to dodge the "cramped", "noisy" downstairs bar and "book
a table upstairs" in the "rustic" dining room.

Ping Pong *Chinese*   21 | 19 | 19 | £28

Bloomsbury | 48 Eastcastle St., W1W 8DX | 020-7079-0550
Bloomsbury | 48 Newman St., W1T 1QQ | 020-7291-3080
Marylebone | 10 Paddington St., W1U 5QL | 020-7009-9600
Marylebone | 29 James St., W1U 1DZ | 020-7034-3100
Soho | Royal Festival Hall | Belvedere Rd., W1F 7JL |
020-7851-6969 ◑
City | 3 Appold St., EC2A 2AF | 020-7422-0780 🗷
City | 3-6 Steward St., E1 6FQ | 020-7422-7650
South Bank | Royal Festival Hall | Belvedere Rd., Festival Terr., SE1 8XX |
020-7960-4160 ◑

(continued)

Ping Pong

Tower Bridge | St. Katherine Docks | St. Katharine's Way, E1W 1BA | 020-7680-7850
Notting Hill | 74-76 Westbourne Grove, W2 5SH | 020-7313-9832
www.pingpongdimsum.com
Additional locations throughout London

"For those who don't want to brave Chinatown", this "crowded", "hip" Chinese chain offers a "wonderful array" of "tasty" dim sum and other "creative morsels" for "reasonable prices"; "enthusiastic", "efficient" service can abet a "quick meal", though unhurried types say it's worth lingering at the "shared tables" over "excellent" gourmet teas and "cocktails with a twist."

☑NEW Pitt Cue Co. ☒ *BBQ*   28 | 18 | 27 | £21

Soho | 1 Newburgh St., W1F 7RB | 020-7287-5578 | www.pittcue.co.uk

It's been a "natural progression" from "emblazoned pig van" to a permanent home in a "Soho basement" for this "superb" purveyor of "serious BBQ meat action", a "destination" for "juicy, tender, smoky" American-style "meaty delights" and "stunning sides"; if "the only quibble" is there are "few tables and usually a queue", "disarming" service and a "fun whisky bar" heighten the "bliss."

Pix Pintxos ◐ *Spanish*   13 | 15 | 10 | £27

Covent Garden | 63 Neal St., WC2H 9PJ | 020-7836-9779
NEW Soho | 16 Bateman St., W1D 3AH | 020-7437-0377
www.pix-bar.com

A "cool" crowd adds "great ambience" to this "chilled" Spanish duo in Covent Garden and Soho, where a "never-ending" array of "good" tapas comes for "low prices"; just bear in mind that, as is the norm with this sort of place, it's easy to "enjoy the concept and run up a bill pretty quickly."

Pizarro *Spanish*   25 | 22 | 21 | £40

Tower Bridge | 194 Bermondsey St., SE1 3TQ | 020-7378-9455 | www.pizarrorestaurant.com

"Robust" tapas and other "Spanish cuisine with a twist" teamed with an "interesting wine list" make chef-owner Jose Pizarro's midpriced Bermondsey Street encore (after José) a "breath of fresh air"; an open kitchen fills the "large, modern space" with "mouth-watering smells", whilst "charming service" aids a "relaxed", "friendly" vibe; P.S. bookings only taken for lunch, so "expect a wait" in the evening.

Pizza East ◐ *Pizza*   20 | 22 | 18 | £27

Shoreditch | Tea Bldg. | 56 Shoreditch High St., E1 6JJ | 020-7729-1888 | www.pizzaeast.com
Notting Hill | 310 Portobello Rd., W10 5TA | 020-8969-4500 | www.pizzaeastportobello.com

It's "always jam-packed" at these "trendy", midpriced Shoreditch and Portobello Road dough-slingers where diners break out of their "pepperoni comfort zone" via "posh", "inventive" thin-crust pies with "meaty" toppings that "satisfy Italian taste buds"; "service can be slow", but that just leaves more time to engage in the "wonderful people-watching"; P.S. it's quite "kid-friendly" too.

Z Pizza Express *Pizza*   21 | 18 | 19 | £22

Covent Garden | 9-12 Bow St., WC2E 7AH | 020-7240-3443 ●
Knightsbridge | 7 Beauchamp Pl., SW3 1NQ | 020-7589-2355
Soho | 29 Wardour St., W1D 6PS | 020-7437-7215
City | 125 Alban Gate, London Wall, EC2Y 5AS | 020-7600-8880
Battersea | 46-54 Battersea Bridge Rd., SW11 3AG | 020-7924-2774
Chelsea | The Pheasantry | 152-154 King's Rd., SW3 4UT |
020-7351-5031
Fulham | 363 Fulham Rd., SW10 9TN | 020-7352-5300
Fulham | 895-896 Fulham Rd., SW6 5HU | 020-7731-3117
Kensington | 35 Earl's Court Rd., W8 6ED | 020-7937-0761
Notting Hill | 137 Notting Hill Gate, W11 3LB | 020-7229-6000 ●
www.pizzaexpress.co.uk
Additional locations throughout London

"Just gets better and better" marvel fans of this long-standing pizza-chain "institution" whose "affordable" menu is so "diverse", "there's something for everyone", "even low-calorie" pies; each location "has a different feel" and "service varies", but since "you always know what you're going to get" in the food and value departments, it remains a "trusted" "standby" for a "quick bite."

PJ's Bar & Grill ● *American*   20 | 20 | 20 | £35

Covent Garden | 30 Wellington St., WC2E 7BD | 020-7240-7529 |
www.pjscoventgarden.co.uk
Chelsea | 52 Fulham Rd., SW3 6HH | 020-7581-0025 |
www.pjsbarandgrill.co.uk

"It's impossible to eat without having a party" at this "atmospheric" Chelsea haunt (decked out with "relics of the polo world and a huge wooden propeller") and separately owned Covent Garden spot where "you may end up sitting next to the cast of a show you've just watched"; the "solid" American "comfort food" is "not bad for the money", whilst the "smiley staff" will "serve you quickly pre-theatre or leave you alone if you've got all night."

Planet Hollywood ● *American*   16 | 19 | 16 | £33

Piccadilly | 57-60 Haymarket, SW1Y 4QX | 020-7437-7639 |
www.planethollywoodlondon.com

"Movie-prop replicas" attract a "tourist"-heavy crowd at this "noisy", "hustle-bustle" Haymarket outpost of the Tinseltown chain, where "predictable" midpriced American eats are "served promptly" by "smiley" if sometimes "overattentive" staff; ok, so it's a "one-trip wonder" for foodies, but for a kid's "birthday bash", it can be "great fun" – and "reasonably priced" too.

Plateau Z *French*   24 | 24 | 22 | £47

Canary Wharf | Canada Pl. | Canada Sq., 4th fl., E14 5ER |
020-7715-7100 | www.plateaurestaurant.co.uk

"Mingle" with a "loud, successful crowd" of "traders and bankers" whilst taking in a "neat view" of "one of the green spots of Canary Wharf" at this "light", "modern" venue, which provides "lovely" New

| | FOOD | DECOR | SERVICE | COST |

French cuisine and staff who "look after you"; as it's priced for "a big spender", some "like the bar better", but whichever section you choose, it's sure "to make a great first impression."

Plum Valley ● *Chinese* ▽ 25 21 19 £26
Chinatown | 20 Gerrard St., W1D 6JQ | 020-7494-4366

"An oasis of calm" amidst "the hustle and bustle of Chinatown", this "upscale, modern" venue provides an "incredible selection" of Chinese fare "for the hard-core food lover", including "excellent dim sum" and "innovative vegetarian dishes"; such a "serious" culinary focus commands costs that some feel are "a bit pricey" for the genre, but it's "worth trying" nonetheless – just prepare for service that can be either "sweet" or "surly."

Poissonnerie de l'Avenue ● *French/Seafood* 25 20 25 £60
Chelsea | 82 Sloane Ave., SW3 3DZ | 020-7589-2457 |
www.poissonneriedelavenue.com

"Right out of the 1960s", this "elegant" Brompton Cross institution "never fails to impress" with the "superb seafood" on its "classic", "pricey" French menu; sure, younger folks may find the experience "a bit staid", but it's "unlikely to upset" the "old-money crowd" that frequents it.

☑ Pollen Street Social ⧈ *British* 25 22 23 £72
Mayfair | 8-10 Pollen St., W1S 1NQ | 020-7290-7600 |
www.jasonatherton.co.uk

"Hats off to Jason Atherton" (ex Maze) who has created a "special" experience with this Mayfair site comprising a tapas bar and "luxe-casual" dining room offering an "inventive" Modern Brit menu, "awesome wine list" and "charming service", all "worth" the "expensive" prices; fans "particularly love the dessert bar" and its "off-the-charts" sweets, but the most "memorable gimmick" found here may be the "whimsical little parting gift" (don't "spoil the surprise").

Polpo *Italian* 22 19 20 £35
Covent Garden | 6 Maiden Ln., WC2E 7NA | 020-7836-8448 ●
Soho | 41 Beak St., W1F 9SB | 020-7734-4479
NEW **Farringdon** | 2-3 Cowcross St., EC1M 6DR | 020-7250-0034
www.polpo.co.uk

Venetian-style small plates and wines that are as "yummy" as they are "good value" make these "buzzy" Italians "fun after work" and "cool enough for a date"; bookings are taken at lunch only, so at night be prepared to queue for a sometimes "excruciatingly long" time amongst "trendy" "twentysomethings"; P.S. the Food score may not reflect the Covent Garden branch's recent transformation from former sibling Da Polpo.

Popeseye ⧈⧈ *Chophouse* ▽ 24 13 23 £37
Putney | 277 Upper Richmond Rd., SW15 6SP | 020-8788-7733
Olympia | 108 Blythe Rd., W14 0HD | 020-7610-4578
www.popeseye.com

"Don't expect a large menu", as these "old-style" chophouses "off the beaten track" in Putney and Olympia "stick to what they're good at": "various cuts of wonderful red meat, chips and a good selection of sauces"; the atmosphere is strictly "no-frills", but it's boosted by "friendly" service and a bill that's "not too pricey"; P.S. cash only.

Portal 🗷 *Portuguese* ▽ 26 | 23 | 21 | £54

Clerkenwell | 88 St. John St., EC1M 4EH | 020-7253-6950 | www.portalrestaurant.com

"Fantastic Portuguese food" with a "modern" slant is served in "satisfying portions" at this "welcoming" Clerkenwell restaurant, which also boasts an "excellent selection" of Iberian wines and a wine bar serving tapas; and with its "enthusiastic service" and "airy" brick-walled conservatory setting, no wonder admirers deem it a "lovely" "option for business and visitors alike."

Porters English Restaurant *British* 18 | 16 | 17 | £29

Covent Garden | 17 Henrietta St., WC2E 8QH | 020-7836-6466 | www.porters-restaurant.com

With "bubble and squeak", "meat pies and puddings" on its "hearty" menu, this "perennial" "standby" in Covent Garden offers a "good-value" introduction to Traditional British cuisine in cheerful, wood-panelled dining rooms; unsurprisingly, it's a magnet for "tourists", what with wares that are "excellent for all ages" and "efficient service" that can handle any "loud and lively group."

Portobello Ristorante 26 | 18 | 21 | £30
Pizzeria ● *Italian*

Notting Hill | 7 Ladbroke Rd., W11 3PA | 020-7221-1373 | www.portobellolondon.co.uk

"Amazing pizza" is served "by the meter or half-meter" at this "casual" Notting Hill Italian also offering "gorgeous" starters and "top-quality" mains to please even "fussy" palates; "value prices" ensure it's "loud" with "tons of kids during the day", but the atmosphere is also "delightfully romantic" at night and, on the "sunny" terrace, "almost like being in Italy" in summer.

Portrait *British* 22 | 26 | 23 | £41

Soho | National Portrait Gallery | 2 St. Martin's Pl., 3rd fl., WC2H 0HE | 020-7312-2490 | www.searcys.co.uk

"How can mere food compete" with "amazing views" that include "Nelson's Column, Big Ben, the London Eye and Parliament"? – that's what diners wonder about this "stylish" Modern British eatery atop the National Portrait Gallery; but the "well-cooked" victuals do a commendable job, and with relatively reasonable costs and "decent" service too, so no surprise, this is one "ferociously popular" place.

Prezzo *Italian* 20 | 18 | 20 | £27

Marylebone | 15 N. Audley St., W1K 6WZ | 020-7493-4990
Mayfair | 17 Hertford St., W1J 7RS | 020-7499-4690 ●
Mayfair | 7-9 Great Cumberland Pl., W1H 7LU | 020-7723-7172
Piccadilly | 8 Haymarket, SW1Y 4BP | 020-7839-1129
Victoria | 22 Terminus Pl., SW1V 1JR | 020-7233-9099 ●
Westminster | 31-32 Northumberland Ave., WC2N 5BW | 020-7930-4288 ●

(continued)

Prezzo

Kensington | 35 Kensington High St., W8 5EB | 020-7937-2800 |
www.prezzorestaurants.co.uk

Regulars are "happy to visit" this "busy" contemporary Italian chain
with numerous locations for its "large, tasty pizzas" and other "no-
frills", "red-sauce" fare; while there are "no surprises" on the menu,
"affordable" costs and "helpful staff" make it "good for a neighbourhood meal out with friends."

Princess Garden ● *Chinese*   24 | 19 | 22 | £43

Mayfair | 8-10 N. Audley St., W1K 6ZD | 020-7493-3223 |
www.princessgardenofmayfair.com

"Palates that appreciate superior Chinese dishes" will revel in the
"fabulous" food at this "high-end" Mayfair Mandarin where the "diverse menu" includes "incredible dim sum"; furthermore, "knowledgeable staff" and a "lively but not overly noisy" ambience help make
the "spacious", minimal room suited for "that special occasion."

Princess of Shoreditch *British*   ∇ 21 | 17 | 21 | £38

Shoreditch | 76-78 Paul St., EC2A 4NE | 020-7729-9270 |
www.theprincessofshoreditch.com

A "comfortable", "candlelit" first-floor dining room serves "well-
prepared", moderately priced Modern British gastropub cuisine at
this "pub conversion" in Shoreditch; meanwhile, the downstairs bar
offers "great draft and bottled beers" and the same "personal", "efficient" service found upstairs.

Princess Victoria *British*   ∇ 25 | 23 | 23 | £33

Shepherd's Bush | 217 Uxbridge Rd., W12 9DH | 020-8749-5886 |
www.princessvictoria.co.uk

"Don't be fooled by the fact it's a pub" – the affordable Traditional
British menu includes some "spectacular dishes" (not to mention
"delicious bar snacks") at this "large, airy" Shepherd's Bush gastropub "landmark"; the "delightful surroundings" include a "pretty"
garden, "charming staff" and, rumour has it, "even the odd celebrity."

Princi London ● *Bakery/Italian*   24 | 23 | 16 | £16

Soho | 135 Wardour St., W1F 0UT | 020-7478-8888 | www.princi.co.uk
For a "quick, uncomplicated" Italian "fix", consider this "sleek",
counter-serve Soho bakery whose "exquisite bread, cakes", sandwiches, salads and pastas are "incredible value"; the marble, slate
and glass-filled setting is as "decadent" as the fare – but be prepared
for an "erratic queuing system" and to "eat standing up", as it's usually "really crowded" and "finding a seat can be frustrating."

Prism 🅱 *British*   ∇ 19 | 21 | 19 | £56

City | 147 Leadenhall St., EC3V 4QT | 020-7256-3888 |
www.harveynichols.com

With its "vast ceiling height, classic columns" and expense-account
pricing, this bank hall-turned-"reliable" Modern British eatery is a
"serviceable" spot for "a business lunch" in the City; after work "can
get noisy when the bar is full", but some folks who've stayed for dinner

say that the "atmosphere leaves something to be desired" the later it gets; P.S. oenophiles say the wine list includes "some good things at reasonable prices."

Providores *Eclectic* 25 | 17 | 19 | £39
Marylebone | 109 Marylebone High St., W1U 4RX | 020-7935-6175 | www.theprovidores.co.uk

"Lively, well-heeled" types seeking "adventurous" dining flock to chef Peter Gordon's "expensive" Marylebone Eclectic for "imaginative" takes on fusion tapas paired with a "terrific" New Zealand-focused wine list; service is mostly "efficient" throughout, but insiders say the more "civilised" upstairs space is better for a "special meal", as the "elbow-to-elbow" ground-floor Tapa Room draws "incredible queues."

Punjab ☻ *Indian* 23 | 18 | 20 | £27
Covent Garden | 80 Neal St., WC2H 9PA | 020-7836-9787 | www.punjab.co.uk

With a "well-deserved reputation" stretching back to the 1940s, this "informal" Covent Garden Indian proffers a "classic" menu that "never disappoints", especially "for the price you're paying"; the place is "a bit cramped" with "miss-able decor", but thanks in part to the "friendly" service, fans vow to "return again and again."

Quadrato *Italian* ▽ 21 | 20 | 21 | £78
Canary Wharf | Four Seasons Canary Wharf | 46 Westferry Circus, E14 8RS | 020-7510-1857 | www.fourseasons.com

"What a beautiful setting" sigh surveyors of this airy Canary Wharf hotel dining room on the Thames, where the "fine" Northern Italian offerings include a "fantastic" Sunday brunch buffet; sure, it's "pricey", but that's to be expected given that it's in the Four Seasons; P.S. a refurb was planned post-Survey, possibly outdating the Decor score.

Quaglino's ☒ *European* 21 | 22 | 20 | £60
St. James's | 16 Bury St., SW1Y 6AJ | 020-7930-6767 | www.quaglinos.co.uk

Accessed down a "grand staircase", this venerable St. James's "gastrodome" boasts an all-around "impressive dining room", with "sumptuous decor", a "see-and-be-seen" scene and "quality", "upper-crust" European fare; modernists say it "needs a few new tricks" (first, for the "patchy" service), but there are kudos for its live entertainment and "dangerously good cocktail bar."

Quilon *Indian* - | - | - | E
Victoria | Crowne Plaza St. James Hotel | 41 Buckingham Gate, SW1E 6AF | 020-7821-1899 | www.quilon.co.uk

Long appreciated for its upscale, refined Southwest coastal Indian cooking that mixes the traditional with the experimental, this pricey venue attached to a Victoria hotel has undergone a plush revamp that introduced comfy banquettes, elegant hues and more tables for larger gatherings; also added is a cosy new entrance bar, with a handful of stools and armchairs.

	FOOD	DECOR	SERVICE	COST

Quirinale 🗗 *Italian*

25 | 17 | 21 | £47

Westminster | 1 Great Peter St., SW1P 3LL | 020-7222-7080 |
www.quirinale.co.uk

People who "work in Whitehall" plan "discreet" "chats with MPs" at
this spot where the Italian fare is "fantastic" and the basement setting is either one of "understated luxury" or "depressing" depending
on whom you ask; there's always "buzz" during the day, and while
the evenings are "more relaxed", bargain-hunters come by for the
early-bird set dinner menu that's an "absolute steal" (similar to the
prix fixe lunch).

Quo Vadis 🗗 *British*

∇ 21 | 21 | 22 | £56

Soho | 26-29 Dean St., W1D 3LL | 020-7437-9585 |
www.quovadissoho.co.uk

Restaurateurs Sam and Eddie Hart (Barrafina, Fino) demonstrate
their "Midas touch" at this Soho "special-occasion" destination,
where new chef Jeremy Lee brings "less fussy, more modern tastes"
to the simple British menu; "outstanding service" and "not-cheap"
prices come with the territory, while a recent refurb of the landmark
building (once home to Karl Marx) reveals a "clean", stylish look.

Racine *French*

24 | 19 | 22 | £51

Knightsbridge | 239 Brompton Rd., SW3 2EP | 020-7584-4477 |
www.racine-restaurant.com

For a "taste of France in Knightsbridge", "upscale" types head for
this "casual, crowded" brasserie, serving "satisfying" "soul food for
the Francophile" and a "comprehensive" wine list at "fair prices"; the
kitchen is supported by "charming" staff, and the "cosy setting" also
adds appeal, shoring up its standing as a "perennial fave."

Randall & Aubin *British/Seafood*

26 | 22 | 23 | £42

Soho | 14-16 Brewer St., W1F 0SQ | 020-7287-4447 |
www.randallandaubin.com

"Don't be fooled" by the "campy", disco-balled setting, "resident drag
queen" and "blatant flirting from the staff" – this "buzzy, no-bookings"
Soho "stalwart" serves an "excellent", "reasonably priced" Modern
Brit menu highlighted by "some of the best seafood around"; "loud
music" and a "hectic atmosphere" complete the "fun" picture.

Ransome's Dock *British/Eclectic*

∇ 21 | 17 | 20 | £48

Battersea | 35-37 Parkgate Rd., SW11 4NP | 020-7223-1611 |
www.ransomesdock.co.uk

"Reliable" Modern British–Eclectic cooking is "carefully married to a
brilliant wine selection" and "promptly served" for "fair prices" at this
"friendly", "folksy restaurant" in Battersea; factor in a "lovely location" "hidden" beside a little-known dock, and no wonder surveyors
ask "what more can you ask for?"

Raoul's *Mediterranean*

17 | 15 | 14 | £36

St. John's Wood | 13 Clifton Rd., W9 1SZ | 020-7289-7313
Hammersmith | 111-115 Hammersmith Grove, W6 0NQ |
020-8741-3692

(continued)

(continued)

Raoul's

Notting Hill | 105-107 Talbot Rd., W11 2AT | 020-7229-2400
www.raoulsgourmet.com

Best known for "great breakfasts" and brunches highlighted by "amazing eggs" imported from Tuscany, this "buzzing" cafe trio can be "quite a scene on weekends", but its "steady" Med menu is available every day (until 6 PM); unfortunately, "uncomfortable" quarters, "loud" decibels, "iffy" service and prices that are "a bit too expensive for what you get" are part of the package.

Rasa *Indian/Vegetarian*   24 | 15 | 20 | £24

Mayfair | 6 Dering St., W1S 1AD | 020-7629-1346
Islington | Holiday Inn King's Cross | 1 King's Cross Rd., WC1X 9HX | 020-7833-9787 🅂
Stoke Newington | 55 Stoke Newington Church St., N16 0AR | 020-7249-0344
www.rasarestaurants.com

Serving "authentic, unusual" Keralan food at "outstanding-value" prices, this South Indian mini-chain is a "vegetarian heaven even if you're not a vegetarian" thanks to "spicy, tangy" curries and dosas (some locations also serve meat and seafood); the food is ferried by "super-friendly" staffers, whilst the "warm atmosphere" overshadows interiors that some say are "looking tired."

🆉 Rasoi Vineet Bhatia *Indian*   27 | 23 | 25 | £90

Chelsea | 10 Lincoln St., SW3 2TS | 020-7225-1881 | www.rasoirestaurant.co.uk

The "sophistication of Mumbai, charm of Rajasthan and imaginative cooking of chef Vineet Bhatia" are all on offer at this "divine" Indian destination, serving "traditional dishes with 21st-century flair" in a "hidden" Chelsea townhouse; it's "ideal for intimate dinners", staff are "eager to please" and though the pricing's certainly "rarefied", diners don't mind given meals that are "dazzling from the start."

Real Greek *Greek*   19 | 17 | 18 | £27

Covent Garden | 60-62 Long Acre, WC2E 9JE | 020-7240-2292
Marylebone | 56 Paddington St., W1U 4HY | 020-7486-0466
Hoxton | 14-15 Hoxton Mkt., N1 6HG | 020-7739-8212 🅂 Ⓜ
Shoreditch | Old Spitalfields Mkt. | 6 Horner Sq., E1 6EW | 020-7375-1364
Southwark | Riverside Hse. | 2 Southwark Bridge Rd., SE1 9HA | 020-7620-0162
Shepherd's Bush | Westfield Shopping Ctr. | Ariel Way, ground fl., W12 7GB | 020-8743-9168
www.therealgreek.com

"Tapas-style" Greek dishes made for "sharing" are the speciality of this "reliable" mini-chain where the "authentic" fare is ferried by "friendly" servers – and "you won't need a bailout to pay for it"; some find the food "not very inspiring" and deem the decor "nothing special", but communal tables and live music at some locations make it a natural for "good times with friends."

	FOOD	DECOR	SERVICE	COST

Red Fort ● *Indian* 25 | 22 | 22 | £48

Soho | 77 Dean St., W1D 3SH | 020-7437-2525 | www.redfort.co.uk
"Refined" "neo-Indian" fare distinguished by "bright flavours" and
"inventive" preparations makes "converts" out of first-time visitors
to this "long-standing" Soho subcontinental; "gracious service" and
a "lovely setting" are boons, and if it's a "bit pricey", the lunch and
pre-theatre set menus are "outstanding deals."

Red Pepper *Italian* 21 | 12 | 18 | £30

St. John's Wood | 8 Formosa St., W9 1EE | 020-7266-2708 |
www.theredpepper.net
Locals pack into this "popular" St. John's Wood Italian for "good-
quality" wood-fired pizza and pasta, overlooking the fact that the
setting is "small, cramped and noisy" ("waiters must be slim in order to weave between the tables"); service is "friendly", but its best
aspect may be "value" pricing.

Refettorio ⓩ *Italian* ▽ 26 | 21 | 21 | £44

City | Crowne Plaza London | 19 New Bridge St., EC4V 6DB |
020-7438-8052 | www.refettorio.com
"Quite amazing" "plates of cured meats and cheeses" and other
"reasonably priced" Italian eats make this City eatery "great for
work or play"; its location in a Blackfriars hotel signifies that once
the "men in suits" have departed, the mood becomes mellow, which
means for dinner, you usually "don't need to book."

Restaurant at the 17 | 19 | 13 | £30
Royal Academy of Arts *British*

Piccadilly | Royal Academy of Arts | Burlington House, Piccadilly,
W1J 0BD | 020-7300-5608 | www.royalacademy.org.uk
What "used to be a very good upmarket cafeteria" in the Royal
Academy of Arts is now a Modern British restaurant in the hands of
Oliver Peyton, who runs similar ventures in other cultural haunts;
whilst supporters deem it a "lovely choice" for a meal amidst "superb
surroundings" (vaulted ceilings, lava-stone bar), critics contend
the "art is all in the gallery", citing "expensive", "so-so" fare and a
"too-formal" ambience.

Reubens *Deli/Jewish* 21 | 12 | 13 | £33

Marylebone | 79 Baker St., W1U 6RG | 020-7486-0035 |
www.reubensrestaurant.co.uk
"All the traditional favourites" can be found at this "reliable kosher
eatery" whose "excellent location" in Marylebone comprises a
"packed" upstairs deli "for takeaway and quick meals" and a "more
formal" downstairs dining area; although "service can be off-hand",
at least the place offers "good value for a West End restaurant."

Rhodes Twenty Four ⓩ *British* 25 | 26 | 25 | £79

City | Tower 42 | 25 Old Broad St., 24th fl., EC2N 1HQ |
020-7877-7703 | www.rhodes24.co.uk
"Superlative" views ("can't be beat for a sunset") are afforded from
the 24th-floor perch of this "very grown up" City dining room, which

serves chef Gary Rhodes' "top-class" Traditional British menu and "excellent" wines to "business groups at lunch and a mixed clientele in the evenings"; it's "expensive", but "worth it" assure respondents who also appreciate the "impeccable" "professional" service.

Rhodes W1 Restaurant 🅱Ⓜ *French*   23 | 18 | 23 | £50

Marylebone | Cumberland Hotel | Great Cumberland Pl., W1H 7DL | 020-7616-5930

Rhodes W1 Brasserie *European*

Marylebone | Cumberland Hotel | Great Cumberland Pl., W1H 7DL | 020-7616-5930

www.rhodesw1.com

"One to keep in mind for a birthday", this "comfortable" spot near Marble Arch offers Gary Rhodes' "quality" Classic French fare in "semi-private spaces" amidst "attractive" Swarovski crystals; the adjacent brasserie is "noisy" by comparison, but "convenient" for "value" Modern Euro eats brought by similarly "diligent staff."

Rib Room *Chophouse*   24 | 22 | 24 | £76

Knightsbridge | Jumeirah Carlton Tower Hotel | Cadogan Pl., SW1X 9PY | 020-7858-7250 | www.theribroom.co.uk

"After all these years", this Knightsbridge hotel "classic" remains an "excellent" choice for a meat-centric meal thanks to "high-quality" chophouse chow enhanced by "exceptional" "old-school" service; happily, lunch and dinner prix fixes can ease the pain of prices that seem aimed at those who "don't look at the bill"; P.S. a refurb of the "dark", "luxurious" space possibly outdates the Decor score.

Riccardo's *Italian*   ▽ 17 | 14 | 18 | £40

Chelsea | 126 Fulham Rd., SW3 6HU | 020-7370-6656 | www.riccardos-italian-restaurant.co.uk

"Simple" Tuscan dishes are served to a "chic" Chelsea clientele at this "standby" "to stop by after shopping" on Fulham Road; however, it's "lost its touch" according to a few punters who complain that "small portions make it more expensive that it seems at first view."

Richoux *British*   16 | 16 | 17 | £28

Knightsbridge | 86 Brompton Rd., SW3 1ER | 020-7584-8300
Mayfair | 41 S. Audley St., W1K 2PS | 020-7629-5228
St. James's | 172 Piccadilly, W1J 9EJ | 020-7493-2204
St. John's Wood | 3 Circus Rd., NW8 6NX | 020-7483-4001

www.richoux.co.uk

"Charmingly old-fashioned", this "cafe-style" chainlet in "convenient areas" doles out "decent" Traditional Brit eats from a "simple", "unchanging" menu (including "all-day breakfasts", high tea and "late-night snacks"); service can be "spotty" and there's debate over the cost, but it remains a "comfortable" "standby" for many.

Riding House Café *European*   21 | 23 | 21 | £38

Fitzrovia | 43-51 Great Titchfield St., W1W 7PQ | 020-7927-0840 | www.ridinghousecafe.co.uk

"Whatever you're in the mood for" – be it "large, hangover-worthy English breakfasts", "sharing plates" fit for a "classy date" or just

| | FOOD | DECOR | SERVICE | COST |

"tea and cake" – the midpriced Modern Euro "comfort-food classics" at this "popular", "laid-back" Fitzrovia brasserie/bar are "great all day"; indeed, the "attention to detail is evident" in everything, from the "quirky" decor ("blue velvet chairs, dark wood and squirrel lamps") to the "swift service" from "friendly" staff.

⊠ The Ritz   British/French   25 | 28 | 26 | £78

Piccadilly | The Ritz | 150 Piccadilly, W1J 9BR | 020-7300-2370 | www.theritzlondon.com

"Comfort and calm rule" at this "luxurious" Louis XVI–style dining room at the famed hotel in Piccadilly, where "superlative service" and "splurge"-worthy, "beautifully prepared" Traditional British–French dishes heighten the "over-the-top opulence"; there's "old-fashioned dancing" with a live band on Fridays (in summer) and Saturdays (year-round), whilst the adjacent Palm Court offers "a step back in time" with afternoon tea; P.S. gentlemen, "don't forget to wear a tie" and jacket.

⊠ River Café   Italian   27 | 23 | 25 | £71

Hammersmith | Thames Wharf Studio | Rainville Rd., W6 9HA | 020-7386-4200 | www.rivercafe.co.uk

"Outstanding depth and complexity of flavour" infuses the "inventive" daily changing Italian fare whipped up in the open kitchen of this "must-visit" in a Hammersmith "warehouse"; it's "not a cheap outing", but "it really is a treat", made even more "special" with "efficient, pleasant" service, "great wines" and a "bright, airy space" that "suits every season" – though it's particularly "sublime" in summer when "picturesque" Thames views can be seen from the "amazing" terrace.

Rivington Grill Bar   British   24 | 21 | 20 | £38

Greenwich | 178 Greenwich High Rd., SE10 8NN | 020-8293-9270
Shoreditch | 28-30 Rivington St., EC2A 3DZ | 020-7729-7053
www.rivingtongrill.co.uk

"Simple" white-walled environs and "chirpy staff" set a "relaxing" tone at this "trendy" Shoreditch brasserie where the all-day Traditional British menu may be "a bit pricey" "for what you get", but at least is "high-quality", with burgers that alone make it "worth visiting"; located by the Greenwich Picturehouse, the younger sibling (with more limited hours) is "one of the more elegant local options."

Roast   British   25 | 23 | 21 | £51

Borough | Borough Mkt. | Floral Hall, Stoney St., SE1 1TL | 0845-034-7300 | www.roast-restaurant.com

At this "buzzy" Traditional Brit, "fabulous natural light" and "stunning views" of "the hubbub of Borough Market" form a "wonderful" backdrop for its "high-quality" menu, featuring many "modern takes" on "classic" meat dishes; lots of "well-heeled" types in the crowd foreshadow a "fairly pricey" bill, which even the masses feel are "worth it" considering the "stellar wine list" and "great people-watching" – and despite service that's often only "pleasant enough."

	FOOD	DECOR	SERVICE	COST

Rocca *Italian* ▽ 19 | 21 | 22 | £33

Dulwich | 75-79 Dulwich Vill., SE21 7BJ | 020-8299-6333
South Kensington | 73 Old Brompton Rd., SW7 3JS | 020-7225-3413 ●
www.roccarestaurants.com

"Attentive", "personable staff" serve "reliably good food and wine" at these "neighbourhood Italians" in South Ken and Dulwich Village, the latter with an "idyllic location"; they particularly make for a "nice night out" with the whole family, as the prices are quite "reasonable."

Rock & Sole Plaice *Seafood* 24 | 9 | 16 | £17

Covent Garden | 47 Endell St., WC2H 9AJ | 020-7836-3785

"Don't pay attention to the silly name" and "don't go for the decor" (it's "dismal"), but do expect "excellent" fish 'n' chips served in "hearty" portions by "rough-and-ready" staff at this Covent Garden seafooder; you have to tolerate a "tight squeeze for a table" inside, so it's "best in nice weather when you can eat outdoors."

Rocket *Mediterranean* 19 | 18 | 19 | £34

Mayfair | 4-6 Lancashire Ct., W1S 1EY | 020-7629-2889 ●
Canary Wharf | 2 Churchill Pl., E14 5RB | 020-3200-2022 🗷
NEW **City** | 201 Bishopsgate, EC2M 3AB | 020-7377-8863 🗷
City | 6 Adam's Ct., EC2N 1DX | 020-7628-0808 🗷
www.rocketrestaurants.co.uk

"Perfect for a catch-up with girlfriends" or a "handy" shopping pit stop, this "trendy", "casual" Mayfair hangout and its more work-orientated offshoots in the City and Canary Wharf (the latter in a "funky glass building") offer "generous portions" of "flavourful" Med fare like "filling salads" and "gorgeous pizzas with fresh rocket"; a few find the menu "nothing to write home about", but it's "value for money", with "lovely decor" and "friendly service" as bonuses.

Rodizio Rico ● *Brazilian* 21 | 14 | 18 | £33

Greenwich | O2 Arena | Greenwich Peninsula, SE10 0DX | 020-8858-6333
Islington | 77-78 Upper St., N1 0NU | 020-7354-1076
Bayswater | 111 Westbourne Grove, W2 4UW | 020-7792-4035
www.rodiziorico.com

"When you're in the mood to pig out", these "taste-bud-tingling" Brazilian churrascarias deliver "never-ending rounds" of "every kind of meat imaginable"; "service is a little slow at times" and the "basic" digs are "not for the faint hearted" (read: "loud"), but "groups" usually find it "great fun", and "wonderful value" to boot.

🖪 Roganic 🗷Ⓜ *British* 28 | 18 | 28 | £94

Marylebone | 19 Blandford St., W1U 3DH | 020-7486-0380 |
www.roganic.co.uk

"Expect the unexpected" at this two-year pop-up "phenomenon" in "minimal" Marylebone environs where Cumbria-based chef Simon Rogan prepares a "gastronomic journey" of "ethereal" Modern British "marvels" ("foraged food is a forte"), all brought by staff so "polished" and "incredibly knowledgeable", they earn London's No. 1 Service rating; the prix fixe–only menus are "expensive" to be sure, but "for what you get", most calculate it's "well worth the price paid."

| | FOOD | DECOR | SERVICE | COST |

Roka *Japanese*
26 | 23 | 23 | £67

Fitzrovia | 37 Charlotte St., W1T 1RR | 020-7580-6464 ◑
Canary Wharf | 4 Park Pavilion, 40 Canada Sq., E14 5FW | 020-7636-5228
www.rokarestaurant.com

"Sit at the beautifully carved wood counter and ask the chefs what to eat" from the menu of "zingingly fresh sushi" and "inspired" robata grill fare at this "vibrant", "theatrical" Japanese sibling of Zuma in Fitzrovia and its "more spacious" Canary Wharf outpost (where it's usually "easier to get a table"); "friendly, efficient" staff serve a "crowd packed with dating couples and groups", who "party the night away" and pay the "premium prices" without care.

Rosa's *Thai*
23 | 16 | 17 | £22

Soho | 48 Dean St., W1D 5BF | 020-7494-1638
NEW **Stratford** | Westfield Stratford City | 2 Stratford Pl., E20 1EJ | 020-8519-1302
Shoreditch | 12 Hanbury St., E1 6QR | 020-7247-1093
www.rosaslondon.com

"Well-prepared, standard" Thai "street food" comes for "reasonable prices" at this trio; though the service is "hit-and-miss", it's usually "fast", making it "a great spot for a quick eat" – that is, "if you can get a seat" in the "cramped", "basic" digs.

Rossopomodoro *Italian*
25 | 19 | 18 | £25

Covent Garden | 50-52 Monmouth St., WC2H 9EP | 020-7240-9095
NEW **Hoxton** | 1 Rufus St., N1 6PE | 020-7739-1899 ◑
NEW **Camden Town** | 10 Jamestown Rd., NW1 7BY | 020-7424-9900 ◑
Chelsea | 214 Fulham Rd., SW10 9NB | 020-7352-7677
Notting Hill | 184 Kensington Park Rd., W11 2ES | 020-7229-9007 ◑
www.rossopomodoro.co.uk

"Whether you speak Italian or not", the "real Neapolitan pizza" and "wonderful" pasta at this "busy, bright" chain offer "good value all around"; those who "give it a shot" say "decent" service ensures it's a "lovely place to spend an evening."

NEW Roti Chai *Indian*
∇ 27 | 22 | 21 | £30

Marylebone | 3 Portman Mews S., W1H 6HS | 020-7408-0101 | www.rotichai.com

In a "quirky, railway cafe-inspired 'street kitchen' on the ground floor" and "elegant, artfully lit dining room and bar" below, this "fantastic addition to the Indian food scene" in Marylebone offers "succulent", "perfectly spiced" small plates, "innovative curries" and more; the service swings between "quick" and "slow", but the prices, thankfully, are always "reasonable"; P.S. there's also a market area selling iconic imports like Parle-G biscuits and Rooh Afza drink.

Rotunda *British*
∇ 23 | 21 | 20 | £32

King's Cross | Kings Pl. | 90 York Way, N1 9AG | 020-7014-2840 | www.rotundabarandrestaurant.co.uk

With "stunning views of the Battlebridge Basin waterfront" and "alfresco seating in season", this "laid-back" venue within the Kings Place arts centre is "perfect before a concert" (though perhaps "a bit out of the way for a stand-alone journey"); whilst "simple", the midpriced Traditional British fare is "delicious" thanks in large part to produce and meat from "its own farm" in Northumberland, all backed by an "interesting wine list."

Roux at Parliament Square ⊠ *European*

▽ 24 | 24 | 24 | £61

Westminster | Royal Institution of Chartered Surveyors | 11 Great George St., SW1P 3AD | 020-7334-3737 | www.rouxatparliamentsquare.co.uk

"MP spot" whilst dining on "fabulous" Modern European fare at this "lovely" Parliament Square option, a Michel Roux Jr. venue in a grand Listed building that "deserves to be better known"; the "efficient service" and "elegant upstairs bar" also earn admirers, and whilst prices are high, the set lunch is "great value."

Roux at The Landau *European*

26 | 26 | 26 | £86

Marylebone | The Langham Hotel | 1 Portland Pl., W1 1JA | 020-7965-0165 | www.thelandau.com

A "classical", "fancy" Modern European menu boasting "high-quality execution" is matched by a "warm", "formal" setting filled with "interesting art" and "beautiful lighting" at this Langham Hotel collaboration between Albert and Michel Roux Jr.; "well-spaced tables" and "attentive" service make it "good for business" as well as "intimate dining", and whilst it's "very expensive", "you get what you pay for"; P.S. the set lunch is more "affordable."

Rowley's *British*

24 | 20 | 22 | £48

St. James's | 113 Jermyn St., SW1Y 6HJ | 020-7930-2707 | www.rowleys.co.uk

A mix of "well-heeled" locals, "business associates" and "tourists" fill this "clubby" St. James's dining room exhibiting "old London flair" to match its "consistent", "hearty" Traditional British menu that majors on "melt-in-the-mouth" steaks with "unlimited chips", accompanied by "pleasant service"; some feel it's "reasonably priced" whilst others deem it "expensive", but most concede it's "worth every penny", especially for a special occasion like "a birthday treat."

Royal China *Chinese*

23 | 17 | 17 | £36

Marylebone | 24-26 Baker St., W1U 7AB | 020-7487-4688
Canary Wharf | 30 Westferry Circus, E14 8RR | 020-7719-0888
Fulham | 805 Fulham Rd., SW6 5HE | 020-7731-0081
Bayswater | 13 Queensway, W2 4QJ | 020-7221-2535
www.royalchinagroup.co.uk

"Top-drawer dim sum" (served daily until 4.45 PM) transcends "outdated decor" and "hurried", "robotic service" at this "noisy" chainlet whose "wide selection" of "good-value" Chinese dishes brings fans "as close as it gets" to the real thing without "a ticket to Hong Kong"; with "no weekend bookings", you should "arrive early" to avoid "long queues", or come for dinner (which is "more expensive").

	FOOD	DECOR	SERVICE	COST

Royal China Club *Chinese* `25` `17` `19` `£48`

Marylebone | 40-42 Baker St., W1U 7AJ | 020-7486-3898 |
www.royalchinagroup.co.uk

Specialising in "high-quality dim sum" and "fish and lobster fresh from
tanks", this Baker Street Cantonese, the compatriot of nearby Royal
China, is playing "in the premier league of fine Chinese dining" – and
charging "relatively high" prices to match; that it accepts reservations is an "added bonus", as are mostly "helpful" staff and the
"comprehensive wine list."

R.S.J. 🗷 *British* `23` `15` `21` `£40`

Waterloo | 33 Coin St., SE1 9NR | 020-7928-4554 | www.rsj.uk.com

"Dine before or after the National Theatre" at this "relaxed" "oasis in a
foodie desert" near Waterloo, where patrons praise the "interesting" Modern British eats, "good-value" prix fixe and "unique" Loire
Valley wine list; a few find it's "nothing special", but "friendly" servers "lift it a grade", lending a "warm welcome" and "getting you out
in time for the curtain."

🗷 Rules *Chophouse* `25` `26` `25` `£63`

Covent Garden | 35 Maiden Ln., WC2E 7LB | 020-7836-5314 |
www.rules.co.uk

"Tradition" rules at this circa-1798 Covent Garden "institution" that
provides a "taste of old England" via its menu of chophouse "classics
that stand the test of time well" ("if game is your game" it's particularly "brilliant") as well as its "opulent" decor that "reeks of history"
and "unobtrusive" service; it may be a "tourist favourite" with decid-
edly modern prices, but most agree it's a "must-do" "at least once."

Sabor ❶ *S American* `▽` `25` `22` `23` `£26`

Islington | 108 Essex Rd., N1 8LX | 020-7226-5551 |
www.sabor.co.uk

"Intriguing South American cuisine" majoring on Argentinean steaks
plus "friendly staff who will do anything to help" make this "zesty",
colourful Argentinean in Islington "worth trekking up the Essex Road
for"; what's more, "great value" abounds, not only in the set lunch
and dinner menus, but also the "fabulous cocktails" and wines.

Saf *Eclectic/Vegan* `21` `20` `20` `£35`

Kensington | Whole Foods Mkt. | 63-97 Kensington High St., W8 5SE |
020-7368-4555 | www.safrestaurant.co.uk

"Innovative without sacrificing taste" is the word on the Eclectic vegan
fare whipped up at this "simple, airy" Kensington option whose eco-
friendliness extends to "awesome botanical drinks", "cool organic
cocktails" and biodynamic wines; "healthy" eaters appreciate that
you leave "far from stuffed", but others baulk that the "small portions" command such relatively "hefty prices."

Sagar *Indian/Vegetarian* `22` `15` `23` `£21`

Covent Garden | 31 Catherine St., WC2B 5JS | 020-7836-6377
Westminster | 17 Percy St., W1T 1DU | 020-7631-3319

(continued)

(continued)

Sagar

Hammersmith | 157 King St., W6 9JT | 020-8741-8563
www.sagarveg.co.uk

The "flavoursome, healthy" eats represent "outstanding value", most notably the "ridiculously cheap lunchtime deals", at this "excellent" South Indian vegetarian trio; if the settings are "not the most inviting" ("cramped", "uncomfortable"), "pleasant staff" make up for it.

Sake No Hana 🖾 *Japanese*   25 | 24 | 21 | £60

St. James's | The Economist | 23 St. James's St., SW1A 1HA | 020-7925-8988 | www.sakenohana.com

"A ride up the escalator" from St. James's reveals this "quiet", "beautiful" Japanese with bamboo galore, "high ceilings" "adorned with wooden geometrical intricacies", "divine sushi" and other "inspired" creations; a "varied" sake list, "innovative cocktails" and mostly "smooth service" complete the experience – one that works best "if money is no object."

Sakura *Japanese*   ▽ 23 | 18 | 19 | £33

Mayfair | 23 Conduit St., W1S 2XS | 020-7629-2961

The relatively new location of this "busy" Mayfair Japanese is "more attractive than the old run-down venue", but the sushi and shabu-shabu are as "amazing" as ever, plus "the wait time for a table seems to have gone down"; "friendly", "knowledgeable" staff are another plus, but its best feature may be that it's "excellent value" (for the neighbourhood, that is).

Sale e Pepe ⬤ *Italian*   23 | 19 | 23 | £50

Knightsbridge | 9-15 Pavilion Rd., SW1X 0HD | 020-7235-0098 | www.saleepepe.co.uk

"Charming" "singing waiters" and "romantic decor" make it feel "like having dinner in an opera house" at this "entertaining" Knightsbridge Italian – indeed, it's all so "joyous", "you don't seem to mind" that it's "noisy", "crowded and cramped"; foodwise, the "classic" menu is "solid", and as for prices, they're "on the high side."

Salloos 🖾 *Pakistani*   24 | 17 | 20 | £57

Belgravia | 62-64 Kinnerton St., SW1X 8ER | 020-7235-4444 | www.salloosrestaurant.co.uk

"Fine spices" "tantalise" in "high-quality Pakistani" dishes, especially "magnificent" tandoori lamb chops, which are "professionally served" at this stalwart Belgravia "hidden gem"; it's "on the expensive side", but "worth it" for the "fantastic" flavours – if not the "somewhat tired decor."

Salt Yard 🖾 *Italian/Spanish*   24 | 19 | 21 | £43

Bloomsbury | 54 Goode St., W1T 4NA | 020-7637-0657 | www.saltyard.co.uk

Belying it's "humble" Bloomsbury location, this "noisy, bohemian" venue offers "top-class" Italian-Spanish tapas, often with "brilliant, avant-garde twists" (the signature courgette flowers with goat cheese and honey are "a dream"); though it's often "full of media

	FOOD	DECOR	SERVICE	COST

types", it's also a "perfect date spot" thanks to mostly "congenial service" and a "broad, well-priced wine list" (the food menu can be 'a little pricey in places").

Sam's Brasserie & Bar *European*   24 | 23 | 23 | £35

Chiswick | Barley Mow Ctr. | 11 Barley Mow Passage, W4 4PH | 020-8987-0555 | www.samsbrasserie.co.uk

Chiswick locals say it's "a joy" to come to this "informal neighbourhood brasserie" delivering Modern European eats that are "well executed and served with style" in a "spacious", "comfortable" restaurant and "laid-back bar"; "lovely staff" further make it a "worthy place" that's especially "good for families" since it's affordable.

Sands End ❷ *British/Irish*   ▽ 23 | 24 | 25 | £36

Fulham | 135-137 Stephendale Rd., SW6 2PR | 020-7731-7823 | www.thesandsend.co.uk

"Off the beaten track" near Imperial Wharf, this "pert boozer" "shines" with an "inviting", "upscale" atmosphere, "fantastic" British-Irish gastropub fare, "well-chosen wine list" and "accommodating" staff; if you're looking for a quiet dinner, best to come early, because word is the bar becomes "loud as the evening wears on."

San Lorenzo 🅉 *Italian*   21 | 19 | 20 | £66

Knightsbridge | 22 Beauchamp Pl., SW3 1NH | 020-7584-1074 | ww.sanlorenzolondon.co.uk

San Lorenzo Fuoriporta *Italian*

Wimbledon | 38 Wimbledon Hill Rd., SW19 7PA | 020-8946-8463 | www.sanlorenzo.com

Though "not as hot as it used to be" in the '90s, there's still "people-watching for sure" at this "vibrant" Knightsbridge venue where an "elite crowd" pays "eyebrow-raising prices" for "pleasantly cooked Italian food"; though the decor feels "dated" to some, "competent service" keeps it a "civilised" option, whilst the offshoot's location makes it a "staple" for tennis "stars during Wimbledon fortnight."

Santa Maria   26 | 18 | 21 | £45
del Sur ❷ *Argentinean/Chophouse*

Battersea | 129 Queenstown Rd., SW8 3RH | 020-7622-2088 | www.santamariadelsur.co.uk

Garufa Grill *Argentinean/Chophouse*

Islington | 104 Highbury Pk., N5 2XE | 020-7226-0070 | www.garufa.co.uk

"Nothing flashy, just great steaks" flown in from Argentina and served with "interesting sides" and a "strong wine list" – that's the recipe at this "friendly" Battersea chophouse and its Islington sib; some say bills "seem a couple of quid more than other local restaurants", but since it "gets it right every time", it's "always buzzing", so "book in advance."

Santini *Italian*   20 | 18 | 19 | £63

Belgravia | 29 Ebury St., SW1W 0NZ | 020-7730-4094 | www.santini-restaurant.com

"If you're feeling flush and like being surrounded by Belgravia aristocracy, it's worth trying" this "expensive", "elegant" eatery where "tasty" Italian cuisine, including "some imaginative items", is delivered by "proficient" staff; "nicely spaced tables" keep the interior "comfortable and quiet", and there's also a patio, set on an olive-tree-bedecked corner.

Sardo ☒ Italian
22 | 18 | 21 | £45

Bloomsbury | 45 Grafton Way, W1T 5DQ | 020-7387-2521 | www.sardo-restaurant.com

"Owner-managed with pride", this "no-fuss" Bloomsbury venue "near Warren Street tube" is a "real find" for "genuine Sardinian cuisine", including "outstanding" bread; "amicable service", "great wines" and relatively "reasonable" prices make it sometimes "difficult to get a table", so "best to book."

Sardo Canale Italian
▽ 20 | 17 | 17 | £44

Primrose Hill | 42 Gloucester Ave., NW1 8JD | 020-7722-2800 | www.sardocanale.com

"Interesting Sardinian dishes" are complemented by a "decent selection of wines" at this only slightly "pricey" sibling of Sardo, run by "lovely people" on Primrose Hill's Regent Canal; surveyors diverge on the brick-lined surrounds ("attractive" vs. "boring"), but all find the olive tree–planted courtyard "nice when the weather is appropriate."

Sartoria ☒ Italian
22 | 22 | 21 | £56

Mayfair | 20 Savile Row, W1S 3PR | 020-7534-7000 | www.sartoriabar.co.uk

"Perfect for Savile Row and the local art-loving crowd", this "comfortable" "Mayfair gem" decked out with "stylish" sartorial displays stitches together a "sophisticated atmosphere" with "elegant Italian" cuisine; a few surveyors find it "pricey" for "small portions", but at least everything's of "great quality", including staff that feature a "helpful sommelier."

Satsuma Japanese
20 | 19 | 17 | £25

Soho | 56 Wardour St., W1D 4JG | 020-7437-8338 | www.osatsuma.com

The trendy recent refurbishment of this "canteen-style" Soho Japanese has introduced "big benches", "long tables" and "quirky", cocoonlike orange pods; meanwhile, the "fab" menu of sashimi and katsu curries is as "good value" as ever (and unfortunately, the service remains "impersonal").

Savoy Grill British/French
25 | 25 | 24 | £73

Covent Garden | Savoy Hotel | The Strand, WC2 0EU | 020-7592-1600 | www.gordonramsay.com

"Glittering with art deco charm since its multimillion pound restoration" in late 2010, this "sleekly luxurious" Strand "institution" exudes "renewed energy", with "impeccable" staffers ferrying Gordon Ramsay's "superb" Classic French and "yummy" Traditional British grill fare (for which you "pay handsomely"); if it's "too chest-thumping, alpha-male dominated" for some, most deem it "a wonderful experience in every way", and "deservedly famous."

	FOOD	DECOR	SERVICE	COST

Savoy River Restaurant *French* — 22 | 26 | 23 | £67

Covent Garden | Savoy Hotel | The Strand, WC2 0EU |
020-7420-2111 | www.fairmont.com

"Take your parents and win brownie points" at this "classy", "art deco–
influenced" dining room where "excellent" Modern French fare is "impeccably served" amidst "romantic" views over the Embankment; its
Covent Garden–area location makes it "ideal for pre-theatre", but the
menu is clearly priced for "special occasions" and "businesspeople."

Scalini *Italian* — 25 | 20 | 24 | £68

Chelsea | 1-3 Walton St., SW3 2JD | 020-7225-2301

"Don't expect a quiet, romantic dinner" or privacy (the "tables are
very close to one another") at this "homey" Chelsea trattoria, but do
count on a "bustling", "jolly atmosphere", "to-die-for" Italian fare
and a possible "neck ache from looking at all the celebs"; true, it's
"not cheap", but "amazing, friendly service" is part of the package.

🄩 Scott's *Seafood* — 26 | 24 | 25 | £79

Mayfair | 20 Mount St., W1K 2HE | 020-7495-7309 |
www.scotts-restaurant.com

"Captains of industry sail" to this "sophisticated" Mayfair seafood
"staple" to "power-lunch" on "interesting combinations" of "exceptional", "sparkling fresh fish", the shelled variety resting on a grand
ice display behind the "hopping bar"; come evening, a "posh" crowd
in "a mix of jeans and cocktail dresses" can be found amongst the
"big draping curtains", enjoying similarly "superlative service" and
"fine wines by the glass" and paying the same "arm and a leg."

Semplice Bar Trattoria *Italian* — ▽ 20 | 15 | 21 | £41

Mayfair | 22 Woodstock St., W1C 2AR | 020-7491-8638 |
www.bartrattoriasemplice.com

Across the street from Semplice Ristorante, this "simple" stripped-
wood younger sib offers "amazing" pastas, antipasti, salumi and other
Italian trattoria fare for prices that are "a great deal" for Mayfair; it's
the sort of place that beckons for "a light supper", with wines that
are just as "affordable" as the food and "friendly" service too.

Semplice Ristorante 🄩 *Italian* — 23 | 20 | 23 | £61

Mayfair | 8-10 Blenheim St., W1S 1LJ | 020-7495-1509 |
www.ristorantesemplice.com

"A well-kept secret worth unearthing", this Mayfair "must" presents
"fantastic, imaginative" Italian cuisine in a "dark", "gold"-hued room
whose "well-spaced tables" and "low-key atmosphere" make it "wonderful" for "a private business conversation or an intimate, romantic
meal"; "the pricing is high", but the cost includes "impeccable" service that's "genuinely concerned with making customers happy."

NEW Sette *Italian* — - | - | - | E

Chelsea | 4 Sydney St., SW3 6PP | 020-7352-3435 |
www.sette-restaurant.com

Top jockey–turned-restaurateur Frankie Dettori has revamped
Chelsea's former Cavallino space into this refined newcomer whose

| | FOOD | DECOR | SERVICE | COST |

minimalist, white-walled setting places the focus squarely on the slightly pricey, classics-centric Italian menu; washing it all down is a selection of mostly Boot-only wines; P.S. the name is a nod to Dettori's seven winning rides at Ascot in 1996.

Shanghai Blues ● *Chinese*   `23` `23` `19` `£46`
Holborn | 193-197 High Holborn, WC1V 7BD | 020-7404-1668 | www.shanghaiblues.co.uk
Devotees praise "innovative, classy dim sum", "spot-on" specials and other "high-quality dishes" at this "stylish", "dark" Holborn Chinese; those who "mainly go for the atmosphere" overlook the "sometimes surly service" and prices "on the high side" since it's "just the place for intimate gatherings" and "big parties" alike; P.S. weekend nights bring live jazz.

Shepherd's ⊠ *British*   ∇ `23` `21` `22` `£49`
Westminster | Marsham Ct., Marsham St., SW1P 4LA | 020-7834-9552 | www.langansrestaurants.co.uk
"Full of political types" "chowing down" on "excellent", "nicely presented" Traditional British "comfort food", this "calm", "old-school eatery" "just 'round the corner" from Parliament is "as cosy as suede shoes"; indeed, it "hasn't changed in years, but nobody seems to mind" – and that's despite the "posh" prices.

NEW Shrimpy's ⇌ *Californian/Mexican*   `-` `-` `-` `M`
King's Cross | King's Cross Filling Station | Good's Way, N1C 4UR | 020-8880-6111 | www.shrimpys.co.uk
The people behind popular Bethnal Green hangout Bistrotheque have taken over an old petrol station in King's Cross for their kitsch new venture, this moderately priced diner whipping up Californian- and Mexican–inspired fare dubbed 'Calexican cuisine'; the simple space sports white walls adorned with cute drawings, a small terrace for when the sun shines and counter seating for walk-ins; P.S. bring a card, they don't take cash.

Signor Sassi ● *Italian*   `23` `19` `22` `£53`
Knightsbridge | 14 Knightsbridge Green, SW1X 7QL | 020-7584-2277 | www.signorsassi.co.uk
"Warm welcomes" from "jovial staff" "brandishing oversized peppermills" set the stage for "ample portions" of "solid, traditional Italian" dishes ("lots of fish") at this long-standing "hideaway near Harrods and Hyde Park" in Knightsbridge; although it's "expensive", advocates assure that it's "worth the price", especially considering the "fun" vibe and all of those "famous patrons."

Simpson's-in-the-Strand *British*   `21` `23` `23` `£59`
Covent Garden | Savoy Hotel | The Strand, WC2R 0EW | 020-7836-9112 | www.simpsonsinthestrand.co.uk
"As British as the changing of the guard", this "properly posh", oak-panelled dining room acts as a "monument" to Traditional British dining on The Strand, highlighted by "travelling silver trolleys" bearing "steaming hunks of meat served by carvers out of a Dickens novel"; if some feel the "expensive" institution is "primarily for tourists"

| | FOOD | DECOR | SERVICE | COST |

these days, no one denies it's got "lots of charm and character"; P.S. a pianist performs nightly.

Singapore Garden *Malaysian/Singaporean* | 23 | 17 | 20 | £34 |

Swiss Cottage | 83 Fairfax Rd., NW6 4DY | 020-7328-5314
Chiswick | 474 Chiswick High Rd., W4 5TT | 020-8994-2222
www.singaporegarden.co.uk

"Popular" on account of its "homely" Singaporean-Malay cooking, this modern Swiss Cottage venue is "great for after work" – and even if "small portions" make it seem "pricey", it "remains a good resource" with "friendly service"; meanwhile, the Chiswick sib is a "small, busy" takeaway/delivery service "of a higher standard than the norm."

⑤ Sketch – The Gallery 🅩 *European* | 22 | 27 | 22 | £70 |

Mayfair | Sketch | 9 Conduit St., W1S 2XG | 020-7659-4500 |
www.sketch.uk.com

"Make sure you dress the part" to "see and be seen" amidst "weird and wonderful" "contemporary decor" – think "exotically lit staircases", "cocoon egg toilets" – at this "over-the-top" Modern European dinner spot inside a "fab" Mayfair townhouse; the fare is just as "original" as the setting, and "delicious" to boot, whilst the service is mostly "friendly" – but "you certainly pay for the privilege."

⑤ Sketch – The Lecture
Room & Library 🅩🅜 *European* | 23 | 28 | 24 | £89 |

Mayfair | Sketch | 9 Conduit St., W1S 2XG | 020-7659-4500 |
www.sketch.uk.com

"All things quirky", "luxurious, decadent" and "bejewelled" come together to create the "out-of-this-world", maroon-heavy setting of this "joyous" Modern European "special-occasion" place in a Mayfair townhouse, rated No. 1 for Decor in London; the "wow moments" continue with "superb service" and consulting chef Pierre Gagnaire's fare, boasting "inventive" "layers of flavours and textures" made "for the adventurous eater with cash to spare."

⑤ Sketch – The Parlour ●🅩 *British* | 21 | 28 | 19 | £46 |

Mayfair | Sketch | 9 Conduit St., W1S 2XG | 020-7659-4500 |
www.sketch.uk.com

"Warm, dreamy" and "magical", this morning and afternoon tearoom in a "stunning" Mayfair townhouse employs "friendly" staff to ferry its "fantastic pastries" and "creative" British light savouries; there's a plea to "reduce prices", but that aside, it's an "amusing" option for a "quaint" repast; P.S. after 9 PM, it's a cocktail-fuelled private club.

Skylon *European* | 20 | 24 | 21 | £47 |

South Bank | Royal Festival Hall | Belvedere Rd., SE1 8XX |
020-7654-7800 | www.skylonrestaurant.co.uk

"Dramatic views" of the Thames "through floor-to-ceiling glass" add to the "delightful experience" of this "huge", "atmospheric" Modern European in the Royal Festival Hall that combines a casual, "reasonable" grill with a "pricey" "fine-dining" destination boasting "slick" service and "a wine list that must be envied"; however, some say the "trendy bar" is "the best part", especially "if cocktails are your thing."

	FOOD	DECOR	SERVICE	COST

Smiths of Smithfield – Dining Room 🅱 *British* — 21 | 20 | 20 | £45

Farringdon | 67-77 Charterhouse St., 2nd fl., EC1M 6HJ | 020-7251-7950 | www.smithsofsmithfield.co.uk

"Chatty" chef John Torode is "often around" this "lively", "industrial style" eatery opposite Smithfield Market, where "fantastic steaks" and other "enjoyable" Modern British dishes are "served with a smile"; though costs are somewhat "expensive", insiders insist it's "well priced", making it a "solid option for work dinners and social gatherings" alike; P.S. it "never gets old" for breakfast either.

Smiths of Smithfield – Top Floor *British* — 23 | 21 | 19 | £62

Farringdon | 67-77 Charterhouse St., 3rd fl., EC1M 6HJ | 020-7251-7950 | www.smithsofsmithfield.co.uk

The "amazing" view over St. Paul's from this chic top-floor dining room in chef John Torode's "multilevel complex" in Smithfield Market complements a "habitually good-quality" Modern British menu majoring on "excellent" meat; service gets mixed reviews ("lovely" and "swift" vs. "spotty"), but surveyors are in agreement about the "buzzy" atmosphere and "high prices."

Smollensky's *American/Chophouse* — 19 | 19 | 19 | £39

Covent Garden | 105 The Strand, WC2R 0AA | 020-7497-2101
Canary Wharf | 1 Reuters Plaza, E14 5AJ | 020-7719-0101 🅱
www.smollenskys.com

"Ribs, ribs and more ribs" are some of the highlights of this "dependable", moderately priced American-style chophouse duo with modern settings; Canary Wharf is geared to "business meetings", whilst The Strand is a "noisy" "party place" that's "ideal for a pre-theatre meal", not least because "pleasant" staff ensure you "finish in time to see the start of the show."

Sofra *Turkish* — 21 | 16 | 18 | £30

Covent Garden | 36 Tavistock St., WC2E 7PB | 020-7240-3773
Marylebone | 1 St. Christophers Pl., W1U 1LT | 020-7224-4080
Mayfair | 18 Shepherd St., W1J 7JG | 020-7493-3320
www.sofra.co.uk

"Tasty", "dependable" Turkish fare that's "great value" draws "pre-theatre"-goers to Covent Garden and "after-shopping" crowds to Marylebone and Mayfair at this trio where the service is "adequate"; "the decor is not the attraction here" (in some areas, "you get squeezed like sardines"), so many prefer to come on a "balmy summer evening" when, depending on locale, you can sit alfresco or under a "retracted roof."

Soho House ●🅓🅱 *British* — 21 | 22 | 24 | £52

Soho | private club | 40 Greek St., W1D 5JJ | 020-7734-5188 | www.sohohouselondon.com

A "hidden entrance" adds to the mystique of this "energetic" private members' club in a "cosy" Soho townhouse where those who can get in "rub up against" "well-known entertainment" figures; "friendly"

	FOOD	DECOR	SERVICE	COST

servers whom you "cannot fault" convey Modern British meals that are "reliably good" if "not exciting" – but that may not matter, as this is more a "place to be seen" than to dine.

NEW Soif *French*
— | — | — | M

Battersea | 27 Battersea Rise, SW11 1HG | 020-7223-1112
New on the scene in Battersea Rise, this Terroirs sibling serves a moderately priced, rustic French menu that changes daily in a flea market–style setting (with a dozen alfresco tables out front); befitting its name, which translates as 'thirst', there's a wide wine selection that includes biodynamic options and a broad choice by the glass.

Solly's *Kosher/Mideastern*
20 | 13 | 16 | £31

Golders Green | 146-150 Golders Green Rd., NW11 8HE | 020-8455-2121
Many diners have "lots of happy memories" at this "busy", basic Golders Green kosher eatery offering "reliable" shawarma, kebabs and the Middle Eastern like alongside "friendly" service; however, others say the "customer attention could be improved", so they just stick to the "small takeaway section."

Song Que Café *Vietnamese*
26 | 9 | 14 | £19

Shoreditch | 134 Kingsland Rd., E2 8DY | 020-7613-3222
"Arrive early to avoid the crowds" for what acolytes assure is the "best Vietnamese food outside of Vietnam" at this Shoreditch "mainstay" whose pho and other "tasty, comforting" fare come for "cheap" prices; what's more, fans "don't mind" that the "street-kitchen" setting is "no-frills" (to say the least) and staff "don't mess about being polite" as they provide "quick" service.

NEW Sonny's Kitchen *European*
— | — | — | M

Barnes | 94 Church Rd., SW13 0DG | 020-8748-0393 | www.sonnyskitchen.co.uk
Flush with the success of their previous pairing at Kitchen W8, owner Rebecca Mascarenhas and chef Philip Howard team up again to convert Barnes favourite Sonny's into this more casual and affordable venture serving a fresh Modern Euro menu of updated comfort-food classics; the airy interior has been lightened up with fresh paint and new banquettes, while the adjacent deli has expanded its offerings to include gourmet takeaway eats.

Sophie's ❶ *American/Chophouse*
22 | 21 | 21 | £41

Covent Garden | 29-31 Wellington St., WC2E 7DB | 020-7836-8836
Chelsea | 311-313 Fulham Rd., SW10 9QH | 020-7352-0088
www.sophiessteakhouse.co.uk
Everyone "knows it's going to be a long wait" at these "no-booking" American chophouses in Chelsea and Covent Garden, yet diners continue to turn up for the "cool vibe" and "hearty food at a fair price", including "quality steaks" and "great ribs (nothing spare about them)"; thankfully, there are "chatty", "attentive" staff and "potent cocktails" to help pass the time; P.S. they're "child-friendly" too.

	FOOD	DECOR	SERVICE	COST

Souk Bazaar ◑ *African*

| 21 | 24 | 21 | £32 |

Soho | 27 Litchfield St., WC2H 9NJ | 020-7240-1796

Souk Medina ◑ *African*

Covent Garden | 1 Short's Gdns., WC2H 9AT | 020-7240-1796
www.soukrestaurant.net

With "quirky" Moroccan furnishings and the "feel of a real souk", it's "like stepping into a genie's lamp" at this "dark" Theatreland duo; many find the staff "lovely" and the North African eats "delicious" – plus the "big" portions make them "good value" – but the real draw may be the "entertaining" "belly dancer later in the evening."

Spice Market *SE Asian*

| 23 | 23 | 20 | £53 |

Chinatown | W London Leicester Square Hotel | 10 Wardour St., W1 6QF | 020-7758-1080 | www.spicemarketlondon.co.uk

There's "plenty of 'wow'" in the "sexy decor", "eye-candy" crowd and "great-looking" staff at chef Jean-Georges Vongerichten's off-shoot of his New York hot spot, spread over two floors of Leicester Square's W Hotel, a "hip, trendy backdrop" for feasting on "upscale" Southeast Asian victuals; although a few think it's more "for the see-and-be-seen crowd than food enthusiasts", the majority proclaim "this place has legs."

Spuntino ◑ *American/Italian*

| 23 | 25 | 21 | £33 |

Soho | 61 Rupert St., W1D 7PW | No phone |
www.spuntino.co.uk

Past the "queue out of the door", the "calculatedly scruffy setting" – "a fabulous cross between a deserted subway station and burnt-out diner" – adds to the "novelty factor" of this "achingly cool" Polpo sibling in Soho; befitting its translated name ('snack'), the menu features "hearty" American-Italian small plates, all "reasonably priced" and offered by "edgy servers" alongside "deadly cocktails"; P.S. with no reservations and not a lot of space, it's "hard to come with a group."

☒ The Square *French*

| 28 | 24 | 27 | £101 |

Mayfair | 6-10 Bruton St., W1J 6PU | 020-7495-7100 |
www.squarerestaurant.com

"Still at the top even after so many years", this "modern", "art-filled" Mayfair "oasis" presents "magnificent" chef Philip Howard's "exqui-site", "artistic" New French dishes, which are "served with style" by a "professional" team that "seldom puts a foot wrong"; considering the "high quality" on offer, the vibe is shockingly "un-square" – though not a surprise is the "very expensive" cost, which can be exacerbated by the "amazing cheese cart" and mitigated by "many reasonably priced alternatives" on the "comprehensive wine list."

Sri Nam ☒ *Thai*

| 22 | 20 | 22 | £32 |

Canary Wharf | 10 Cabot Sq., E14 4EY | 020-7715-9515

"Conducive for a quiet dinner" or a "group" lunch in Canary Wharf, this silk-swathed, bi-level eatery produces "yum" Thai fare; there's "good service" too, but its best feature may be that it's "quite afford-able given the location."

	FOOD	DECOR	SERVICE	COST

Star of India ● *Indian* | 26 | 18 | 21 | £39

South Kensington | 154 Old Brompton Rd., SW5 0BE |
020-7373-2901 | www.starofindia.eu

As "gourmet Indians" go, "there are newer but none better" – or so
say acolytes of this 60-year-old South Ken institution crafting "consistent", "wonderful" "dishes with flair"; indeed, not many mind that
the "space is small" and "packed tight" and the decor's a little
"frumpy" in light of the mostly "excellent service" and relative value.

Sticky Fingers *American* | 19 | 20 | 18 | £34

Kensington | 1 Phillimore Gdns., W8 7QB | 020-7938-5338 |
www.stickyfingers.co.uk

"If you like rock memorabilia", there's lots to check out at musician-
turned-restaurateur Bill Wyman's "noisy", midpriced Kensington
hangout, which lures "Rolling Stones fans" and "tourists" with
"standard burger bar" eats in "American-sized portions"; what's
more, "children love it" – as do their parents when it comes to the
"variety of cocktails" and Monday night discounts.

St. John *British* | 26 | 18 | 23 | £55

Farringdon | 26 St. John St., EC1M 4AY | 020-3301-8069 |
www.stjohnrestaurant.com

"Ignore the operating-room decor and concentrate" on chef Fergus
Henderson's "inspiring way" of turning "unusual cuts of meat" into
"unexpectedly tasty delicacies" ("not for the faint of heart") at this
"bustling" Modern British venue in Farringdon where the "freshness
of ingredients and ideas excite every time"; the "committed" staff
"appreciate you liking what they do", and even if a few sceptics "do
not think the price is justified", the "iconic" venue remains the "gold
standard for hedonism."

St. John Bread & Wine *British* | 25 | 19 | 23 | £43

Shoreditch | 94-96 Commercial St., E1 6LZ | 020-3301-8069 |
www.stjohnbreadandwine.com

Celebrating "weird and wonderful parts of the animal", this all-day
Shoreditch Modern British "meat-lover's paradise" from chef Fergus
Henderson is "less expensive" than the original St. John, but just as
"amazing"; furthermore, "amiable, informal service" reflects the
"lively", "casual" atmosphere – and belies the merely "functional"
decor; P.S. "breakfast here is monumentally good."

St. John
Hotel Restaurant ● *British* | 25 | 17 | 24 | £54

Soho | St. John Hotel | 1 Leicester St., WC2H 7BL | 020-3301-8020 |
www.stjohnhotellondon.com

Offering culinary "sanity amidst the craziness of Leicester Square",
Fergus Henderson's latest outpost of the St. John mini-chain is
"superb in every way", from the "impeccable", "expensive" menu of
"back-to-basics", meat-centric Modern British eats to the "confident,
competent" staff; although the "crowded dining room" with "decor
so plain it's nearly nonexistent" frustrates a few, most call it a "joy" –
and "brilliant" for after the theatre thanks to a 2 AM licence.

| | FOOD | DECOR | SERVICE | COST |

St. Pancras Grand Restaurant *British* `18` `22` `17` `£49`

King's Cross | St. Pancras Int'l | Euston Rd., upper concourse, NW1 2QP | 020-7870-9900 | www.searcys.co.uk

"Whether you're off to Paris or Peterborough", this "grand" art deco-inspired eatery and bar in the "wonderful, historic" St. Pancras International makes a "chic place to dine" on "fine" all-day Modern British cuisine; some complain of "cold service" and "not-cheap" prices, but all things considered, the package is "much better than the average station restaurant."

Strada *Italian* `20` `18` `19` `£25`

Holborn | 6 Great Queen St., WC2B 5DH | 020-7405-6293
Marylebone | 31 Marylebone High St., W1M 4PY | 020-7935-1004 ●
Piccadilly | Panton Honor | 39 Panton St., SW1Y 4EA | 020-7930-8535 ●
City | 156 Chiswick High Rd., W4 1PR | 020-8995-0004 ●
Clerkenwell | 8-10 Exmouth Mkt., EC1 4QR | 020-7278-0800
Islington | 105-106 Upper St., N1 1QN | 020-7226-9742
Barnes | 375 Lonsdale Rd., SW13 9PY | 020-8392-9216 ●
Clapham | 102-104 Clapham High St., SW4 7UL | 020-7627-4847
Earl's Court | 237 Earl's Court Rd., SW5 9AH | 020-7835-1180
Wimbledon | 91 Wimbledon High St., SW19 5EG | 020-8946-4363
www.strada.co.uk
Additional locations throughout London

With "something for everyone" on its "reasonably priced" Italian menu of "creditable pastas, salads, pizzas" and the like, this "buzzy", "modern" chain is a "firm favourite" for a "smart" meal; "service could be better at busier times", but it does "try hard to please", which is another reason it's "perfect for a family."

NEW Suda *Thai* ▽ `22` `20` `17` `£25`

Covent Garden | 23 Slingsby Pl., WC2E 9AB | 020-7240-8010 | www.suda-thai.com

"Well-presented" Thai dishes with "complex" flavours are the draw at this "attractive" spot spread across two "spacious" floors in Covent Garden, with tables spilling onto "a small pedestrian square"; service is "quick", and prices are "moderate", making it "good for groups"; P.S. there's also a lineup of exotic cocktails and healthy shakes.

Sumosan ● *Japanese* `23` `20` `18` `£58`

Mayfair | 26 Albemarle St., W1S 4HY | 020-7495-5999 | www.sumosan.com

"For those more interested in food than the whole 'who's who'" of more "flamboyant" Mayfair restaurants, this modern, minimalist Japanese with a six-seat sushi bar offers a "wonderful menu" of "artistically presented" dishes that "never disappoint" (unlike the service, which is occasionally "slow"); "yes, you pay for it", but loyalists assure "it's worth every penny."

Sushi-Say Ⓜ *Japanese* ▽ `28` `21` `22` `£47`

Kilburn | 33 Walm Ln., NW2 5SH | 020-8459-2971

It "might seem unassuming from the outside", but inside this "cosy" Kilburn venue, an "amazing" "husband-and-wife team" produce "fabulous sushi" and other Japanese dishes of the "highest quality", packed by a "great sake list"; despite the "Mayfair prices", it's "always full", so try to "book well in advance."

Sweetings ⊠ *Seafood* | 23 | 16 | 21 | £50 |

City | 39 Queen Victoria St., EC4N 4SA | 020-7248-3062 |
www.sweetingsrestaurant.com

Looking like something out of "olde England" with its Victorian decor, this "venerable" City "time capsule" (est. 1889) serves "superb", "straightforward" seafood via "friendly" staff who cater for "the business set"; it's "expensive but a real treat" for visitors – "just get there early", before the queue forms, as reservations aren't accepted.

Tamarind *Indian* | 25 | 21 | 23 | £58 |

Mayfair | 20 Queen St., W1J 5PR | 020-7629-3561 |
www.tamarindrestaurant.com

"In India, you would have to be a maharaja" to feast on such "complex" dishes, but Londoners can enjoy the "crème de la crème of fine Indian cuisine" at this "high-end" haunt hidden in an "elegant" Mayfair basement; yes, it's "a bit of a splurge", but "attentive, professional" service and a "well-defined" wine list help keep it on the list for "a celebration, a proposal or to impress visitors."

NEW Tapasia *Asian* | - | - | - | E |

Soho | 32 Old Compton St., W1D 4TP | 020-7287-0213

The team behind Tsunami brings this pricey newcomer serving Pan-Asian tapas to the heart of Soho, where the menu concept is very different than its parent's, but the decor is similarly simple; the bi-level setting features black leather seats and bare, low lights, plus a long bar whipping up fruity, spice-infused house cocktails.

Taqueria *Mexican* | 23 | 11 | 16 | £29 |

Notting Hill | 139-143 Westbourne Grove, W11 2RS |
020-7229-4734 | www.taqueria.co.uk

"If only it had more locations" sigh devotees of this "authentic" Notting Hill "Mexican food mecca" where the "sense-tingling" small plates are "great for sharing" (though the "prices are a little large"); "refreshing" margaritas are another "highlight", as are "friendly" staff who encourage a "laid-back" vibe that "puts a smile on your face"; P.S. be "prepared to wait, since it doesn't take reservations."

Taro *Japanese* | 24 | 16 | 20 | £19 |

Soho | 10 Old Compton St., W1D 4TF | 020-7439-2275
Soho | 61 Brewer St., W1F 9UW | 020-7734-5826
www.tarorestaurants.co.uk

"Melt-in-the-mouth-delicious" sushi and other "excellent" Japanese dishes are the draws at this "no-frills" duo in Soho, which "hits all the right notes" for a "quick bite to eat", especially if you don't mind "sharing a table or bench"; with "competitive" prices and solid service to ensure a "friendly" atmosphere, no wonder it's "bustling."

Tas ● *Turkish* | 22 | 18 | 21 | £25 |

Bloomsbury | 22 Bloomsbury St., WC1B 3QJ | 020-7637-4555
(continued)

(continued)

Tas

Farringdon | 37 Farringdon Rd., EC1M 3JB | 020-7430-9721
Borough | 72 Borough High St., SE1 1XF | 020-7403-7200
Waterloo | 33 The Cut, SE1 8LF | 020-7928-1444

Tas Pide ● *Turkish*

South Bank | 20-22 New Globe Walk, SE1 9DR | 020-7928-3300
www.tasrestaurants.co.uk

"Ideal for meeting friends after work" or when "on a tight budget",
these "swift, reliable" "standbys" around town promise "generous"
portions of "satisfying", "tasty" Turkish fare with "lots of vegetarian
choices"; they "can get loud at times", but "courteous" staff help
keep the environs as "cheerful" as they are "welcoming"; P.S. they're
open late too.

Tate Modern Restaurant *European* | 20 | 23 | 19 | £36 |

South Bank | Tate Modern | Bankside, 7th fl., SE1 9PG |
020-7887-8888 | www.tate.org.uk

Before or after hitting the galleries at the Tate, head up to this "lively"
all-day canteen on the seventh floor of the South Bank museum, offering "quality" Modern European fare amidst "celestial views" across
the Thames; although "long queues" can make it "less comfortable
than it should be", you're bound to have a "relaxing" experience once
seated, as "you're not rushed."

Tayyabs ● *Pakistani* | 26 | 15 | 15 | £22 |

Whitechapel | 83-89 Fieldgate St., E1 1JU | 020-7247-6400 |
www.tayyabs.co.uk

"Beautifully spiced" eats have "zing" at this "legendary", "no-frills"
Whitechapel Pakistani ("mecca for grilled lamb"); unless you've
"booked in advance" or "arrive before 6.30 PM", expect a "manic
queue to get in", "super-noisy" acoustics and service that ranges
from "hurried" to "utter chaos" – but whenever you come, count on
"tremendous value", thanks in part to BYO with "no corkage."

Tempo *Italian* | ∇ 24 | 18 | 19 | £61 |

Mayfair | 54 Curzon St., W1J 8PG | 020-7629-2742 |
www.tempomayfair.co.uk

"Exquisitely prepared" Italian dishes with "some unusual taste combinations" are supported by a "small, well-chosen wine list" and
"friendly service" at this "quiet", "elegant", somewhat "hidden"
Mayfair venue; although it's "eye-wateringly expensive", most agree
that it's overall "delightful"; P.S. there's also a "gem of a bar" serving
small plates on the first floor.

NEW 10 Cases ☒ *European* | 23 | 21 | 22 | £41 |

Covent Garden | 16 Endell St., WC2H 9BD | 020-7836-6801 |
www.the10cases.co.uk

Overflowing with "character and charm", this "welcome" Covent
Garden newcomer takes an "original idea" – spotlighting 10 cases
each of 10 "delicious" red and white wines, all served by the glass,
carafe and bottle – and pairs it with "appealing" European eats; even

if the choices are "limited" and the "few tables" sometimes full, fans toast the "cool" "bistro atmosphere" and servers who ensure you're "well looked after."

Tendido Cero *Spanish*   ▽ 22 | 18 | 20 | £44

South Kensington | 174 Old Brompton Rd., SW5 0BA | 020-7370-3685 | www.cambiodetercio.co.uk

"Tantalising tapas served with style" are the specialities of this "always busy" (hence "noisy"), hip South Kensington Spanish "landmark" from the same folks as Cambio de Tercio; a "reasonable bill" and "excellent wine choices" bolster the "feel-good factor", not to mention the "efficient, friendly" staff.

Tendido Cuatro *Spanish*   ▽ 21 | 18 | 21 | £37

Fulham | 108-110 New King's Rd., SW6 4LY | 020-7371-5147 | www.cambiodetercio.co.uk

"Traditional tapas", paella and other Spanish fare are "done to a high standard" and "wonderfully presented" by "polite" servers at this "stylish, modern" Fulham offshoot of Cambio de Tercio; reasonable prices help it attract its fair share of "noisy groups" in the evening, whilst it's also "recommended" for a "decent" weekend brunch.

NEW 10 Greek Street 🗷 *European*   - | - | - | M

Soho | 10 Greek St., W1D 4DH | 020-7734-4677 | www.10greekstreet.com

In terms of looks, lighting and comfort, simplicity reigns at this plucky Soho addition where an Aussie chef prepares a short, midpriced Modern European menu, displayed on a daily changing blackboard; as for libations, the highlight is a good-value wine list that takes an interesting meander around the world.

Tentazioni 🗷 *Italian*   ▽ 24 | 19 | 23 | £46

Tower Bridge | Lloyd's Wharf | 2 Mill St., SE1 2BD | 020-7237-1100 | www.tentazioni.co.uk

"Gorgeous" "homemade Italian food" "served with flair" makes it "worth the trek" to this venue "hidden in a side street" near Tower Bridge; although some find the decor a bit of "a letdown" ("too red"), it's trumped by the "leisurely" atmosphere, informed by "lovely staff" who "cope with big groups quite well"; P.S. it's pricey, save for the "excellent inexpensive lunch."

Ten Ten Tei 🗷 *Japanese*   ▽ 25 | 12 | 21 | £24

Soho | 56 Brewer St., W1 9TJ | 020-7287-1738

A "fantastic array" of "well-executed" Japanese "classics", including "tasty sushi" and tempura, and "dependable" staff are "the stars" at this "unpretentious" Soho venue with "basic decor (especially downstairs)"; factor in "incredible value for money", and no wonder it's often "very busy", with "a queue out the door."

Terroirs 🗷 *Mediterranean*   21 | 17 | 18 | £37

Covent Garden | 5 William IV St., WC2N 4DW | 020-7036-0660 | www.terroirswinebar.com

The "rustic" Med menus of "ingredient-driven small plates" and "top-quality charcuterie" are "worth seeking out" as much as the "bewildering, genuinely exciting" wine list ("mostly biodynamic") at this "lively", bi-level Covent Garden "hangout"; although service gets mixed marks, "reasonable" prices and a "buzzy", "French-bistro" vibe make it a "great place to meet friends" – and "perfect post-theatre."

Texture ●◙Ⅿ *European* | 25 | 23 | 25 | £70 |

Marylebone | 34 Portman St., W1H 7BY | 020-7224-0028 | www.texture-restaurant.co.uk

"Each dish is a work of art" on the Modern European menu laced with "lots of surprises" and "bold" Scandinavian influences at this "well-appointed" Marylebone "gem"; yes, "it's pricey, particularly if you dig into the excellent champagne list", but given the "refined, attentive" service, it's "definitely worth it"; P.S. the lunch menu's a "deal."

Thai Square *Thai* | 22 | 21 | 20 | £30 |

Covent Garden | 148 The Strand, WC2R 1JA | 020-7497-0904 ◙
Mayfair | 5 Princes St., W1B 2LF | 020-7499-3333 ◙
St. James's | 21-24 Cockspur St., SW1Y 5BL | 020-7839-4000 ●
City | 136-138 Minories, EC3N 1NT | 020-7680-1111 ◙
City | 1-7 Great St. Thomas Apostle, EC4V 2BH | 020-7329-0001 ◙
Islington | 347-349 Upper St., N1 0PD | 020-7704-2000
Putney | 2-4 Lower Richmond Rd., SW15 1LB | 020-8780-1811
Richmond | 29 Kew Rd., TW9 2NQ | 020-8940-5253
South Kensington | 19 Exhibition Rd., SW7 2HE | 020-7584-8359
Soho Thai ◙ *Thai*
Soho | 27-28 St. Anne's Ct., W1F 0BN | 020-7287-2000
www.thaisq.com
Additional locations throughout London

"Generous portions" of "delicious" "classic Thai food" make this "welcoming", "well-priced" chain an "easy go-to", with "polite" servers who "efficiently" handle "small groups or large parties" alike; ok, it's "hardly an exciting or exotic choice", but loyalists say its numerous "handy" locations are "good to have around" for a "quick fix."

Thai Thai *Thai* | 24 | 24 | 21 | £31 |

Shoreditch | 110 Old St., EC1V 9BD | 020-7490-5230 | www.thaithaieast.co.uk

From soups to stir-fries, the "enjoyable", "expertly cooked" Thai cuisine at this spacious Shoreditch standby hits the spot for reasonable prices; "nicely laid out", with "lovely" modern decor, it "tends to get busy", but "efficient" service keeps things moving.

Theo Randall at The InterContinental ◙ *Italian* | 26 | 21 | 24 | £53 |

Mayfair | InterContinental Park Ln. | 1 Hamilton Pl., W1J 7QY | 020-7318-8747 | www.theorandall.com

"Superb" pastas, "well-executed meats and fish" and other "earthy" Italian cooking, plus "gracious service" and a "serene ambience" add up to a "special treat" at chef Theo Randall's InterContinental Park Lane venue; although a few find the "underground location" "dreary" and warn that "the price can rack up", most "can't fault the experience"; P.S. the set menu is "superlative."

	FOOD	DECOR	SERVICE	COST

NEW 34 *Chophouse* | 23 | 24 | 23 | £62 |

Mayfair | 34 Grosvenor Sq., W1K 2HD | 020-3350-3434 |
www.34-restaurant.co.uk

"All the glamour you'd expect" from a Mayfair chophouse overseen by the Caprice group comes via "splendid", "elegant" Edwardian and art deco–inspired adornments at this "buzzy" newcomer offering "a fabulous selection" of "succulent" mains and "divine" desserts; what's more, it's all presented with the sort of "spot-on" service "London oligarchs" demand – at the kind of "expensive" prices they have no trouble paying.

Thomas Cubitt *British* | 21 | 20 | 19 | £42 |

Belgravia | 44 Elizabeth St., SW1W 9PA | 020-7730-6060 |
www.thethomascubitt.co.uk

With a "solid" Traditional British menu downstairs, "fantastic" Modern British fare upstairs and a "thoughtful wine list", this Belgravia venue "defines all that's good about gastropubs"; "popular with the beautiful people", "the pub section is more packed than a London tube at rush hour", whilst the "tranquil" dining room resembles "the posh townhouse you can't afford"; whichever area you choose, expect "competent" service and "make a reservation – otherwise, you'll salivate as an onlooker."

Timo 🗷 *Italian* | ∇ 25 | 18 | 24 | £52 |

Kensington | 343 Kensington High St., W8 6NW | 020-7603-3888 |
www.timorestaurant.net

"Smartly dressed" regulars promise that they "will go back forever" to this "understated", cream-and-green-hued Kensington spot offering a "simple" yet "top-quality" Italian menu and "wonderful" service; it's a bit "expensive", but the prices probably "won't kill you", especially if you "choose the lunchtime menu."

Tinello 🗷 *Italian* | 26 | 21 | 22 | £49 |

Pimlico | 87 Pimlico Rd., SW1W 8PH | 020-7730-3663 |
www.tinello.co.uk

What was once an "excellent find" by Pimlico cognoscenti is "now emerging as a go-to Italian", where "fabulous, thoughtful Tuscan cooking", a "lovely wine list" and "attentive service" ensure the place gets "jammed"; the "low-key but stylish space" with "exposed brick and subdued lighting" attracts a "chic, business-casual clientele" who venture "upstairs for atmosphere, downstairs to hold a conversation" and pay "slightly pricey" costs throughout.

Tokyo Diner ◑ *Japanese* | 22 | 14 | 19 | £20 |

Chinatown | 2 Newport Pl., WC2H 7JJ | 020-7287-8777 |
www.tokyodiner.com

Resembling a "typical workingman's place" in Tokyo, this "crowded", "no-frills" Theatreland Japanese endeavour "does a good line in noodles, sushi" and other "tasty" dishes – all served "fast", with a "no-tip rule", making it "great value"; what's more, there's "extra rice if you want it", "Japanese newspapers at hand" and "unlimited complimentary green tea."

Tom Aikens ☒ *French*
25 | 22 | 24 | £81

Chelsea | 43 Elystan St., SW3 3NT | 020-7584-2003 |
www.tomaikens.co.uk

The eponymous celeb chef's "cutting-edge" style is "clearly visible"
in the "innovative", "fabulous" dishes at his Chelsea New French, an
"expense-account" affair that's undergone "quite a transformation"
in a recent refurb – "gone are the white tablecloths, replaced by bare
wood tables"; staff are as "knowledgeable" and "relaxed" as ever,
whilst a "sensational" wine list is the icing on the cake, all of which
adds up to a "thrilling gastro experience."

Tom Ilic ☑ *European*
▽ 24 | 17 | 22 | £40

Battersea | 123 Queenstown Rd., SW8 3RH | 020-7622-0555 |
www.tomilic.com

Foodies "don't mind travelling across two postcodes" for the namesake chef's "inventive", "deliciously cooked" Modern European
dishes (pork is a speciality) and staff's "informed", "friendly" service
at this Battersea site; they also "don't worry about the room" (it's
"down-to-earth") because pricewise, it's "a definite steal."

Tom's Deli *Eclectic*
24 | 17 | 22 | £22

Notting Hill | 226 Westbourne Grove, W11 2RH | 020-7221-8818 |
www.tomsdelilondon.co.uk

"You'll want to linger all day" over the "awesome" Eclectic eats at
Tom Conran's Notting Hill venue comprising a ground-floor deli
"crammed" with "treats", and an art-filled upstairs cafe; although it
"looks tired" to some eyes, don't be surprised if it's "crowded" right
up until closing time, 6.30 PM daily.

Tom's Kitchen *British*
23 | 19 | 20 | £45

Covent Garden | Somerset Hse. | The Strand, WC2R 1LA | 020-7845-4646
Chelsea | 27 Cale St., SW3 3QP | 020-7349-0202
www.tomskitchen.co.uk

"Upscale" Modern British "comfort food" offers "little taste surprises at every turn" at chef Tom Aikens' "fabulous farm-to-table"
duo in Chelsea and Covent Garden; "attentive" service creates a
"homey feeling", whilst the "young", "trendy" clientele bring a "satisfying buzz" to the "casual" experience – which is "popular for good
reason" and particularly "perfect with kids."

Tortilla *Mexican*
24 | 19 | 22 | £11

Bloomsbury | 6 Market Pl., W1W 8AH | 020-7637-2800
Stratford | The Gallery, Westfield Stratford City | 213 The Balcony,
E20 1ES | 020-8555-3663
Canary Wharf | 18 N. Colonnade, E14 4EU | 020-7719-9160
City | 28 Leadenhall Mkt., EC3V 1LR | 020-7929-7837 ☒
South Bank | 106 Southwark St., SE1 0TA | 020-7620-0285 ☒
Islington | 13 Islington High St., N1 9LQ | 020-7833-3130
Wimbledon | 22 The Broadway, SW19 1RE | 020-8947-3589
Hammersmith | 6 King St., W6 0QA | 020-8741-7959
www.tortilla.co.uk

"The highlight of many a drab office-bound day", this chain provides
"hunger-afflicted workers" with "filling", "fast, straightforward

| | FOOD | DECOR | SERVICE | COST |

Mexican food" for "bargain-basement prices"; the "amazing burritos" are complemented by "a fine selection of beers", and all is proffered by "smiling staff" amidst "modern" environs.

NEW Tramshed British
- | - | - | M

Shoreditch | 32 Rivington St., EC2A 3EQ | 020-7749-0478 | www.chickenandsteak.co.uk

Startling Damien Hirst artwork – a formaldehyde-encased cow and cock set on a pedestal – makes Mark Hix's new Shoreditch eatery in a former tram-generator building hard to ignore; the art is a nod to the Modern British menu, which is restricted to dry-aged steak and slow-reared chicken mains, plus three seasonal starters for sharing, all served at unadorned wooden tables and for reasonable prices; P.S. there's a cosy cocktail bar, and takeaway is available too.

Trinity European
26 | 22 | 25 | £57

Clapham | 4 The Polygon, SW4 0JG | 020-7622-1199 | www.trinityrestaurant.co.uk

"Adventurous tastes" ("bone marrow, pig's trotters") abound on Adam Byatt's "fantastic-value" Modern Euro menu at this "laid-back" "gem" on the "edge of Clapham Common"; "slick service" and "cool decor" complete the "memorable" picture, one that's "smart without being stuffy, and indulgent without being excessive."

Trishna Indian
26 | 19 | 22 | £48

Marylebone | 15-17 Blandford St., W1U 3DG | 020-7935-5624 | www.trishnalondon.com

"Providing a light, refreshing touch to the upscale Indian scene", this "low-key" Marylebone offshoot of a Mumbai mainstay "steps outside the humdrum" with "sublime" "coastal" cuisine ("emphasis on seafood"); surveyors call it "pricey but worth it", and with an "interesting" wine list and "friendly service" as added enticements, small wonder they "want to go back for more and more."

The Troubadour Eclectic
22 | 24 | 22 | £23

Earl's Court | 265 Old Brompton Rd., SW5 9JA | 020-7370-1434 | www.troubadour.co.uk

There's "something addictive" about the "arty", "bohemian feel" of this "quirky" Earl's Court cultural "haunt" from 1954, a "chilled-out place to relax" all day over "quality" Eclectic eats, "awesome coffee" and "great cocktails"; additional features include a "lovely" garden and a downstairs club that usually has "decent singer/songwriters on the bill", following in the footsteps of famous past headliners.

Truc Vert French
∇ 18 | 15 | 16 | £35

Mayfair | 42 N. Audley St., W1K 6ZR | 020-7491-9988 | www.trucvert.co.uk

When you'd like a "respite from the Oxford Street crowds", this Mayfair cafe is a "soothing" "place to hang your hat for a while" and tuck into "nicely prepared", daily changing French bistro fare with "creative undertones", and all "for less money than you'd expect"; a "comprehensive wine list" is a plus, and "great brunch" is yet another, especially if you snag a table outside in summer.

| | FOOD | DECOR | SERVICE | COST |

Trullo *Italian*   24 | 20 | 22 | £43

Islington | 300-302 St. Paul's Rd., N1 2LH | 020-7226-2733 | www.trullorestaurant.com

"Vibrant" Italian dishes are crafted with "skilful hands" and served by "cheery" staff at this Islingtonian where the "paper-topped tables" are "crowded" with the local "intelligentsia celebrating birthdays or their latest book deals"; and not only is it a "bargain for the quality", but there's also a "great tapas bar" in the "cosy" cellar.

Tsunami ● *Japanese*   24 | 21 | 23 | £39

Bloomsbury | 93 Charlotte St., W1T 4PY | 020-7637-0050 🗷
Clapham | 5-7 Voltaire Rd., SW4 6DQ | 020-7978-1610
www.tsunamirestaurant.co.uk

There's a "chilled vibe" at this "dark", "intimate" Japanese duo in Clapham and Charlotte Street, but it's the "brilliant", "beautifully presented" sushi and such, "superb service" and "fantastic cocktails" that make it a "perfect date" venue; whilst "not super-expensive or super-cheap", it's a "reliable" backup for "trendy" dining in "lovely" environs; P.S. the "takeaway option is a lifesaver for lazy nights in."

Tsuru 🗷 *Japanese*   ▽ 23 | 16 | 18 | £21

City | 10 Queen St., EC4N 1TX | 020-7248-1525
City | 201 Bishopsgate, EC2M 3UG | 020-7377-1166
South Bank | 4 Canvey St., SE1 9AN | 020-7928-2228
www.tsuru-sushi.co.uk

They're "concerned with the provenance of the ingredients" at these "minimalist" Japanese spots by the Tate Modern and in the City, which are "like fast-food restaurants during lunchtime", when most folks take the "super-fresh", "sustainably sourced sushi" to go; the "good-value" menu expands with "mouth-watering katsu curries" and teriyaki in the evening, when you should "expect to be finished by 9 PM", because that's when it closes.

Tuttons ● *British*   ▽ 19 | 18 | 18 | £33

Covent Garden | 11-12 Russell St., WC2B 5HZ | 020-7836-4141 | www.tuttons.com

"Whether you're looking for a pre-meeting breakfast or post-opera supper, the location is hard to beat" at this "lively" stalwart "right at the edge" of the Covent Garden piazza, which revamped its "reliable", midpriced menu post-Survey to focus on Traditional British dishes and refurbished its brasserielike setting (out-dating Food and Decor scores); what shouldn't have changed is "charming service" that's perhaps best "when not busy" – a rare occurrence, especially in summer when the "delightful" outdoor terrace is mobbed.

28-50 Wine Workshop & Kitchen 🗷 *French*   22 | 20 | 22 | £48

Holborn | 140 Fetter Ln., EC4A 1BT | 020-7242-8877
NEW Marylebone | 15-17 Marylebone Ln., W1U 2NE |
020-7486-7922 Ⓜ
www.2850.co.uk

Staff "dazzle" with their "excellent" oenological knowledge at this "hidden basement gem" in Holborn, where the "amazing", "ever-changing" list of "fairly priced" wines is complemented by "rustic" French bistro dishes that are "a cut above"; "fashionable", casual decor makes it "great for a quiet drink, impressing a client" or a "late bite" post-work; P.S. the Marylebone offshoot is new.

Two Brothers Fish Ⓜ *Seafood*   23 | 16 | 21 | £30

Finchley | 297-303 Regent's Park Rd., N3 1DP | 020-8346-0469 | www.twobrothers.co.uk

Finchley seafood fans turn up at this "long-standing" local joint that's renowned for "delicious" fish 'n' chips breaded with matzo meal, along with other "good-quality" catch and side dishes; the "drab decor" and "crowded, noisy" conditions mean it's probably "not the place for a long, leisurely meal", but at least service is "fast and helpful."

202 *European*   19 | 20 | 18 | £34

Notting Hill | 202 Westbourne Grove, W11 2RH | 020-7727-2722 | www.202london.com

"Food and fashion mix" at this Modern European set inside a "stylishly casual" Notting Hill "concept store" where "cool, funky locals" "shop, be seen" and have a "delicious" "quick" meal ferried to them by "friendly" staff; at weekends, "expect a wait", as seemingly all the local "mummies" stop in for a "girlie brunch."

222 Veggie Vegan *Vegan*   24 | 19 | 23 | £32

Earl's Court | 222 North End Rd., W14 9NU | 020-7381-2322 | www.222veggievegan.com

The "varied selection" of "tasty", "nutritious" vegan fare on offer at this "friendly" Earl's Court cafe "might even persuade carnivores" to "take the plunge", and it all comes "without any trace" of "pretentiousness"; prices are "competitive for the quality", particularly a lunchtime buffet that's "really good value for money."

2 Veneti Ⓩ *Italian*   24 | 21 | 22 | £39

Marylebone | 10 Wigmore St., W1U 2RD | 020-7637-0789 | www.2veneti.com

"Medics" from nearby Harley Street rub shoulders with "concert performers from Wigmore Hall" next door at this "cosy" brick-walled Marylebone Venetian, where "unique dishes" offer "a genuine taste of the region", and the "fresh pasta is a dream"; "cheerful" staff are on hand to "discuss the ingredients and make useful suggestions", and best of all, it's "affordable."

Ⓩ Umu Ⓩ *Japanese*   27 | 25 | 25 | £96

Mayfair | 14-16 Bruton Pl., W1J 6LX | 020-7499-8881 | www.umurestaurant.com

For a "true celebration" of "traditional" Kyoto-style kaiseki along with "glorious sushi", this "civilised" Mayfair Japanese offers a "unique" dining experience that's well "worth the steep price"; with its "personal service", "great sake list" and "dark", "elegant" ambience, it's a "special place for a special night" – and "lovely" set-price lunches supply the same "upmarket" experience at a lower cost.

	FOOD	DECOR	SERVICE	COST

Union Cafe ● *British/Mediterranean* **21 | 16 | 20 | £41**

Marylebone | 96 Marylebone Ln., W1U 2QA | 020-7486-4860 |
www.brinkleys.com

For a "chat with friends" or an "informal business lunch", this
"buzzy" Marylebone local is "reliable but never boring", thanks to
an "interesting" menu of Modern British–Mediterranean comfort
dishes; the setting may be "bland", and the "friendly" staff "a bit off
hand" when it's full, but an "outstanding-value wine list" keeps the
"repeat" trade brisk.

NEW Union Jacks *British* **20 | 18 | 21 | £28**

Holborn | 4 Central St. Giles Piazza, WC2H 8AB |
020-3597-7888
Chiswick | 217-221 Chiswick, W4 2DW | 020-3617-9988
www.unionjacksrestaurants.com

Jamie Oliver is behind these Chiswick and Holborn yearlings distrib-
uting a midpriced selection of "fancy" flatbreads ("essentially pizza"),
whose "innovative combinations" of toppings recall "traditional"
British recipes (some deem the concept "slightly strange", others
assure that it "really works"); "old-school decor, cool background
tunes" and "zippy service" ensure a "fun", "relaxed" time.

Vanilla Black ☒ *Vegetarian* **24 | 18 | 24 | £49**

Holborn | 17-18 Tooks Ct., EC4A 1LB | 020-7242-2622 |
www.vanillablack.co.uk

"Surprising and delighting even the most devout carnivores", this
"out-of-the-way wonder" in Holborn creates "exciting", "original",
"gourmet vegetarian" eats, which arrive via "polite", "attentive
service"; it comes "highly recommended" for a "fancy date night",
despite a "plain", "sparsely furnished" setting – and perhaps because it's "not an everyday" kind of place pricewise.

Vapiano ● *Italian* **23 | 20 | 18 | £18**

Marylebone | 19-21 Great Portland St., W1W 8QB |
020-7268-0080 | www.vapiano.co.uk
Southwark | 90 Southwark St., SE1 0FD | 020-7593-2010 |
www.vapiano.de

"Stand at the counter" whilst the "delicious" Italian pizzas, pastas
and salads are made "to your specifications before your eyes" at
these "light-on-the-wallet" Marylebone and Southwark outposts of
the international "quick-bite" chain; sceptics sigh "gimmicky", but
fans say the formula "works well", save for "bottlenecks at the till"
and "long" lunchtime queues.

Vasco & Piero's Pavilion ☒ *Italian* **∇ 26 | 21 | 27 | £36**

Soho | 15 Poland St., W1F 8QE | 020-7437-8774 |
www.vascosfood.com

Supporters who've been going to this "low-key treat" in Soho for
"donkey's years" (it's been around since 1971) say they've "never
been disappointed" in its "high-quality" Umbrian fare, "impeccable
service" or value; the "simple" "decor is ok" for a "neighbourhood"
place – and it's a "popular" one at that, so "booking is advisable."

	FOOD	DECOR	SERVICE	COST

Veeraswamy *Indian*
25 | 24 | 24 | £52

Mayfair | Victory Hse. | 99 Regent St., W1B 4RS | 020-7734-1401 |
www.veeraswamy.com

Snare a "window table overlooking Regent Street" at this "iconic"
Mayfair "landmark" in Victory House (since 1926) that tenders a
"spectacular array" of "inventive" Indian dishes presented with
"verve" by "skilled" staffers; the "glittering", "luxurious" setting
suits "business lunches and couples' dinners" alike, and even
though the pricing is "high-end", it's "highly recommended" for a
"first-class" experience.

Verru *E European/Scandinavian*
∇ 24 | 22 | 24 | £38

Marylebone | 69 Marylebone Ln., W1U 2PH | 020-7935-0858 |
www.verru.co.uk

A "highly original" Scandinavian-Baltic menu on which "traditional
fare" gets "gourmet, artistic twists" is offered by "friendly, attentive"
folks at this bare-brick-walled Marylebone haunt with a "romantic,
cosy atmosphere"; lunchtime and pre-theatre set menus are a "bargain", but "the à la carte is not far off", and "the wine list is varied
enough for all palates and budgets."

Viajante ◐ *Eclectic*
26 | 22 | 25 | £96

Bethnal Green | Town Hall Hotel | Patriot Sq., E2 9NF |
020-7871-0461 | www.viajante.co.uk

Chef Nuno Mendes takes diners on a "surprise"-filled "gastronomic
journey" at this "experimental" Eclectic set in the former Bethnal
Green Town Hall, a "real foodie's restaurant", where the "daring"
dishes are prepared in a "theatrical" open kitchen and offered in a
"tasting-menu-only" format; the "limited wine list", rather "austere"
premises and "sky-high" price tags are counterbalanced by a "relaxing" ambience and "incredible" service; P.S. those "on a budget"
head for the Corner Room adjunct or the "small cocktail bar" for
equally "intriguing" nibbles.

Viet Hoa ◐ *Vietnamese*
23 | 17 | 18 | £21

Shoreditch | 70-72 Kingsland Rd., E2 8DP | 020-7729-8293 |
www.viethoarestaurant.co.uk

"Jostle with East London types" seeking "pre-clubbing noodles" at this
Shoreditch standard for "ridiculously reasonably priced" Vietnamese
eats like a "cure-all hot-and-sour soup"; the "cavernous" space has
had a "trendy makeover", introducing "plenty of wood and unadorned
walls", whilst service is often "attentive"; P.S. downstairs is the Mess,
a "cook-your-own-BBQ affair."

Village East ◐ *British*
23 | 24 | 20 | £41

Tower Bridge | 171-173 Bermondsey St., SE1 3UW |
020-7357-6082 | www.villageeast.co.uk

"New York City" in style, this "lively", "trendy Bermondsey Street
haunt" is "worth seeking out" for "quality" Modern British eats
served all day; there's a "big bar to just drop in for a drink" – ask
"helpful" staff what's recommended from the "strong, affordable
wine list" or "amazing cocktails."

	FOOD	DECOR	SERVICE	COST

Villandry French
19 17 18 £38

Bloomsbury | 170 Great Portland St., W1W 5QB | 020-7631-3131 |
www.villandry.com

Whether for a "business breakfast, lunch or glass of wine after work",
this "upmarket" Bloomsbury venue covers all bases, with a "relaxed"
cafe and a "white-tablecloth" restaurant serving "simple" French
fare, along with a "gourmet deli" vending "fresh foods and unusual
gifts"; though critics find the setting "plain" and the tariffs "pricey",
"friendly" staff, who are always "willing to help", redeem.

Vinoteca European
23 20 22 £37

Marylebone | 15 Seymour Pl., W1H 5BD | 020-7724-7288
NEW **Soho** | 53-55 Beak St., W1F 9SH | 020-3544-7411
Farringdon | 7 St. John St., EC1M 4AA | 020-7253-8786 Ⓢ
www.vinoteca.co.uk

An "interesting" vino selection (including a "terrific range by the
glass") makes these "super-casual" wine bars oenophile magnets,
whilst an "artful" Modern European menu of "frequently changing"
dishes delights diners; "fantastic" sommeliers, "convivial" compa-
triots and prices that are "reasonable for the quality" support the
view that it's "worth a try."

Vivat Bacchus ⓈEuropean
21 17 20 £38

Holborn | 47 Farringdon St., EC4A 4LL | 020-7353-2648
Tower Bridge | 4 Hays Ln., SE1 2HB | 020-7234-0891
www.vivatbacchus.co.uk

An "amazing" cheese cave and a wine list as thick as a "novel" are the
draws at this South African–owned duo in Holborn and near Tower
Bridge, which also turn out an "interesting", midpriced Modern
European menu (including a few "off-*piste*" dishes); "friendly",
"knowledgeable" service and a "bright, lively" atmosphere further
enhance the "thoroughly enjoyable experience."

ⓏWagamama Japanese
21 15 19 £20

Bloomsbury | 4 Streatham St., WC1A 1JB | 020-7323-9223
Covent Garden | 1 Tavistock St., WC2E 7PG | 020-7836-3330
Knightsbridge | Harvey Nichols | 109-125 Knightsbridge,
lower ground fl., SW1X 7RJ | 020-7201-8000
Marylebone | 101 Wigmore St., W1U 1QR | 020-7409-0111
Soho | 10 Lexington St., W1F 0LD | 020-7292-0990
City | 1 Ropemaker St., EC2V 0HR | 020-7588-2688 Ⓢ
City | 109 Fleet St., EC4A 2AF | 020-7583-7889 Ⓢ
South Bank | Southbank Ctr. | Belvedere Rd., SE1 8XX |
020-7021-0877
Camden Town | 11 Jamestown Rd., NW1 7BW | 020-7428-0800
Islington | N1 Ctr. | 40 Parkfield St., N1 0PS | 020-7226-2664
www.wagamama.com
Additional locations throughout London

Waga-maniacs say they're "never disappointed" with the "heart-
warming", "healthy" Japanese fare, "brisk", "helpful" service or
"cheap" bills that make this "addictive noodle house" a "weekly
stomping ground" – and London's Favourite chain; you'll probably "sit
next to a complete stranger" at a "huge" communal table in the "no-

rills" environs, but that's part of the "fun", and though some diners
are "a bit annoyed" when dishes come "at different times", "you are
warned, so you can't complain."

☑ Wahaca *Mexican*   23 | 20 | 20 | £24

Covent Garden | 66 Chandos Pl., WC2N 4HG | 020-7240-1883
Soho | 80 Wardour St., W1F OTF | 020-7734-0195
NEW Stratford | Westfield Stratford City | 6 Chestnut Plaza, E20 1GL |
020-3288-1025
Canary Wharf | Park Pavilion, 40 Canada Sq., E14 5FW |
020-7516-9145
Shepherd's Bush | Westfield Shopping Ctr. | Ariel Way, W12 7GB |
020-8749-4517
www.wahaca.co.uk

"Fast, fresh and fabulous" sums up this "vibrant", "funky" "chain
with soul", which "satisfies Mexican cravings" via chef Thomasina
Miers' "consistent", "interesting" selection of "affordable" "street
food" that is served "always with a smile"; caveats include the
"no-reservations policy", "long waits" and "loud noise", but you
really should "beware the tequila mojitos", lest you "end up on the
wrong night bus."

The Wallace *French*   18 | 23 | 15 | £30

Marylebone | Wallace Collection | Hertford Hse., Manchester Sq.,
W1U 3BN | 020-7563-9505 | www.thewallacerestaurant.co.uk
"A treat at any time, but especially on a gray day", this "gorgeous",
glass-roofed atrium inside Marylebone's "wonderful" Wallace
Collection is a "beautiful setting for a light luncheon" of "simple,
tasty" French fare, or "high tea after a visit to the museum"; whilst
critical types lament that the cuisine doesn't match "the standards
of the surroundings" and service can be "slow", the moderate prices
make amends for most.

Wapping Food *European*   20 | 26 | 20 | £43

Wapping | Wapping Hydraulic Power Station | Wapping Wall, E1W 3ST |
020-7680-2080 | www.thewappingproject.com
"Set in the cool confines of an old power station", this "engaging"
Wapping venue features "Victorian industrial machinery interspersed
with the tables", "ever-changing" art exhibitions and an "accomplished" Modern European menu with "reasonable" prices; "friendly,
quirky" staff and an "interesting Australian wine list" bolster its reputation as a "unique gem", "especially for weekend brunch."

The Warrington *British*   ▽ 20 | 20 | 19 | £33

St. John's Wood | 93 Warrington Cres., W9 1EH | 020-7286-8282 |
www.faucetinn.com
"Fantastic pub downstairs, light and airy dining room upstairs" is the
makeup of this "wonderfully restored" Victorian landmark in Maida
Vale, a "relaxing", "family-friendly" venue whose "quality" Traditional
British menu covers "everything from pub grub to fine dining";
surveyors say service is "ok", whilst the "selection of properly
stored ales and beers" is "fine" indeed; P.S. no longer part of the
Gordon Ramsay portfolio.

	FOOD	DECOR	SERVICE	COST

Wasabi *Japanese*   22 | 17 | 20 | £15

Covent Garden | 34 Villiers St., WC2N 6NJ | 020-7807-9992
Marylebone | 439 Oxford St., W1C 2PN | 020-7493-6422
Soho | 58 Oxford St., W1D 1BH | 020-7580-0062
Westminster | Victoria Station | 115 Buckingham Palace Rd., SW1V 1JU | 020-7630-0311 ●
City | 52 Old Broad St., EC2M 1RX | 020-7374-8337 🖼
City | 69 Fleet St., EC4Y 1EU | 020-7353-9992
Camden Town | 127 Tottenham Court Rd., W1T 5AU | 020-7383-7772
Islington | 74-76 Finsbury Pavement, EC2A 1AT | 020-7256-5111 🖼
Brixton | Waterloo Station | York Rd., SE1 7LY | 020-7928-0743
Hammersmith | The Broadway Shopping Ctr., W6 9YE | 020-8748-8675
www.wasabi.uk.com
Additional locations throughout London

Though "worth waiting to sit down for", the "delicious sushi" and "tasty noodles" at this "speedy", "efficient" Japanese chain make for a "reliable" meal "on the go", so regulars often "end up taking it home"; with "enormous portion sizes", it's a "good deal", and whilst the streamlined settings are often "crowded", "helpful" staff maintain a "friendly" vibe.

Waterloo Bar & Grill 🖼 *British*   20 | 18 | 20 | £34

Waterloo | 119 Waterloo Rd., SE1 8UL | 020-7960-0202 | www.waterloobarandgrill.com

"Well-prepared and -presented" Modern British "comfort food" at moderate prices and "cocktails in abundance" are highlights at this "cosy", contemporary Waterloo venue that's "well sited for the Old Vic and Southbank theatres"; what's more, the "warm welcome" and "quick in-and-out" ensure that most "would certainly go again."

🅉 Waterside Inn   29 | 28 | 28 | £120
Restaurant 🅜 *French*

Bray | Waterside Inn | Ferry Rd., Berkshire | 01628-620 691 | www.waterside-inn.co.uk

"Fine dining is taken to another level" at this "magical", "romantic" Roux family venue "on the banks of the river in Bray", where the Classic French cuisine is so "impeccably prepared", it's been voted No. 1 for Food in the London area; in fact, it's "breathtaking in every way, including the price", but for a "flawless experience" - complemented by "excellent" wines and "immaculate service" - it's "more than worth it"; P.S. for a really "big treat", "arrive by boat", order *le menu exceptionnel* and spend the night.

The Waterway *European*   ▽ 21 | 20 | 19 | £35

St. John's Wood | 54 Formosa St., W9 2JU | 020-7266-3557 | www.thewaterway.co.uk

In summer, the "super terrace is the draw" at this "picturesque" St. John's Wood Modern European with a "beautiful view of Little Venice", but it's also "hopping" at other times, like Sunday brunch and Thursday live music; as for the gastropub fare, though "well executed", a few folks feel it's "expensive for what you get" and when factoring in the "patchy" service (sometimes "rude", sometimes "friendly").

| | FOOD | DECOR | SERVICE | COST |

The Wells *European*

22 | 21 | 21 | £46

Hampstead | 30 Well Walk, NW3 1BX | 020-7794-3785 |
www.thewellshampstead.co.uk

"Wonderfully welcoming (especially to dogs)" and "pleasantly decorated", this Modern European gastropub "not far from the heath" in
Hampstead is more than just "a neighbourhood joint", it's a "destination", thanks to "imaginative", "tasty" cooking served in a ground-
floor pub and an upstairs dining room (where the menu is "a little
expensive"); a "good wine selection", "places for backgammon
and chess" and a "great Sunday roast" are some more reasons it's
"worth the trek."

Wheeler's of St. James's 🗷 *Seafood*

23 | 19 | 22 | £56

St. James's | 72-73 St. James's St., SW1A 1PH | 020-7408-1440 |
www.wheelersrestaurant.org

"Casual diners mix with suits" at chef-owner Marco Pierre White's
spacious, "traditional" St. James's seafooder, "the place to go" for
an "excellent selection" of "top-dollar, top-quality" fin fare; the "prix
fixe menus can be a real bargain", especially for "this neck of the
woods", and it's a "lovely place for a group" too, with "delightful"
service that adds to its "classic London" appeal.

Whitechapel Gallery
Dining Room 🅼 *European*

▽ 19 | 18 | 18 | £42

Whitechapel | Whitechapel Gallery | 77-82 Whitechapel High St.,
E1 7QX | 020-7522-7888 | www.whitechapelgallery.org

A "great resource" for Whitechapel, this "cosy" oak-panelled "oasis" in a "significant" art gallery boasts the talents of chef Angela
Hartnett (Murano), who consults on the "limited but quite good"
Modern European menu; what's more, the "relatively quiet" atmosphere benefits from "warm" service from staff who make customers
feel "well looked after."

Wild Honey *British*

23 | 19 | 21 | £49

Mayfair | 12 St. George St., W1S 2FB | 020-7758-9160 |
www.wildhoneyrestaurant.co.uk

Mavens are just "wild about" this "cosy" "wood-panelled" Mayfair
spin-off of Arbutus, praising its "understated elegance" and "fantastic" seasonal Modern British cooking that's "reasonably priced
given the quality"; more accolades are earned for its "attentive, helpful
service" and "superb" selection of wines, each available by the bottle or 250-ml carafe, all helping to make it a "dependable go-to" for
"entertaining" or a "quiet" dinner "pre-theatre."

Wilton's 🗷 *British/Seafood*

26 | 25 | 26 | £80

St. James's | 55 Jermyn St., SW1Y 6LX | 020-7629-9955 |
www.wiltons.co.uk

"One gets the sense King Edward might sit down" alongside "the
cast of *Downton Abbey*" at this "bastion of Britishness" in "refined",
"reserved" St. James's digs, a "time machine" "operating continu-
ously since 1742", where "outstanding seafood" (like "excellent
oysters") and "incredible game" lead a "superb" traditional menu

that's "served with a deft touch" by "respectful" staff; sure, it's "budget-busting", but for a "grown-up", "fine-dining experience", it's "worth it."

☑ The Wolseley ◐ European

| 23 | 26 | 23 | £55 |

Piccadilly | 160 Piccadilly, W1J 9EB | 020-7499-6996 | www.thewolseley.com

"Blissful for breakfast, tea, an assignation, celebration or dining alone", this "grand Viennese-style brasserie" (voted London's Favourite restaurant) in "sophisticated" Piccadilly premises attracts "its fair share of glitterati" with "consistent" all-day Modern European eats, which are "not terribly pricey" given the "exquisite" "quality", and matched by an "extensive wine list"; "it all feels so effortless" thanks to the "slick" service, but "make sure you get a reservation well in advance" to avoid a "long wait" – or pray that one of the few "tables kept free for walk-ins" is available.

Wong Kei ◐⊟ Chinese

| 19 | 7 | 10 | £16 |

Chinatown | 41-43 Wardour St., W1D 6PY | 020-7437-8408

"Huge portions" of "divine" noodles and other "reliable", "student-priced" Cantonese eats come at "a rapid pace" at this "multifloor" Chinatown "legend"; "you won't want to linger" due to "service with a growl" (considered "part of its great charm") and the "atmosphere of a bus station", but still, loyalists "can't resist", it being such a "quintessential London experience."

Woodlands Indian/Vegetarian

| 23 | 15 | 20 | £26 |

Marylebone | 77 Marylebone Ln., W1U 2PS | 020-7486-3862
Leicester Square | 37 Panton St., SW1Y 4EA | 020-7839-7258
Hampstead | 102 Heath St., NW3 1DR | 020-7794-3080
www.woodlandsrestaurant.co.uk

"Recommended for vegetarians" and "committed meat eaters" alike, this "convivial" India-based chain offers "excellent South Indian specialities such as dosas" and other "tasty" veggie fare; even if the decor "could use some sprucing up", "reasonable" prices and a "warm welcome" make it "worth the time" to pop in for a bite.

Wright Brothers
Oyster & Porter House Seafood

| 24 | 22 | 22 | £42 |

Borough | Borough Mkt. | 11 Stoney St., SE1 9AD | 020-7403-9554
Wright Brothers
Soho Oyster House ◐ Seafood

Soho | 12-13 Kingly St., W1 5PW | 020-7434-3611
www.thewrightbrothers.co.uk

"Jostle at the bar for a plate of oysters" and other "seafood delights" at this "fish-lover's paradise" in Borough Market, a "buzzing", "casual" place with "plain wood tables", "reasonable prices" and "knowledge-able staff who remember your face"; likewise, the "unpretentious", equally "crowded" Soho offshoot (a three-floor endeavour combining a restaurant and raw bar) is "well worth a trip" for "when you want to splurge."

	FOOD	DECOR	SERVICE	COST

NEW Wulumuchi *Chinese*
— | — | — | M

Chinatown | 16 Lisle St., WC2H 7BE | 020-7287-6606

Xinjiang in Northwest China – where wheat and lamb rather than rice and pork are king – provides the culinary influence at this sensibly priced Chinatown newcomer; set behind an unassuming wood facade, the bi-level digs have an easy East-meets-West aesthetic, with wood and silk screens mingling comfortably with multicolored Tiffany lamps.

XO *Asian*
21 | 20 | 19 | £40

Hampstead | 29 Belsize Ln., NW3 5AS | 020-7433-0888 | www.rickerrestaurants.com

"A touch of glamour" in Belsize Park, this spot from Ricker Restaurants (E&O, Great Eastern Dining Room, et al.) hits the mark for a "girls' night out or post-movie date" with its "smart", "modern" look, "notable wine list" and "variety"-packed Pan-Asian menu that's only "a bit expensive"; a few think the "great formula is now dating gently", but it's "reliable", "fast" and "friendly" too.

Yalla Yalla *Lebanese*
24 | 18 | 19 | £20

Soho | 1 Greens Ct., W1F 0HA | 020-7287-7663
Soho | 12 Winsley St., W1 8HQ | 020-7637-4748 🗷
NEW King's Cross | King's Cross Station, Unit 47, N1C 4AL | 020-7837-3680
www.yalla-yalla.co.uk

"Generous portions" of "healthy" Mideastern eats are "perfect for sharing with a group of friends" and "priced reasonably" at these three "popular" Lebanese spots; "enthusiastic" staff "aim for a high turnover", but since there's "limited seating" in the "slightly spartan" environs, you can expect a "long wait" – though "delicious takeaway" is another option.

⊠ Yashin Sushi *Japanese*
28 | 23 | 25 | £60

Kensington | 1 Argyll Rd., W8 7DB | 020-7938-1536 | www.yashinsushi.com

"You'll find yourself eating things you never imagined" at this "expensive" Kensington purveyor of "gorgeous" edible Japanese "art", where the "superb, inventive" sushi and sashimi come "without soy sauce", and the miso soup's served "in a teacup"; "attentive" staff also present a "great sake selection" in the "elegant setting", where insiders feel the "upstairs is more convivial than the basement."

⊠ Yauatcha ⏺ *Chinese*
27 | 24 | 21 | £52

Soho | 15 Broadwick St., W1F 0DL | 020-7494-8888 | www.yauatcha.com

The "buzzing nightclub atmosphere doesn't overshadow" the "inventive" Chinese menu – led by a "diverse" range of "swoon-making", "expertly crafted dim sum" – at this "glorious experience" in Soho, where the "glamourous" digs are patrolled by servers who can be "charming" or "lax" "depending on when you go"; afternoon tea with "addictive macarons" and "amazing" "warm scones" is "pretty special" and "great value" too (otherwise, the "bill adds up").

	FOOD	DECOR	SERVICE	COST

Yming ●⏹ *Chinese* ▽ | 24 | 16 | 23 | £37 |

Soho | 35-36 Greek St., W1D 5DL | 020-7734-2721 |
www.yminglondon.com

It's "nothing much to look at", but this spot in a "little corner of Soho"
is "not your average" Chinese thanks to "courteous" staff who "make
everyone feel special", "fantastic", "reliable" "Sichuan-influenced"
dishes and "reasonable prices"; as "casual" and "relaxed" as it is, it's
still quite "popular", so you "must book."

Yo! Sushi *Japanese* | 18 | 15 | 15 | £24 |

Knightsbridge | Harrods 102 | 102-104 Brompton Rd., SW3 1ER |
020-7841-0742
Knightsbridge | Harvey Nichols | 109-125 Knightsbridge, 5th fl.,
SW1X 7RJ | 020-7201-8641
Marylebone | Selfridges | 400 Oxford St., ground fl., W1C 1JS |
020-7318-3944
Mayfair | Sedley Pl. | 15 Woodstock St., W1C 2AQ | 020-7629-0051
Soho | 52 Poland St., W1F 7NQ | 020-7287-0443
Westminster | County Hall | Belvedere Rd., SE1 7GP | 020-7928-8871
Farringdon | 95 Farringdon Rd., EC1R 3BT | 020-7841-0785
Fulham | Fulham Broadway Ctr. | 472 Fulham Rd., 1st fl., SW6 1BW |
020-7385-6077
Bayswater | Whiteleys Shopping Ctr. | 151 Queensway, W2 4YN |
020-7727-9392
Paddington | The Lawn | Paddington Station, W2 1HB | 020-7262-7408
www.yosushi.com
Additional locations throughout London

"Just help yourself" as colour-coded plates of "basic" sushi "zoom
past on a conveyor belt" at this "convenient", "no-nonsense" Japanese
chain where "you can't go wrong" for "cheap", "instant gratification"
(though it becomes "pricey if you don't watch the plates racking up");
it's "no longer the novelty it once was", and service "varies between
branches", yet it remains a "quirky", "funky" option that's "fun for
kids" and the "young at heart" alike.

York & Albany *European* | 20 | 19 | 18 | £42 |

Camden Town | 127-129 Parkway, NW1 7PS | 020-7388-3344 |
www.gordonramsay.com

Set in a John Nash–designed former coach inn near Regent's Park, this
Gordon Ramsay venue boasts a "plush" setting and an "enjoyable",
"sensibly priced" Modern European menu, which is delivered by
mostly "commendable" staffers; admirers say it's "best for breakfast"
or a "leisurely lunch" in the "cosy" red-hued dining room, whilst others stick to the "fabulous" street-level bar or the "rustic deli."

Yoshino ⏹ *Japanese* | 25 | 14 | 20 | £30 |

Piccadilly | 3 Piccadilly Pl., W1J 0DB | 020-7287-6622 | www.yoshino.net

"Charming", "friendly staff" "greet customers with smiles and advice"
at this "well-hidden secret off Piccadilly", where the "excellent"
sushi complements a "wide variety" of "traditional", "beautifully
presented" Japanese eats; what's more, it's "great value" (especially the bento boxes), and there's also a "packed deli counter"
for "delicious" takeaway lunches.

	FOOD	DECOR	SERVICE	COST

Yum Yum *Thai*
23 | 21 | 21 | £27

Stoke Newington | 187 Stoke Newington High St., N16 0LH |
020-7254-6751 | www.yumyum.co.uk

"It's all in the name" according to admirers of the "brilliant" Thai treats
sold at this "calm" Stoke Newington haunt; though some deem it
"slightly on the expensive side" if you don't catch the "excellent-value"
lunch menu, it's "popular with locals" and "large parties" at all times,
due to "warm" service and "charming" indoor/outdoor seating.

Zafferano *Italian*
25 | 21 | 23 | £66

Belgravia | 15 Lowndes St., SW1X 9EY | 020-7235-5800 |
www.zafferanorestaurant.com

"You can come here to people-watch, but the food is much better"
pronounce "well-heeled" habitués of this "venerable" "gourmets'
delight" in Belgravia, where "brilliant", "refined" Italian cuisine is
delivered in "attractive" brick-walled environs; "your bill at the end
won't be cheap", but most find it "well worth it", with "warm, professional service" and a "superb wine carte" as added incentives.

Zaika *Indian*
25 | 23 | 23 | £52

Kensington | 1 Kensington High St., W8 5NP | 020-7795-6533 |
www.zaika-restaurant.co.uk

"Surprising taste combinations" abound on the "amazing", "innovative" modern Indian menu offered at this "upscale" "treat", a "dark",
"exotic setting" in a former Kensington bank, with a "wonderful bar"
and "superb servers" who "treat you like royalty"; yes, "it comes at
a price", but since it's "not your typical" "special-occasion" destination, most find it "worth every pence."

Zayna *Indian/Pakistani*
∇ 28 | 21 | 21 | £44

Marylebone | 25 New Quebec St., W1H 7SF | 020-7723-2229 |
www.zaynarestaurant.co.uk

"Extraordinary", "beautiful" North Indian–Pakistani cuisine "always
pleases", as do the "reasonable prices" at this Marylebone "neighbourhood gem" near Marble Arch; the "intimate" setting features
wood carvings, a basement seating area (if you're "claustrophobic",
"try to avoid") and staff who provide "service with a smile" even
when it gets "crowded."

Ziani ◐ *Italian*
25 | 18 | 23 | £56

Chelsea | 45 Radnor Walk, SW3 4BP | 020-7351-5297 | www.ziani.co.uk

"Bring the kids, they're honoured guests" as far as "bantering",
"energetic staff" are concerned at this "fast and furious" Chelsea
Italian dispensing "excellent" Venetian victuals; on the downside,
it's somewhat "pricey", and the "cramped", "noisy" digs "fill up
quickly", but otherwise "everything works" here, solidifying its sta-
us as a "dependable neighbourhood favourite."

⧉ Zizzi *Italian*
20 | 19 | 19 | £26

Bloomsbury | 33-41 Charlotte St., W1T 1RX | 020-7436-9440
Covent Garden | 20 Bow St., WC2E 7AW | 020-7836-6101

(continued)

(continued)

Zizzi

Covent Garden | 73-75 The Strand, WC2R 0DE | 020-7240-1717 🌓
Marylebone | 110-116 Wigmore St., W1U 3RS | 020-7935-2336
Marylebone | 35-38 Paddington St., W1 4HQ | 020-7224-1450
Victoria | Cardinal Walk, Unit 15, SW1E 5JE | 020-7821-0402
Finchley | 202-208 Regent's Park Rd., N3 3HP | 020-8371-6777
Highgate | 1 Hampstead Ln., N6 4RS | 020-8347-0090
Earl's Court | 194-196 Earl's Court Rd., SW5 9QF | 020-7370-1999
Chiswick | 231 Chiswick High Rd., W4 2DL | 020-8747-9400
www.zizzi.co.uk
Additional locations throughout London

A "great place to hang with the family", this "trustworthy" chain offers "reliable" pizza and other Italian "standards" with "interesting seasonal changes" in "lively", "informal" settings; naturally, service is "hit-and-miss" depending on the branch, but it's mostly "acceptable", and as far as value goes, it's "hard to beat."

🇿 Zucca Ⓜ *Italian*   27 | 20 | 23 | £42

Tower Bridge | 184 Bermondsey St., SE1 3TQ | 020-7378-6809 |
www.zuccalondon.com

"Passion for provenance" yields "big flavours" at this Bermondsey Street eatery where the "frequently changing menu" always delivers "a refreshing twist on Italian classics", and "cool staff" carry things off "with aplomb"; the "bustling", "canteen-ish" setting may be "nothing special", but no one really cares with such "affordable prices" – and by the way, "what a wine list!"

🇿 Zuma *Japanese*   27 | 24 | 21 | £74

Knightsbridge | 5 Raphael St., SW7 1DL | 020-7584-1010 |
www.zumarestaurant.com

After "jostling for high-end cocktails" or "amazing" sake at the "vivacious" bar of this "fancy Japanese hot spot" in Knightsbridge, its many "gorgeous" customers dig into the "exciting", "taste bud–tickling" fare at the tables or wait "patiently" for a seat at the counter for "yummy sushi" (the bill commands "a fortune", but is "worth every penny"); "efficient" service is one more reason it's roundly considered to be a "sure thing" – "if you can get in."

Wine Vintage Chart

This chart is based on a 30-point scale. The ratings (by U. of South Carolina law professor **Howard Stravitz**) reflect vintage quality and the wine's readiness to drink. A dash means the wine is past its peak or too young to rate. Loire ratings are for dry whites.

Whites	95	96	97	98	99	00	01	02	03	04	05	06	07	08	09	10
France:																
Alsace	24	23	23	25	23	25	26	22	21	22	23	21	26	26	23	26
Burgundy	27	26	22	21	24	24	23	27	23	26	26	25	26	25	25	-
Loire Valley	-	-	-	-	-	-	-	25	20	22	27	23	24	24	24	25
Champagne	26	27	24	25	25	25	21	26	21	-	-	-	-	-	-	-
Sauternes	21	23	25	23	24	24	29	24	26	21	26	25	27	24	27	-
California:																
Chardonnay	-	-	-	-	22	21	24	25	22	26	29	24	27	23	27	-
Sauvignon Blanc	-	-	-	-	-	-	-	-	-	25	24	27	25	24	25	-
Austria:																
Grüner V./Riesl.	22	-	25	22	26	22	23	25	25	24	23	26	25	24	25	-
Germany:	22	26	22	25	24	-	29	25	26	27	28	26	26	26	26	-

Reds	95	96	97	98	99	00	01	02	03	04	05	06	07	08	09
France:															
Bordeaux	25	25	24	25	24	29	26	24	26	25	28	24	24	25	27
Burgundy	26	27	25	24	27	22	23	25	25	23	28	24	24	25	27
Rhône	26	22	23	27	26	27	26	-	26	25	27	25	26	23	27
Beaujolais	-	-	-	-	-	-	-	-	-	27	25	24	23	28	25
California:															
Cab./Merlot	27	24	28	23	25	-	27	26	25	24	26	24	27	26	25
Pinot Noir	-	-	-	-	-	-	26	25	24	25	26	24	27	24	26
Zinfandel	-	-	-	-	-	-	25	24	26	24	23	21	26	23	25
Oregon:															
Pinot Noir	-	-	-	-	-	-	-	26	24	25	24	25	24	27	24
Italy:															
Tuscany	25	24	29	24	27	24	27	-	24	27	25	26	25	24	-
Piedmont	21	27	26	25	26	28	27	-	24	27	26	26	27	26	-
Spain:															
Rioja	26	24	25	22	25	24	28	-	23	27	26	24	24	25	26
Ribera del Duero/Priorat	25	26	24	25	25	24	27	-	24	27	26	24	25	27	-
Australia:															
Shiraz/Cab.	23	25	24	26	24	24	26	26	25	25	26	21	23	26	24
Chile:	-	-	-	-	24	22	25	23	24	24	27	25	24	26	24
Argentina:															
Malbec	-	-	-	-	-	-	-	-	25	26	27	26	26	25	-